LANDSCAPING

PRINCIPLES AND PRACTICES

FOURTH EDITION

Jack E. Ingels

State University of New York
Agricultural and Technical College
Cobleskill, New York

DELMAR PUBLISHERS INC.®

Cover photo by Bob Wands, courtesy of
Marie Selby Botanical Gardens, Sarasota, FL.

Delmar Staff

    Executive Editor: David Gordon
    Senior Administrative Editor: Joan Gill
    Project Editor: Carol Micheli
    Production Coordinator: Wendy A. Troeger
    Design Supervisor: Susan C. Mathews

For more information, address Delmar Publishers Inc.
3 Columbia Circle, Box 15-015
Albany, New York 12212-5015

Printed in the United States of America
Published simultaneously in Canada
by Nelson Canada,
A Division of The Thomson Corporation

10   9   8   7   6   5

Library of Congress Cataloging-in-Publication Data

Ingels, Jack E.
    Landscaping: principles and practices / Jack E. Ingels. — 4th
ed.
    p.   cm.
  Includes index.
  ISBN 0-8273-4683-2 (textbook)
  1. Landscape architecture. 2. Landscape gardening.
3. Landscaping industry. I. Title.
SB472.I53 1992   91-8503
712—dc20   CIP

CONTENTS

NOTICE TO THE READER

PREFACE

The landscapes of the nation are rich and diverse. They include unspoiled natural regions, recreational areas, suburban neighborhoods, and intensely developed cityscapes. The individual who pursues a career in landscaping is a service person, whose professional objective is to satisfy the needs of those who use and enjoy landscapes. Determining what the needs of people are and how they can be satisfied without harm to others or the environment is the challenge of the trained landscaper. The response to that challenge may be expressed in the design, the installation, or the maintenance of our landscapes. Separate professions have developed around the different services of landscaping.

Landscaping: Principles and Practices is intended as an overview of a complex and rapidly growing industry. The text directs students to an understanding of what constitutes a high quality landscape in harmony with its surroundings, and explains how such a landscape is developed, installed, and maintained.

As an introductory text, *Landscaping: Principles and Practices* is directed to traditional and nontraditional students who wish to begin their training as landscape professionals. By following the text, students progress from the basic principles of landscape design and graphics, through methods of installation and maintenance to specific business methods of beginning in the business, bidding, and cost estimating.

The text aids student learning through the use of specific learning objectives, end-of-unit reviews, numerous photographs, tables and drawings, and supplemental classroom activities. Technical terms are defined as they are introduced within the unit and again in the Glossary at the back of the text.

FEATURES OF THE FOURTH EDITION

- Additional Suggested Activities are provided in selected units. These activities provide opportunities for students to expand their knowledge about the landscape professions and to gain useful skills for their professional practice.

- Sample landscape designs show completed designs for residential and commercial installations. These designs demonstrate the principles of landscape design presented in the text and also provide samples of different drawing and lettering styles.

- Color photographs show existing residential, commercial, and institutional landscape installations. These photos demonstrate the principles of landscape design, particularly the use of color to emphasize the landscape and complement the item being landscaped.

- Botanical names were added to tables of trees, shrubs, vines, ground covers, and flowers commonly used in landscape plantings. Botanical names were also added to the table of plants used in arid landscapes. The use of the botanical names will facilitate student use of the terminology and aid in plant identification.

- Unit 2 was revised to describe the work of landscape contractors, list the skills needed for landscape construction, explain the need for landscape contracts, and describe design-build firms.

- Unit 4, "Starting Your Own Business," is new to this edition. It describes the advantages/disadvantages of owning a business, compares three legal forms of business operation, lists sources of money to finance a new business, lists factors that influence the location of a business, and discusses uses for computers in a landscape business.

- Unit 6 now includes a discussion of the use of a lettering tape machine in preparing landscape plans and as a factor in selecting the best lettering

method for the work being prepared.

- A table was added in Unit 19 to describe surfacing materials and summarize their preferred uses.

- Unit 22, "Selecting the Proper Grass," was extensively revised to reflect current information. The unit lists comparison factors for turfgrasses, describes information required by law on grass seed labels, and explains differences between single species plantings, single species blends, and mixtures of species. "A Comparison Chart for Turfgrasses" summarizes comparison factors for common turfgrass species.

- In Unit 23, "Lawn Construction," updated information is provided on lawn installation using the following methods: seeding, sodding, plugging, sprigging, and stolonizing.

- Unit 24, "Pricing the Proposed Design," explains the difference between a cost estimate and a bid, describes landscape specifications, and works through a typical cost estimate. Current costs are used for materials and labor.

- Landscape pricing and bidding methods utilize the unit pricing techniques commonly used in the industry.

- Unit 25, "Pricing Landscape Maintenance," emphasizes the importance of a cost analysis for maintenance. Unit pricing techniques are used in a sample cost analysis.

- Unit 27, "Care of the Lawn," was revised to provide updated recommendations for patching the lawn, vertical mowing, watering, and mowing the lawn. Lawn damage caused by weeds, pests, drought, and vandalism is discussed.

- A new Appendix listing professional and trade organizations for horticulture and landscaping is included.

- Pedagogical features include performance objectives, appropriate reading level, review questions to test student understanding, and suggested activities.
- All-new Unit 30, "Interior Plantscaping," introduces students to the interior plantscape.
- New irrigation unit describes all kinds of sprinkler and watering systems.
- Students are introduced to computers and their business uses in a new chapter that also covers applications.

ABOUT THE AUTHOR

Jack E. Ingels is a Professor of Landscaping at the State University of New York Agricultural and Technical College at Cobleskill. He is responsible for the campus landscaping program which prepares students for career-track positions in all areas of the landscape industry throughout the nation.

Professor Ingels completed his undergraduate schooling at Purdue University and his graduate studies at Rutgers University. Postgraduate training was at Ball State University. His fields of specialization include ornamental horticulture, landscape design, plant physiology, and plant pathology. In addition to his extensive teaching experience, Mr. Ingels has a diverse practical background in industry. He is also the author of *Ornamental Horticulture: Principles and Practices*, another successful text in Delmar's agricultural series.

ACKNOWLEDGMENTS

Consulting Editor, Agricultural Series: H. Edward Reiley, Woodsboro, MD

The author wishes to thank the following for providing illustrations for this textbook:

Goldberg and Rodler Landscape Contractors, Huntington, NY (2 color plates)
Millard Irwin
Anthony Markey, Figures 13–6, 13–7, 16–1, 16–2, 23–2, 23–3
Alan R. Nason, Figure 1–5
Stanley Pendrak, Figure 2–3
J. S. Staedtler Co., Inc., Figures 5–1, 5–5, 5–7
State University of New York at Cobleskill, Figure 20–3
Joseph Tardi Associates
Harold Toles, Figure 2–4
United States Department of Agriculture, Figures 13–1, 15–1, 16–5, 18–6, 22–2, 22–3, 23–8
Ray Wyatt, Figures 17–2, 17–3, 17–4, 17–6

LANDCADD software, Figures 31–5, 31–6
Richard Kreh, Figure 30–1
From Reiley and Shry, *Introductory Horticulture*, 4th edition, copyright 1991 by Delmar Publishers Inc., Figures 30–2, 30–3, and 30–4
From Boodley, *The Commercial Greenhouse*, copyright 1981 by Delmar Publishers Inc., Figures 30–5, 30–9, 30–10, and 30–11
From Ingels, *Ornamental Horticulture: Principles and Practices*, copyright 1985 by Delmar Publishers Inc., Figure 31–1

The remaining photographs are the original work of the author.

The author wishes to express appreciation to the following for their help in the preparation of this text:

Stewart Allen, Director, The Allen Organization
E. Mark Barry
Robert C. Bigler Associates, Architects

Eric Blamphin, Designer
Michael Boice, Designer
Harriet Brewster
Richard Centolella
Cooperative Extension Service, Cornell
    University, Ithaca, New York
Joann Cornish, L. A.
Bernard Cushman
Vickie Davis
Gustave Deblasio
Edward Dennehy, Designer
Albert Glowacki Landscaping
Vicki Harris
Russell Ireland, Landscape Contractor
John Krieg, L. A.
Peter Lee
Mark Magnone, L. A.
Anthony Markey, L. A.
Joye Noth
Stanley Pendrak
Daniel Pierro, Designer
Olga Ressler
Robert Rodler, Landscape Contractor
Frederick Smith
Ricky Sowell
Paul Stacey
State University of New York Agricultural
    and Technical College, Cobleskill, NY
David Thomas
David Wakeman, Designer

Unit 25, "Pricing Landscape Maintenance," was based on an original chart by David Lofgren which appeared in *Grounds Maintenance Magazine*, January 1968.

Landscaping: Principles and Practices was classroom tested at the State University of New York Agricultural and Technical College at Cobleskill, New York.

The following individuals devoted their time and considerable professional experience to reviewing the manuscript for the fourth edition of this text:

Edward L. Wright
Graves County High School
Mayfield, KY 42066

Carl E. Mitchell
Lee-Davis High School
Mechanicsville, VA 23111

Don C. Leibelt
Green Bay East High School
Green Bay, WI 54301

Bryan Starr
Jefferson High School
Jefferson, OR 97352

David Briggs
Jefferson-Scranton & East Greene
Jefferson, IA 50129

SECTION 1

THE SCOPE OF THE LANDSCAPE BUSINESS

UNIT 1
LANDSCAPE DESIGNING

OBJECTIVES

After studying this unit, you will be able to

- explain the need for landscape designers.
- list landscape professions in which designing is all or part of the job.
- identify the tools used in landscape designing.

The term *landscaping* has many different meanings to different people. Some picture a business that grows and installs plants. Others see landscapers sitting before large drawing boards planning beautiful gardens. Still others see landscapers as those who mow lawns, prune shrubs, build patios, and erect fences. These and other tasks are a part of landscaping. For learning purposes, landscaping will be presented in three categories: design, installation, and maintenance.

THE NEED FOR PROFESSIONAL DESIGNERS

In theory, if human beings had never altered the natural world, there would be no need for designers. Nature is such a perfect designer that, left unchanged by human beings, the earth's beauty and natural system of operation would never have required improvement. This idea, however, is not realistic in the modern world. Centuries ago, people developed life-styles which set them permanently apart from the natural world. They began to grow their own food, no longer accepting what was provided naturally. They grouped themselves into living units which are our neighborhoods, cities, and suburbs. Such modern inventions as firearms, automobiles, highways, airplanes, and factories illustrate that we no longer live in a natural environment. Our population is so large that the greatest influence on our day-to-day life is not nature, but other people. The activities of each person influence the lives and activities of many others. Our activities also influence the natural world, even if the activity is limited to the immediate surroundings of the home landscape.

The interrelationship that exists between the individual and the environment is complicated by the individual's desire to assert his or her own personality on the landscape. Evidence of this is seen in our business districts where every sign seems to be bigger and brighter than the others around it. It is seen in our unzoned neighborhoods where hamburger stands spring up next to churches and private homes. It is also seen in our home landscapes where every house in the neighborhood may exhibit a different landscape style, attesting to the owners' particular preferences.

Our civilized world is no longer natural and no longer in a state of ecological balance. Every time an individual digs, plants, paves, or in some other way changes the land, the landscape is altered somewhat for the rest of the population. It is unrealistic to believe that all of the daily altera-

tions people make to the land are wise and beneficial. For this reason, professional planners and designers must take a large part of the responsibility for directing society's use of land.

Good quality planning and designing are not new ideas—they have been with us for several centuries. The merits and benefits of planning and good design were understood and practiced by the wealthy and aristocratic for hundreds of years. As figures 1–1 and 1–2 illustrate, wealthy classes in the sixteenth, seventeenth, and eighteenth centuries made great changes in the landscape to create attractive outdoor spaces for their personal pleasure. These

Figure 1–1. This historic garden at Drummond Castle in Scotland is styled after the sixteenth century Italian Renaissance gardens.

Figure 1–2. The gardens of Versailles represent the peak of formal garden design in seventeenth century France.

gardens were usually many acres in area and were often measures of the owners' influence and position. Certain ancient cities in Egypt, Greece, Spain, Britain, and Italy also display evidence of community planning which was sensitive to the local environment and the needs of the average city dwellers, not just the wealthy and aristocratic.

Only in the latter half of the twentieth century has the need for good planning and design been recognized at all levels of American society, including the very important middle class. Citizen involvement in community development is growing. Zoning boards of community residents are beginning to direct the growth of their cities and towns. Strict regulation of billboard placement and sign sizes is giving a new look to many business districts. Big city skyscrapers are now required to observe certain spacing regulations that allow for the development of pedestrian plazas at their bases, figure 1–3. Many towns are developing shopping malls where streets once were as one means of renewing midtown business districts, figure 1–4.

There is a need for professional landscape designing at all levels of modern society. Yet someone who is interested in working with home properties and other small sites may not be interested or trained

Figure 1–3. The large open area, used to balance the massive buildings, is a recent development in American urban planning.

to work with large parks, urban plazas, or large geographic regions. Therefore, different types of landscape designers exist.

THE DESIGN PROFESSIONS

The Landscape Architect

The *landscape architect* is involved with the development of all the space outside buildings. That covers a lot of territory. It can include a home's front yard and backyard. It can also include park-lands, ski resorts, golf courses, and hundreds of other sites. The differences in the size and scope of the projects are easily seen.

Nearly two-thirds of the states now require landscape architects to be certified and licensed to practice in the state. The licensing requirements include the completion of four or five years of study at a university whose program is accredited by the American Society of Landscape Architects. The course of study leads to a B.L.A. and/or M.L.A. degree (Bachelor or Master of Landscape Architecture). Completion of the degree is usually followed by a period of apprenticeship in the office of a practicing professional. Later, the prospective landscape architect must pass a state licensing examination. The requirements for landscape architects are safeguards, as are the requirements for those who would be lawyers, doctors, or architects. They protect the reputation of landscape architecture as

Figure 1–4. This was once a decaying city center. The streets have been replaced by a well-planned pedestrian mall.

a profession and the investments of clients who pay for those professional services.

The landscape architect is the client's direct representative on a project. It is the landscape architect who must identify the needs of the client and the other users of the landscape. Analysis of the character, the potential, and the limitations of the site is also the responsibility of the landscape architect. Finally, the landscape architect creates new outdoor areas that fit the needs of the client to the capabilities of the site. In creating those areas, the landscape architect often not only does the design, but also selects the landscape contractor and oversees the project through its completion.

While some landscape architects operate at the residential level, most do not. Those who do usually work with large estates or multifamily complexes. They seldom work with typical middle-income home lots, figure 1–5.

The Landscape Designer

The term *landscape designer* is regulated with less consistency than the term landscape architect. In some states, they mean the same thing and are both governed by the same licensing requirements. In other states, landscape designers can practice at the residential and the small commercial level, but cannot get involved with larger projects. Landscape designers may not be trained as landscape architects, but may attain their design training through two-year and four-year college programs in landscaping or ornamental horticulture. In a few states there are no restrictions for the use of the term, so landscape designers may practice with no formal schooling.

Figure 1–5. A landscape architect presents his plan for a new community park to a group of interested citizens.

Landscape designers often work with landscape contractors. The designers make the first contacts with the clients, design the landscapes, and gain the customers' approval to begin the installation. That is a vital service in a landscape contracting firm, where emphasis is on both the designing and building of landscapes.

Landscape designers often work on residential properties and within a smaller geographic area than landscape architects, figure 1–6. Therefore, it is especially important that they have full knowledge of local life-styles, plant materials, soil and climate characteristics, and sources of material supply. Equally important is practical experience in the installation and maintenance of landscapes. Observing techniques in developed landscapes can help designers in their own planning of future gardens.

Landscape Nursery Workers

Some landscape designing is done at retail nurseries and garden centers. Since these businesses make their profits from the sale and installation of plants, the designs are often sales tools more than full-site plans. The quality of the graphics is not as important, nor is the precision of the planning. *Landscape nursery workers* are often least skilled in garden design since it is not their primary area of concern.

THE TOOLS OF THE DESIGNER

The creation of a professional landscape plan requires time, training, and talent. The design combines the creativity of

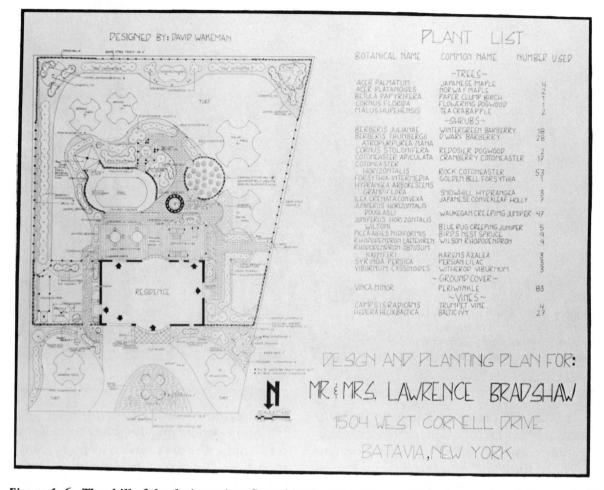

Figure 1–6. The skill of the designer is reflected in the plan. The carefully drawn plan is the mark of a design professional.

the designer with data about the site and the needs and desires of the client. To organize all of this information into a form which others can see and understand requires techniques of graphic art.

Unlike a fine art, graphic art relies heavily on drawing tools. It is the skillful use of these tools which creates the sharp, crisp plans of the professional designer.

Figure 1–7 illustrates the basic drawing tools used by the landscape designer. While many of them are available in more complicated forms, their functions remain the same.

Unit 5 explains the use of the designer's instruments. At this time, the student should be able to recognize and label the design tools required by all those entering the landscape professions:

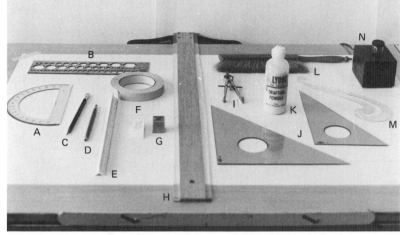

Figure 1–7. Tools of the landscape designer placed on a large drawing table: (A) protractor, (B) circle template, (C) drawing pencil, (D) lead holder, (E) scale, (F) drafting tape, (G) erasers, (H) T-square, (I) compass, (J) triangles, (K) drafting powder, (L) drafting brush, (M) French curve, and (N) lead sharpener.

- drawing board
- T-square
- triangles
- drawing pencils
- erasers and erasure shield

- drafting tape
- scale
- protractor
- compass
- circle template

ACHIEVEMENT REVIEW

A. Write a short essay on the reasons professionally trained landscape designers are needed today. Include: (a) the relationship of the individual with nature; (b) the interrelationship among people within the environment; (c) examples of good planning and design throughout the country; and (d) examples of good and poor planning in your local community.

B. Match each job on the left with its characteristic(s) on the right.

a. Landscape architects
b. Landscape designers
c. Landscape nursery workers

1. Their main interest is selling plants.
2. This profession usually requires the greatest number of years of schooling.
3. They often work on small residential projects.
4. They are often involved in planning large urban projects.
5. They usually are not too concerned about the appearance of a design; it is mainly a selling tool for them.

C.   Identify each of the following drawing tools.

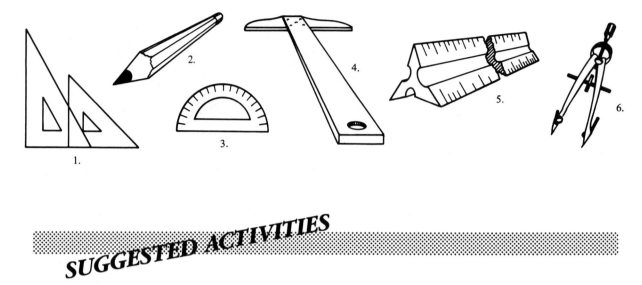

SUGGESTED ACTIVITIES

1.   Visit a drafting supply store or have a salesperson visit the class so that students can observe the variety of graphic materials available and their prices.

2.   Invite different types of landscape designers to meet with the class for a panel discussion of their work. Ask questions to distinguish differences in the types of designing done by the representatives. Select as panel members a landscape architect, a non-architect landscape designer, and a landscape nursery worker. Encourage them to bring samples of their designs for the students to study and to promote discussion.

UNIT 2

LANDSCAPE CONSTRUCTION

OBJECTIVES

After studying this unit, you will be able to

- describe the work of landscape contractors.
- list the skills needed for landscape construction.
- explain the need for landscape contracts.
- describe design-build firms.

Landscape contractors build landscapes in accordance with the terms of written contracts. Beginning with designs, created either by their own designers or by a landscape architect, landscape contractors bring the plans into reality. The work is done outdoors most of the time. The workers are usually organized into crews under the leadership of a supervisor. Frequently the supervisor has a college degree in landscaping. A crew may be comprised of workers with a diversity of skills and ed-

ucational preparation. The particular crew assigned to a landscape job depends upon the type of work to be done. There is a great difference in the skills required to install plants and those needed to lay a flagstone patio.

LANDSCAPING AS A BUILDING TRADE

Those who earn a living by installing landscapes are similar in many ways to people who work in other building trades, figures 2–1 and 2–2. The major difference is that landscape contracting also requires horticultural knowledge. To exemplify the kinship with other building trades, consider a poured concrete patio and a brick wall. Both are common elements of landscapes. What questions must be answered by the landscape contractor before construction can begin?

Poured Concrete Patio

- How is concrete made?
- How much concrete is needed?

Figure 2–1.   Wood forms hold the concrete being poured as a footing for a stone retaining wall.

- How thick must the concrete be to avoid cracking without being too thick?
- How is the wooden form to be constructed?
- Is some wood better than others for construction of the form?
- How much time is required for concrete to harden?
- Should methods that force concrete to harden more quickly or slowly than is natural be employed?
- Should the patio surface be smooth or rough, and how is either accomplished?
- How can the patio be constructed so that water drains off, yet it still appears level?
- Is concrete poured directly onto the soil or does it require a base?

Brick Wall

- Are all bricks the same size?
- Are all bricks the same strength?
- Should hardness of the brick be considered?
- How high can a wall which has a thickness of a single brick be built? At what height is a second thickness needed?
- Does turning a corner weaken or strengthen a brick wall?
- What are the ingredients of mortar?
- Should brick be moist or dry during installation?
- Is it preferable for mortar to dry quickly or slowly?
- How much space should be left between bricks?
- How are bricks cut?

Figure 2–2. Stone is spread as part of the construction of a patio. Landscape contractors bring the landscape design into being.

LANDSCAPE CONSTRUCTION SKILLS

A partial listing of the skills needed to install a sizeable landscape could include the following construction techniques:

- modular masonry (flagstones, bricks, stones, paving units)
- concrete and asphalt mixing and spreading
- heavy equipment operation
- carpentry
- plumbing and pipe fitting
- electrical wiring
- grading
- surveying

It may also require some or all of these horticultural skills:

- balling and burlapping
- soil conditioning
- transplanting and staking
- seeding, sodding, and sprigging of turf grass
- watering
- fertilizing
- mulching

Figures 2–3 and 2–4 illustrate several of these skills.

Not every landscape contracting firm attempts to build all parts of all landscapes. Often special skills or specialized equipment is required that the company does not possess. To accomplish the work required, a landscape contractor may hire another individual or firm to construct that special portion of the landscape. The hired firm is called a *subcontractor.*

Figure 2-3. Large trees may require special handling to assure successful relocation. Here, a tree spade is used to prepare the ground for planting of a large maple.

Figure 2-4. A large tree is felled to prepare the site for landscaping. The landscaper wears protective clothing and sound mufflers for safeguarding her hearing.

LANDSCAPE CONTRACTS

A *contract* is an agreement between two parties in which one party agrees to pay for materials and/or services provided by the other. Without a contract, disputes may arise and neither party can prove the conditions of the agreement.

Landscape contracts may exist between

- the landscape architect and the client.
- the landscape architect and the landscape contractor.
- the landscape contractor and suppliers.
- the landscape contractor and subcontractors.

Proposal

DANIEL L. PIERRO
PRESIDENT

DANIEL L. PIERRO
INC.
LANDSCAPE
DESIGN & CONSTRUCTION

227 SHADYSIDE RD.
RAMSEY, N.J. 07446
(201) 825-1959

PROPOSAL SUBMITTED TO	PHONE	DATE
STREET	JOB NAME	
CITY, STATE AND ZIP CODE	JOB LOCATION	

We hereby submit specifications and estimates for:

We Propose hereby to furnish material and labor — complete in accordance with above specifications and the following guarantees for the sum of:

_____ dollars ($ _____).

Payment to be made as follows:

All material is guaranteed to be as specified. Plant guarantee is as follows: provided payment in full is made upon completion of work, plant material planted by us which has received recommended and appropriate care and fails to survive the first——months after date of planting will be replaced. Plants will be replaced once which fail to survive the first ____ months. The customer assumes all responsibilities for keeping plants in good health (watering, fertilizing, or insecticide treatment) upon completion of jobs. All work to be completed in a workmanlike manner according to standard practices. Any alteration or deviation from above specifications involving extra costs will be executed only upon written orders, and will become an extra charge over and above the estimate. All agreements contingent upon strikes, accidents, weather conditions or delays beyond our control. Owner to carry fire, tornado and other necessary insurance. Our workers are fully covered by Workmen's Compensation Insurance. Title to all materials remains with the seller until payment in full has been made by the owner. The owner hereby grants the seller right of entry to the lands and premises. There is a minimum $30.00 labor fee for replacements under guarantee.

DANIEL L. PIERRO, INC.

Authorized
Signature _____

Acceptance of Proposal — The above prices, specifications and conditions are satisfactory and are hereby accepted. You are authorized to do the work as specified. Payment will be made as outlined above.

Signature _____

Signature _____

Date of Acceptance: _____

Figure 2–5. A typical landscape contract form (Courtesy of Daniel L. Pierro, Inc.)

A contract between the landscape architect (as the client's representative) and the landscape contractor selected to build the landscape will usually cover these items:

- quantity, size, and quality of all plant and nonplant materials specified
- methods of installation
- pre and post transplant care
- guarantees required
- restrictions imposed
- time of completion
- the price agreed to
- terms of payment
- provision for unforeseen changes

Most of the requirements for actual installation of the landscape are included in the *specifications,* prepared by the landscape architect at the time of designing. These specifications are made available to all contractors interested in bidding on the job. Therefore, they are known to all parties before the contract is signed and becomes binding.

Small installation projects can utilize simple, standard contract forms, figure 2–5. Larger projects usually require longer forms. Much of the technical information of both specifications and contracts is standardized and repetitive from one project to another. Thus, it is adaptable to use with a word processor, figure 2–6.

DESIGN-BUILD FIRMS

In recent years, certain companies have evolved from solely installation firms into organizations that design as well. Frequently they are landscape contractors who

Figure 2–6. A word processor can simplify much of the paperwork of a landscape firm. Its keyboard is similar to a typewriter.

employ landscape architects to do the design work as full-time staff members. Usually the designs are residential or small commercial in scope. They do not attempt to compete with the landscape architect offices in large-site development.

Design-build firms provide the design service as one means of dealing directly with a client, rather than working through a landscape architect. They often eliminate the need for the contractor to bid a project, since there may be no other competitors for the job. At this time, the landscape architects and the design-build firms seem to be coexisting compatibly.

ACHIEVEMENT REVIEW

A. Select the best answer from the choices offered to complete each statement.

1. Those who earn a living by installing landscapes are similar to those who work in the _____ trades.
   a. maintenance
   c. artistic
   b. building
   d. nonskilled

2. A landscape contractor is often subcontracted by a _____.
   a. foreman
   c. client
   b. landscape architect
   d. subcontractor

3. Landscape contractors differ from other construction specialists due to their knowledge of _____.
   a. building materials
   c. design
   b. outdoor work
   d. horticulture

4. An agreement between two parties is termed a _____.
   a. contract
   c. relationship
   b. arrangement
   d. specification

5. Most of the requirements for actual installation that are covered by a landscape contract are detailed in the _____.
   a. subcontract
   c. specifications
   b. contract
   d. word processor

B. Define the following terms.

1. subcontractor
2. landscape contractor
3. design-build firm

C. List fifteen skills commonly required in landscape construction.

SUGGESTED ACTIVITY

Select several constructed landscape items near the classroom or from magazines. These items might be walls, fences, fountains, pools, or light fixtures. Discuss the many questions that must be answered during the construction of these particular features. Arrange the questions in the order they must be answered to permit construction.

LANDSCAPE MAINTENANCE

OBJECTIVES

After studying this unit, you will be able to

- list the types of jobs done in landscape maintenance.
- list the types of positions which involve landscape maintenance.
- identify tools commonly used in landscaping.
- explain the relationship between the designer and the maintainer of landscapes.

Landscape maintenance is the care and upkeep of the landscape after its installation. Since landscapes are *dynamic* (constantly growing and changing), they alter their appearance and size each season, thereby requiring different types of maintenance at different times of the year.

The following is a partial listing of the jobs necessary for year-round maintenance of a landscape.

- mowing of the lawn
- pruning of trees and shrubs
- application of fertilizer to lawn and plantings
- weed control in lawn and plantings
- spraying and/or dusting for insect and disease control
- planting and care of flower beds and borders
- replacement of dead plants
- painting or staining of fences and outdoor furnishings
- repairing of walls and paved surfaces
- cleaning of fountain and pool basins
- irrigation of lawn
- cultivation of soil around trees and shrubs
- replacement of mulches
- removal of lawn thatch
- rolling and reseeding of lawn
- raking of leaves in fall
- winterization of trees and shrubs
- snow removal
- preventive maintenance on equipment

Several of these jobs can be done by the homeowner or by an untrained employee. Most, however, require specialized equipment and training. This places complete and top quality landscape maintenance beyond the capability of the amateur. Because of the increasing demand for professional grounds maintenance, certain landscapers direct most or all of their time to this work. Full-time landscape maintenance persons are usually called *grounds keepers* or *gardeners.*

It might be expected that all landscape architects, contractors, and nursery workers offer landscape maintenance services to their clients. Certainly some of them do. However, the majority are not involved in grounds maintenance because they do not want to purchase the necessary specialized equipment. Much of this equipment is not usable in other types of landscape work. Also, the profit per hour of landscape maintenance is often not as great as that for design and installation.

In most areas of the country today, the public demand for professional landscape maintenance exceeds the number of properly trained landscapers willing to provide those services. This gap between supply and demand is being filled by an assortment of skilled and unskilled amateurs working part time or full time at the business. The limited services usually offered by the amateur include lawn mowing, pruning, weeding, and yard cleanup.

The public has been led to believe that landscaping, as represented by the part-time amateur, is a low-cost service which requires no formal training or knowledge. The amateur, however, simply cannot provide the full line of services required of the professional. When clients encounter a fully qualified landscape maintenance professional, they are often surprised by the scope and cost of proper landscape care.

For a person interested in beginning a career in the landscape business with a relatively small cash investment, landscape maintenance is a good choice. There is no need for land, greenhouses, or extensive building space. Most of the money initially invested is placed toward the purchase of proper equipment necessary to do a high quality job. Materials such as fertilizer, grass seed, and mulches can be bought from a supplier and their cost charged back to the customer. The charge for services is the major source of income for the independent landscape grounds keeper.

In addition to self-employment, there are other ways to become involved in landscape maintenance. The two largest landscape firms in the United States are maintenance operations. They are contracted to maintain the landscapes of many of America's corporate giants, university campuses, and military bases. Still other park systems, businesses, and institutions maintain their own grounds crews. Employment as a grounds supervisor for such landscapes can be very rewarding. It provides the opportunity to see the landscape grow and mature through several seasons. The landscape grounds keeper who moves from job to job misses that opportunity.

There are also a limited number of jobs available as gardeners on private estates. Although the position of resident gardener remains strong in various European countries, it is declining in America.

TOOLS OF THE TRADE

High quality landscape maintenance requires a wide variety of tools, some of which serve many purposes. Others are very specialized. Many items, such as trucks, lawn mowers, wheelbarrows, and

Specialized Hand Tools and their Functions

Tool and Name	Function	Tool and Name	Function
Grass Shears	Used to trim grass along walks, roadways, the edge of planting beds, and around trees, posts, etc.	**Hedge Shears**	Prunes shrubs grown closely spaced as hedges. These shears are only used on young, tender new growth.
Pruning Shears	Used to trim tree and shrub twigs up to one-half inch in diameter.	**Pruning Saw**	Removes any tree or shrub part which cannot be easily cut with the lopping shears. Usually parts are an inch or more in diameter.
Lopping Shears	Used to trim tree and shrub twigs from one inch to one and one-half inches in diameter.	**Crosscut Saw**	Removes large limbs and small trees. The saw has additional general uses.

Tool and Name	Function
Spades	Obvious general uses in digging. Spades have flatter shapes than shovels. They penetrate the soil more easily but have less scooping capability.
Shovel	Used for cleaning loose soil from planting holes and other scooping uses. A shovel has sides that a spade does not have.
Spading Shovel	A combination tool having uses similar to both spades and shovel. It can be used for digging as well as scooping.

Tool and Name	Function
Grass Hook	For reducing the height of overgrown grass areas. It requires the user to bend over.
Grass Whip	For reducing grass height without bending over. (Once reduced in height, a lawn mower can be used on the grass.)
Spading Fork	Used for turning over the soil when it is not too hard or compacted. Also used for lifting bulbs in the fall.

Chart continues on pages 22–24

Tool and Name	Function	Tool and Name	Function
Weed Cutter	Removes annual weeds by cutting them off at ground level. Not very effective against biennial and perennial weeds.	Scoop	Good for moving loose materials such as crushed stone, peat moss, soil, etc. Scoops have high sides. They are not used for digging.
Toothed Rakes	Used for heavy duty raking which requires a strong tool. Commonly used in preparation of lawn seed beds and cultivation of planted beds.	Manure Fork	The best tool for moving coarse, lightweight materials such as straw, wood chips, etc.
Broom Rake	Very useful in places where a lightweight springy rake is needed. Very good for collecting debris and clippings from lawn surface.	Single-Bit and Double-Bit Axes	Obvious chopping uses. Especially useful in tree removal and for cutting up fallen timber.

Tool and Name	Function	Tool and Name	Function
Hand Trowel	Used for transplanting bedding plants into flower beds, borders, and boxes.	Lawn Comb	An excellent rake for collection of leaves and coarse debris from lawn surface.
Transplanting Hoe	Uses are similar to those of a hand trowel. It has less adaptability for other types of digging.	Shrub Comb	Used for raking debris from small areas between shrubs.
Scuffle Hoe	Useful in weeding and cultivating in planted beds. It cuts off weeds and loosens surface soil.	Bulb Planter	Used to install flowering bulbs.
Post Hole Digger	Prepares holes for the support posts of fences.	Push Hoe	Similar to a scuffle hoe. It is good for rooting out weeds.

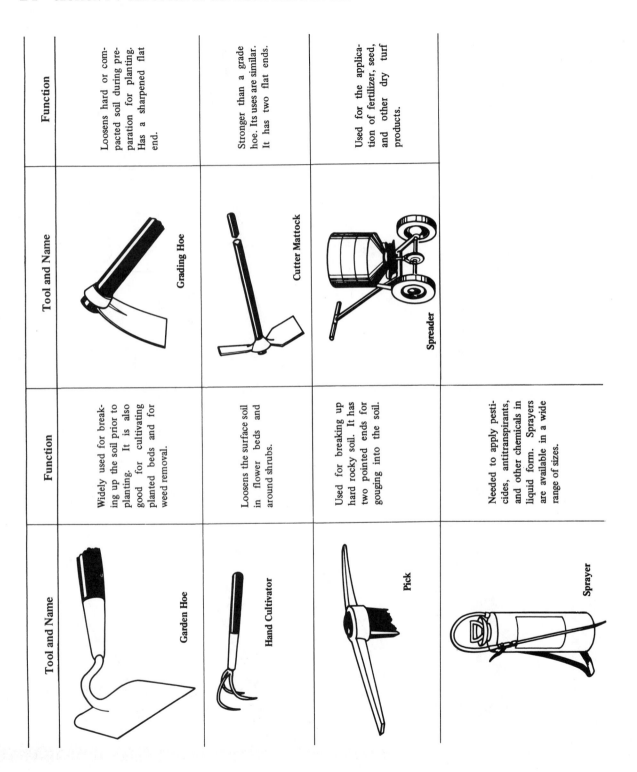

Tool and Name	Function	Tool and Name	Function
Garden Hoe	Widely used for breaking up the soil prior to planting. It is also good for cultivating planted beds and for weed removal.	Grading Hoe	Loosens hard or compacted soil during preparation for planting. Has a sharpened flat end.
Hand Cultivator	Loosens the surface soil in flower beds and around shrubs.	Cutter Mattock	Stronger than a grade hoe. Its uses are similar. It has two flat ends.
Pick	Used for breaking up hard rocky soil. It has two pointed ends for gouging into the soil.	Spreader	Used for the application of fertilizer, seed, and other dry turf products.
Sprayer	Needed to apply pesticides, antitranspirants, and other chemicals in liquid form. Sprayers are available in a wide range of sizes.		

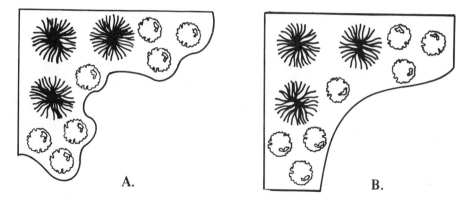

A.   B.

Figure 3–1. Landscape maintenance can be made easier by a thoughtful designer. Bedline A is fussy and complex. Mowing along this bedline would be a time-consuming process. Bedline B, more thoughtfully designed, would be easier to maintain.

hoses, are in common use. The chart on pages 20–24 shows some of the more specialized hand tools. Students should learn to recognize each tool and know its proper name and function.

THE RELATIONSHIP BETWEEN LANDSCAPE DESIGN AND LANDSCAPE MAINTENANCE

It is important that the landscape designer be concerned with the amount of care necessary to keep the landscape attractive. If designers are thoughtless in their planning, the grounds keeper may be faced with many problems. For example, some plants are known to be especially apt to attract insects and disease, requiring a great deal of costly spraying to keep them healthy looking. Other plants which are less susceptible can be used to fill the same role, thereby reducing maintenance. Certain plants have demanding soil requirements. The use of these plants can also cause extra work for the grounds keeper. The designer might specify other plants which require less attention.

Other design specifications can act to lighten or burden the job of the landscape grounds keeper. A smooth-edged, flowing bedline is easier to mow along than a fussy complex bedline, figure 3–1. Where walks intersect at 90-degree angles, a specific design can minimize wear on the lawn; this in turn requires less maintenance time, figure 3–2.

In brief, the amount of care required by a landscape can be controlled to some extent by the designer. It is the responsibility of the designer to know the requirements of landscape maintenance so that maintenance time can be kept to a minimum. If possible, grounds keepers responsible for maintenance should be given the opportunity to review landscape plans early in their development so that their suggestions for easier maintenance can be taken into consideration.

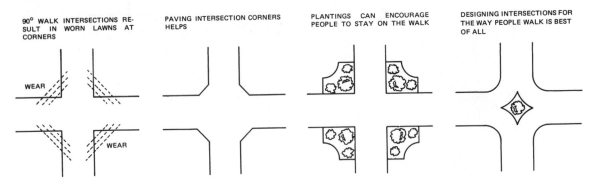

Figure 3–2. Various design techniques used to reduce wear on lawns.

ACHIEVEMENT REVIEW

A. Select from the list below only those jobs which are done as a part of land-scape maintenance.

constructing patios
mowing lawns
pruning dead tree limbs
designing landscape plans
fertilizing lawns

raking leaves
preparing new planting beds
adding fresh mulch to plantings
installing swimming pools
building fences

B. Identify each of the following hand tools.

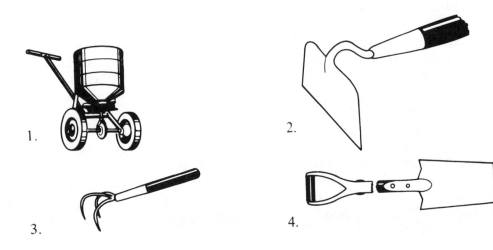

1.

2.

3.

4.

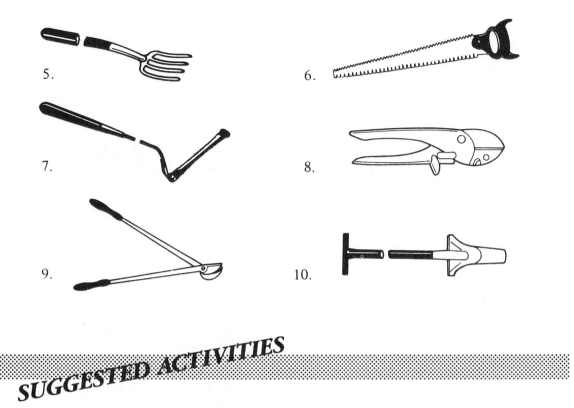

5.

6.

7.

8.

9.

10.

SUGGESTED ACTIVITIES

1. Do a study of maintenance requirements of your school's landscape. Select ten different features (such as shrub beds, trees, parking lots, and entrances) and rank them in order of ease or difficulty of maintenance.

2. Itemize all of the maintenance requirements necessary for the proper upkeep of each feature given in your answer to question 1.

3. Match the maintenance requirements listed in question 2 with the proper tools needed to accomplish the job.

STARTING YOUR OWN BUSINESS

WHY HAVE YOUR OWN BUSINESS?

It is not necessary to have your own business in order to find success and satisfaction as a landscaper. Most landscapers work for someone else. Still, the landscape industry is a small business industry, so there are many who do choose to have their own companies.

For those who desire their own businesses, there may be one or more of the following advantages:

- the opportunity to offer leadership and make all major management decisions
- the opportunity to build the business around your interests and personal talents
- job security
- certain tax advantages
- greater income

Those who do not have the desire or opportunity to have their own businesses also have certain advantages:

- no responsibility for making major management decisions
- the opportunity to pursue a career without the problems of ownership
- freedom to change jobs and relocate as the desire or opportunity develops

Just as personal ownership of a business only appeals to some landscapers, there are also certain personal qualities that make some people better suited to being owners. Owners must like people, both workers and customers. They must possess strong leadership skills as well as a thorough knowledge of landscaping. Owners must be skilled personnel managers and be able to promote positive attitudes among the employees. Someone who prefers working alone or is unusually shy might be better advised not to seek a career as an owner.

FORMS OF BUSINESS ORGANIZATION

There are three ways that landscape firms are commonly organized: the sole proprietorship, the partnership, and the corporation. Each form has certain advantages for an owner. The type of organization is not necessarily a measure of the size of a business.

Sole Proprietorship

The *sole proprietorship* is the simplest form of doing business. It is the easiest to begin and the most private. The part-time landscaper who mows lawns on weekends and has no employees is a sole proprietor. This form is also suited to a person just beginning full-time in the business. For many, the sole proprietorship form of business is suitable even as the company grows in size.

In a sole proprietorship, the owner puts up the capital (money to finance the business), hires and directs all employees, reaps all profits, and absorbs all losses. He or she is totally responsible for all debts of the business as well. There is no separation between the sole proprietor's personal finances and those of the business. Should the business fail, the owner's personal finances can be affected.

Sole proprietorships have other disadvantages. One is that the business can be limited by the weaknesses of the owner. The business usually grows at the outset, then levels off due to the owner's inability to direct its growth further. Another disadvantage is that the business ends with the death of the owner. If the death is unexpected and no arrangement has been made for the business to continue, it usually ends too.

Partnership

A landscape *partnership* is a business engaged in by two or more persons. It is a good way of doing business for individuals with similar ownership interests and complementary skills. For example, one partner might look after designing and sales, while the other partner oversees all construction and installation. Should the partners decide to expand the business and add a landscape maintenance service, they might take in another partner.

In modern partnerships, all agreements between partners are put in writing before the business begins. The terms of agreement should include the percentage of original capital to be provided by each partner. They should also specify the responsibilities of each partner and the business objectives of the partnership. Finally, the terms of partnership must provide for ending the partnership in the event one of the partners dies or wishes to leave the business. Agreeing to the terms of partnership in advance does not guarantee that the partners will work together well. It does help expose possible areas of misunderstanding or disagreement before they arise.

In a traditional partnership, the partners contribute equal amounts of capital and divide the work equally. They each draw the same weekly salary, and at the end of the year they divide the profits equally. Each partner is identical in the eyes of the law and can act on behalf of the business. Either partner can contract with other firms, receive credit, and obligate the company. Thus both partners become responsible for the actions of either partner.

Another type of partnership is one in which a single partner provides most or all of the capital, and the other(s) provide the technical or administrative skills. There are also limited partnerships in which one partner may perform a function, such as partial capitalization, but has a limited claim on the profits or liabilities of the business. Where liability is limited for one or more of the partners, at least one partner must agree to be legally responsible for all the liabilities of the company. Limited partnerships usually restrict the right of the limited partner(s) to obligate the firm.

Corporation

A *corporation* is the third way that a business can be organized. It is the most public method of doing business and is more closely governed by state and federal laws than are sole proprietorships or partnerships. There is an expense involved in becoming incorporated, but it is not excessive. A corporation is given its existence by the state. Therefore, to the state, the corporation is a legal entity, and is regarded as being separate from its owners and managers. The profits of the corporation are taxed independently of the incomes of the owners. The corporation's liabilities are also separate from the personal debts of its owners. Therefore, a corporation can file a lawsuit or be sued without affecting the personal finances of the owners or managers. One of the greatest advantages of the corporate form of business is the liability protection it offers to its owners and managers.

Since the corporation is a separate entity, it has more flexibility than other forms of business. Some corporations are completely managed by nonowners. In this case, wise management decisions are often more easily made since they are not limited to the strengths and weaknesses of the owners. Objective decisions often are more easily made by trained management personnel than by less skilled owners.

The ownership of a corporation is obtained through the purchase of shares, with each share having a certain monetary value. When major decisions must be made requiring a vote of the owners, each shareholder's vote is weighted by the number of shares and percentage of the business owned. At the end of the fiscal year, the profits of the corporation are paid to the shareholders on the basis of the number of shares owned. The profits are termed dividends. If the corporation does not make a profit, no dividends are paid, and the value of the stock may be reduced.

There are two types of corporations common to the landscape industry. A *private corporation* sells its stock publicly and can be owned by many people, often as an investment. Some of the large landscape maintenance firms are private corporations. Most landscape corporations are *closed corporations.* In a closed corporation the stock is not sold publicly. It is often owned by members of a single family. If additional capital is needed to finance expansion of the business, either corporation may sell more stock.

Operating decisions are made by a board of directors, elected by the stockholders. Stockholders cannot obligate the company. Since most landscape corporations are the closed type and have few stockholders, the election of directors and the conduct of meetings are usually informal.

SOURCES OF FUNDS

For someone considering starting a new business, the early excitement of plans and dreams can be quickly replaced by questions of financing. Where does the money come from to start a new business? How much money is needed to start and support the business until it begins to make a profit?

Capital is needed for two reasons. One is to purchase *fixed assets* such as real estate, furniture, vehicles, equipment, and similar items. The other is to pay wages, purchase supplies, and pay utility bills. Such funds are termed *working capital.*

There are three ways to obtain capital for a business:

- Use the owners' own money or that of other people willing to invest money in the business.
- Borrow from lending institutions such as banks, insurance companies, or loan companies; or borrow from people seeking to buy into the business as limited partners.
- Return the profits of the firm to the business for use as capital.

Of the three sources of capital, the best one is the use of personal funds whenever possible. First, there is no interest charge when the owners use their own money. Using personal funds also displays a serious commitment to the business.

Frequently, young people have little of their own money to invest in a new busi-

ness. That is why many begin their careers working for someone else. For new business owners as well as established ones, borrowing may be the only way to obtain capital. It is also the most expensive and most public way to obtain money. This is because interest is charged on the loans and detailed information about the borrower, the business, and the use of the money is required by the lender. *Collateral,* which is something of equal or greater value, is also required as security for a loan. Usually accepted as collateral are such things as land, buildings, vehicles, or equipment.

SELECTING A BUSINESS SITE

One of the first uses of capital is to obtain a site for the new business. Many part-time landscapers use their homes as bases of operations and carry most of their fixed assets in the back of their pick-up trucks. However, the full-time professional landscaper needs a permanent and separate business location. The specific business site selected depends greatly upon the types of landscape services offered. The following factors should be considered when selecting a site.

Size. A small landscape architecture firm may operate efficiently in a two- or three-room office suite. A landscape contractor will require not only office space, but space for equipment and supply storage. If bulk inventory items, such as bales of peat moss, pallets of bricks, or piles of sand are kept in quantity, a sizeable amount of space will be required. Should there be a nursery included in the operation, even more space is needed. Thus, the size of the site must be judged in terms of how much area the business needs at the beginning and how much expansion is planned if the business is successful. Selecting a site that is larger than the business is ever likely to need only increases the costs of maintenance and taxation.

Proximity to the Market.   The geographic area from which a business attracts most of its customers is termed its *market*. Since most Americans live in urban and suburban communities, the landscaper who wants to be successful must locate there also, figure 4–1. Selecting a rural location for a design-build or maintenance firm would require long distance transport of materials and workers to each job site. This adds greatly to the cost of doing business. Since the market region of a landscape architect may reach across county or state lines, it is not critical that the office be located amidst a large population.

Zoning Regulations.   Zoning regulations determine what use can be made of a site. Some areas of a community may be zoned only for residential development.

Other areas may be zoned for heavy industry. Still others will allow light commercial businesses, which is how landscape contractors are usually regarded. Because zoning ordinances can and do change over time, it is important to investigate the present and possible future zoning of an area before buying. Being in an area that adjoins a large zone of single family residences is an advantage. That advantage could be lost if the residential area is suddenly rezoned to permit boarding houses.

Access.   Access to the site is of prime concern. Customers may choose to visit the business personally, rather than telephoning. A landscape nursery needs to be on a major road near the community of clients. Also, delivery trucks need easy access to the landscape firm.

Competition.   A site that has all of the desired physical features could still be a poor choice if located in an area that has too many similar firms. A market area that is being served by an adequate number of

Figure 4–1. Proximity to residential neighborhoods is an important factor in the success of this landscape nursery business.

established, competent landscapers is not the place to begin a new business. In a saturated market area, someone must eventually close each time a new business opens. The chances are good that it will be the new business.

COMPUTERS AND THE NEW BUSINESS

The computer is a data storage and retrieval system. It can also calculate and may have a graphic capability. It can accelerate office and drafting procedures that once required more people and more time, figure 4–2. Use of a computer may reduce errors, since it suffers no fatigue, needs no vacation, and has no personal problems. Some computers can talk to us, translate for us, project costs, and find structural flaws. They can also do tedious, repetitive work indefinitely without boredom or complaint.

Common applications of the computer to landscape businesses include:

- inventory records
- accounts receivable
- accounts payable
- payroll
- taxes
- profit and loss statements
- billing
- time records
- mailing lists
- sales analysis
- cost estimates
- bidding
- graphic assistance

Not long ago, the question facing many small landscape firms was "Should we invest in a computer?" Technology and training have advanced so rapidly that the question now is "When should we invest in

Figure 4–2. The microcomputer accelerates many office procedures for the landscape firm.

a computer?'' The question requires a two-fold answer for a new business person. First, the use of a computer should begin when the business begins. It will save time and improve efficiency if all records of the business are stored in the computer from the beginning. Second, the use of a computer and the purchase of a computer need not be the same. There are computer service bureaus in most major cities that permit use of a computer on a rental basis to supply the same services that private ownership could provide. The landscaper is responsible for supplying accurate information to the bureau so that the required services can be provided.

Small computers, called *microcomputers,* are expensive (up to $10,000) but the prices are steadily declining. One should be purchased as soon as the business can afford it. When the decision is made to purchase a computer, the landscape manager should do some comparison shopping. Computer consultants can be hired to study the business and advise on which system and model to purchase. Valuable advice can also be obtained from computer stores. Most stores carry several manufacturers' products, so their advice is not as likely to be biased as the advice of a manufacturer's representative. However, they may be tempted to try to sell a more complicated system than is needed.

In selecting the best computer for the business, the business manager must consider three factors:

- Are the available funds adequate to cover both the computer and the necessary software, accessories, and supplies required to make it usable?
- Will the system meet the present and future needs of the business?

- Can the system be operated easily by the firm's staff? If additional training is needed, how complicated is it and is there someone in the firm willing to learn it?

The microcomputer system requires an input device, a central processing unit, external and internal memories, and an output unit(s). Common examples of each part are given in the following table.

Computer Part	Examples
Input device	Keyboard (resembles a typewriter) Cash register Video camera Light pens Tape drive
Central processing unit	Microprocessor (There may be more than one per computer.)
External memory	Floppy disk Hard disk
Internal memory	Random access memory (RAM) for temporary data storage Read only memory (ROM) for permanent data storage
Output unit	Monitor (resembles a television screen) Printer Modem (serves as both an input and output device and permits intercomputer communication via telephone lines)

As essential as the computer hardware is, it has no usability until directed to perform a specific operation by the appropriate software. Therefore, the microcomputer system selected should be supported by comprehensive and interrelated software programs of use to the landscape firm. Use of the system should not always depend upon a trained programmer to create the needed software.

It is worth noting that there is a lot of computer-assisted technology being developed to aid the landscaper. One example, is the computer assisted planimeter with a light pen input device that accelerates area and volume measurement. The convenience is a definite asset, but it is expensive. Such high tech features should not be purchased without checking first for their acceptability to the firm's computer system.

ACHIEVEMENT REVIEW

A. Write an essay comparing the advantages and disadvantages of business ownership with those of non-ownership. Explain why you do or do not want to own your own business someday.

B. Indicate whether the following characteristics apply most often to sole proprietorships (S), partnerships (P), or corporations (C):

1. the most public method of operation
2. work and profits are divided evenly among the owners
3. the simplest form of doing business
4. offers the greatest protection to the owners' personal finances
5. the most private method of operation
6. closely governed by state and federal laws

C. List three common ways to obtain money to begin a new business.

D. Define the following terms.

1. capital
2. collateral
3. closed corporation

E. List five factors to consider when evaluating a site as a location for a landscape business.

F. List at least ten different uses of a computer in a landscape business.

G. What three factors must be considered prior to selecting a computer system for a landscape business?

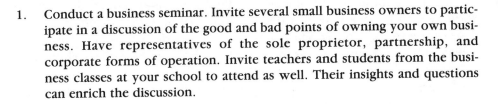

SUGGESTED ACTIVITIES

1. Conduct a business seminar. Invite several small business owners to participate in a discussion of the good and bad points of owning your own business. Have representatives of the sole proprietor, partnership, and corporate forms of operation. Invite teachers and students from the business classes at your school to attend as well. Their insights and questions can enrich the discussion.

2. Select three available business sites near the school. Evaluate them in terms of their suitability as locations for either a design-build firm or a maintenance firm. Discuss as a group why each site is or is not a good location to begin a new business. Include an analysis of the competition and the market area in the evaluation.

3. Visit a computer store and ask the sales staff to compare the advantages of each of the several systems on display. Let each student select the system that he or she would purchase for a new landscape business. Then ask the salesperson for a recommendation of the most appropriate system. Compare the selections of students and sales staff.

SECTION 2

PRINCIPLES OF LANDSCAPE DESIGNING

USING DRAWING INSTRUMENTS

OBJECTIVES

After studying this unit, you will be able to

- properly use the instruments important in landscape designing.
- measure and duplicate angles.
- measure and interpret lengths and distances to scale.

The landscape designer is concerned with the creation of the landscape plan. After an idea originates mentally, it is transferred into a form in which it relates to the total project. Still later, the designer presents plans for the landscape that the client can see and understand.

Landscape designers use several different mechanical drawing instruments to transfer their ideas from their minds onto paper. The *T-square* is a long straightedge which takes its name from its shape, figure 5–1. When used with a smooth-surfaced *drawing board,* with four 90-degree corners, the T-square can be used to draw a series of horizontal or vertical lines which are

parallel, figure 5–2. It is important that the T-square be kept flush with the edge of the drawing board at all times when parallel or perpendicular lines are being drawn. The T-square is used by the landscape designer to create lines to represent property lines, walks, roads, driveways, and fences.

The *drawing pencil,* a basic tool of the landscape designer, may be an expensive or inexpensive instrument, depending upon the quality selected. The designer may select from wooden pencils with leads of varying hardness or plastic and/or metal lead holders whose various leads are purchased separately and inserted. It is recommended that the beginning designer select inexpensive wooden drawing pencils. Both 2H and 3H leads should be obtained. The *H rating* of a pencil is a measure of its hardness. The higher the H rating, the harder the lead is. The lead should have a sharp point at all times.

A *compass* is used to create circles, figure 5–3. For the landscape designer, these circles form the guidelines for creating tree and shrub symbols. (Explained in Unit 7.) The metal pointed leg of the compass is

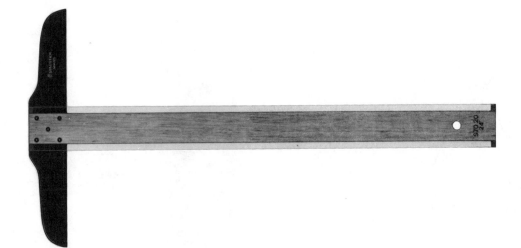

Figure 5–1. T-square

placed in the center of the circle. The pencil or leaded leg of the compass creates the arc. When drawing circles, it is important to remember that the distance between the two legs of the compass should be one-half the desired diameter of the circle. For example, if a circle with a 4-inch diameter is

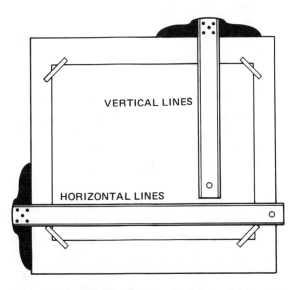

Figure 5–2. The T-square may be used to create parallel horizontal or vertical lines.

Figure 5–3. Compass

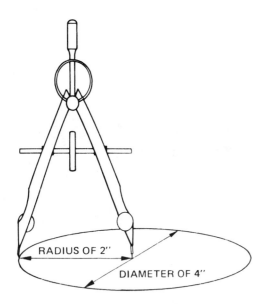

Figure 5–4. To create a circle with a diameter of 4 inches, the legs of the compass are spaced 2 inches apart. The radius of this circle measures 2 inches.

Figure 5–5. A 360-degree protractor. It is also available in a 180-degree model.

to be the result, the compass legs are set at a spacing of 2 inches, figure 5–4.

A *protractor,* figure 5–5, measures the relationship between two joined lines. This relationship is known as an *angle;* the unit of measurement is a *degree.* To measure an angle, the center notch at the base of the protractor is placed upon the point at which the two lines join. The 0-degree mark of the protractor's baseline is aligned along the lower line being measured. The angle is determined by reading up from 0° to the point at which the second line intersects the protractor. In figure 5–6, the protractor is measuring a 25-degree angle. It is important to remember that the reading is always taken between two existing lines, starting at 0°. In this way, confusion over the protractor's double scale is avoided.

Several plastic or metal *triangles* are also used by landscape designers. The two

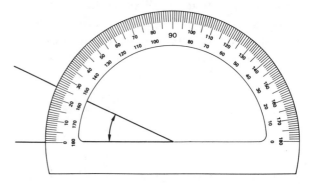

Figure 5–6. The protractor is placed along one line of the angle and aligned with zero (0°). The angle is read at the point of intersection of the second line.

most common triangles are those having 30°-60°-90° and 45°-45°-90° angle combinations, figure 5–7. The triangles are frequently used as straightedges by themselves, but are also used in combination with the T-square to create angles of 30, 45, 60, or 90 degrees, figure 5–8.

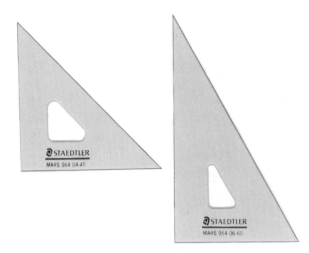

Figure 5–7. The 45°-90° triangle (left) and the 30°-60° triangle (right).

Figure 5–8. The triangle can be used with the T-square to create angles of 30, 45, 60, or 90 degrees.

The most vital instrument used by landscape designers is a measuring tool known as a *scale,* figure 5–9. While the scale resembles an ordinary ruler, it has many more uses than simply measuring inches. The engineer's scale, which divides the inch into units ranging from ten to sixty parts, is the most easily read scale.

The scale instrument is used by the landscape designer to represent or reproduce actual land dimensions and objects on the drawing paper at a size convenient for working. For example, if a property line is 90 feet long, it can be represented on the designer's paper as a line 9 inches long if the scale of the drawing is 1″ = 10′. The same length can be represented by a line 4½ inches long if the scale of the drawing is 1″ = 20′. In figure 5–10, the same measurement of 60 feet is located on each of the six sides of the scale instrument. Note that each unit represents 1 linear foot regardless of the side of the instrument used, as long as the scale of the drawing corresponds to the proper side of the scale instrument.

Once its use is mastered, the scale instrument permits the designer to represent entire building lots, houses, walks, plants, and other items on paper. If the same scale is used throughout, all objects will be in the proper relationship to one another.

Many other drawing tools are available to the landscape designer. Most are used to keep the drawing neat and clean. Included are such items as erasers, erasure shields, drafting powder, and pens.

Beginning designers can purchase the basic instruments fairly inexpensively. Many of the items can be found in variety stores. Several of the items, such as the drawing board, T-square, and scale, can be purchased at drafting supply stores or art supply stores.

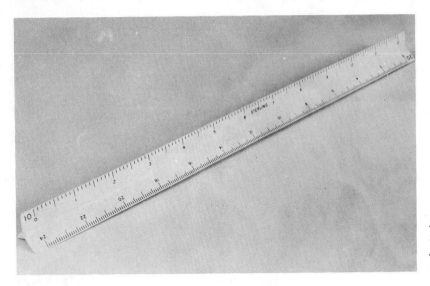

Figure 5–9. The scale. The triangular shape of this instrument creates six measuring sides.

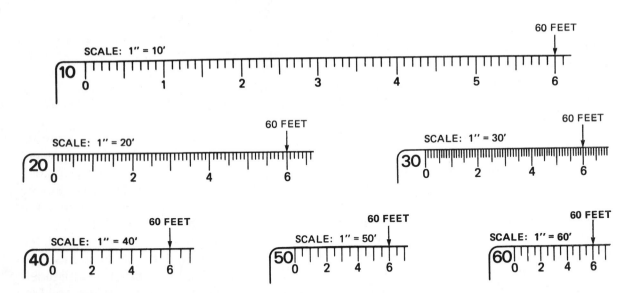

Figure 5–10. Reading the scale. The six views show where one measurement (60 feet) appears on each side of the scale instrument. Individual foot units are not shown in the scales on the bottom line. (Drawing not to scale)

PRACTICE EXERCISES

A. Tape a piece of drawing paper onto a drawing board. Practice drawing parallel horizontal lines and vertical lines using a T-square. Use a 2H pencil first and then a 3H or 4H pencil. Which pencil marks smear most easily? Which are easiest to erase?

B. With your protractor, measure the angles in the figure below. Duplicate the angles on a separate sheet of paper.

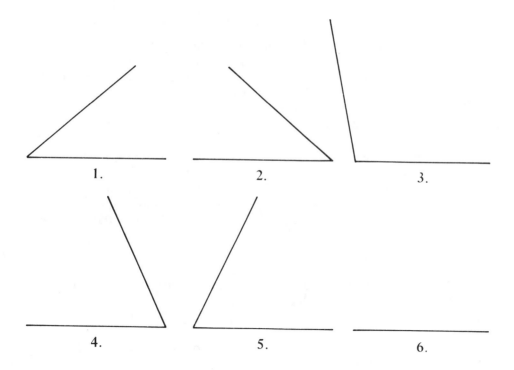

C. Using a scale instrument to measure and a triangle as a straightedge, draw a line 30 feet long to the scale of 1″ = 10′. Draw another 30-foot line to the scale of 1″ = 50′. Draw an 87-foot line to the scale of 1″ = 40′ and another to the scale of 1″ = 30′.

D. Use a compass and a scale instrument to create a circle with a 20-foot diameter drawn to the scale of 1″ = 10′. What is the radius setting for the compass? Draw another circle with a 20-foot diameter to the scale of 1″ = 20′.

ACHIEVEMENT REVIEW

A.   Explain the function of each drawing instrument listed.

1.   T-square
2.   triangle
3.   compass
4.   protractor
5.   scale

B.   From the choices offered, select the best answer to each question.

1.   A compass set for a 2-inch radius forms a circle of what diameter?
     a.   2 inches   b.   4 inches   c.   1 inch   d.   6 inches
2.   If the scale of the drawing is $1'' = 5'$, the completed circle described in question 1 would be how many feet wide?
     a.   5 feet   b.   10 feet   c.   15 feet   d.   20 feet
3.   Which of the following indicates the hardest pencil lead?
     a.   2H   b.   3H   c.   4H   d.   5H
4.   Which two instruments combine most easily to make a 90-degree angle?
     a.   compass and scale   c.   protractor and scale
     b.   T-square and triangle   d.   compass and T-square
5.   What is the most logical way to measure an angle when the lines are too short to intersect the protractor?
     a.   Do not measure it; simply estimate it.
     b.   Attempt to trace the angle.
     c.   Extend the lines of the angle until they intersect the protractor.
     d.   Measure it with the scale instrument.

LETTERING

After studying this unit, you will be able to

- name four methods of lettering used in landscape designs.
- compare the advantages and disadvantages of each method.
- create four different styles of freehand lettering.

THE IMPORTANCE OF LETTERING

A quick glance at a professionally prepared landscape plan reveals that it is a blend of both symbols and lettering. The symbols suggest how the proposed objects and landscape will appear. The lettering usually identifies the objects and often explains how they are used or installed. The lettering requires the same care and quality that is applied to the formation of the symbols. A plan that is used as a device for selling the landscaper's ideas to the client must be prepared with the highest graphic standards. This includes the neatest and most at-

tractive lettering. To the client, shoddy lettering will suggest shoddy design, although that association may not be totally fair or logical.

METHODS OF LETTERING

Today's sophisticated advertising layouts fill magazines, newspapers, and television with intricately styled lettering that is colorful, and both difficult and time consuming to create. In contrast, the labeling of a landscape plan requires lettering that is

- easy to create.
- rapid to apply.
- attractive.
- compatible with the symbol styling, without overpowering it.

Four methods of lettering that fulfill these requirements are: waxed press-on letters, lettering tape machines, letters created with stencil guides, and letters created by the designer's own hand. These methods are commonly referred to, respectively, as press-ons, lettering machine, lettering guides, and freehand. Each method has its advantages and disadvantages as compared to the others.

35 **Folio Extra Bold**	45 **Gill Extra Bold**	61 **News Gothic Bold**	15 *Berling Italic*
36 **Folio Bold Condensed**	47 Grotesque 7	61 News Gothic Condensed	16 **Berling Bold**
36 **Franklin Gothic**	47 GROTESQUE 9	66 **Pump Medium**	16 Beton Medium
37 *Franklin Gothic Italic*	47 *Grotesque 9 Italic*	66 **Pump**	16 **Beton Bold**
37 **Franklin Gothic Cond.**	48 Grotesque 215	69 **Simplex Bold**	17 **Beton Extra Bold**
38 FRANKLIN GOTHIC EX COND	48 **Grotesque 216**	71 **Standard Medium**	17 Bookman Bold
39 FRANKLIN GOTHIC COND	49 Helvetica Ex Light	72 **Standard Extra Bold Cond.**	18 *Bookman Bold It.*
39 Futura Light	50 Helvetica Light	75 Univers 45	20 **Carousel**
40 Futura Medium	51 Helvetica Medium	75 Univers 53	20 Caslon 540
40 *Futura Medium Italic*	52 **Helvetica Bold**	76 Univers 55	21 **Caslon Black**
41 **Futura Bold**	52 *Helvetica Light Italic*	76 Univers 57	21 **Century Schoolbook Bold**
41 ***Futura Bold Italic***	53 *Helvetica Med. Italic*	76 Univers 59	22 Cheltenham Old Style
42 **Futura Demi Bold**	53 ***Helvetica Bold It.***	77 Univers 65	22 Cheltenham Med

Figure 6–1. Styles and sizes of press-on letters

Waxed Press-on Letters

When a landscape plan requires a highly refined, professional lettering style, the *waxed press-on letters* are the quickest and easiest method to use. They are commercially manufactured in an assortment of styles and sizes, figure 6–1. The letters are mounted and sold on sheets of plastic or waxed paper, figure 6–2. They are transferred onto the drawing surface by the heat of friction created when a pencil is rubbed over the surface of the sheet, figure 6–3. To improve their adhesion, the letters are then rubbed again with the pencil through a sheet of waxed paper that usually accompanies each sheet of letters, figure 6–4.

The following are the major advantages of press-on letters:

- They are easy to apply.
- They create a highly refined graphic impression.
- They are easily removed, permitting the correction of mistakes.

The following are the major disadvantages of press-on letters:

- They are expensive.
- Frequently used letters run out before others are used, causing costly waste.
- They crack with age.

Press-on letters are commonly used for presentation drawings and for important concept drawings where the graphic appearance of the designer's work must be first-rate. They are often used both by landscape architects and landscape contractors.

Lettering Machines

The newest and most expensive method of lettering a landscape plan is the *lettering tape machine.* Its mode of operation is simple. An assortment of letter sizes and styles are available. Each size and style is on a separate plastic disc that fits onto the machine. Functioning much like a typewriter, the machine imprints letters onto a

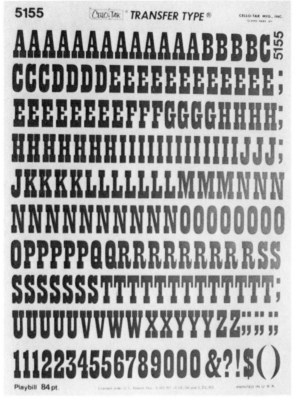

Figure 6–2. *A sheet of one style of press-on letters*

Figure 6–3. Press-on letters are transferred onto the design by the heat of friction.

clear tape that is contained in a cartridge. The tape then adheres to the landscape plan. It is nearly invisible after application, allowing only the letters to be seen, figures 6–5 and 6–6.

The following are the major advantages of lettering machines:

- They are easy to use.
- They create a highly refined graphic presentation.
- There are no wasted letters.
- The letters do not age in storage.

The major disadvantage of the system is its expense. There is the initial purchase cost. In addition, each lettering disc is sold

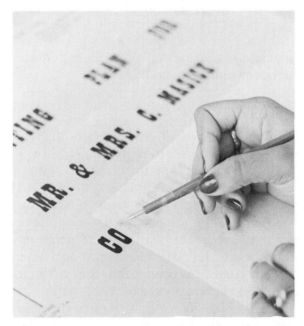

Figure 6–4. To secure them to the surface, the letters are rubbed again through a sheet of waxed paper.

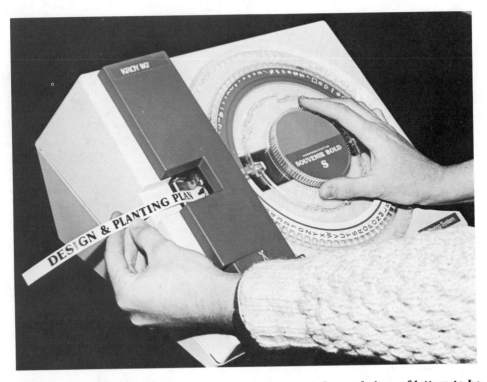

Figure 6–5. The lettering machine permits many styles and sizes of letters to be produced without waste.

separately and the tape cartridges require frequent replacement.

Lettering Guides

Lettering guides are templates that reproduce the same letter size and style over and over again. They may be used with a drawing pencil or lead holder, but are most often used with technical pens. If a technical pen and ink are used, a lettering guide sized to match the width of the pen's tip must be selected. The guide must also have raised edges to permit its use without smearing the ink, figure 6–7.

Lettering guides in several styles and sizes are available on the commercial market. A single landscape drawing may require letters of varied sizes. Thus, a selection of lettering guides may be needed. The drawing usually looks best if the same style of letters is used throughout. Using mixed brands of guides should be avoided, since this can result in varied styles.

The following are the major advantages of lettering guides:

- They are less expensive than press-on letters once the initial investment has been made.
- There are no leftover letters; therefore, there is no waste.
- They allow a designer who letters poorly by hand to produce an attractive plan.

The following are the major disadvantages of lettering guides:

Figure 6–6. The lettered tape is peeled from its backing and applied to the tracing surface.

- They are time-consuming for some people to use.
- They remove the human element that makes freehand lettering interesting; thus, the design often looks too mechanical.

Freehand Lettering

The *freehand* method is the most common and most important method used for lettering a landscape drawing. The styles of freehand lettering can be described and studied. However, no two people will form the letters in exactly the same way. As a result, good freehand lettering has a personality and quality as unique and stylized as a person's handwriting.

Students can develop a good freehand lettering style by carefully analyzing how the letters are constructed, and by repeatedly practicing the new lettering styles so as to replace the ones learned earlier in life.

STYLES OF FREEHAND LETTERING

The styles of freehand lettering used by most landscape designers are usually based upon four traditional styles:

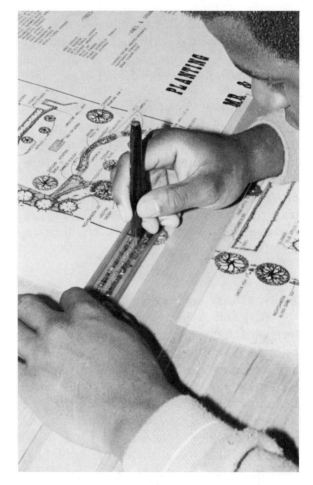

Figure 6–7. Using a lettering guide

- Basic block letters
- Distorted block letters
- Slanted block letters
- Slanted, distorted block letters

Each of these basic styles is merely a variation of the others. All four styles create single-stroke letters the width and thickness of one pen or pencil line. Because they are simple to construct, the letters may be produced quickly and with consistency of width and style. All styles require the use of horizontal guidelines and, when large in size, the support of straightedges may be needed. Generally, in common practice, the letters are created without the need for straightedges; the designer relies only upon the T-square to keep the lettering properly aligned.

Each of the freehand styles described here creates letters that are either equal in height and width or else slightly higher than they are wide. All are based upon three horizontal guidelines. The *placement of the horizontal midline* is one determining factor in creating the styles. The *angle of the vertical slant* of each letter is the other determining factor.

Basic Block Letters

Basic block letters are the basis of all freehand lettering styles. The horizontal midline is equidistant between the upper and lower lines. All vertical lines are drawn at a 90-degree angle to the horizontal lines. Figure 6–8 illustrates the complete alphabet lettered in the basic block style. Note that the midlines of the letters A, B, E, F, G, H, P, R, and Y touch the center guideline. Certain letters, such as M, O, Q, and W are as wide as they are tall. Others, except the

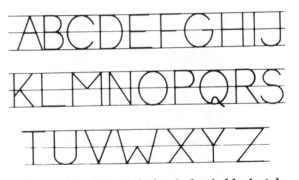
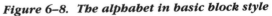

Figure 6–8. The alphabet in basic block style

I, are about two-thirds to three-quarters as wide as they are tall. To keep the letters properly vertical, some designers strike 90-degree reference lines at random intervals along the line being lettered as a guide for their eyes.

Figure 6–9 shows a line of letters being developed. Note the placement of the T-square for construction of the horizontal guidelines and the use of the 90-degree triangle to provide the vertical reference lines. Still, the actual letters are created freehand.

If a technical pen is used for the lettering, the line width will remain consistent, as it should. If a pencil or lead holder is used, the designer must frequently repoint the lead in a sharpener or by rolling the point across a sandpaper pad, figure 6–10.

Another aspect of freehand lettering that applies to the basic block style, as well as the three variations, concerns serifs. *Serifs* are decorative strokes attached to letters to create a more ornate style. Serif-style type, which is common to most typewriters and newspapers, is used in this text. It is so common that many students apply serifs to certain letters, notably the I and J, even when lettering in a nonserif style. Since landscape freehand lettering is a nonserif style, there are no serifs on the I and J or any other letters.

Figure 6–9. Developing basic block letters using the T-square and 90-degree triangle

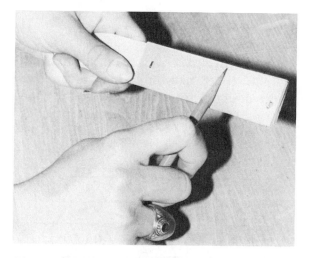

Figure 6–10. Sharpening the point of a drawing pencil on a sandpaper pad

Distorted Block Letters

One variation of the basic block style is created by either raising or lowering the horizontal midline from its center position. Letters which touched the midline at center before now touch a raised or lowered midline. The result is a distortion of the basic block lettering, a style preferred by many designers. Figures 6–11 and 6–12 show the alphabet in distorted lettering styles.

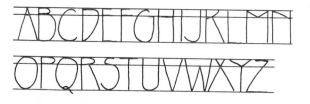

Figure 6–11. Distorted block alphabet with midline raised

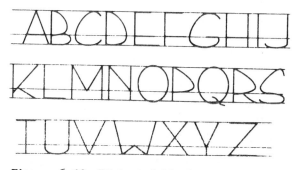

Figure 6–12. Distorted block alphabet with midline lowered

Slanted Block Letters

In the basic block style the three horizontal guidelines are equidistant and the vertical reference lines are at a 90-degree angle in relation to the horizontal lines. Another lettering variation can be created by angling the vertical reference lines and the vertical sides of the letters at 60 degrees instead of 90 degrees. The result is a slanted block style of lettering, figure 6–13. Some designers prefer this style, especially if their own handwriting tends to be more slanted than vertical.

In figure 6–14, the letters are shown being constructed with a T-square and a 60-degree triangle in place to provide guidelines and reference lines. A student attempting slanted block lettering is likely, at first, to find it difficult to maintain a consistent 60-degree slant. Mastering this style takes time and practice. The 60-degree reference lines can be of great help.

Slanted, Distorted Block Letters

The final variation of the basic block style is actually a combination of the variations described earlier. In this style, the horizontal midline is raised or lowered from the center, *and* the vertical orientation of the letters and reference lines is 60 degrees. Figure 6–15 illustrates the alphabet lettered in the slanted, distorted block style.

DEVELOPING A LETTERING STYLE

A textbook can only offer guidance to a new designer seeking to develop a good lettering style. Each designer must practice and modify his or her style until the de-

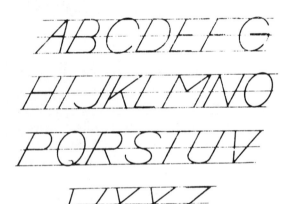

Figure 6–13. Slanted block alphabet

Figure 6–14. A T-square and 60-degree triangle are used to place the guidelines and reference lines for slanted block lettering.

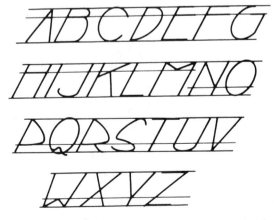

Figure 6–15. Slanted, distorted block alphabet with guidelines. Half of the alphabet has the midline above center, and half has the midline below center.

sired results are attained. The style that develops is likely to be a personalized version of one of the four freehand styles previously described. It may be further modified to suit the designer's own preference and style. Lettering styles used by some professional landscape designers are shown in figure 6–16. Sense the life and vitality of these letters. There is not a dull, mechanical sameness about them as there is with letters produced by a lettering guide; neither is there a childish quality about them.

Once the four basic styles of freehand lettering have been studied and mastered, students should look for examples of interesting lettering based upon these styles and try to duplicate them. One of the best ways to learn a new style is by copying those that you admire. Since a copy is never exact, a customized lettering style usually develops which then becomes the new designer's own.

Deliberate Line Width Variation

In the section describing the freehand styles, it was mentioned that line width should be consistent. Such is the case when a round-lead pencil or technical pen is being used. However, careful study of some of the styles shown in figure 6–16 reveals noticeable variations in the line widths within a single letter. These letters are styled by using a *wedge* or *chisel point,* not a rounded lead. The wedge point has a beveled end, similar to a chisel, figure 6–17.

By using a wedge point, both broad and narrow lines can be made with the same pencil, figure 6–18. A simple version of this style can be developed by holding the wedge point in a fixed position: vertical strokes create a wide line and horizontal strokes create a thin line. Further practice with the chisel tip held at different

angles gives the designer one more variation upon the basic block lettering style.

The following are the advantages of a good freehand lettering style:

- There is no initial or recurring expense for supplies.
- It can be used with all drawing media, such as pencils, technical pens, and felt-tip pens.
- The letters have the human touch not found in press-on or stenciled letters. They look handcrafted, not manufactured. Thus, the finished design has a customized appearance.

The disadvantages of good freehand lettering are almost nonexistent. However, freehand lettering does not look good on the same drawing where lettering guides have been used. The contrast between the two methods is not attractive.

SELECTING THE APPROPRIATE LETTERING METHOD

The time and expense involved in the lettering of a landscape plan are determined by the type and importance of the work being lettered. Press-on letters and those made on a lettering machine are regularly used on concept drawings and presentation plans. On those plans, the graphic quality is often important to the acceptance of the designer's proposal. The same may be said for the use of lettering guides. If the potential value of the project warrants the time needed to use the lettering guides, then their use is justified.

Freehand lettering is the best choice when the potential value of the project is

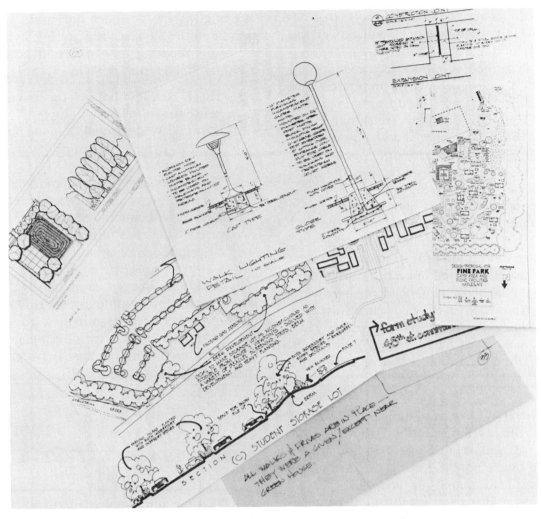

Figure 6–16. Lettering styles used by professional designers

such that the expense of press-on letters or the time it takes for stenciled letters cannot be justified. Working drawings vital to the installation of the landscape do not need stylized lettering, only complete information. They are almost always lettered freehand.

It should not be assumed that freehand lettering is inappropriate on important presentation work. When done well, it is not only appropriate but preferred by many landscape designers over the other methods. Some designers never use lettering guides, and only use press-on letters to highlight such features as the client's name and address or the name of the designer or firm.

CREATING WORDS

Since the purpose of the landscape plan is to communicate the designer's ideas and intent to the client and the landscape installers, the letters must be formed into

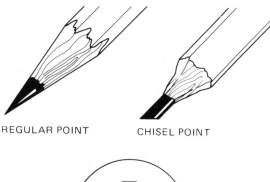

REGULAR POINT   CHISEL POINT

CHISEL POINT—SIDE VIEW

Figure 6–17. Wedge-point drawing pencil

words. To create words correctly, the letters must be spaced properly. Proper spacing is basically a visual skill; that is, if it looks good, it is probably correct.

The following guidelines may help to insure attractive word formation:

- The letters within a word should not be crowded; neither should they be spaced so far apart that gaps are created, figure 6–19.
- The spaces between words should be greater than the spaces between letters within a word, figure 6–20.
- The same style of lettering should be used throughout the plan.
- Uppercase letters (capitals) and lowercase letters (noncapitals) should not be mixed within a word or label, figure 6–21.

Figure 6–18. Wedge-point lettering

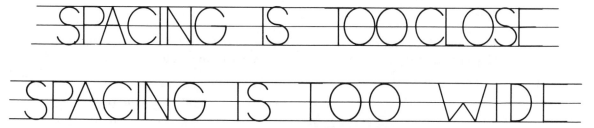

Figure 6–19. Incorrect spacing

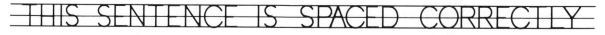

Figure 6–20. Correct spacing

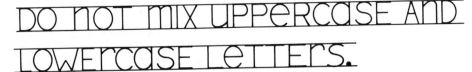

Figure 6–21. Mixing uppercase and lowercase letters is improper.

A. On a sheet of drawing paper, lay out two horizontal lines one-fourth inch apart. Following the examples shown in this unit, letter a complete alphabet in the basic block style. Space the midline equidistant between the two horizontal lines and strike 90-degree vertical reference lines before beginning. Letter the alphabet several times. Repeat any letters you find difficult as often as necessary.

B. Repeat exercise A, altering the placement of the midline and/or the angle of the vertical reference lines to create the full alphabet in (1) distorted block, (2) slanted block, and (3) slanted, distorted block styles.

C. Select the lettering style that seems most comfortable to you. Using a rounded lead point, letter the Objectives of this unit using that style. Make the letters one-fourth inch tall. Be careful to keep to the same style, and to space the letters and words properly.

D. Repeat exercise C using a wedge point on the pencil instead of a rounded point.

E. Select one of the lettering styles illustrated in figure 6–16 and letter the alphabet in that style. Make the letters one-quarter inch tall.

A. List four factors that determine the suitability of a lettering method for a landscape plan.

B. List the four methods of lettering commonly used by landscape designers.

C. Indicate if the following advantages or disadvantages apply to the lettering machine (M), press-on letters (P), lettering guides (G), or freehand lettering (F).

1. time-consuming for some to use
2. most expensive investment
3. has the human touch
4. excess, unused letters remain
5. helpful to designers with poor freehand lettering, and not expensive after the initial investment
6. maintains a consistent pen or pencil line

D. Answer briefly each of the following questions.

1. When a stylized, professional lettering appearance is needed, which methods are best?
2. Lettering guides that are to be used with technical pens should have what type of edge to prevent them from smearing?
3. Two factors of construction determine the style of freehand lettering. One is the angle of the slant of the vertical reference lines. What is the other factor?
4. Should the spaces between words be greater or smaller than the spaces between letters within a word?

SYMBOLIZING LANDSCAPE FEATURES

OBJECTIVES

After studying this unit, you will be able to

- symbolize all major features of the landscape.
- interpret a landscape plan.

When landscape designers are ready to present their ideas to clients, it is important that the plans be both attractive and easy to read. If a plan is accurate in suggesting how the finished landscape will look, there is a greater chance that the client will accept the designer's ideas.

To obtain an accurate picture, landscape designers use their drawing instruments to create symbols. *Symbols* are drawings which represent overhead views of trees, shrubs, and other items that make up a landscape. If the symbols are neatly constructed and all are drawn to the same scale, the final plan can be very impressive, figure 7–1.

When symbolizing landscape features, it is important to keep the symbols as simple as possible. At the same time, they should be suggestive of the actual appearance of the landscape features.

LANDSCAPE SYMBOLS

Needled Evergreens. When thinking of the appearance of a pine or spruce tree or a prickly juniper, it becomes easy to understand the symbol used for the needled evergreen, figure 7–2. The symbol suggests the spiny leaves and rigid growth habit of these plants which are green throughout the year.

Deciduous Shrubs. The word *deciduous* indicates a plant that drops its leaves in the autumn. *Shrub* usually refers to a multi-stemmed plant. It differs from a tree, which usually has only one main stem or trunk. The symbol for deciduous shrubs, figure 7–3, suggests their larger leaves and loose habit of growth. Notice that there is an X or dot in the center of this and other symbols.

Figure 7–1. A completed landscape plan

This mark locates the exact center of the plant and indicates the point at which it is later to be set into the ground by the landscape contractor.

Deciduous Trees. Trees are usually larger than shrubs and play a different role in the landscape. The symbols for deciduous trees, figure 7–4, suggest their size and importance.

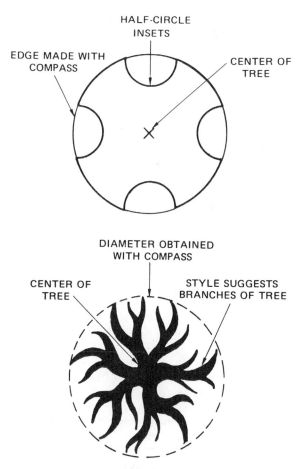

Figure 7–4. Deciduous tree symbols, one more complex than the other

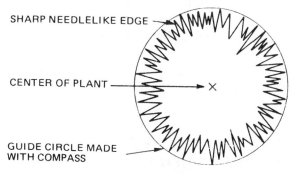

Figure 7–2. Needled evergreen symbol

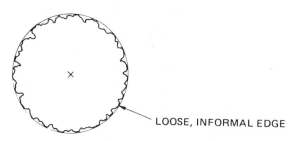

Figure 7–3. Deciduous shrub symbol

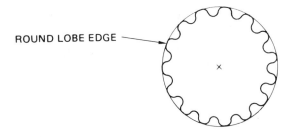

Figure 7–5. Broad-leaved evergreen symbol

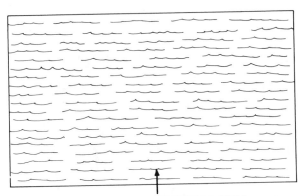

WAVELIKE PATTERN FILLS AREA
TO BE PLANTED WITH GROUND COVER

Figure 7–7. Trailing ground cover symbol

Broad-leaved Evergreens. Another group of plants keeps its leaves all year (evergreen), but has larger, wider leaves than pines, hemlocks, or junipers. These are the broad-leaved evergreens. They are found in the warmer, milder regions of the country. Their mature appearance is less rigid than the needled evergreens and yet somewhat more rigid than deciduous shrubs, as illustrated by the symbol in figure 7–5.

Vines. Trees and shrubs tend to grow in a circular manner. This is why the compass is so useful in forming their symbols. Vines, on the other hand, are wide and thin. The symbol for the vine is based more upon a sausage-shaped guideline, figure 7–6.

Ground Covers. The small trailing plants which cover the ground beneath shrubs and trees are called *ground covers.* There are many different types of plants which fall into this category. Some resem-

ble vines; others are short and stalky. The symbol used to represent trailing ground covers does not show an individual plant, but rather a group of plants, figure 7–7.

Construction Materials. The key to symbolizing constructed items of the landscape is to imagine how the item would appear if viewed from an airplane. That overhead view is how the drawn symbol should appear. Some common construction items are shown in figure 7–8. Students should practice drawing these and other symbols.

EXPLAINING AN IDEA WITH SYMBOLS

Once students have mastered the technique of symbol development, they can begin to use their skills to explain an idea. For example, figure 7–9 illustrates arrangements containing shrubs, trees, plants, and construction materials. Where plants touch (and the symbols merge) the plants are said to be *massed.* Where they do not touch, they are *side by side.* As illustrated in the drawings, it is sometimes necessary to in-

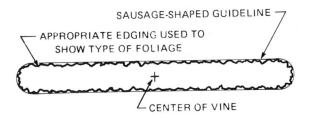

SAUSAGE-SHAPED GUIDELINE

APPROPRIATE EDGING USED TO
SHOW TYPE OF FOLIAGE

CENTER OF VINE

Figure 7–6. Vine symbol

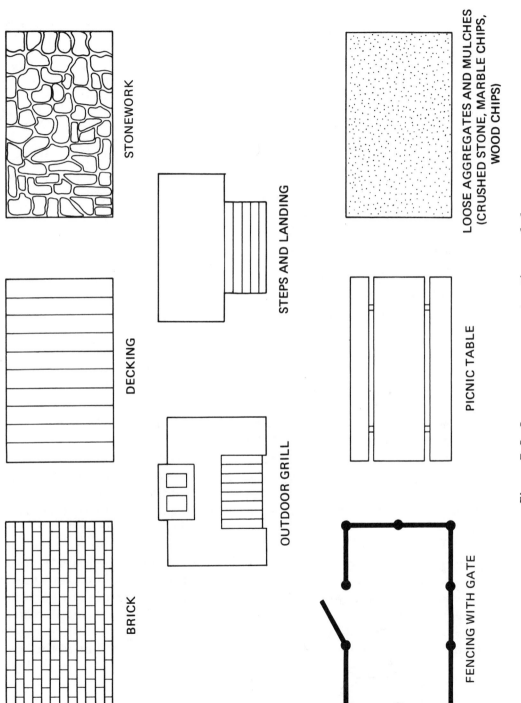

Figure 7–8. Some common construction symbols

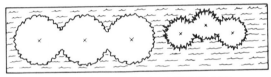

TWO SPECIES MASSED IN A BED WHICH
IS SURFACED WITH GROUND COVER.

SHRUBS AND VINE AGAINST STONE WALL.
BED IS SURFACED WITH MULCH.

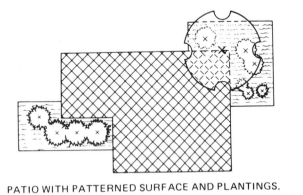

PATIO WITH PATTERNED SURFACE AND PLANTINGS.

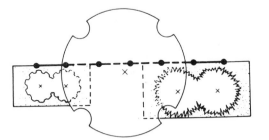

PLANTING BED AND FENCE PASSING BENEATH TREE.
BROKEN LINES ARE USED FOR HIDDEN FEATURES.

Figure 7–9. Symbols are grouped together to convey the designer's idea.

dicate that one landscape feature is to be located beneath another. The symbol for the feature partially covered is drawn with a broken line where it passes beneath the more expansive feature. Hidden features are always shown as broken lines in symbolization.

SYMBOLIZING TO SCALE

The final step in learning the technique of landscape symbolization is learning to draw the symbols so that they fit a certain scale. In developing a landscape plan, the landscape designer must draw all dimensions of buildings, property lines, and symbols to the same scale.

At this point, the student should demonstrate the techniques involved in drawing plant symbols to scale. The method is simple. Using the scale instrument, select the proper dimension for the compass (one-half the diameter desired). Form the guide circle with the compass and develop the appropriate symbol around the circle. The result will be a symbol which indicates the type of plant desired by the designer and the size it will be in the landscape.

PRACTICE EXERCISES

A. Using the proper instruments, draw the symbols below to the given scale.

1. Deciduous tree, 25 feet wide, to the scale of $1'' = 10'$.
2. Needled evergreen shrub, 10 feet wide, to the scale of $1'' = 10'$.
3. Deciduous shrub, 8 feet wide, to the scale of $1'' = 5'$.
4. Broad-leaved evergreen shrub, 6 feet wide, to the scale of $1'' = 5'$.

B. Using drawing instruments, symbolize the features below to the proper scale.

1. Three massed needled evergreens (each 5 feet wide). Draw to the scale of $1'' = 5'$.
2. A 25-foot wide deciduous tree with three deciduous shrubs each 8 feet wide beneath it. Draw to the scale of $1'' = 10'$.
3. A patio, 10 feet × 15 feet, paved with brick. Draw to the scale of $1'' = 5'$.
4. A side-by-side planting of the following, drawn to the scale of $1'' = 10'$: three broad-leaved evergreens (each 5 feet wide), a needled evergreen tree (15 feet wide), four deciduous shrubs, massed, (each 6 feet wide), and a needled evergreen shrub (8 feet wide). Place the plants in front of a fence 65 feet long.

ACHIEVEMENT REVIEW

A. Select the best answer from the choices offered for each question.

1. What do landscape designers use most often to convey their ideas to their clients?
    a. photographs   b. symbols   c. magazine pictures
2. The landscape plan is drawn to show what type of view?
    a. an overhead view   b. a ground-level view   c. an interior view
3. What term describes a plant which is not evergreen?
    a. dead   b. vine   c. deciduous

4. Why is an *X* or dot placed in the exact center of each symbol?
   a. to cover the hole made by the compass
   b. to locate the center of the plant and the point at which it will be installed in the ground
   c. to make the symbol more noticeable
5. To symbolize an evergreen shrub 8 feet in diameter, what should be the radius setting for the compass?
   a. 8 feet   b. 6 feet   c. 4 feet

B. Study the completed landscape plan below and answer the questions on page 65.

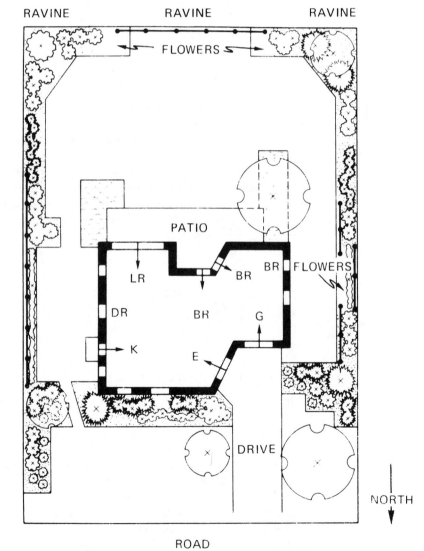

1. How many deciduous shrubs should be purchased for the plan?
2. How many deciduous trees are needed?
3. How many needled evergreens and broad-leaved evergreens are needed?
4. What is the difference in the symbolization used for ground covers and that used for mulches?
5. On which side of the house are the most trees located? Consult the plan's directional arrow to answer.
6. Knowing that the sun moves from east to west, which rooms of the house will be hottest in the afternoon?

SUGGESTED ACTIVITIES

1. Observe several different plants outside. Determine if they are needled or broad-leaved evergreens, deciduous trees or shrubs, vines, or ground covers. Make a tally to determine which types are found most commonly in your area.

2. Visit a nursery or garden center where a wide assortment of plants can be examined side by side.

3. Take drawing instruments outside. Select a planting near the school and draw it to the scale of 1″ = 10′. Use the correct symbol for each landscape feature.

4. Borrow a set of landscape plans from a landscape designer or landscape architect. Compare the symbols used with the ones illustrated in this unit. Note the difference between the symbols used in working plans and those used in presentation plans.

5. Symbolization is a method of explaining ideas without words. Create your own symbols for the following landscape features: a fountain, a flagpole, a car, a storage shed, a swimming pool, a statue on a pedestal. Ask someone outside the class to identify the features being symbolized. Redesign those that are not easily identified.

EXAMPLES OF LANDSCAPE DESIGNS

The illustrations that follow are examples of landscape designs done by professionals currently working in the landscape industry. The designs include residential areas, small commercial sites, and recreational areas. These plans are the work of designers having college preparation ranging from two to five years. The designers are employed as landscape contractors, landscape architects, or recreational planners.

Students will gain several insights by studying the plans. First, each plan can be seen as a graphic explanation of the designer's ideas. Some are mainly concepts, with few precise details, aimed at selling the designer's proposals to a client. Others are detailed instructions of what, where, and how elements of the landscape are to be developed.

Second, notice how the graphics vary. Some of the plans are highly mechanical in appearance, due to the use of lettering guides and waxed press-on letters. Others are less rigid in appearance, due to freehand lettering and a looser graphic style. All of the designs are of professional quality. The graphic technique used depends upon how much time the project warrants at a particular stage in its development, and how much competition there is among designers to gain a potential client.

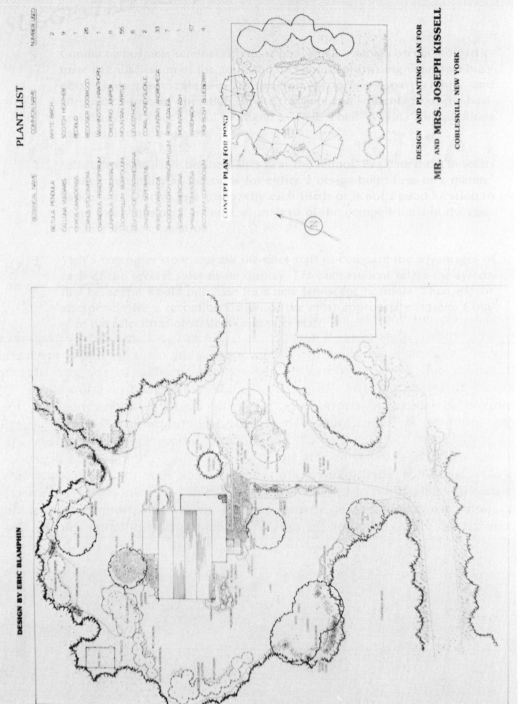

PLANT LIST

BOTANICAL NAME	COMMON NAME	NUMBER USED
BETULA PENDULA	WHITE BIRCH	2
CALLUNA VULGARIS	SCOTCH HEATHER	9
CERCIS CANADENSIS	REDBUD	1
CORNUS STOLONIFERA	REDOSIER DOGWOOD	28
CRATAEGUS PHAENOPYRUM	WASHINGTON HAWTHORN	1
JUNIPERUS HORIZONTALIS	CREEPING JUNIPER	8
LEUCOTHOE FONTANESIANA	MOUNTAIN MYRTLE	55
LEUCOTHOE	LEUCOTHOE	6
DIERVILLA SESSILIFOLIA	CORAL HONEYSUCKLE	2
PIERIS FLORIBUNDA	MOUNTAIN ANDROMEDA	33
RHODODENDRON PRINOPHYLLUM	ROXY AZALEA	7
SORBUS AMERICANA	MOUNTAIN ASH	1
SPIRAEA TOMENTOSA	HARDHACK	67
VACCINIUM CORYMBOSUM	HIG-BUSH BLUEBERRY	4

CONCEPT PLAN FOR POND

DESIGN AND PLANTING PLAN FOR
MR. AND MRS. JOSEPH KISSELL
COBLESKILL, NEW YORK

SCALE 1:10

N

DESIGN BY ERIC BLAMPHIN

DESIGNED BY ERIC BLAMPHIN
CALEDONIA, NY

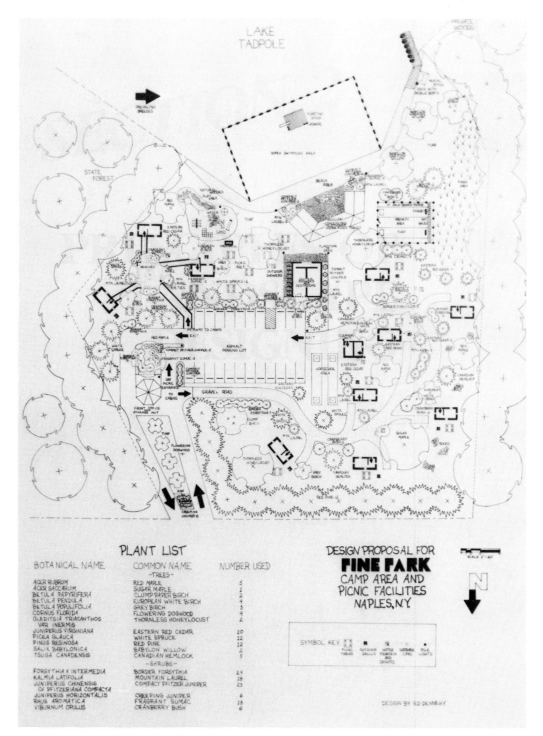

PLANT LIST

BOTANICAL NAME	COMMON NAME	NUMBER USED
	—TREES—	
ACER RUBRUM	RED MAPLE	5
ACER SACCARUM	SUGAR MAPLE	2
BETULA PAPYRIFERA	CLUMP PAPER BIRCH	2
BETULA PENDULA	EUROPEAN WHITE BIRCH	4
BETULA POPULIFOLIA	GREY BIRCH	3
CORNUS FLORIDA	FLOWERING DOGWOOD	4
GLEDITSIA TRIACANTHOS VAR. INERMIS	THORNLESS HONEYLOCUST	2
JUNIPERUS VIRGINIANA	EASTERN RED CEDAR	10
PICEA GLAUCA	WHITE SPRUCE	12
PINUS RESINOSA	RED PINE	12
SALIX BABYLONICA	BABYLON WILLOW	2
TSUGA CANADENSIS	CANADIAN HEMLOCK	5
	—SHRUBS—	
FORSYTHIA X INTERMEDIA	BORDER FORSYTHIA	24
KALMIA LATIFOLIA	MOUNTAIN LAUREL	18
JUNIPERUS CHINENSIS CV. PFITZERIANA COMPACTA	COMPACT PFITZER JUNIPER	23
JUNIPERUS HORIZONTALIS	CREEPING JUNIPER	6
RHUS AROMATICA	FRAGRANT SUMAC	15
VIBURNUM OPULUS	CRANBERRY BUSH	6

DESIGN PROPOSAL FOR
PINE PARK
CAMP AREA AND
PICNIC FACILITIES
NAPLES, N.Y.

SCALE 1" = 40'

N

SYMBOL KEY: PICNIC TABLES | OUTDOOR GRILLS | WATER FOUNTAIN AND SPIGOTS | GARBAGE CANS | POLE LIGHTS

DESIGN BY ED DENNEHY

DESIGNED BY EDWARD DENNEHY
DANBURY, CT

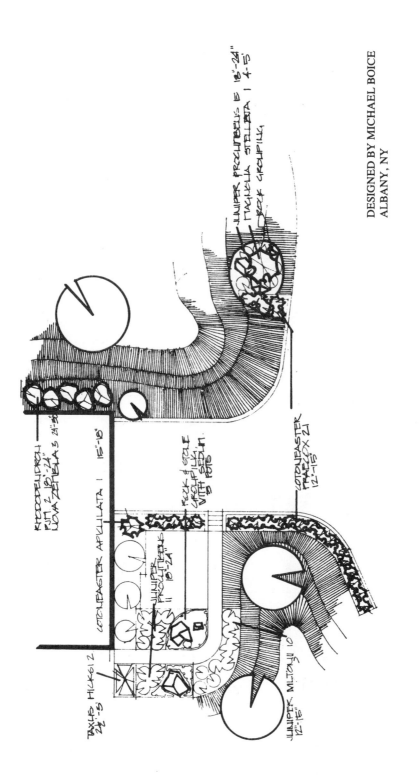

DESIGNED BY MICHAEL BOICE
ALBANY, NY

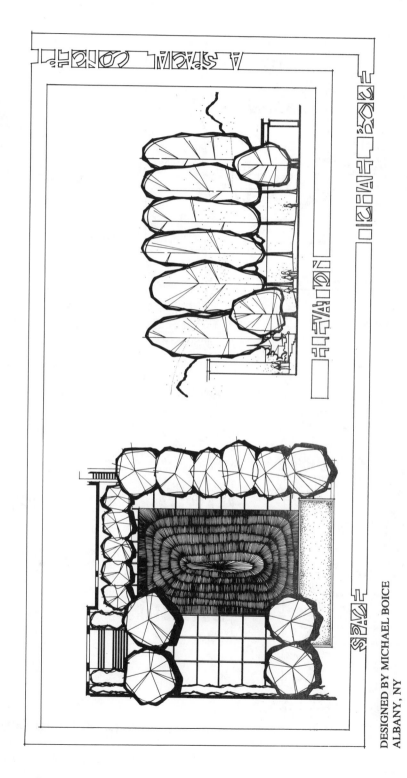

DESIGNED BY MICHAEL BOICE
ALBANY, NY

PLANTING PLAN FOR

MR. & MRS. C. MASICK

COBLESKILL, N.Y.

DESIGNED BY MICHAEL BOICE
ALBANY, NY

SITE PLAN

DESIGNED BY MARK MAGNONE
SCHENECTADY, NY

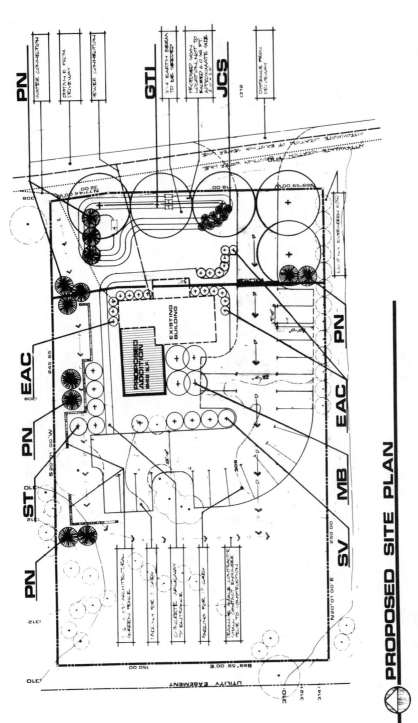

PROPOSED SITE PLAN

DESIGNED BY MARK MAGNONE
SCHENECTADY, NY

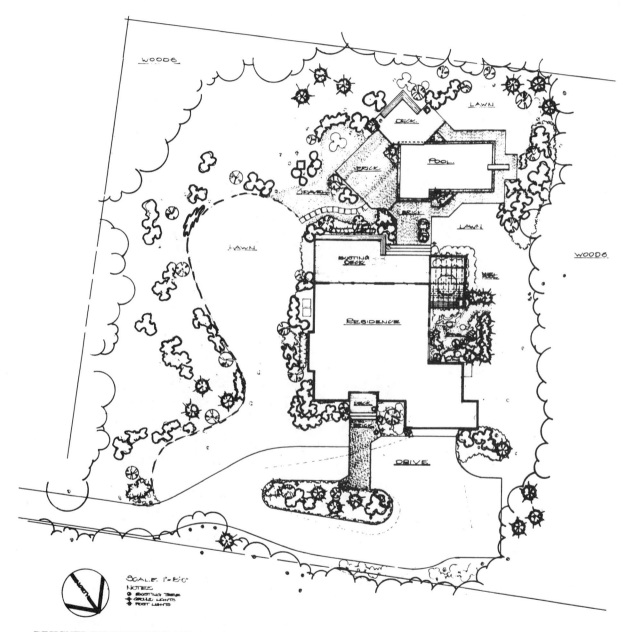

DESIGNED BY GOLDBERG AND RODLER
HUNTINGTON, NY

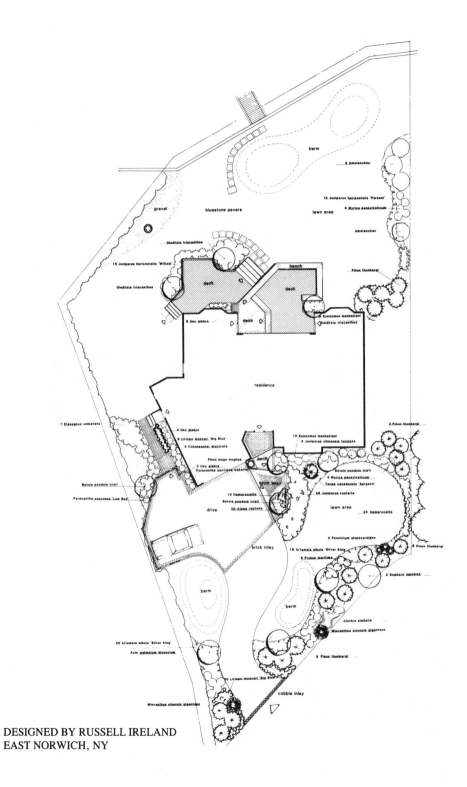

DESIGNED BY RUSSELL IRELAND
EAST NORWICH, NY

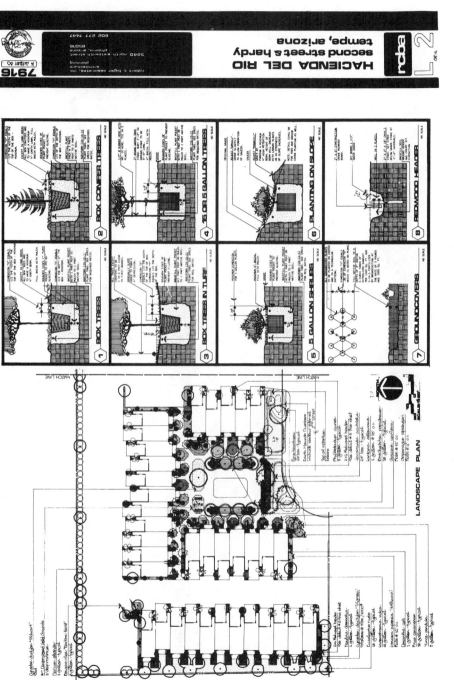

DESIGNED BY JOHN KRIEG, LANDSCAPE ARCHITECT
ROBT. C. BIGLER ASSOC., ARCHITECTS
PHOENIX, ARIZONA

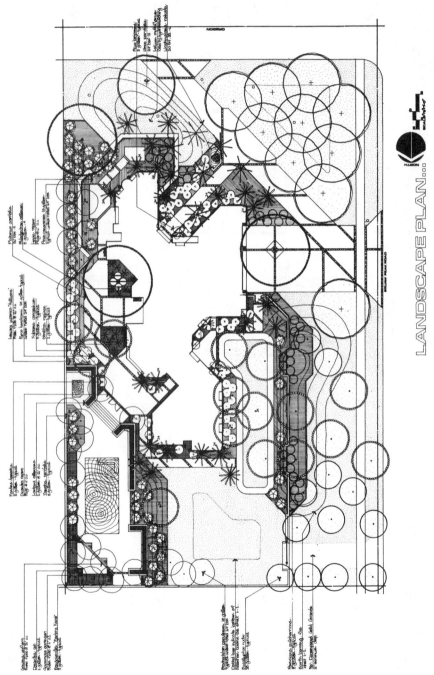

LANDSCAPE PLAN...

DESIGNED BY JOHN KRIEG, LANDSCAPE ARCHITECT
ROBT. C. BIGLER ASSOC., ARCHITECTS
PHOENIX, ARIZONA

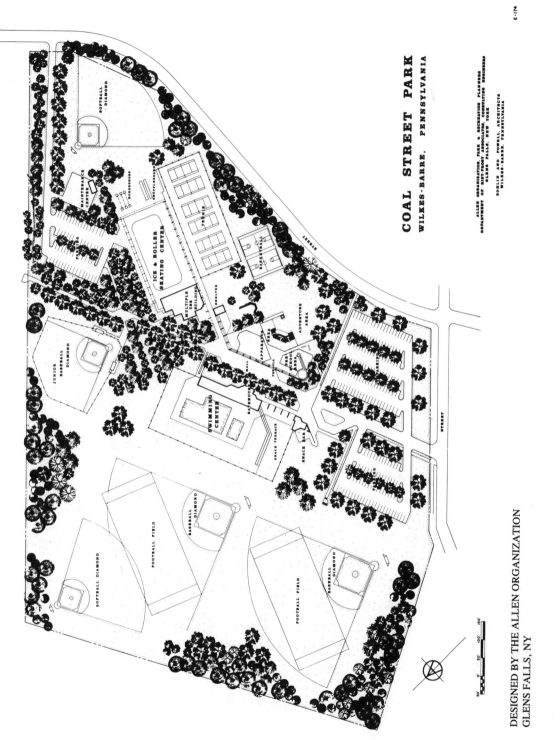

COAL STREET PARK
WILKES-BARRE, PENNSYLVANIA

ALLEN ORGANIZATION, PARK & RECREATION PLANNERS
DEPARTMENT OF RUST-FROST ASSOCIATES, CONSULTING ENGINEERS
GLENS FALLS, NEW YORK

ROSLIN AND POWELL, ARCHITECTS
WILKES-BARRE, PENNSYLVANIA

E-174

DESIGNED BY THE ALLEN ORGANIZATION
GLENS FALLS, NY

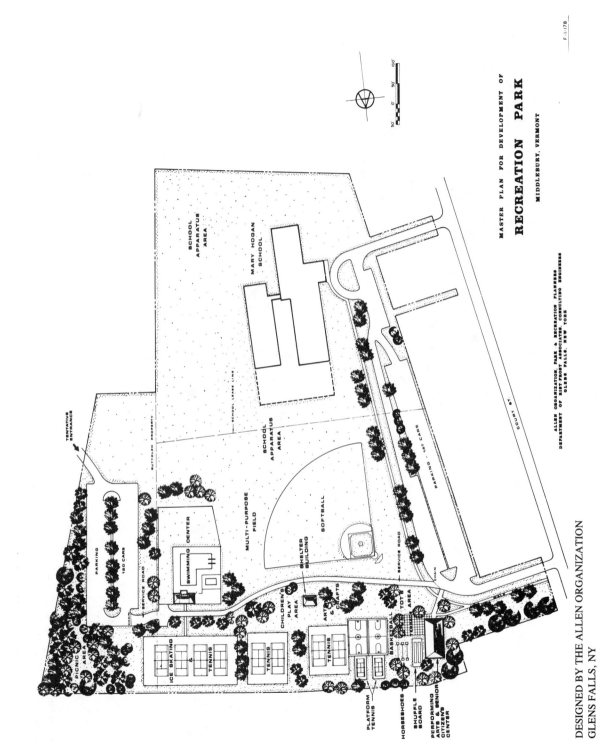

MASTER PLAN FOR DEVELOPMENT OF

RECREATION PARK

MIDDLEBURY, VERMONT

ALLEN ORGANIZATION, PARK & RECREATION PLANNERS
DEPARTMENT OF RIST-FRONT ASSOCIATES, CONSULTING ENGINEERS
GLENS FALLS, NEW YORK

DESIGNED BY THE ALLEN ORGANIZATION
GLENS FALLS, NY

ANALYZING THE LANDSCAPE SITE

OBJECTIVES

After studying this unit, you will be able to

- define the word *site,* and explain its significance in the development of a landscape.
- list the features by which a site can be evaluated.
- describe the limitations that the terrain imposes upon human activities.
- understand the basic concepts of land grading.

THE SITE

The word *site* refers to a piece of land that has the potential for development. The evaluation of a site involves any or all of the following factors:

- A comparison of the characteristics of two or more possible land areas
- An analysis of the features of a single piece of land

- A comparison of the potential uses for a site
- Selection of a site, and a final detailed analysis of it

Site comparisons and analyses are part of the responsibilities of professional *site planners.*

The following examples illustrate how site analysis functions in the landscape process.

Comparing Sites

A religious organization plans to build a facility which will serve as a summer camp for its members and their families. The facility is intended to provide space for thirty residential cabins, a center for worship services, assorted woodland recreational areas, adequate parking, and all necessary public utilities. Privacy is also deemed to be a necessity.

Two sites are available, both of which are within the financial means of the organization. The principal characteristics of the two sites are listed on page 82.

Site A	Site B
The site consists of 500 acres; 400 are wooded and rolling, 100 are cleared and level.	The site consists of 550 acres, all of which are wooded and rolling.
The site adjoins a major state highway.	The site is near a state highway, but actually adjoins a secondary road.
Land adjacent to the site is presently wooded, but is zoned commercial.	Land adjacent to the site is state forest land which is not likely to be rezoned.
A small stream runs through the property.	The property has no surface water, but it borders on a large lake.
Utility lines are already installed near the property.	Utility lines are farther from the site than they are in Site A.
The soil is heavy clay, and one section of the wooded acreage has major rock outcroppings.	The soil is loamy to sandy and without rock formations.

Once the characteristics are noted, the site planner can begin a comparative analysis to determine which site will best satisfy the client's needs. This process is not like fitting a pair of shoes or solving a puzzle. There is never a perfect solution. The 100% perfect site does not exist among the available choices. Site analysis often results in reshaping the client's needs. Though failing to meet certain needs, the analysis may introduce new possibilities of the land that had not occurred to the client originally.

In this example, neither site is totally right or wrong for the organization. Site A would permit the construction of cabins and other buildings, plus parking lots, on the 100 acres of cleared flat land, without the need for extensive and costly clearing and grading of the land. Site B would need to be cleared and leveled before building could begin. Site A is reached more easily than Site B. However, the better site could depend upon the client's attitude toward remoteness and privacy.

Both sites offer sizeable woodlands, but the commercial zoning of the land around Site A could result in a great change in the character of the area over a period of years. Site B, surrounded by state-owned forest land, is unlikely to change as much as Site A, if at all, through the years. As a financial investment, Site A, because of the nearby commercial zoning, would increase in value faster than Site B. The preferable site could depend upon the client's concern or lack of concern about the land as an investment.

Finally, the lake in Site B would probably be considered as a more desirable feature for water recreation than the small stream in Site A. Whether the client would favor Site B over Site A would depend upon the importance of the lake as a positive site feature, as compared to the negative features of Site B and the positive features of Site A.

Analyzing One Site

A farmer wants to utilize 400 acres of marginally productive farmland in a way that will increase its profitability. The farmer seeks suggestions for potential use of the site as a recreational facility.

The principal features of the site are as follows.

- The site consists of 400 acres; 200 acres are cleared and level, and 200 acres are wooded but open beneath the canopy. The wooded acres were used as a grazing woodlot for cattle. The two 200-acre portions are separated by a stream where the trout fishing is good.

- The stream flows into a nearby public reservoir where recreational boating and swimming are allowed.
- Small wildlife abounds on the site.
- The soil is somewhat rocky and drains well.
- One corner of the woodlot is swampy and contains a growth of vegetation rare to the area.
- The site receives substantial snow accumulation during the winter.
- The land around the site is agricultural in character.
- The area is zoned for agriculture and small business.
- The site and adjacent areas were the scenes of many local skirmishes during the Civil War.
- The site is a rich source of American Indian artifacts, as well as prehistoric fossils.

In this example, the site analysis becomes an itemized account of the property's characteristics. Most of them cannot be rated as positive or negative, since the client has not yet decided how to put the property to use. The site's characteristics of themselves may suggest the best use. The terrain is suitable for all types of camping. Canoeing and boating are possibilities. Nature studies or hunting could take place in the swampy areas and habitats (living and growing areas). The historical and archaeological features could be developed as tourist attractions.

In short, the site analysis can help to suggest uses for the land that the client had not thought of before.

THE CHARACTERISTICS OF A SITE

No two sites are identical. Although some may appear to be quite similar, each has a combination of qualities that sets it apart from other properties. A landscape planner should have an organized method to assess the hundreds of characteristics pertaining to each site.

Separating the factors into categories is a logical place to begin. Some of the site's characteristics are *natural* features, while others are *man-made*. Other features are *cultural* (associated with human society). Still others are basically *physical* features. Some other characteristics are most important as *visual* features. Some features are unmistakably *positive* factors, and others are definitely *negative* in impact. Many have a *neutral* quality until they are judged in the context of the proposed design.

A checklist is one way to compile the factors of a site analysis, figure 9–1. In this example, the information, when filled in, will be both complete and concise. The checklist can then be taken to the drawing table to provide essential input for the design process.

The analysis checklist is a flexible tool for the designer. An item can be simply checked (✓) to indicate its presence, or additional notations can be made to indicate its size, direction, quality, state of repair, importance, prominence, possible uses, and so on. The more notations there are, the more helpful is the data in producing a landscape plan that will fit the site.

READING THE TERRAIN

The rise and fall of the land describes its *terrain*. The record of an area's terrain

Site Analysis for the Property of

Client's Name _Mr. & Mrs. John Doe_

Client's Address _1234 Main Street_

Tucson, Arizona

Taken By _JCA_ Date Taken _April 12, 1982_

Site Characteristics	Physical Importance	Visual Importance	Pos. +	Neg. -	Neutral ?
NATURAL FACTORS					
Existing vegetation	2 SHADE TREES IN RA. 1 FL. TREE OFF S.W REAR CORNER	ALL IN GOOD HEALTH AND ATTRACTIVE	✓		
Stones, boulders, rock outcroppings	NONE	NONE			
Wind, breezes	WESTERLY / GUSTY			✓	
Surface water features	NONE	NONE			
Groundwater	TOO DEEP TO BE USABLE				✓
Soil conditions	CALICHE LAYER			✓	
Birds and small game	✓	✓	✓		
Large game	NONE				
Existing shade	FAIRLY GOOD		✓		
Turf plantings	NONE OF QUALITY				✓
Terrain features	LEVEL				✓
Direct sunlight	LOTS OF IT / ALL DAY				✓
Off-site views		MOUNTAINS IN DISTANCE	✓		
Others					
Hardiness zone 9					
Soil pH 8.4					
Soil texture SANDY DOWN TO THE CALICHE					
MAN-MADE FACTORS					
Architectural style of building(s)		SPANISH			✓
Presence of outbuildings	NONE				✓
Existing patios	10x15 CONCRETE	NOTHING SPECIAL			✓
Existing walks, paths, steps, ramps	DRIVEWAY IN / WALKS IN / CONCRETE		✓		
Swimming pool	YES	OVAL / 30' LONG	✓		
Fountains, reflecting pools	NONE	NONE			
Statuary	NONE	NONE			
Fences, walls	NONE	NONE			
Existing lighting	NONE	NONE			
Off-site features		HOMES ON ALL SIDES			✓
Others FIRE HYDRANT	FRONT CORNER OF LOT			✓	
CULTURAL FACTORS					
Power lines (aboveground)	YES	UNATTRACTIVE		✓	
Power lines (belowground)	NO	NO			
Telephone lines	YES			✓	
Water lines	INSTALLED				✓
Historical features	NONE	NONE			
Archaeological features		ATTRACTIVE SPANISH STYLING	✓		
Nearby roadways	IN FRONT OF HOUSE				✓
Neighbors	GOOD RELATIONSHIP /	ELDERLY ON N SIDE FAMILIES + KIDS ON E+W	✓		
Off-site benefits		GOOD DISTANT VIEWS	✓		
Off-site nuisances	WIND IS TOO STRONG			✓	
Zoning regulations	YES / PROTECTIVE		✓		
Nearby public transportation	NO				✓

Figure 9–1. Site analysis checklist

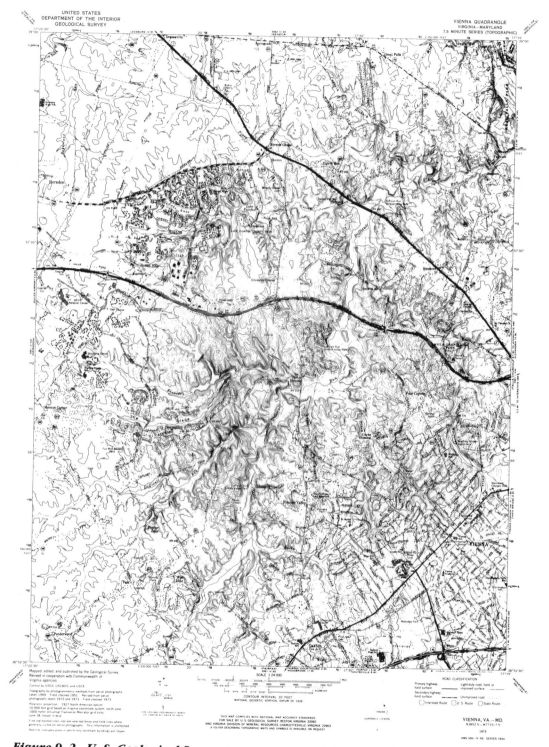

Figure 9–2. U. S. Geological Survey topographic map *(Courtesy of U. S. Geological Survey)*

is its *topography.* Topography is charted and recorded nationally by the United States Geological Survey, in the form of topographic maps, figure 9–2.

The maps are drawn to a scale of 1 inch = 2,000 feet. The broken lines on the map are *contour lines,* representing a vertical rise or fall of 10 feet over the horizontal distance measured from the map's scale. Each contour line connects all of the points of equal elevation on that map, and is labeled to indicate its elevation. The vertical distance between contour lines, *the contour interval,* is always stated on the map (10 feet in the U.S. Geological Survey topographic maps). Steep slopes are identified by closely spaced contour lines. Gradual slopes are denoted by more widely spaced contour lines. See figure 9–3.

For large sites, the U.S. Geological Survey maps may provide satisfactory data for a designer to use in planning the landscape. These maps are available for most areas of the United States, and may be purchased at a nominal cost from regional offices of the Survey. For smaller sites, the scale of the map may need to be 1 inch = 50 feet, or smaller, and the contour interval as precise as 1 foot between lines. To obtain such precise data, the landscape planner may have to hire a private surveyor.

Figure 9–4 illustrates some of the land forms recognizable from a topographic map. In order to interpret the map fully, students should know the following points regarding contours and contour lines:

- Existing contours are always shown as broken lines.
- Proposed contours are always shown as solid lines.
- Contours are labeled either on the

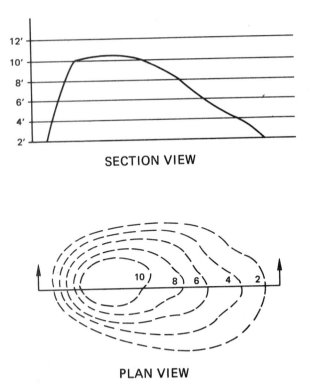

SECTION VIEW

PLAN VIEW

Figure 9–3. The contour interval is 2 feet. Closely spaced contour lines represent a steep slope. Widely spaced lines show a gradual slope.

high side of the contour or in the middle of the line.
- Spot elevations are used to mark important points.
- Contour lines neither split nor overlap (except in overhangs).
- Contour lines always close on themselves. The site map may not be large enough to show the closing, but it does occur on the land.
- Run-off water always flows downhill along a line that is perpendicular to the contour lines.

Once the contours of a site are known and plotted, then slopes can be measured and analyzed. *Slopes* are measurements that

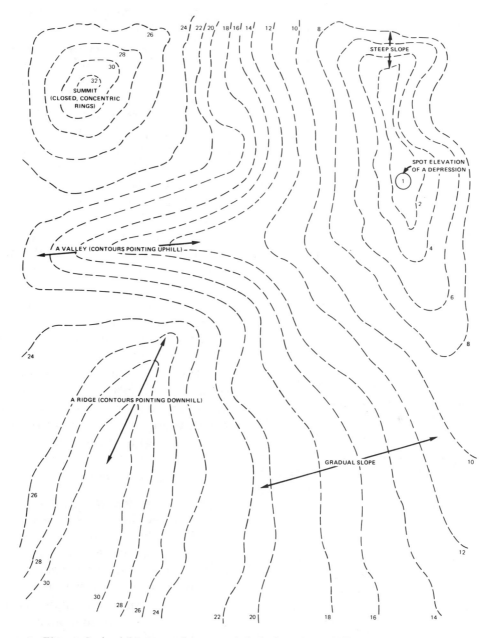

Figure 9–4. A topographic map labeled to show different land forms

compare the horizontal length (measured from the map's scale) to vertical rise or fall (as determined by the contour lines and contour interval). Slopes may be stated as

ratios or percents. As a *ratio,* the horizontal space required for each foot of vertical change in elevation is commonly expressed as 3:1, 4:1, and so forth, figure 9–5. As a

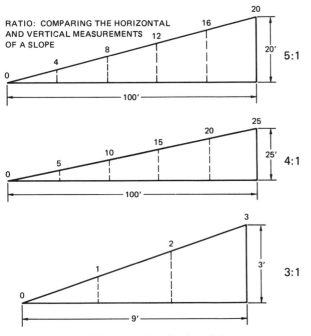

Figure 9–5. Ratio of slope

percent, the vertical distance is divided by the horizontal distance, and the answer is expressed as 33%, 25%, and so forth. Another way to visualize percent of slope is to picture the slope extending along a horizontal distance of 100 feet. The vertical distance then becomes comparable to the percent of slope, figure 9–6.

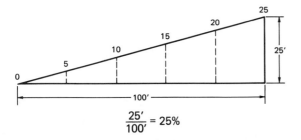

Figure 9–6. Percent of slope

THE NEED FOR TERRAIN INFORMATION

The ease or difficulty of development depends upon whether the land is level or rolling, rocky or sandy, forested or open. A study of the terrain also supplies answers to such basic questions as: Where does the surface water flow? Will water collect in puddles anywhere? What types of human activities can take place? Will grass grow on that slope? Can a car be parked safely on that slope?

Most human activities require that the land is flat or nearly flat. Land which is 5% or less in slope is perceived by users as flat. Flat land is the easiest terrain to develop, but it may be difficult to move off surface water. A slope of at least 1% is usually necessary to drain off surface water on turf and other planted landscape areas.

Human activities can usually take place on a slope of 5% to 10%, but users will sense the nonlevel footing. Land which slopes more than 10% may require alteration (grading) to make it more usable. Figure 9–7 lists the acceptable slopes for various landscape components.

GRADING THE LAND

When the terrain is not suitable for the activities planned for the site, it may be necessary to reshape it. The form of the land is changed by a process called *grading.* Grading can be as simple as one worker leveling and smoothing a small area of earth with a spade and a rake, and hauling away the leftover soil in a cart. It also can be so extensive that massive bulldozers and dump trucks are required to chew up and haul away entire mountains. Regardless of the extent of the project, grading is usually done for one of four reasons:

Landscape Component	Percent of Slope		Illustrated Example
	Allowable	Ideal	
Sitting areas, patios, terraces and decks	1/2% to 3%	1/2% to 2%	2%
Lawns	1% to 5%	2% to 3%	3%
Walks	1/2% to 8%	1% to 4%	4%
Driveways and ramps	1/2% to 11%	1% to 11%	10%
Banks planted with grass	Up to 33%	16% to 33%	30%
Banks planted with groundcovers and shrubs	Up to 50%	20% to 33%	33%
Steps	Up to 65%	33% to 50%	50%

Figure 9–7. Recommended slopes for common landscape components

- To create level spaces for the construction of buildings
- To create the level spaces required for activities and facilities such as parking

lots, swimming pools, and playing fields

- To introduce special effects into the landscape, such as better drainage, earth berms, tree wells, and ponds
- To improve the rate and pattern of circulation by means of better roads, ramps, tracks or paths

When earth is *removed* from a slope, the grading practice is called *cutting*. When earth is *added* to a slope, the practice is called *filling*. On a contour map, a cut is shown as (1) a solid line diverting from and then returning to an existing contour line, and (2) moving in the direction of a higher contour. A fill is shown as (1) a solid line diverting from and then returning to an existing contour line, but (2) moving in the direction of a lower contour line. See figure 9–8. A typical graded slope is illustrated in figure 9–9.

Since the grading process can involve the movement of tons of soil and rocks, designers should approach such specifications cautiously. In cut and fill operations, the

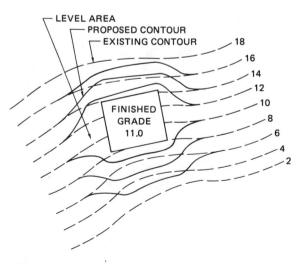

Figure 9–8. Cut and fill as shown on a topographic map

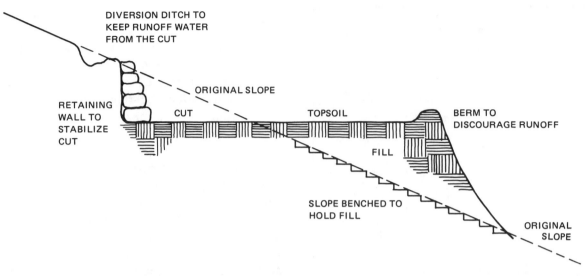

Figure 9–9. Cross-sectional view of a typical graded slope

soil that is removed from the cut should be used to create the fill whenever possible. This practice minimizes the need for hauling. If possible, the topsoil layer should be stripped away and stockpiled before grading begins. The topsoil can then be spread over the finished grade before the site is replanted.

When land is graded, not only is the topsoil disturbed, but the surface water drainage and vegetation are disturbed as well. Water must drain away from buildings, not toward them. Freshly graded slopes must be stabilized to guard against erosion. The surface roots of valuable trees must be protected from the destruction of

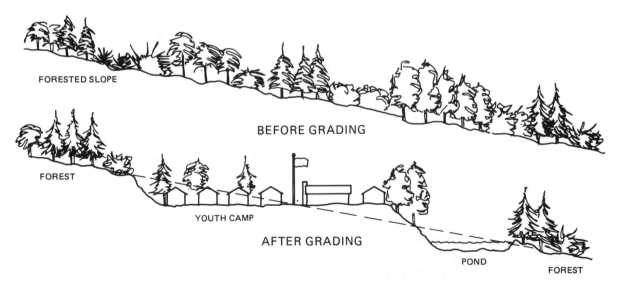

Figure 9–10. A typical slope before and after grading

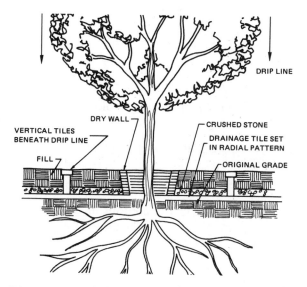

Figure 9–11. *Raising the grade around an existing tree*

Figure 9–12. Although the level of the lawn has been lowered, the tree's roots remain at the original level because of the retaining wall.

cutting and the suffocation of filling. Figure 9–10 shows a typical slope before and after grading. Figures 9–11 and 9–12 show common techniques for dealing with trees that exist prior to the grading of a site.

ACHIEVEMENT REVIEW

A. Indicate if the site characteristics listed are natural (N), man-made (M), or cultural (C).

1. condition of the turf
2. nearness of public transportation
3. rock outcroppings
4. swimming pool
5. terrain features
6. off-site views
7. buildings on the site
8. style of the architecture
9. existing shade
10. prevailing breezes
11. soil conditions
12. historical features
13. provisions for parking
14. nearness of neighbors
15. presence of wildlife
16. traffic sounds
17. zoning regulations
18. presence of large, old trees
19. existing lighting
20. surface water patterns

B.   Define the following terms.

1.   terrain
2.   topography
3.   contour line

4.   contour interval
5.   slope

C.   Complete the following sentences that describe the characteristics of contours and contour lines.

1.   Existing contours are always shown as _____ lines on topographic maps.
2.   Proposed contours are always shown as _____ lines on topographic maps.
3.   Contours are always labeled on the _____ side of the contour or in the _____ of the line.
4.   Important points on topographic maps are marked by _____.
5.   A 3:1 or 4:1 comparison is the _____ of a slope.

D.   Label the parts of a typical cut and fill shown in the following diagram.

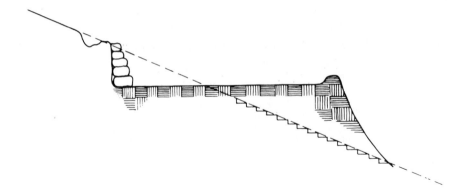

E.   Identify the land forms A through E on the contour map on page 93.

SUGGESTED ACTIVITIES

1.   Fill several greenhouse flats with loamy soil and plant with grass seed. Tip the flats to create various slopes up to 50%. Water all flats with the same amount of water, applied from a sprinkling can. Record the erosion noted over the weeks at each degree of slope. Record also the quantity and quality of grass that grows.

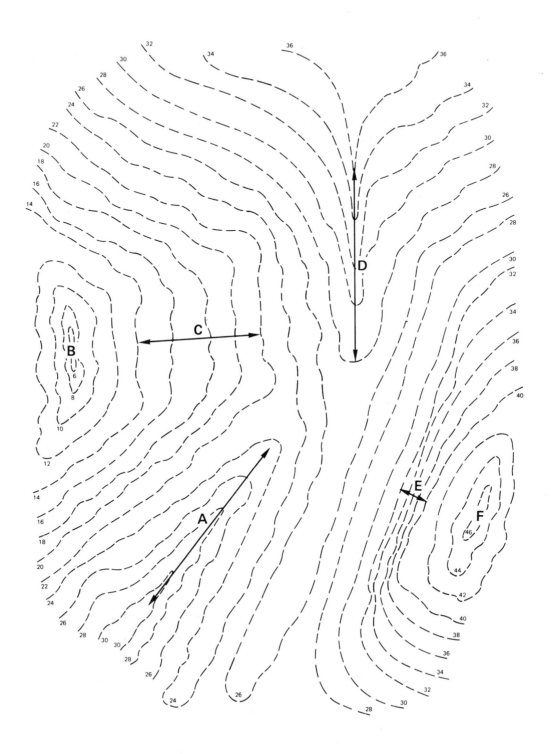

2. Build a small contour model from information on a topographic map. Use cardboard of a thickness comparable to the contour interval on the map.

3. Using a sand table, the instructor can set up site situations that require alterations before landscaping can begin. Teams of students can alter the sites and discuss their reasoning with the class.

4. Order topographic maps of the local area from the U. S. Geological Survey. Find recognizable local features on the map to help students visualize how the contour lines describe terrain variations.

5. Invite a land surveyor to visit the class to demonstrate the use of surveying instruments and explain how land surveys are done.

THE OUTDOOR ROOM CONCEPT

OBJECTIVES

After studying this unit, you will be able to

- identify indoor and outdoor use areas.
- list and define the features of the outdoor room.

Modern American homes may vary in size from three or four rooms to several dozen. Regardless of the simplicity or complexity of the home, the rooms are usually divided into four different categories of use, figure 10–1. The *public area* of the home is that portion which is seen by anyone coming to the house. The public area includes the entry foyer, reception room, and enclosed porch. The *family living area* includes those rooms of the house which are used for family activities and for entertaining friends. Rooms such as the living room, dining room, family room, and game room fall into this category. The *service area* includes those rooms of the house which are used to meet the family's operating needs. These include the laundry room, sewing room, kitchen, and utility room. The *private living area* of the home is used only by the members of the family for their personal activities. The bedrooms comprise the major rooms of this area. Dressing rooms, if present, are also included.

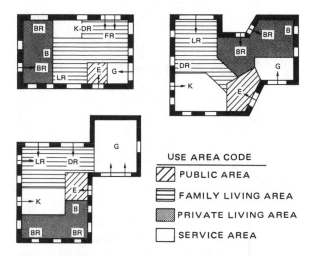

Figure 10–1. Examples of use area categories within the home

OUTDOOR USE AREAS

Just as a house is divided into different areas of use, so is the property around it. The public area of the landscape is the front yard. It is that portion of the landscape which is seen by everyone who drives or walks past the house. It is also the one area of the landscape through which everyone passes who enters the house. Ideally, the public area of the landscape connects with the public area of the home, figure 10–2. The public area should be large enough to

place the house into an attractive setting, but not so large that a usable family living area is sacrificed.

The family living area of the landscape should also connect with the indoor family area whenever possible. This is often difficult because of the layout of some houses. The outdoor family living area is usually located toward the rear and often toward the side of the house. It is that portion of the landscape where the family relaxes and entertains guests. It includes space for patio, barbecuing, swimming, or whatever activities interest the family members. It is the largest of the outdoor use areas. Because of its location and its purpose, this portion of the landscape is seen by fewer people than the public area. It is developed for full or partial privacy. However, the quality of the design in both the family area and public area is important. They are both major areas of the landscape serving different purposes for the family.

The service area of the landscape plays a functional role for the family. It provides space to hang clothes, store garbage, house a dog, or grow a vegetable garden. Since it is used for service rather than beauty, the service area is usually screened from view. It is located near the kitchen or other indoor service room. The outdoor service area should be big enough to accomplish its purpose, but no larger.

All of the outdoor use areas described so far are most successful if they are connected directly to the indoor rooms they serve. A visual connection by way of a window is almost a necessity. A physical connection through a doorway is highly desirable. To be able to walk directly from the living room or family room into the outdoor family living area is a pleasure; to have to go through the kitchen or garage

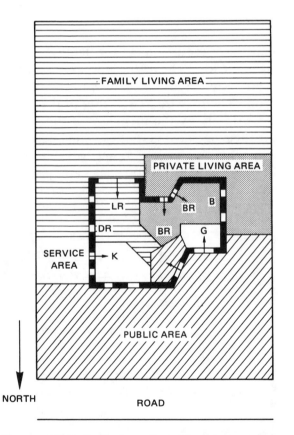

Figure 10–2. Indoor and outdoor use areas should be matched in location as closely as possible. For example, notice that in this drawing, the outdoor service area adjoins the kitchen, the indoor service area.

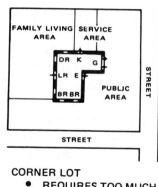

CORNER LOT
- REQUIRES TOO MUCH PUBLIC AREA

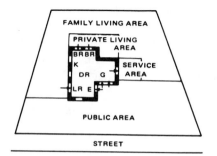

WIDE FRONT LOT
- ALSO WASTES SPACE AS PUBLIC AREA

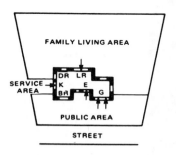

NARROW FRONT LOT
- MINIMIZES PUBLIC AREA
- MAXIMIZES FAMILY LIVING AREA

Figure 10-3. Assigning landscape use areas is easier on some lots than on others.

first is not so pleasant and may be a nuisance.

The one outdoor use area which requires a direct physical link to the indoor room it serves is the private living area. This outdoor living area is developed for total privacy. The view of outsiders is screened. This is the area of the landscape where the family may sunbathe or relax in private. If the outdoor area is to serve the bedrooms of the house, it must be possible to reach the outdoor area without walking through another part of the house or yard. Therefore, a door off the bedroom is necessary if this area is being planned.

Figure 10-3 shows several different houses and lots divided into outdoor living areas. Note the sizes of the use areas and their relationship to indoor rooms, exits, and windows.

THE OUTDOOR ROOM CONCEPT

Once the use areas have been assigned to the property, the next step is to design and develop those areas into livable outdoor spaces. To accomplish this, it is helpful to think of the outdoor space as an outdoor room. In this way, students can apply some of what they know about indoor rooms to the outdoors.

The composition of the indoor room is the same whether it is simple or ornate, consisting of walls, a ceiling, and a floor. While the materials may vary from room to room, the basic structure remains the same.

The outdoor room also has walls, a ceiling, and a floor, figure 10-4. The materials are usually different from those used indoors, but they accomplish the same purpose. The *outdoor wall* defines the limits or size of the outdoor room. It can also

Figure 10–4. A typical outdoor room, containing wall, ceiling, and floor elements

slow or prevent movement in a certain direction. The walls of the outdoor room determine the vertical sides of the room in the same manner as the walls of an indoor room. Thus, outdoor wall materials should not be placed in the middle of the lawn, where a wall would not logically be located. Materials used to form outdoor walls may be natural (shrubs, small trees, ground covers, and flowers) or man-made (fencing and masonry).

The *outdoor floor* provides the surfacing for the outdoor room. The materials used for the outdoor floor might be natural surfacings such as grass, ground covers, sand, gravel, or water. They might also be man-made surfacings such as brick, concrete, patio blocks, or tile.

The *outdoor ceiling* defines the upper limits of the outdoor room. It may offer physical protection, such as an awning or

Figure 10–5A. Example of a public area

aluminum covering, or merely provide shade, such as a tree. In temperate regions, a deciduous tree is an ideal ceiling material for placement near the home. It gives shade from the hot summer sun, and then drops its leaves in the winter to allow the sunlight through, which warms the house.

Figures 10–5 and 10–6 illustrate two

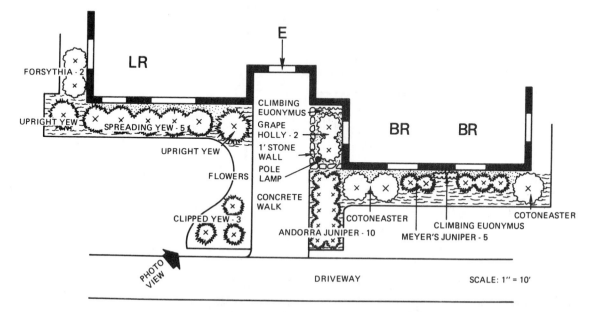

Figure 10–5B. Plan view of the public area

Figure 10–6A. Example of a family living area

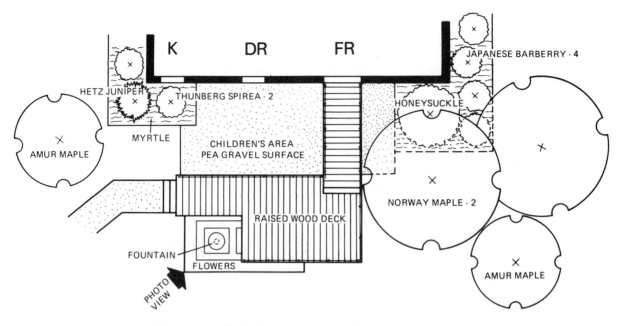

Figure 10–6B. *Plan view of the family living area*

use areas around a home landscape. Carefully analyze the development of these areas as outdoor rooms, noting the different materials used for the walls, ceilings, and floors. Also examine the corresponding landscape plan for each area.

PRACTICE EXERCISES

A.   Figure 10–7 shows three individual houses on their own lots. All windows, doors, and rooms are marked. Also provided is information on the family living in each house. Trace each house and its lot on tracing paper. Using a straightedge and pencil, divide each lot into the three or four use areas that seem appropriate for the family. With a scale instrument, determine the approximate square footage of each area you lay out. Is each area a practical size? Are the shapes such that rooms could later be developed if necessary? Is the family living area going to receive a good deal of sunshine? (It should be located on the south or west side of the property if possible.) Is the private living area receiving morning sun from the east? If it is intended as a morning use area, western afternoon sun is of little value.

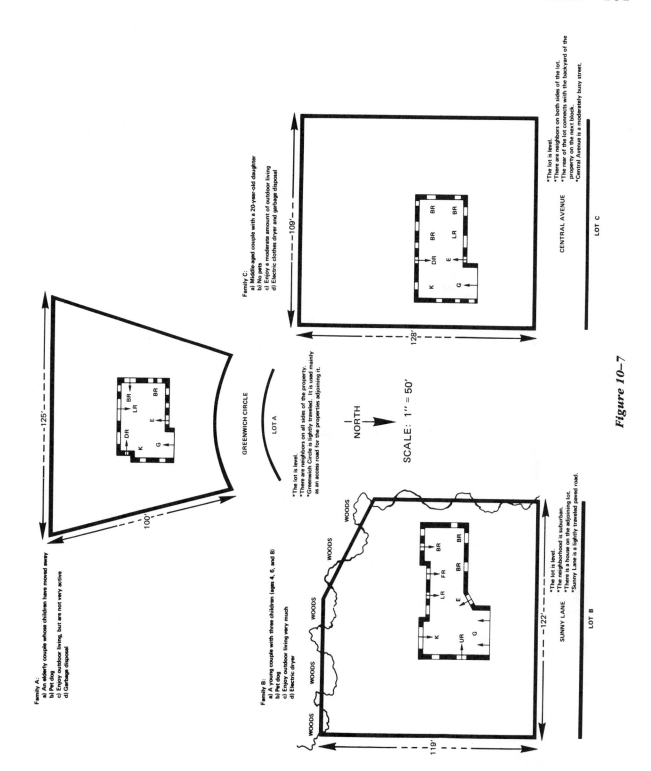

Family A:
a) An elderly couple whose children have moved away
b) Pet dog
c) Enjoy outdoor living, but are not very active
d) Garbage disposal

Family B:
a) A young couple with three children (ages 4, 6, and 8)
b) Pet dog
c) Enjoy outdoor living very much
d) Electric dryer

Family C:
a) Middle-aged couple with a 20-year-old daughter
b) No pets
c) Enjoy a moderate amount of outdoor living
d) Electric clothes dryer and garbage disposal

*The lot is level.
*There are neighbors on all sides of the property.
*Greenwich Circle is lightly traveled. It is used mainly as an access road for the properties adjoining it.

*The lot is level.
*The neighborhood is suburban.
*There is a house on the adjoining lot.
*Sunny Lane is a lightly traveled paved road.

*The lot is level.
*There are neighbors on both sides of the lot.
*The rear of the lot connects with the backyard of the property on the next block.
*Central Avenue is a moderately busy street.

NORTH

SCALE: 1" = 50'

GREENWICH CIRCLE

LOT A

SUNNY LANE

LOT B

CENTRAL AVENUE

LOT C

Figure 10–7

B. Figures 10–8 and 10–9 illustrate two partially completed landscapes. Trace each landscape onto paper. Applying your knowledge of symbolization and the outdoor room concept, complete the landscape plans. As you insert symbols for trees, shrubs, and construction materials into the plans, be certain that each feature is playing the role of a wall, ceiling, or floor element.

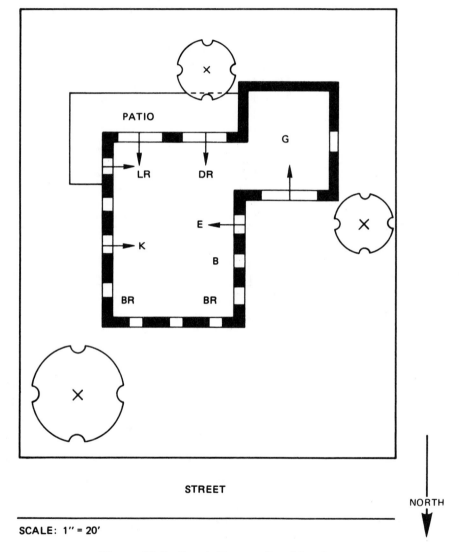

Figure 10–8. Partially completed landscape

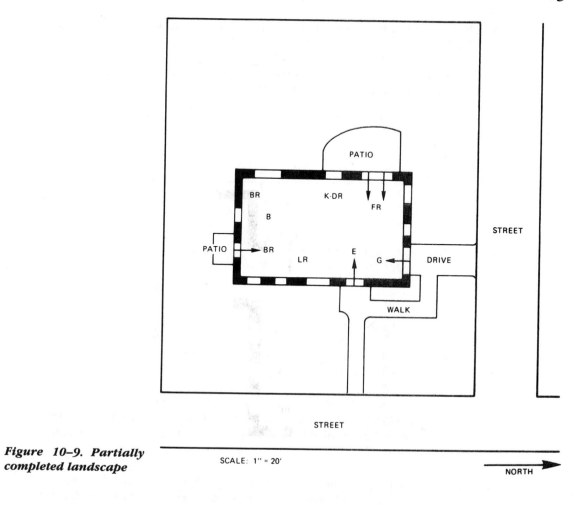

Figure 10–9. Partially completed landscape

SCALE: 1″ = 20′

NORTH

ACHIEVEMENT REVIEW

A. Indicate in which use area the following activities occur.

Activity	Public Area	Family Living Area	Service Area	Private Living Area
picnicking				
welcoming guests				
hanging laundry				
breakfast, coffee				
badminton				
pitch and catch				
trash can storage				

B.   Indicate if the following materials are used for outdoor walls, ceilings, or floors.

Material	Outdoor Wall	Outdoor Ceiling	Outdoor Floor
brick wall shrubs crushed stone high-branching tree turf grass fencing			

SUGGESTED ACTIVITIES

1.   Study various types of house floor plans. (These can be found in numerous magazines.) Which ones provide the best access to the outdoors through doorways? Which ones have only visual connection between the house and garden through windows?

2.   Walk down a neighborhood street. Evaluate the public areas of the homes. Have the houses been placed in attractive settings? Are the wall elements where they should be or do they project into the center of the outdoor room?

3.   Evaluate the property on which your school is located. Can different use areas be seen? Does the landscape appear to be a series of connecting outdoor rooms?

UNIT 11

DESIGNING PLANTINGS

OBJECTIVES

After studying this unit, you will be able to

- identify the five principles of design and explain how they are applied to landscaping.
- arrange plant materials in linear and corner designs.
- explain the basic techniques involved in foundation planting design.

THE PRINCIPLES OF DESIGN

The landscape designer engages in a form of applied art, much as an architect or interior decorator does. Any form of art, including landscape designing, is guided by several basic principles. These *principles of design* have been applied by artists for centuries and are as relevant for today's students as they were for ancient Greeks.

Simplicity

The first principle of design is *simplicity*. To apply this principle, the landscaper must first realize that there may be com-

plexities in the property before he or she even begins work. For example, a client may own a highly ornate home or desire the use of many different plants, flowers, and statues. In a case such as this, it is the task of the landscaper to develop simplicity in the property so that it provides a restful setting for outdoor living.

Simplicity may be incorporated in several ways. Repetition of the same species of plant, construction material, or color is one of the easiest ways to keep a landscape simple. It is not necessary, as some individuals believe, to use a great number of plants to have a well-landscaped home. Massing plants is another way to create simplicity. Massing can give the landscape a sense of unity not otherwise possible, since the individual plants do not have to compete with one another for attention.

Simplicity in design does not necessarily suggest a boring or limited landscape. The design can be simple, yet still show full outdoor room development with a variety of plants and other landscape features. Figure 11–1 illustrates two *plantings* (groupings of plants), each containing the same plants. Notice how simplicity is achieved in planting (B) through the use of a smooth,

105

A. CHOPPY SILHOUETTE – NO MASSING

B. FLOWING SILHOUETTE – SPECIES MASSED

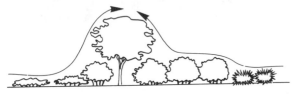

Figure 11–1. Simplicity in plant arrangement. Grouping B allows the viewer's eye to move smoothly along the planting.

Figure 11–2. Symmetric balance. One side of the outdoor room is a mirror image of the opposite side.

flowing silhouette and the grouping of plant species.

Balance

The second principle of design is *balance*. To understand this principle, the student should imagine the outdoor room cut in half and placed upon a scale. If both sides of the outdoor room attract the eye of the viewer equally, the design is well balanced. There are two types of balance useful in residential designing: symmetric and asymmetric. With *symmetric balance*, figure 11–2, one side of the outdoor room is planted and built exactly the same as the side opposite it. While symmetric balance is still used in landscape designing, it some-

times creates a formal appearance which may be undesirable. For this reason, asymmetric balance is more commonly used. As figure 11–3 shows, *asymmetric balance* creates the same amount of interest on both sides of the outdoor room, but does not create an exact duplication.

Proportion

Third among the principles of design is *proportion*. Proportion is concerned with the size relationship of the features of the landscape. In figure 11–4, a tree is shown between two houses. The tree is out of proportion with house (A), but is in proper proportion with house (B). Next to house (A), the tree looks gigantic, even threatening. With house (B), however, the tree seems appropriate and comfortable. The principle of proportion can be applied to plants, constructed features, and buildings.

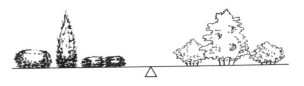

Figure 11–3. Asymmetric balance. One side of the outdoor room has as much interest as the opposite side but does not duplicate it exactly.

A   B

Figure 11–4. Proportion. Each element of the landscape must be in the proper size relationship with all other elements.

All must be in the proper size relationship with each other and, in a general sense, with the persons using the landscape.

Focalization

The principle of *focalization* is applied to every outdoor room in one or two selected spots. It is based upon the knowledge that when the human eye views a scene, it is attracted immediately to one feature, then gradually begins to take in the adjacent items. The feature which first attracts the eye is known as a *focal point*. It may draw attention through its shape, color, size, texture, sound, or motion. Examples of landscape focal points include *specimen plants* (highly attractive, unusual plants), flowers, statues, and fountains.

In the public area of the landscape, the most important feature is the front door of the house. Therefore, the focal point is already established and all other parts of the outdoor room are designed to bring the viewer's attention to the focal point, not compete against it, figure 11–5.

In other outdoor use areas, the designer may enjoy the freedom of creating the focal point. Figure 11–6 illustrates a backyard family living area with one corner developed as the major focal point. Many times, there is a temptation among new designers to include too many focal points in

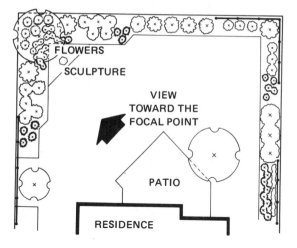

Figure 11–6. Focalization draws the eye of the viewer to one major feature in each use area.

a design. It should be remembered that there is never more than one focal point per view.

Rhythm and Line

The final design principle is *rhythm and line*. This principle is used to create a sense of movement for the viewer's eye. Gently rolling bedlines and stepped plant arrangements are methods by which this sense of motion is created within an outdoor room. When walking from one use area into another, viewers should have the feeling that the design is transporting them from outdoor room to room. If the planting beds flow from one area to another, the principle of rhythm and line has been applied well, figure 11–7.

ARRANGING PLANT MATERIALS

No two properties should ever be regarded in exactly the same way, since different clients are being served in every case. Every landscape problem requires a fresh,

Figure 11–5. Focalization. Plants are arranged in an asymmetrical step-down manner to move the viewer's eye toward the entry, the focal point.

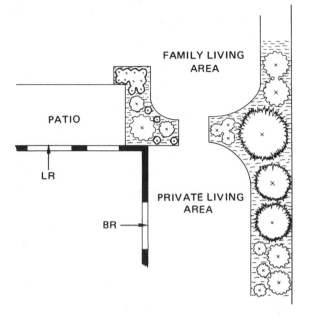

Figure 11–7. Rhythm and line. Two use areas are shown sharing a common planting whose bedline flows smoothly from one area to the next.

new solution. Nevertheless, there are several basic ways of arranging trees and shrubs which can be applied to nearly all design problems.

A general rule of thumb for the student designer is that all shrubs belong in cultivated beds. The immediate reaction of a new designer to the above statement is often one of disagreement since in actuality, shrubs are not placed within beds in many instances. It is often wise, however, for students to avoid using what they see around them as examples when developing their landscape plans. The cultivated bed protects the shrubs from lawn mower damage by excluding the grass. It is mulched with peat moss, marble chips, wood chips, or similar material which helps to keep weeds out and moisture in. In this way, the cultivated bed helps to reduce the time and expense of landscape maintenance. In the examples of plant arrangements which follow, all shrubs and trees are placed in cultivated beds.

The Corner Planting

Defining the corners of the outdoor living room are the *corner plantings*. Depending upon how much privacy is desired, the corner planting may or may not be connected to other plantings which make up the walls of the outdoor room.

The corner planting bed has two parts, the *incurve* and the *outcurves*, figure 11–8. The incurve is the most desirable place for the location of a highly attractive plant (specimen plant) because it is a natural focal point. The plants in the outcurve should be selected and placed to draw attention even more strongly to the incurve.

The incurve plant is usually the tallest plant in the bed, figure 11–9. If the corner planting is not being used as the major focal point of the outdoor room, a less attracting accent plant can be selected for the

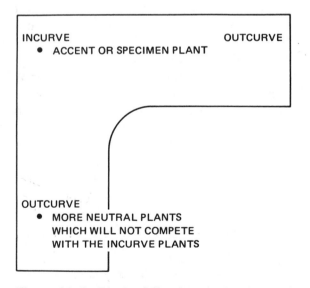

Figure 11–8. Parts of the corner planting bed: the incurve and the outcurves.

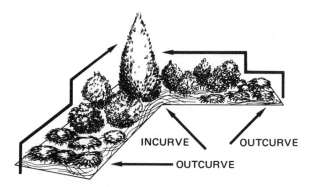

Figure 11–9. In a corner planting, attention is drawn from the outcurves to the incurve by stair-stepping plants.

incurve. An *accent plant* has a greater attraction than the outcurve plants, but not as great an attraction as the focal point (in a different location).

There are many variations possible with the corner planting, figure 11–10. Shorter plants can be placed in front of taller plants, or a statue or bench might be used instead of a plant at the incurve. Whatever is done, it is important that the design remain simple. The number of plant species used should be limited to three or four unless the bed is exceptionally large.

The Line Planting

The *line* or *linear planting* is the basic means of forming outdoor walls with plants. Depending upon the types of plants selected and their placement, the outdoor wall can accomplish many purposes. It can provide total privacy, partial privacy, or no privacy. The linear planting can also provide protection from the effects of the weather. It can create a view, block a view, or frame a view. Figure 11–11 illustrates some of the many functions of the line planting.

The line planting, like the corner planting, should be within a cultivated bed.

Figure 11–10. Three variations of the corner planting. Notice that in each example, the eye is drawn from the ends of the planting to the center and from the front to the rear.

The height and thickness of the outdoor wall depend upon the size and number of plants used. When arranging plants in this or any arrangement, remember to space the plants far enough apart so that they have sufficient room to grow to maturity. Crowded spacing creates unnecessary maintenance requirements.

Figure 11–12 illustrates the design approach to line planting. It is important that the plant species be limited and the plants

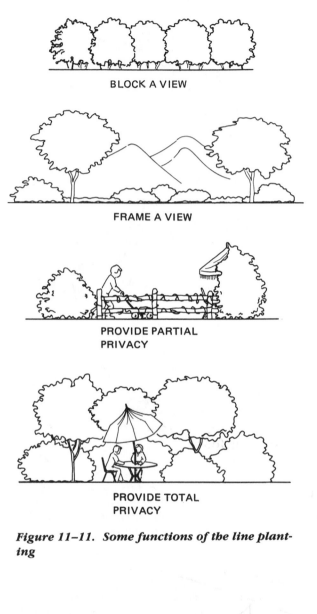

Figure 11-11. *Some functions of the line planting*

grouped. The staggered placement of the plants makes the planting more interesting to the viewer's eye. Likewise, the small tree alters the silhouette of the planting, adding interest.

The line planting can be made more attractive by placing small shrubs in front of taller ones, figure 11-13. This creates a stepped effect, which can be further enhanced with ground cover placed below the smaller shrubs.

Skillful designing of the line planting requires practice and experience. Designers should try to avoid the monotony which develops when too few plant species are used, figure 11-14. Likewise, they must resist the temptation to use too many species, which destroys the simplicity of the design, figure 11-15.

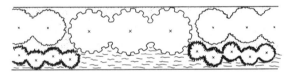

Figure 11-13. The placement of low shrubs in front of taller ones adds a stepped effect to the line planting.

Figure 11-14. A monotonous view results when there is not enough variation in plant height or texture.

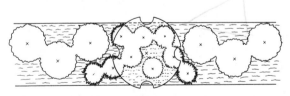

Figure 11-12. An effective line planting consists of (1) only a few species, (2) massed groupings, and (3) staggered placement.

Figure 11-15. The simplicity of a line planting is destroyed by too many plant species and too much variation in height.

Figure 11–16. A common, unimaginative foundation planting. Upright shrubs at the corners of the house and spreaders beneath the windows create a rigid appearance.

Figure 11–17. This foundation planting, with informal plant shapes, creates a modern appearance. The planting extends outward from the house to tie the structure more closely to the landscape.

The Foundation Planting

Many years ago, houses were built on high, unattractive foundations. The foundation planting developed as a way to hide the concrete block base of these older homes. Now, it is common practice to build homes so that the foundation does not show. The foundation planting is still used, though with a slightly different purpose.

The modern foundation planting plays an important role in tying the house in with the rest of the landscape. No longer ending at the corners of the house, the foundation planting reaches out from the house toward the garden. It attracts the eye of the viewer and leads it toward the entry in the public area.

The beginning designer should avoid one common, unimaginative practice in the design of foundation plantings. This is the placement of spreading evergreens under the picture windows and upright pyramidal evergreens on the corners of the house, figure 11–16. By using greater imagination, the designer can create more attractive foundation plantings. Figure 11–17 shows the same house as figure 11–16, but with a more modern planting. The taller plants are placed at the corners and the height of the other plants gradually descends toward the entry. Figure 11–18 illustrates how a well-designed foundation planting can contribute to the beauty of a home.

Figure 11–18. This planting, consisting of shrubs, ground covers, and raised planters, carries the viewer's eye easily to the entrance of the home.

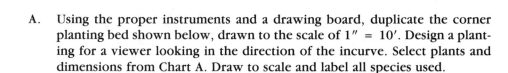

A.   Using the proper instruments and a drawing board, duplicate the corner planting bed shown below, drawn to the scale of 1″ = 10′. Design a planting for a viewer looking in the direction of the incurve. Select plants and dimensions from Chart A. Draw to scale and label all species used.

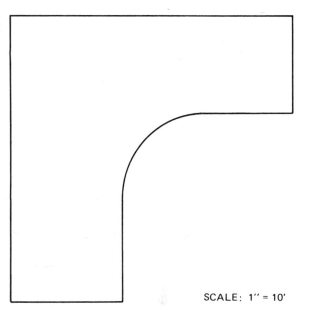

SCALE: 1″ = 10′

Figure 11–19. Corner planting bed

Chart A

Species		Width	Height
Redbud tree	(D)	20 ft.	25 ft.
Viburnum	(D)	10 ft.	12 ft.
Forsythia	(D)	10 ft.	9 ft.
Cotoneaster	(D)	5 ft.	5 ft.
Spirea	(D)	5 ft.	4 ft.
Grape holly	(BLE)	3 ft.	3 ft.
Andorra juniper	(NE)	3 ft.	1½ ft.
Myrtle	(G)	Vining	1 ft.

D: Deciduous   BLE: Broad-Leaved Evergreen
G: Ground Cover   NE: Needled Evergreen

B. With the proper equipment, duplicate the planting bed shown below. Assume that the viewer is located south of the bed and that there is an attractive mountain scene north of the bed. Design a planting which frames but does not block the view. Select plants from Chart A. Draw to the scale of $1'' = 10'$.

NORTH

SCALE: 1″ = 10′

Figure 11–20. Planting bed

C. Figure 11–21 illustrates the entry portion of a house. The garage and driveway are also shown. With the proper instruments, design the public area portion of the foundation planting. Use the plants in Chart A. Design to the scale of $1'' = 10'$.

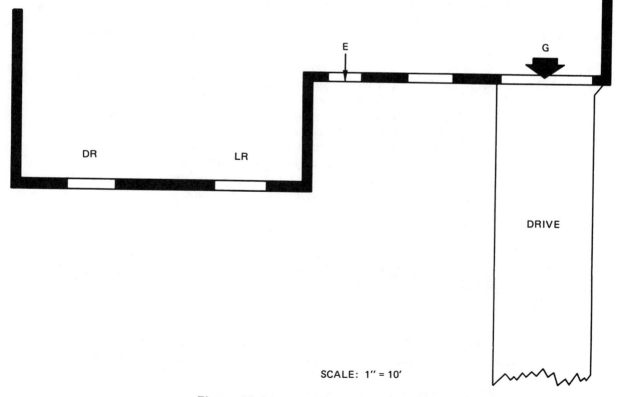

SCALE: 1″ = 10′

Figure 11–21. Entry portion of house

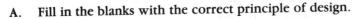

ACHIEVEMENT REVIEW

A.   Fill in the blanks with the correct principle of design.

1.   Drawing attention to the front door of a house is demonstrating the principle of _____.
2.   Repeating materials or plants in different areas of the landscape is demonstrating the principle of _____.
3.   The principle of design being ignored when a tree that will eventually grow to be 100 feet tall is planted next to a 15-foot house is _____.
4.   A landscape which suggests smoothness and unity is demonstrating the principle of _____.
5.   If one side of a landscape attracts the same attention as the opposite side, the designer has used the principle of _____.

B.   Select the best answer from the choices offered for each question.

1.   Which of the following is not a function of a good mulch?
 a.   inhibits weeds b.   attracts insects c.   retains moisture
2.   Which of the following plants would not work well at the incurve of a corner bed?
 a.   vine   b.   specimen plant c.   accent plant
3.   Which is the proper way to space shrubs in a planting bed?
 a.   so that the landscape appears completed the day it is installed
 b.   so that shrubs are able to grow to maturity without crowding
 c.   so that shrubs crowd together and require a great deal of pruning
4.   Which is the function of the modern foundation planting?
 a.   to hide the unsightly foundation of the modern house
 b.   to prevent the house from being seen from the street
 c.   to tie the house in with the rest of the landscape

SUGGESTED ACTIVITIES

1.   Collect dried weed flowers or similar natural materials that resemble small trees and shrubs. Spray paint them green and arrange them on a styrofoam base cut into the shape of a corner or linear planting bed. See how many different ways the same bed shape can be designed.

2. Evaluate your home landscape plantings. How well have the plants been selected and arranged?

3. Evaluate the plantings of ten different home landscapes in a single neighborhood. Rate them on a one to ten rating basis, with ten representing an ideal landscape and one representing almost no development. Let five represent a very ordinary style, such as the one shown in figure 11–16. Average the scores to determine the rating for the neighborhood. Compare your average with other members of the class. If the neighborhood ratings vary greatly, determine the reasons why.

UNIT 12

COMPLETING THE LANDSCAPE PLAN

OBJECTIVES

After studying this unit, you will be able to

- label a landscape plan.
- prepare a final landscape plan.

Since the plan is the major contribution of the designer to the landscaping process, it is important that it look professional. Generally, plans must be of better quality than clients could produce themselves. For this reason, the student designer should learn to incorporate some small but important final touches to complete the plan.

The finished design plan should be labeled throughout. This enables clients to read and understand the plan. It also aids the landscape contractor who is responsible for installing the design once it has been accepted by the client. There are several types of labels which appear on the finished plan. Included are symbol labels, directional arrow, scale, designer's name, client's name and address, and plant list.

Symbol labeling identifies each plant, construction item, installation detail, and building which appears on the plan. Nothing must be left unexplained. To avoid confusion, it is always best to label directly on or near the symbol. It may not always be possible to fit the entire label directly on the symbol; therefore, all of the examples shown in figure 12–1 are acceptable. These methods of symbol labeling are most desirable because they allow for immediate reading of the plan.

Coding, figure 12–2, is sometimes necessary when the scale of the plan is 1″ = 20′ or smaller. Coding is a less satisfactory method since it requires a separate listing to explain the code. Should the list be lost, the design is unreadable.

Following the name of a plant or its coded number is the number of plants to which that label applies, figure 12–3. By using one label for several plants of the same species, the number of labels can be reduced and confusion avoided. An overabundance of labeling lines also can be con-

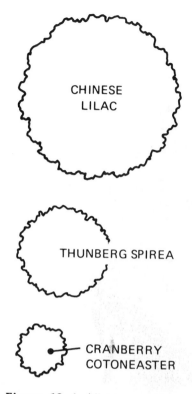

Figure 12–1. *Three accepta-ble methods of direct symbol labeling*

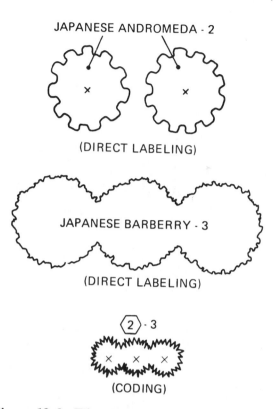

Figure 12–3. *When the label or code applies to more than one plant of that species, the number should be indicated.*

 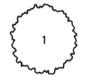

PLANT SPECIES CODE

#1 COMMON LILAC   SYRINGA VULGARIS
#2 CREEPING JUNIPER   JUNIPERUS
                        HORIZONTALIS

Figure 12–2. *Coding the labeling of plant symbols is less desirable than direct labeling but is sometimes necessary. Never use the techniques of direct labeling and coding on the same landscape plan.*

fusing, and should be eliminated whenever possible.

Construction materials are labeled as plant materials are, but are seldom coded. While there is no need to indicate specific numbers (such as 30 bricks or 6 stones), the object to be constructed should be described according to such features as height, width, and color. For example, one labeling might read *basket weave fence—5' tall, redwood stained.* Another might read *concrete patio with natural redwood strips @ 2' intervals.*

From the symbol labels, a tally can be made of how many of each species of plant are used in the total plan. Following the tally, the plant list is made. A *plant list* is an

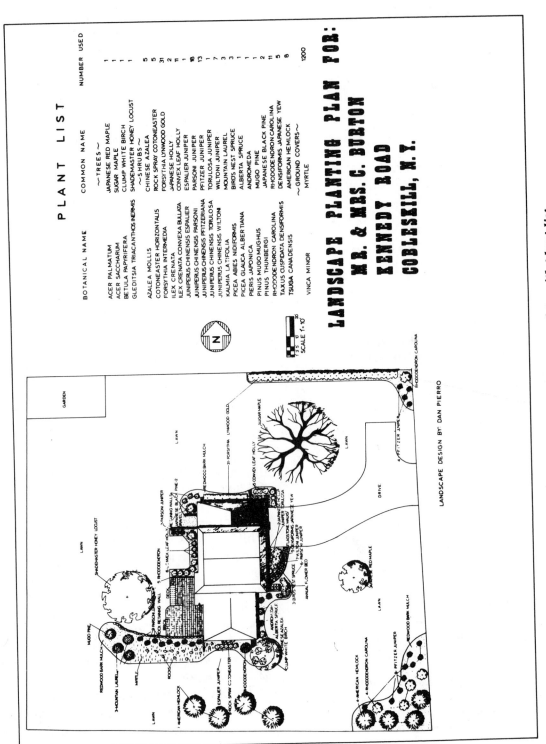

Figure 12–4. A landscape plan complete with plant list

alphabetical listing of the botanical names of the plants planned for the landscape, their common names, and the total number used. Plant lists are used most frequently by the persons responsible for purchasing the plants.

On the completed final plan, the plant list is located opposite the design. Figure 12–4 illustrates the plant list and how it coordinates with the final plan.

Figure 12–4 also illustrates the other important landscape labels and their suggested positions. The directional arrow is a necessity. It provides the physical orientation for the property and permits the sun movement to be interpreted. The scale in-

dicator is also vital. The largest lettering on the plan is reserved for the client's name. The designer's name is also included, but in smaller letters. Finally, the plan is bordered with a line running around the edge of the drawing. This border does the same thing that a frame does for a picture—it gives the entire plan a sense of unity.

Professional designers usually do their original design work on heavy, often gridded, paper. Then a sheet of thin, transparent tracing paper or *vellum* (a strong, cream-colored paper) is placed over it and the entire work traced, figure 12–5. The transparent tracing can then be copied on a duplicating device such as the diazo ma-

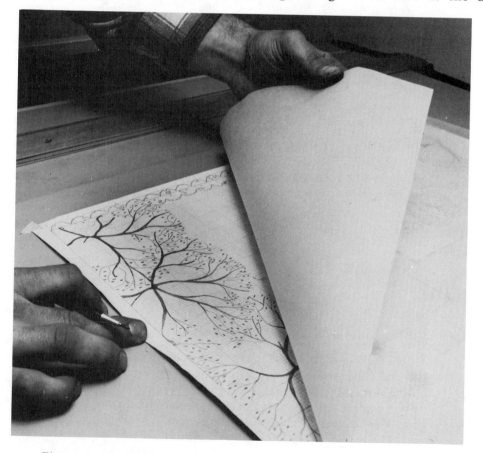

Figure 12–5. Vellum is placed over the original design for tracing.

chine, figure 12–6. The diazo duplicator can be used to make unlimited copies of the plan on heavy paper or plastic film. Copies are then given to the landscape contractor who is responsible for the installation of the landscape.

Figure 12–6. A diazo copier duplicates the landscape plan from vellum onto heavy paper in seconds.

ACHIEVEMENT REVIEW

Select the best answer from the choices offered for each question.

1. What is the most desirable method of labeling plant symbols?
   a. near the symbol   b. by coding   c. on the symbol
2. What does the label *hemlock-3* mean?
   a. A total of three hemlocks are referred to by the one label.
   b. The hemlocks are to be three feet apart.
   c. The hemlocks are to be three years old.

3. Which part of the plant list is alphabetized?
   a. The total number of plants used
   b. The common names of the plants
   c. The botanical names of the plants
4. Why is the directional arrow necessary on the final plan?
   a. It is ornate and attractive.
   b. It orients the property on the plan.
   c. It tells which way the wind blows across the property.
5. Which of the following is not a part of the final presentation plan labeling?
   a. plant list   b. designer's name   c. price list

SUGGESTED ACTIVITIES

1. Visit the office of a landscape architect. Ask to see examples of his or her work and request a demonstration of the use of the diazo duplicator.

2. Visit a drafting supplies store. Observe the many types of drawing instruments, papers, and furniture available to landscape designers.

3. Do a complete landscape design of your home, from the beginning drawings to the final tracing.

4. Trace a simple landscape plan onto vellum three different times using a pencil, a felt pen, and a technical drawing pen. Compare their appearances for clarity, ease of smudging, and the quality of diazo copy which they make.

SECTION 3

THE SELECTION AND USE OF PLANT MATERIALS IN THE LANDSCAPE

TREES

OBJECTIVES

After studying this unit, you will be able to

- select the proper tree to fill a certain role in a landscape.
- evaluate the possible strengths and weaknesses of a specific tree in a landscape.
- distinguish between bare-rooted, balled and burlapped, and containerized plants.
- explain the proper method of planting a tree.

As discussed in Section 2, one function of trees is to act as the ceiling of the outdoor living room. In that role, a tree may provide full or partial shade, while creating a feeling of intimacy or openness. To function correctly, trees must be selected with careful thought, not merely because the designer happens to like their appearance. The selection of a tree is determined by a combination of several factors:

- the height of the tree
- how low to the ground it branches
- the density of its foliage
- whether it is deciduous or evergreen
- seasonal color, foliage texture, and whether it bears flowers and/or fruit
- hardiness
- ease of transplanting
- resistance to insects or diseases

TYPES OF TREES AND SHRUBS

Trees (and shrubs) are available and usable as native, exotic, or naturalized materials. *Native* plants are those which evolved through nature within a certain locale. Examples are the eastern white pine of the northeastern United States and the Douglas fir of the Pacific Northwest. *Exotic* plants are those that have been introduced to an area by individuals, not nature. For example, many of the junipers and yews used in landscaping in the United States actually evolved in China or Japan. However, they have adapted very well to America. *Naturalized* plants are those which were brought into an area as exotic, but have adapted so well that they have *escaped cultivation*. This means that they now occur commonly both in and out of planned landscape settings. The bird of paradise bush is such a plant. Native to South America, it grows like a native plant in the desert of the southwestern United States.

Exotics have certain advantages over many of the native plants. They often transplant more easily than the natives. Also, they often have fewer insect and disease problems. Such positive features are probably why over 60 percent of the trees and shrubs used in American landscaping are exotic in origin.

HOW TO SELECT A TREE

One important reason for selecting a particular tree is its hardiness rating. The *hardiness rating* determines whether or not the plant will survive the winter in the location desired. The United States Depart-

ment of Agriculture has prepared a Hardiness Zone Map, figure 13–1, which shows the average annual minimum temperatures for all of the United States (except Alaska and Hawaii) and Canada. Notice on the map that the continent is divided into ten hardiness zones.

Each zone has an average annual minimum temperature variation of ten degrees Fahrenheit. As the hardiness zone number increases, so does the temperature minimum. For example, northern Kansas temperatures (Zone 5) drop to between – 10° and – 20° F in the winter, but southern Kansas (Zone 6) drops only to between 0° and – 10° F during the same months. Zone 10 regions are the warmest areas of the U.S.

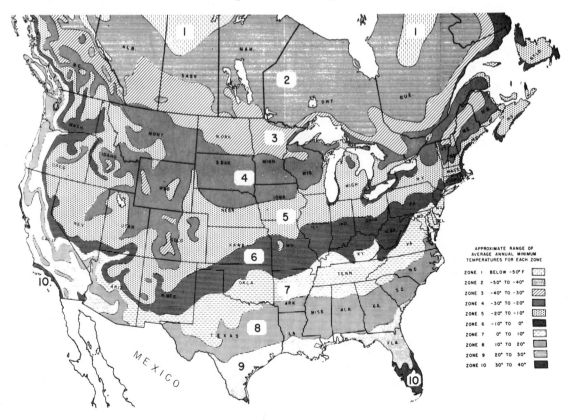

Figure 13–1. U.S.D.A. plant hardiness zone map

When a plant is assigned a hardiness zone rating, it means that the tree or shrub may survive the winter in that zone or any zone having a higher numbered rating. Thus, a tree rated as a Zone 5 plant may survive the winters in Zones 5 through 10, but not in Zones 4 through 1.

Students should be aware that temperature hardiness is more complicated than the examples here may imply; therefore, the Hardiness Zone Map should be used as only one method of measuring the plant's chance of survival. (For example, some plants will not survive if the winter is too warm, while others may survive in colder areas than expected because they are planted in sheltered locations. These small, unusual planting areas are known as *microclimates.*)

The shape or silhouette of the tree may also determine its suitability for use in the landscape. Figure 13-2 illustrates some of the shapes trees may take. Some of the more common species, their characteristics, and recommended uses are also listed. Students should study each silhouette in the figure and then think of additional examples common to their areas of the country.

Closely associated with the silhouette of a tree is its *branching habit,* or the way in which the branches tend to grow. Some trees have low, sweeping branches, such as the pin oak and willows, figure 13-3. It is difficult to walk, picnic, or play under such trees.

When human activity is expected to occur beneath trees, a high-branching species should be selected. For example, small, high-branching trees (25 to 30 feet tall) make excellent patio trees. They provide shade while keeping the ceiling effect low and intimate.

The size of the tree is another important measure of its suitability for the landscape. A tree that grows to be 100 feet tall would dwarf a small, one-story house. However, that same tree could be attractive if planted near a much taller building. To assure that the tree selected is in the correct proportion to the rest of the landscape and any surrounding structures, the design principle of scale and proportion (discussed in Unit 11) must be applied. Figure 13-4 illustrates some common uses and misuses of trees based on their size.

The texture and density of the plant's *foliage* (leaves) should be considered when analyzing the qualities of a tree. Texture may be determined by touch, sight, or both. Visually, *texture* is a combination of the size of the leaves and the shadow effect of sunlight falling upon the leaves. Foliage *density* determines how much sunlight or wind actually passes through the foliage. As a general rule, large trees with coarse textures (large leaves, heavy shade effects) look best when placed away from small buildings. Finer textures, for use nearer to buildings, are present on smaller trees.

When selecting a tree for a landscape, the foliage density should be considered in relation to the function of the tree. Is it to serve as a windbreak? Is it to provide shade? For example, a deciduous tree placed off the southwest corner of a house provides cooling shade on hot summer days. Later in the winter, it drops its leaves and allows the sunlight to warm the house, thereby reducing fuel consumption.

Seasonal color is also a consideration in tree selection. Some trees, such as the flowering crabapple, dogwood, crape myrtle, pear, redbud, and cherry, are truly spectacular in the springtime when they bloom.

Silhouette and Examples	Characteristics	Possible Landscape Uses	Silhouette and Examples	Characteristics	Possible Landscape Uses
wide-oval Flowering crabapple Silk tree Cockspur hawthorn Flowering dogwood	• spreads to be much wider than it is tall • often a small tree • horizontal branching pattern • branches low to the ground	• focal point plant • works well to frame and screen • can be grouped with spreading shrubs beneath	round Shinyleaf magnolia Cornelian cherry dogwood American yellow wood Norway maple	• width and height are nearly equal at maturity • usually dense foliage • if the tree is large, a heavy shade is cast	• lawn trees • mass well to create grove effect • larger growing species may be used for street plantings • smaller growing species can be pruned and used as patio trees
vase-shaped American elm	• high, wide-spreading branches • majestic appearance • usually gives excellent shade • an uncommon tree shape	• excellent street trees • allows human activities underneath • frames structures • use above large shrubs or small trees • *note:* the American elm is easily killed by Dutch elm disease; this limits its use	columnar Columnar Norway maple Columnar Chinese juniper Fastigiata European birch	• somewhat rigid in appearance • much taller than wide • branching strongly vertical	• useful in formal settings • accent plant • group with less formal shrubs to soften its appearance • frames views and structures
pyramidal Pines Fir Spruce Hemlock Filbert Sweetgum Pin oak Sprenger magnolia	• pyramidal evergreen trees are geometric in early years • pyramidal deciduous trees are less geometric • pyramidal shape is less noticeable as the trees mature	• accent plant • large, high-branching trees allow human activity beneath • older trees may be valued for their irregular shapes • *note:* avoid planting large trees near small buildings	weeping Weeping willow Weeping hemlock Weeping cherry Weeping beech	• very graceful appearance • branching to the ground • easily attracts the eye • grass or other plants cannot be grown beneath them	• focal point plant • screens • attractive lawn trees • *note:* avoid grouping with other plants

Figure 13–2. Typical tree silhouettes, characteristics, and landscaping uses

Figure 13–3. The graceful silhouette of the weeping willow is attractive to the eye, but walking beneath it is difficult.

Others are colorful in the autumn and/or winter season because of their fruit (crabapple, mountain ash, and holly) or their foliage (maples, oaks, and sweet gum). A few trees give bright color during several seasons in the same year from the flowers, leaves, or fruit. These include the dogwood, flowering crabapple, hawthorn, and others.

Color can also be present on the bark of the tree or shrub. For example, the white, peeling bark of the white birch or sycamore is a very appealing characteristic. Both trees contrast effectively with evergreens planted behind or beneath. Likewise, the shiny red bark of cherry trees and the silvery gray bark of the red and silver maple trees are important reasons for selecting these trees for use in the landscape.

The chart on pages 130–135 (A Guide to Landscape Trees) summarizes some of the more common trees used in landscaping in the United States. While the list does not completely cover any section of the country, it can serve as a beginning point for students when selecting trees. Those students whose interest in plants extends beyond the scope of this text should seek a more in-depth study of the identification and use of plants.

PROPERLY SIZED TREES PROVIDE A VISUALLY APPEALING FRAME FOR HOMES.

OVERSIZED TREES DWARF AND DEHUMANIZE A RESIDENTIAL LANDSCAPE.

LARGE TREES PROVIDE AN EXCELLENT HIGH CEILING FOR THE RECREATIONAL LANDSCAPE.

Figure 13–4. Size is an important factor in tree selection.

HOW TREES AND SHRUBS ARE SOLD

Trees and shrubs purchased from a nursery are sold in one of three forms: bare rooted, balled and burlapped, or growing in containers. Because each form has certain advantages and disadvantages, students should learn which form to select under which conditions.

A *bare-rooted* plant is one that has been dug from the nursery field with the soil washed away from its root system, figure 13–5. It may be wrapped in moss and a plastic covering, dipped in wax, or be completely free of covering. The bare-rooted plant is usually dormant, young, and deciduous. The advantage of this type of plant to

Figure 13–5. Bare-rooted plant

the nursery worker is that it is lightweight and can be stored easily. Its major advantage to landscapers and their clients is that it is the least expensive way to purchase trees and shrubs.

The disadvantages of bare-root stock are (1) the severe reduction of the root system caused by the processing and (2) the fact that planting is limited to the early spring and late fall.

In the *balled and burlapped* (or *B & B*) method, the plant is removed from the ground with a ball of earth intact around the root system, figure 13–6. The soil ball is then wrapped with burlap and tied. This process increases the weight of the plant and makes it more difficult to handle and store. However, it disturbs the plant's root system to a lesser extent than the bare-rooted method, thereby increasing the landscaper's chance for a successful transplant. Balled and burlapped plants cost more, but can be planted later into the spring season. Some very large plants which otherwise could not be transplanted can be by use of this technique.

Container-grown plants, figure 13–7, are plants that are purchased while they are actually growing in a tar paper, metal, or plastic container. These plants are usually young; seldom are they more than three or four years old. Although small, they can be transplanted into the ground at almost any season since their entire root system is intact. Therefore, the landscaper is able to extend the planting season beyond the traditional spring and autumn limits. The cost of using container-grown plants is less than that for the B & B method, but more than that for the bare-root method.

Figure 13–7. Containerized plant

Figure 13–6. Balled and burlapped plants

A Guide to Landscape Trees

Tree		Evergreen	Deciduous	Maximum Height		
Common Name	Botanical Name			10'–25'	25'–60'	60' and up
Almond	Prunus amygdalus		X	X		
Amur corktree	Phellodendron amurense		X	X		
Apples 　Summer 　Fall 　Winter	Malus species		X X X		X X X	
Apricot	Prunus armeniaca		X		X	
Arborvitae	Thuja occidentalis	X			X	
Ash 　Arizona 　Green 　White 　Flowering	Fraxinus species 　F. velutina 　F. pennsylvanica 　F. americana 　F. ornus		X X X X		X X X	X
Beech 　American 　European	Fagus species 　F. grandifolia 　F. sylvatica		X X			X X
Birch 　Canoe 　European 　Sweet	Betula species 　B. papyrifera 　B. pendula 　B. lenta		X X X		X	X X
Cherry	Prunus padus		X		X	
Chinese chestnut	Castanea mollissima		X		X	
Crabapple 　Flowering 　Fruiting	Malus species		X X	X X		
Crape Myrtle	Lagerstroemia indica		X	X		
Cypress 　Italian 　Monterey 　Sawara false	Cupressus sempervirens Cupressus macrocarpa Chamaecyparis pisifera	X X X				X X X
Dogwood 　Flowering	Cornus florida		X	X		
Douglas fir	Pseudotsuga menziesi	X				X
Elm	Ulmus americana		X			X
Fig	Ficus carica	X			X	
Fir 　Balsam 　White	Abies species 　A. balsamea 　A. concolor	X X				X X
Fringe tree	Chionanthus virginicus		X	X		
Ginkgo	Ginkgo biloba		X			X

Time of Flowering			Fruiting Time			Good Fall Color	Hardiness Zone Rating	Comment
Early Spring	Late Spring	Early Fall	Late Summer	Early Fall	Late Fall			
	X			X			8	edible fruit
	X			X			4	
X			X				4	does not fruit in warmer zones
X				X			4	
X					X		4	
X			X				5	edible fruit
							3	prunes well
	X			X		X	5	heavy seed formation
	X			X			2	
	X			X			3	
	X			X			5	
						X	3	low branching
						X	4	does not do well in city air
X						X	2	attractive but often short lived because of certain insect damage
X						X	2	
X						X	3	
X			X				4	edible fruit attracts birds
	X			X			4	disease resistant edible fruit
	X			X		X	3	edible fruit attractive flowers
	X			X		X	4	
		X					7	difficult to transplant
							7	pyramidal growth habit
							7	
							3	
X						X	6	good patio tree
							4	dense foliage pyramidal shape
							2	susceptible to several diseases
X			X				6	edible fruit
							4	
							4	
	X			X			4	may also be grown as a shrub
						X	4	plant only male trees good for city conditions

A Guide to Landscape Trees (continued)

Tree		Evergreen	Deciduous	Maximum Height		
Common Name	Botanical Name			10'–25'	25'–60'	60' and up
Goldenchain	Laburnum anagyroides		X	X		
Goldenrain tree	Koelreuteria paniculata		X	X		
Hawthorn	Crataegus species					
Cockspur	C. crusgalli		X		X	
English	C. oxyacantha		X	X		
Washington	C. phaenopyrum		X		X	
Hemlock	Tsuga canadensis	X				X
Holly	Ilex species					
American	I. opaca	X			X	
English	I. aquifolium	X				X
Honeylocust	Gleditsia triacanthos inermis		X			X
Hornbeam	Carpinus species					
American	C. caroliniana		X		X	
European	C. betulus		X		X	
Larch	Larix decidua		X			X
Linden	Tilia species					
American	T. americana		X			X
Little leaf	T. cordata		X			X
Silver	T. tomentosa		X			X
Magnolia	Magnolia species					
Saucer	M. soulangeana		X	X		
Southern	M. grandiflora	X				X
Star	M. stellata		X	X		
Maple	Acer species					
Amur	A. ginnala		X	X		
Hedge	A. campestre		X	X		
Japanese	A. palmatum		X	X		
Norway	A. platanoides		X			X
Red	A. rubrum		X			X
Sugar	A. saccharum		X			X
Mountain ash (European)	Sorbus aucuparia		X		X	
Oak	Quercus species					
Live	Q. virginiana	X			X	
Pin	Q. palustris		X			X
Red	Q. rubra		X			X
Scarlet	Q. coccinea		X			X
Peach	Prunus persica		X		X	
Pear	Pyrus communis		X		X	
Pecan	Carya illinoensis		X			X

Time of Flowering			Fruiting Time			Good Fall Color	Hardiness Zone Rating	Comment
Early Spring	Late Spring	Early Fall	Late Summer	Early Fall	Late Fall			
	X						5	
	X				X		5	coarse textured
	X			X		X	4	avoid using near
	X			X			4	children's area; plants
	X			X		X	4	are thorny
							3	grows best in full sunlight
					X		5	male and female plants are needed for fruit set
					X		6	pyramidal silhouette
				X			4	good city tree
			X			X	2	
			X			X	5	
						X	2	a deciduous, needled conifer
	X						2	
	X						3	good street trees
	X						4	
X				X			5	large, showy flowers
	X			X			7	
X				X		X	5	
X			X			X	2	has spectacular autumn
X			X				5	foilage color where
X			X			X	5	autumn days are cool
X			X				3	and crisp
X						X	3	
X			X			X	3	
	X		X			X	3	susceptible to borer insects
							7	strong trees
						X	4	used widely as lawn
						X	3	and shade trees
						X	4	good for attracting squirrels
X			X				5	edible fruit, but may not bear if winters are too warm
X			X				4	edible fruit
	X			X			5	may not bear mature fruit outside of southeastern states.

A Guide to Landscape Trees (continued)

| Tree | | Evergreen | Deciduous | Maximum Height | | |
Common Name	Botanical Name			10'–25'	25'–60'	60' and up
Pine	Pinus species					
Austrian	P. nigra	X				X
Red	P. resinosa	X				X
Scotch	P. sylvestris	X				X
White	P. strobus	X				X
Plum	Prunus species					
Fruiting	P. domestica		X	X		
Purple	P. pissardi		X	X		
Redbud	Cercis canadensis		X		X	
Russian olive	Elaeagnus angustifolia		X	X		
Sapodilla	Achras zapota	X			X	
Spruce	Picea species					
Black Hills	P. glauca densata	X				X
Blue	P. pungens glauca	X				X
Colorado	P. pungens	X				X
Norway	P. abies	X				X
White	P. glauca	X				X
Sweet gum	Liquidambar styraciflua		X			X
Sycamore	Platanus occidentalis		X			X
Tulip tree	Liriodendron tulipifera		X			X
Walnut	Juglans species					
Black	J. nigra		X			X
English	J. cinerea		X			X
Willow	Salix species					
Babylon weeping	S. babylonica		X		X	
Pussy	S. discolor		X	X		
Thurlow weeping	S. elegantissima		X		X	
Zelkova (Japanese)	Zelkova serrata		X			X

Time of Flowering			Fruiting Time			Good Fall Color	Hardiness Zone Rating	Comment
Early Spring	Late Spring	Early Fall	Late Summer	Early Fall	Late Fall			
							4 2 2 3	good for use as windbreaks most effective when used in groups of three or more
X			X				4	
X			X				4	
X							4	attractive, delicate flowers
	X			X			2	silver foliage color
X				X			10	
							3 2 2 2 2	rigid, pyramidal trees
			X			X	5	spectacular fall color mixed shades
	X				X		5	white peeling bark
	X		X				4	needs room to grow and spread
				X X			4 6	edible fruit roots of black walnut kill most plants growing beneath the tree
X X X						X X	6 4 4	grows quickly weak wood
						X	5	good substitute for American elm

INSTALLING TREES AND SHRUBS

The success and survival of the tree or shrub in the landscape is determined by (1) preparation of the planting site, (2) proper installation, and (3) good post-transplant care. Each is critical in assuring that the plant will survive its first year after transplanting.

Preparation of the Planting Site

The place where the tree is to be planted (the *site*) should be well drained. The soil should not be too compacted or heavy with clay. It is very likely that the soil will require preparation (called *conditioning*) to make it suitable for the tree. If the soil contains too much clay, water will not pass through it quickly enough. It may be necessary to add sand and peat moss (or other organic material) to loosen and lighten the soil. If the drainage is very poor, the site may require the installation of drainage tile. If the soil is excessively sandy, it may drain too quickly. In this case, the addition of organic material may be necessary to increase the soil's ability to hold water.

The hole which is dug should be at least 50 percent larger than the root system or soil ball it is receiving. If a bare-root plant is being transplanted, the hole should be prepared with a mounded bottom to allow the roots to spread in a natural fashion. If a B & B or containerized plant is being used, the hole should be flat bottomed. See figure 13–8 for an illustration of these two methods.

Proper Installation

The plant should be set into the ground to the same depth at which it was originally

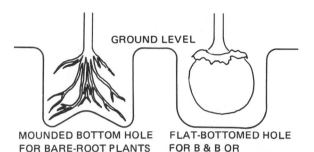

Figure 13–8. Different forms of nursery stock require differently shaped planting holes.

growing, or slightly higher if drainage is poor. With a balled and burlapped or container-grown tree, the top of the soil ball represents the original ground level, figure 13–9. With a bare-rooted tree, there is usually a natural stain on the bark marking the former soil level. Duplicating this original soil level is very important because the plant will die if placement is too deep or too shallow.

The roots of the bare-rooted plant are pruned to remove dead, diseased, or damaged parts. Once set into the hole, its roots are spread carefully over the mound. The burlap of a B & B plant is loosened but not removed. (It rots eventually and adds organic matter to the soil.) The container of a container-grown plant is removed before planting. Care should be taken to disturb the root system as little as possible.

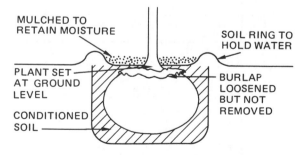

Figure 13–9. The finished planting

After the hole has been backfilled with properly conditioned soil, the soil is tamped very carefully with the foot. This assures that there are no unseen air pockets below the soil to collapse after the landscaper has left the site. Gently raising and lowering the plant helps to settle the soil. *Caution:* The soil should not be firmly packed.

A thorough, deep watering at the time of transplanting is essential. If a doughnut-shaped ring of soil is built up around the new plant, rainwater is more easily caught and held. This gives the tree a better chance of survival.

Deciduous trees and shrubs may benefit from several handfuls of a slow-release, complete fertilizer mixed into the soil during its conditioning. This type of fertilizer provides nitrogen, phosphorus, and potassium gradually throughout the first year. Application of fertilizer at the time of planting is never recommended when transplanting evergreens. Their roots are severely harmed by the harsh chemicals until the plant has had at least a year to become established. *Caution:* Excessive amounts of any fertilizer applied to new plantings can cause serious damage to their root systems.

The final step of installation, staking the tree, is to assure that the tree remains straight until the soil has settled and the roots grow enough to stabilize it. Figure 13–10 illustrates the two staking methods commonly used by landscapers. Technique A, used for large trees, offers the greatest strength. However, it also presents a hazard, so the wires must be flagged for safety. Technique B is effective with smaller trees and does not create a hazard. In both techniques, the wire must be wrapped in rubber or plastic hosing where it touches the tree. This prevents injury to the tree. Shrubs rarely require staking.

Many times, an application of *mulch* (a porous, coarse material such as peat moss, wood chips, marble chips, shredded corncobs or peanut hulls) is made after the tree is staked. Mulching reduces evaporation and helps the soil to maintain a more even temperature.

Post-transplant Care

Following transplanting, it may be necessary to prune back as much as one-quarter to one-third of the plant's branch length. This is often necessary to reduce the water demands made by the leaves on the root system. Another way of reducing water loss is to spray the plant with an antitranspirant. An *antitranspirant* is a liquid which forms a plasticlike seal over the leaves, temporarily reducing their water loss.

Wrapping the tree trunk with a *tree wrap* of burlap stripping or heavy paper can also help reduce water loss and prevent *sunscald* (drying and blistering of the bark caused by winter sunlight), figure 13–11. The wrap should either be removed or allowed to decompose in no more than a year and a half. *Caution:* Before wrapping the tree, be sure to remove any labels, cord, or wire from the branches or trunk. Allowing them to remain could cause serious injury as the tree grows.

Deep and thorough watering of the plant is necessary throughout the first growing season. Enough water should be used to wet the soil to a depth of 12 to 16 inches. Infrequent deep watering is preferable to frequent shallow watering.

TECHNIQUE A

TECHNIQUE B

Figure 13–10. Two staking techniques commonly used by landscapers

Figure 13–11. Tree wrapping is begun at the bottom and proceeds to the top of the tree. This assures that there are no exposed edges through which water can enter, encouraging disease.

ACHIEVEMENT REVIEW

A.   List eight factors that are considered when selecting a tree for a landscape.

B.   Explain the difference between exotic and native plants.

C.   What is indicated if a tree has a hardiness zone rating of 6?

D.   Of the following characteristics, state which ones apply to trees purchased as bare-rooted (BR), balled and burlapped (BB), or containerized (C).

1.   least expensive
2.   greatest chance of a successful transplant

3. most cumbersome to handle
4. commonly used only for deciduous plants
5. keeps the entire root system intact
6. must be planted in a mounded hole

SUGGESTED ACTIVITIES

1. Consult the Hardiness Zone Map to determine:

   a. the hardiness zone rating of your home county.
   b. other regions of the country having winter temperatures similar to those of your home county.

2. Compare the Hardiness Zone Map with a geographic map. Determine what can influence winter temperatures in an area besides the north-south location.

3. Determine why the coast of Maine has a warmer hardiness zone rating than upstate New York, even though Maine is farther north.

4. Study tree silhouettes by matching trees near the classroom with the diagrams in figure 13–2.

5. If a light meter is available, take readings beneath several different types of trees. Be sure that the day selected for taking the readings is clear and sunny. Temperature readings can be taken as well. Rate the foliage density of the trees tested.

6. Make a collection of tree flowers, fruits, or colored leaves. Rate them on the basis of how colorful they are.

7. Plant a tree near the school. Follow the preparation and installation techniques described in this unit.

8. Practice wrapping trees. Trees which are already planted may be used if new ones are not available. Likewise, inexpensive strip crepe paper can be used if tree wrap is not available. Secure the wrap with strips of cloth.

UNIT 14

SHRUBS

OBJECTIVES

After studying this unit, you will be able to

- explain the basis of plant nomenclature.
- select and use shrubs for specific functions in the landscape.
- describe the proper methods for planting shrubs.
- describe the role of mulches and fertilizers in plant maintenance.

Shrubs are plants that are smaller in size than trees and usually multistemmed. Shrubs are most commonly used as a wall element in the outdoor room. Much of the information in Unit 13 which pertains to trees also applies to shrubs. Therefore, various parts of this unit will be a brief review of material discussed earlier.

PLANT NOMENCLATURE

Shrubs (and all other plants) usually have two types of names. One is a common name by which the plant is known in each country or region of a country. Winged eu-onymus is an example of a common name. Grey dogwood is another. Plants also have a botanical name, which is recognized internationally. The botanical name is expressed in Latin and is assigned to the plant by a *taxonomist* (a person who specializes in the classification of plants and animals). Taxonomists are governed by International Rules of Botanical Nomenclature, which are established by an international botanic congress. Botanical names are recognized in all countries, regardless of native language. For example, the botanical name of winged eu-onymus is *Euonymus alatus;* the botanical name of grey dogwood is *Cornus racemosa.*

In *botanical nomenclature* (naming of plants), each plant is referred to as a *species.* The name of each species is unique to that one type of plant. The first part of the name (such as *Cornus*) is called the *genus.* The second part is called the *epithet* (such as *racemosa*). A genus (plural is *genera*) name may be applied to several closely related types of plants. For example, all pines are in the genus *Pinus.* It is the epithet which eliminates all other types but one and creates the unique species. Thus, *Pinus sylvestris, Pinus resinosa, Pinus nigra,* and

Pinus strobus are four distinctly different plants.

It is important that landscapers know both the common and botanical names of the plants with which they work. It is the common name which is most easily recognized by the customer. However, to assure that the nursery delivers the correct plant for installation, the landscaper must order under the botanical name. This is necessary because many common names are localized in their usage, and because a single plant may have numerous common names, even within one locality.

REASONS FOR SELECTING CERTAIN SHRUBS

There are numerous reasons for selecting a certain species of shrub for use in the landscape. However, as with trees, each individual case should be carefully thought out by the landscaper before a decision is made.

The following are some points to consider before selecting a certain shrub for a landscape.

* the silhouette of the shrub
* its branching structure
* size
* texture and density
* color contributions
* attraction of birds and other wildlife
* existing soil conditions
* hardiness
* resistance to attacks by insects and disease

Many shrubs, especially needled evergreens, have rigid geometric shapes. As such, they function in the role of specimen or accent plants and must be used cautiously. Other shrubs are softer and less defined in their silhouettes. They mass easily; therefore, several can be used in one landscape to create a desired effect. Figure 14–1 illustrates a number of shrub silhouettes and lists some common examples of each, their characteristics, and some recommended uses.

Sometimes the branching structure of the shrub must be considered at the time of selection. A shrub having stiff, upright branches could be easily broken by heavy snow piled on top of it. In these conditions, a *prostrate* shrub (one with horizontal branches) is preferable, since the branches bend, rather than break, under the weight of the snow and ice.

If traffic control is expected of the shrub, the branching pattern should probably be more vertical and intertwined. The thorniness of the shrub might also be a desirable feature for traffic control.

The size of the mature, or fully grown, plant determines how much security or privacy the shrubs will provide. To offer full visual privacy to an outdoor living room, the shrubs must be at least 6 feet tall. Privacy increases as the width of the shrub and its branching density increase.

Foliage texture and density determine the visual effect of the shrub and the ability of the shrub to absorb noise, dust, and wind. Generally, coarse-textured shrubs attract the eye more than fine-textured shrubs. Thus, more fine-textured plants are required to counterbalance the effect of coarse textures in the landscape. Fine-textured shrubs are especially well suited for providing a background for flowers.

Thick, coarse-textured shrubs also aid in noise absorption and help to break strong winds. Leaves with finely haired surfaces can help to purify the air by collecting dust particles from it.

Shrub Silhouette and Examples	Characteristics	Recommended Landscape Uses
globular Brown's yew Globe arborvitae Burford holly Globosa red cedar	• as wide as it is tall • geometric-shape • attracts attention • does not mass very well	• accent plant • use several with a single pyramidal shrub for strong eye attraction • avoid overuse
low and creeping 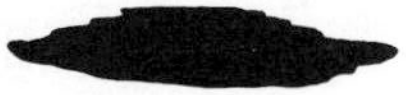 Andorra juniper Bar-Harbor juniper Cranberry cotoneaster Prostrate holly	• low growing • much wider than it is tall • masses well • irregular shape • loose, informal shape	• use to edge walks • cascades over walls • controls erosion on banks • grown in front of taller shrubs
spreading Hetz junipers Pfitzer junipers Spreading yew Mugo pine	• wider than it is tall • medium to large shrub • masses well • usually dense foliage	• use at outcurve • place at corners of buildings • useful for screening, privacy, and traffic control
arching 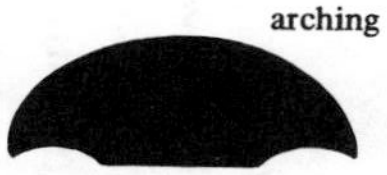 Forsythia Beautybush Vanhoutte spirea Large cotoneaster	• wider than it is tall • prevents the growth of other plants beneath itself • graceful silhouette • usually requires yearly thinning	• provides screening and dense enclosure • softens building corners and lines • background for flowers, statuary, fountains

Shrub Silhouette and Examples	Characteristics	Recommended Landscape Uses
pyramidal 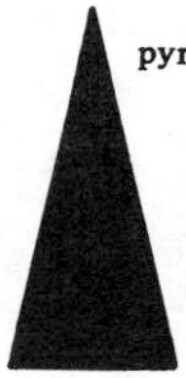 Upright yew Pyramidal junipers False cypress Arborvitae	• taller than it is wide • rigid and stiff • attracts attention • geometric shape • usually evergreen	• accent plant • focal point • use to mark entries and at incurves • group with less formal spreading shrubs
upright and loose 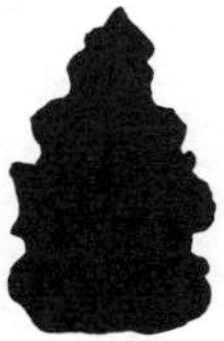 Lilac Smoke bush Rose of Sharon Rhododendron	• taller than it is wide • loose, informal shape • usually requires pruning to prevent leggy growth	• closely spaced for privacy • use to soften building corners and lines • useful for screening and framing views
columnar 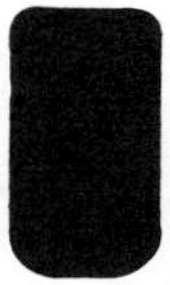 Hicks yew Italian cypress Arizona cypress	• width is about half the height • geometric, flat topped, and dense	• accent plant • foundation plantings • closely spaced for hedges • mass closely when a solid wall is desired

Figure 14–1. Shrub silhouettes

Hardiness, disease and insect resistance, and color were all mentioned as important aspects in tree selection. The same logic applies in selecting shrubs. All are important factors demanding knowledge and good judgment.

The existing soil conditions often limit the usefulness of shrubs. For example, if the pH of the soil (a measure of its acidity or alkalinity) is extreme, only a few shrubs or trees can be grown unless the soil is properly conditioned. To grow well, azaleas and rhododendrons require soil which is somewhat acidic and which contains large amounts of rich organic material. Likewise, yews should not be grown in poorly drained soil, since their roots cannot tolerate standing water. The soil in some areas, such as beneath black walnut trees, will not support the growth of any shrubs at all. (The walnut roots secrete a substance injurious to most plants that might be growing nearby.)

An increasingly popular reason for selecting certain shrubs is to provide a *habitat* (living and growing area) or food for birds and other small wildlife so that they are encouraged to remain in a particular area. For example, certain shrubs are ideal nesting sites due to their branching habits. Others produce tasty fruit which attracts birds, chipmunks, and rabbits. Most state colleges of agriculture can provide students with the names of shrubs in their states that are used for this purpose.

TRANSPLANTING SHRUBS

Successful transplanting of shrubs requires a procedure similar to the one described for trees in Unit 13. The important points are highlighted here.

- Purchase the shrubs as bare rooted, balled and burlapped, or container grown. The transplanting season, temperatures in the area, and budget determine which type is specified by the landscape designer.
- Prepare the planting site properly. Develop a rich, loose, loamy soil with the pH properly balanced. Make the planting hole at least 50 percent larger than the ball or root system it is to receive. Avoid the application of fertilizer to evergreens for the first year after transplanting. Use nonburning organic fertilizer if necessary for deciduous shrubs.
- Tamp the soil down around the shrubs when backfilling. Build a ring of soil around the shrub to catch and hold rainwater. Use of an antitranspirant is advised with shrubs as well as trees.
- Keep the shrub watered deeply and regularly for the first year. The use of an organic mulch around the shrub aids in moisture retention.

THE USE OF MULCHES

A *mulch* is a material placed on top of soil to

- aid in water retention.
- prevent soil temperature fluctuations.
- discourage weed growth.
- improve landscape appearance.

Mulches may be either *organic* (consisting of modified plant or animal materials) or *inorganic* (consisting of nonliving materials), figure 14–2. Organic mulches are more varied than inorganic mulches and are more commonly used.

Organic Mulches (peat moss, wood chips, shredded bark, chipped corncobs, pine needles)	Inorganic Mulches (marble chips, crushed stone, brick chips)
reduce soil moisture loss	also reduce moisture loss
often contribute slightly to soil nutrition	do not improve soil nutrition
may alter soil pH	seldom alter pH
are not a mowing hazard if kicked into the lawn	are a hazard if thrown by a mower blade
may be flammable when too dry	are inflammable
may temporarily reduce the nitrogen content of the soil	have no effect upon the nitrogen content of the soil

Figure 14–2. Comparison of organic and inorganic mulches

When mulching shrubs (and trees), the mulch should be applied 3 to 4 inches deep for maximum effectiveness. A very shallow layer of mulch does not discourage weed seed germination, offer much water retention, or prevent constant changes in the soil temperature. Repeated freezing and thawing of the soil around the plant's base can damage the bark and allow the entrance of disease or insects.

If a shallower layer of mulch is desired, weed control and water retention can still be accomplished by spreading black plastic around the plant first and then adding enough mulch to weight down the plastic. It is essential that the plastic be black to prevent sunlight from penetrating and promoting weed growth. This mulching technique works well on flat land. However, it is not advised for use on slopes because rainwater tends to wash the mulch off the slick plastic. It must also be used cautiously on heavy clay soils; in these cases, the plastic may collect and hold too much water and drown the shrub or tree.

FERTILIZING SHRUBS

The nutrients found in soil are used by plants as they grow. Often, it is necessary to replace those nutrients by the application of chemical fertilizers. The fertilizers most commonly used by landscapers are those needed for maintenance of the garden. They are called *complete fertilizers,* which means that they contain the three primary nutrients needed in the greatest amounts by growing plants: nitrogen, phosphorus, and potassium.

For shrubs growing in cultivated beds, fertilizer may be applied in late March or early April. Depending upon the needs of the particular plants involved, each 100 square feet of bed area receives between 1 and 3 pounds of a low analysis, complete fertilizer (one which contains less than 30 percent total nitrogen, phosphorus, and potassium). The fertilizer is distributed uniformly on the soil beneath the shrubs. Care should be taken to place most of the fertilizer beneath the outer edge of the shrub rather than around the base. This is because the special roots which absorb the nutrients are centralized there. The fertilizer should not be allowed to touch the shrub's foliage, or foliar burn may result. *Foliar burn,* as described here, is a reaction of the leaf tissue to the harsh fertilizer chemicals. The tissue dies where it is touched by the fertilizer.

If the soil is dry, the fertilizer can be worked into the soil by use of a hoe. If the weather has not been abnormally dry, the fertilizer can be left untilled since the next rainfall will wash it into the soil.

All fertilization of shrubs and trees should be completed by July 1st. Application of the nutrients after that can cause *succulent* (fleshy) growth too late into the summer, making the plant more likely to receive injuries due to harsh winter weather.

THE USE OF SHRUBS IN LANDSCAPE DESIGN

Traffic control comprises a major use of the shrub planting as an outdoor wall. Figure 14–3 illustrates a shrub wall used to control pedestrian traffic. Figure 14–4 shows a similar use but displays the results of poor positioning of the shrubs.

Providing a background for flowers, sculpture, and fountains is another way in which shrubs are used for design purposes, figure 14–5. Most flowers and other enrichment items are displayed more attractively when contrasted against the rich green of a shrub mass.

Softening harsh building lines is a common function of shrub plantings, figure 14–6. The improvement in the overall appearance of the house is apparent.

In reducing wind velocity, shrubs are usually more desirable than a solid fence next to a patio. If the designer wishes to slow a strong prevailing wind to a soft

Figure 14–3. This hedge, bordering the sidewalk, prevents pedestrians from cutting across the corner of the lawn.

Figure 14–4. This hedge is set back too far from the sidewalk to function as an outdoor wall. Pedestrians have cut across the corner, destroying the lawn.

breeze, large shrubs can be effective, figure 14–7. A solid structure such as a fence or wall blocks the wind, but may not reduce its velocity unless it is designed with openings.

The fragrance of blooming shrubs such as roses, honeysuckle, and lilacs is sometimes a desirable landscape quality. When used near patios or under bedroom or kitchen windows, an aromatic shrub can add appeal to a home. Some landscape designers keep a list of fragrant trees and shrubs that are hardy in their area.

Screening is an important function where privacy or blockage of a view is de-

sired by the designer. To screen properly, the shrubs must be dense and spaced closely enough that no one can see through them. Also, the height of the shrubs must be as high as the eye level of the tallest viewer (around 6 feet). Figure 14–8 shows some of the instances in which shrub masses (often in combination with trees) are used to create visual screens.

The use of shrubs as a focal point and accent to the landscape was described earlier in the text. Because of their bright colors and various shapes, foliage textures, and branching patterns, many shrubs can be used alone to create points of interest. Thus, the shrub becomes an item of individual appreciation.

Figure 14–5. The dark foliage of shrubs provides an excellent background against which to contrast sculpture.

GENTLE BREEZE

WIND

Figure 14–7. Shrubs can reduce the velocity of wind, turning a gust into a breeze.

WITHOUT CORNER SHRUBS, THE LINES OF THE HOUSE SEEM STARK AND HARSH.

WITH CORNER SHRUBS, THE CORNERS ARE SOFTER AND LESS APPARENT.

Figure 14–6. Shrubs can be used to soften harsh building lines.

The chart on pages 150–155 (A Guide to Landscape Shrubs) lists some of the more common landscape shrubs used in various parts of the country. This listing does not include every shrub available; rather, it is meant to act as an introduction. For a more complete chart, the student should make a separate list of the *flora* (plant life) which is not already included and which is common to his or her own area.

WITH FENCING...
TO PROVIDE SCREENING AND SECURITY

WITH TREES...
TO SCREEN AN UNSIGHTLY AREA

AS A HEDGE FOR PRIVACY

Figure 14–8. Various ways to screen with shrubs

A Guide to Landscape Shrubs

Shrub		Evergreen*	Deciduous	Mature Height		
Common Name	Botanical Name			3'–5'	5'–8'	8' and up
Almond, Flowering	Prunus glandulosa		X	X		
Azaelas	Rhododendron species					
Gable	R. poukanense hybrid		X	X		
Hiryu	R. obtusum 'Hiryu'		X			
Indica	R. indicum	X			X	
Kurume	R. obtusum 'Kurume'	X		X		
Mollis	R. kosterianum		X	X		
Torch	R. calendulaceum		X	X		
Barberry	Berberis species					
Japanese	B. thunbergi		X		X	
Mentor	B. mentorensis	semi			X	
Red leaved	B. thunbergi atropurpurea		X		X	
Bayberry	Myrica pennsylvanica	semi				X
Boxwood	Buxus species					
Common	B. sempervirens	X				X
Little leaf	B. microphylla	X		X		
Camellia	Camellia japonica	X				X
Coralberry	Symphoricarpos orbiculatus		X	X		
Cotoneaster	Cotoneaster species					
Cranberry	C. apiculata		X	X		
Rockspray	C. horizontalis	semi		X		
Spreading	C. divaricata		X		X	
Deutzia, slender	Deutzia gracilis		X	X		
Dogwood	Cornus species					
Cornelian cherry	C. mas		X			X
Grey	C. racemosa		X			X
Red twig	C. stolonifera		X			X
Firethorn	Pyracantha species					
Scarlet	P. coccinea	semi			X	
Formosa	P. formosana	X				X
Forsythia	Forsythia species					
Early	F. ovata		X		X	
Lynwood	F. intermedia 'Lynwood'		X			X
Showy border	F. intermedia spectabilis		X			X

Semi-evergreen indicates that the plants retain their leaves all year in warmer climates, but drop them during the winter in colder areas.

Season of Bloom**			Light Tolerance			Good Fall Color	Zone of Hardiness	Comment
Early Spring	Late Spring	Early Fall	Sun	Semi-shade	Heavy Shade			
X			X				4	very showy blooms
	X		X	X			6	requires an acidic soil condition and often iron chelate fertilizers
	X			X			7	
X				X			8	
	X			X			7	
	X		X	X			6	
	X			X		X	6	
	X		X	X		X	4	good plants for traffic control; thorny
	X		X	X			5	
	X		X	X			4	
			X	X			2	fragrant leaves and fruit good for seashore areas
			X	X			5	prunes well; good for formal hedges
			X	X			5	
X				X	X		7	blooms from late October to April
		X		X		X	2	good on banks for erosion control
	X		X	X		X	4	fall color comes from bright red fruit
	X		X	X		X	4	
	X		X	X		X	5	
	X		X				4	white flowers
X			X			X	4	red twig is very good for erosion control. All dogwoods have good fall color
X			X			X	4	
X			X			X	2	
	X		X			X	6	fall color comes from brightly colored fruit
	X		X			X	8	
X			X				4	bright yellow flowers cascading branching patterns
X			X				5	
X			X				5	

**Where no rating is given, flowers are either not produced or are not of importance.

A Guide to Landscape Shrubs (continued)

Shrub		Evergreen*	Deciduous	Mature Height		
Common Name	Botanical Name			3'–5'	5'–8'	8' and up
Gardenia	Gardenia jasminoides	X		X		
Hibiscus	Hibiscus species					
Chinese	H. rosa-sinensis	X				X
Shrub althea	H. syriacus		X			X
Holly	Ilex species					
Chinese	I. cornuta	X				X
Inkberry	I. glabra	X				X
Japanese	I. crenata	X				X
Honeysuckle	Lonicera species					
Blue leaf	L. korolkowii zabel		X			X
Morrow	L. morrowii		X		X	
Tatarian	L. tatarica		X			X
Hydrangea	Hydrangea species					
Hills of Snow	H. aborescens grandiflora		X	X		
Oak leaf	H. quercifolia		X		X	
Pee gee	H. paniculata grandiflora		X			X
Jasmine	Jasminum species					
Common white	J. officinale	semi				X
Italian		X				X
Primrose	J. primulinum	semi				X
Juniper	Juniperus species					
Andorra	J. horizontalis plumosa	X		X		
Hetz	J. chinensis hetzi	X			X	
Japanese garden	J. procumbens	X		X		
Savin	J. sabina	X			X	
Pfitzer	J. chinensis pfitzeriana	X				X
Lilac	Syringa vulgaris		X			X
Mahonia	Mahonia species					
Leatherleaf	M. bealei	X				X
Oregon grape	M. aquifolium	X		X		
Mock orange, sweet	Philadelphus coronarius		X			X
Nandina	Nandina domestica	X			X	
Ninebark	Physocarpus opulifolius		X			X
Pieris (Andromeda)	Pieris species					
Japanese	P. japonica	X			X	
Mountain	P. floribunda	X			X	
Pine, Mugo	Pinus mugo	X			X	
Poinsettia	Euphorbia pulcherrima	X				X
Pomegranate	Punica granatum		X			X
Potentilla (Cinquefoil)	Potentilla fruticosa		X	X		

Semi-evergreen indicates that the plants retain their leaves all year in warmer climates, but drop them during the winter in colder areas.

Season of Bloom**			Light Tolerance			Good Fall Color	Zone of Hardiness	Comment
Early Spring	Late Spring	Early Fall	Sun	Semi-shade	Heavy Shade			
	X	X		X			8	very fragrant flowers
	X		X				9	
		X	X				5	
							7	fruit color is most attractive in the fall
							3	
							6	
	X		X	X			5	
	X		X	X			4	
	X		X	X			3	
	X		X				4	coarse-textured shrubs
		X	X			X	5	
		X	X			X	4	
	X		X				7	
	X		X				8	
	X		X				8	
			X				2	grows well in hot, dry soil
			X				4	
			X				5	
			X				4	
			X				4	
	X		X				3	large, fragrant flowers
X				X			6	holly-like foliage
X				X			5	bluish, grapelike fruit
	X		X				4	creamy white fragrant flower
		X	X	X		X	7	very attractive in flower and fruit stage
	X		X			X	2	
X			X	X			5	
X				X			4	
			X	X			2	
		late fall	X				9	long-lasting blooms
	X		X	X		X	8	colorful in both spring and fall
	X	X	X				2	produces yellow flower all summer

**Where no rating is given, flowers are either not produced or are not of importance.

A Guide to Landscape Shrubs (continued)

Shrub		Evergreen*	Deciduous	Mature Height		
Common Name	Botanical Name			3'–5'	5'–8'	8' and up
Privet	Ligustrum species					
Amur	L. amurense		X			X
California	L. ovalifolium	semi				X
Glossy	L. lucidum	X				X
Regal	L. obtusifolium regelianum		X		X	
Quince, Flowering	Chaenomeles species					
Common	C. speciosa		X		X	
Japanese	C. japonica		X	X		
Rhododendron	Rhododendron species					
Carolina	R. carolinianum	X			X	
Catawba	R. catawbiense	X			X	
Rosebay	R. maximum	X				X
Rose, Hybrid tea	Rosa species		X	X		
Spirea	Spiraea species					
Anthony Waterer	S. bumalda 'Anthony Waterer'		X	X		
Bridal wreath	S. prunifolia		X			X
Billiard	S. billardi		X		X	
Frobel	S. bumalda 'Froebelii'		X	X		
Thunberg	S. thunbergi		X	X		
Vanhoutte	S. vanhouttei		X		X	
Viburnum	Viburnum species					
Arrowwood	V. dentatum		X			X
Black haw	V. prunifolium		X			X
Cranberrybush	V. opulus		X			X
Doublefile	V. plicatum tomentosum		X			X
Fragrant	V. carlcephalum		X			X
Japanese snowball	V. plicatum		X			X
Leatherleaf	V. rhytidophyllum	X				X
Sandankwa	V. suspensum	X			X	
Weigela	Weigela florida		X			X
Winged Euonymus	Euonymus alatus		X		X	
Wintercreeper	Euonymus fortunei vegetus	X		X		
Yew	Taxus species					
Spreading Anglo-Japanese	T. media	X				X
Upright Anglo-Japanese	T. media hatfield	X				X
Spreading Japanese	T. cuspidata	X				X
Upright Japanese	T. cuspidata capitata	X				X
English	T. baccata	X				X
Canada	T. canadensis	X		X		

Semi-evergreen indicates that the plants retain their leaves all year in warmer climates, but drop them during the winter in colder areas.

Season of Bloom**			Light Tolerance			Good Fall Color	Zone of Hardiness	Comment
Early Spring	Late Spring	Early Fall	Sun	Semi-shade	Heavy Shade			
	X		X	X			3	prunes well
	X		X	X			5	popular hedge plants
		X	X				7	
	X		X	X			3	
X			X	X			4	densely branched, thorned plants
X			X	X			4	good for traffic control
	X			X			5	
	X			X			4	
	X			X			3	
	X	X	X				varies	very diversified group of plants / special culture required
	X		X	X			5	very attractive when blooming
	X		X	X		X	4	most are resistant to
	X		X	X			4	disease and insect pests
	X		X	X			5	
X			X	X		X	4	
	X		X	X		X	4	
	X		X	X		X	2	attractive spring flowers
	X		X	X		X	3	good fall foliage color
	X		X	X		X	2	many are good as wildlife food
	X		X	X		X	4	
	X		X	X		X	5	
	X		X	X		X	4	
	X		X	X			5	
	X		X	X			9	
	X		X				5	blooms late
			X			X	3	spectacular crimson fall color
				X		X	5	
			X	X			4	excellent for foundation plantings and hedges / prunes well / long lived
			X	X			4	
			X	X			4	will not tolerate poorly drained soil
			X	X			4	
			X	X			6	
				X			2	

**Where no rating is given, flowers are either not produced or are not of importance.

ACHIEVEMENT REVIEW

Select the best answer(s) from the choices offered for each question.

1. Which two items are Latin botanical names of plants?
   - a. Chinese juniper
   - b. *Juniperus chinensis*
   - c. Carolina rhododendron
   - c. *Rhododendron caroliniana*

2. Why must a landscaper know both the common and the botanical name of plants?
   - a. Clients are impressed by the use of botanical names.
   - b. Some common names are localized and only the botanical name is reliable.
   - c. Some plants have only common names.
   - d. Clients recognize only botanical names.

3. In what landscape role do rigid, geometric shrubs function best?
   - a. as accent or specimen plants
   - b. as softeners of harsh building lines
   - c. on corners of buildings
   - d. as wildlife attractants

4. In what landscape role do soft, loose shrubs function best?
   - a. as accent or specimen plants
   - b. as softeners of harsh building lines
   - c. at the incurve of corner plantings
   - d. as windbreaks

5. Which of the following plants is not likely to be the same genus as all of the others?
   - a. grey dogwood
   - b. red twig dogwood
   - c. blue spruce
   - d. flowering dogwood
   - e. yellow-osier dogwood

6. Which two of the following plants are most closely related?
   - a. *Quercus rubra*
   - b. *Acer rubrum*
   - c. *Quercus borealis*
   - d. *Symphoricarpos albus*

7. How large should the planting hole be when transplanting shrubs?
   - a. slightly smaller than the root system or soil ball being set into it
   - b. the same size as the soil ball or root system being set into it
   - c. at least 50 percent larger than the root system or soil ball being set into it
   - d. The size of the hole is not important.

8. What technique used in planting trees is not needed in transplanting shrubs?
   - a. soil conditioning
   - b. watering
   - c. mulching
   - d. staking

9. Which of the following are reasons to use a mulch around newly planted shrubs?
   - a. It holds moisture in the soil.
   - b. It reduces weed growth.
   - c. It reduces soil freezing and thawing.
   - d. all of these reasons

10. What role do fertilizers play in good shrub care?
    a. They replace lost soil nutrients.   c. They prevent water loss.
    b. They reduce weed growth.   d. They prevent windburn.
11. When should shrubs be fertilized?
    a. middle of summer   c. late March to early April
    b. July and August   d. whenever it is convenient

SUGGESTED ACTIVITIES

1. Collect the fruit of ten or more different shrubs. Place each type in old plates or pie tins and set them outside. Observe which shrubs produce fruit most attractive to the wildlife in your area. Which fruits are of no interest?

2. During the winter months, cut branches from early flowering shrubs. Bring them into the classroom and place in vases of water. Change the water every day. In this way, the shapes, sizes, and colors of the flowers can be observed before spring arrives. Which shrubs produce flowers before leaves? Which produce the leaves first?

3. Practice mixing good planting soil in the classroom. Collect soil from the home or school yard. Have a quantity of peat moss and sand also available. In a separate container, mix equal amounts of the three ingredients. Moisten the mix *slightly* and roll some between your fingers. If it sticks like modeling clay, more sand or peat is needed. If it crumbles, more soil is needed. When it rolls, but cracks slightly, the mixture is a *loam* and suitable for planting.

4. To demonstrate how mulch aids in water retention, fill two deep glass jars with equal amounts of dry soil. Leave about 4 inches unfilled. Slowly add enough water to thoroughly moisten the soil, without leaving water standing in the jar. Fill one jar to the top with a moistened mulch. Leave the other jar unmulched. Observe the two soils for the next week. Which soil dries out first?

5. Using drawing tools, design a corner planting with shrubs which would remain hardy in Zone 5. Select the shrubs from ''A Guide to Landscape Shrubs.''

6. Design a line planting of shrubs suitable for a semishaded location in Zone 6.

7. Visit a nursery and compare the wide selection of shrubs available in your area.

GROUND COVERS AND VINES

After studying this unit, you will be able to

- distinguish ground covers and vines from other landscape plants.
- explain ways in which ground covers and vines are used to solve special landscape problems.
- list the methods for the installation and maintenance of ground cover and vine plantings.

The term *ground cover* is applied to small plants (less than 18 inches tall) which cover the ground in place of turf. The width of the plant does not matter; the definition is based upon the height and the use of the plant. There is a great variety of plants regarded as ground covers. Some such plants are small shrubs. Others are vinelike with long, trailing growth habits. Ground covers can be needled or broad-leaved evergreens, or deciduous. They can be *herbaceous* (nonwoody plants which die back every fall) or *woody* (leaving dormant stems and branches aboveground all winter). Some ground covers ease the maintenance requirements of gardens; others increase maintenance needs. Some ground covers yield attractive flowers; others do not.

Ground covers are generally regarded as special purpose plants, since many times they are used where other types of plants are not workable. Certainly turf grass is the most common material for covering the land's surface (although it is not classified as a ground cover). There are some conditions, however, under which grass does not grow well, such as places in which the soil is too dry, too acidic or alkaline, too steeply sloped, or too shaded. In such places, ground covers may be a better choice than grass. Figures 15–1 and 15–2 show successful ground cover plantings serving in functional roles. In figure 15–3, ground cover can be seen in an additional role, that of a beautifying design element.

Figure 15–1. Ground cover holds this steep bank and provides a lawn that does not require mowing.

Figure 15–2. This ground cover retains the slope, fills the space where mowing would be difficult, and provides color all year round.

Figure 15–3. Ground cover in a raised bed provides an aesthetic quality while allowing water to reach tree roots.

HARDINESS OF GROUND COVERS

Although there are hardiness zone ratings for ground covers, they are often unreliable. The lack of reliability is due to the fact that ground covers grow so close to the soil. Soil holds both high and low winter temperatures longer than the atmosphere. As a result, there can be frequent thawing and refreezing of the ground during the winter. Repeated thawing and freezing can be very harmful to ground cover plants in that it *heaves* them to the surface of the soil, exposing their root systems to cold air and drying. Therefore, some ground covers may have a hardiness zone rating which implies that they will survive in an area, when they will not.

In other parts of the country, a heavy snow blanket is predictable throughout the winter. This blanket serves to insulate the ground and keep it frozen all winter. Without the freezing and thawing, the plants do not heave. The snow also protects the plants from the drying winds. Thus, some ground covers survive in regions colder than their hardiness zone rating suggests. Should there be a winter without the usual heavy snowfall, many ground cover plantings might die.

INSTALLING AND MAINTAINING GROUND COVERS

Soil Preparation

The soil for ground covers must have the ability to retain moisture. It should not be poorly drained, however. Since soil varies greatly throughout the country, the landscaper must analyze the needs of each particular soil at the planting site.

If the soil repels or fails to hold natural moisture, large quantities of organic material (peat moss, leaf mold, manure) should be worked into it. If the soil is compacted or heavy with clay, the addition of organic matter and sand may be helpful.

Adjustment of Soil pH

With over two hundred species of ground covers from which to select, there is no one pH suitable for them all. The landscaper must know the pH which is appropriate for the plants being installed. Likewise, the existing pH of the soil must be determined. A simple pH test kit can be of great help in this.

If it is necessary to lower the pH of the soil, the addition of aluminum sulfate is recommended. About 2 to 4 pounds per hundred square feet is a good rate with which to begin. The actual rate depends upon the particular need at the time. The planting site should be thoroughly watered immediately after application of the aluminum sulfate.

The pH of soil can be raised by adding lime. It is best if the lime is applied in the form of dolomitic limestone. Depending upon how much adjustment is needed, from 10 to 25 pounds per hundred square feet are recommended.

Fertilizer Requirements

Most ground covers grow best if given some type of fertilization. Those growing near trees and shrubs are especially in need of it, since the roots of the larger plants compete with the ground covers for available nutrients. Cornell University recommends between 2 and 4 pounds of a 5 percent nitrogen fertilizer per hundred square feet. A 5 percent nitrogen fertilizer is one having an analysis such as 5-8-7 or 5-10-5.

The best time of year to apply fertilizer to ground covers is in the early spring when the most rapid growth occurs. If there has been any winter injury to the ground covers, the nutrients help the plants recover. The fertilizer should be watered in right away to prevent the foliage from being burned.

Spacing Ground Covers

If ground covers are used extensively in a garden plan, they can easily become the most costly of all plantings. Therefore, their spacing becomes important when the landscaper has a limited budget. The more closely the ground cover is planted, the more quickly a solid cover is formed. It also requires weeding over fewer years since the shade of a solid planting of ground cover prevents the growth of many weeds. The major drawback to close spacing at the time of planting is cost.

A planting of vining ground covers set 15 to 18 inches apart may take three or four years to fill in solidly. While the initial cost is less, there is much more weeding by hand or with costly herbicides needed over a longer period of time.

For small, vinelike ground covers (myrtle, Baltic English ivy, pachysandra), the most common spacings are 6, 12, or 18 inches. At a spacing of 6 inches, the planting requires approximately 6 plants per square foot. At a spacing of 12 inches, only 2½ plants per square foot are required, while an 18-inch spacing needs only one plant per square foot. The differences in the cost of installation are quickly apparent.

If the ground cover plants are wide spreading but low growing shrubs (such as andorra juniper or rockspray cotoneaster), spacing is calculated in feet rather than inches. Regardless of the size of the plants, the planting arrangement is important. Greater coverage with fewer plants results if the plants are placed in a staggered fashion, figure 15–4.

Watering and Mulching Ground Covers

Ground covers must be encouraged to develop their roots deep into the soil as quickly as possible. In this way, they are able to survive warm, dry summer periods more easily. It is better to give ground cover plantings deep, thorough waterings at infrequent intervals than to give them frequent shallow waterings.

Figure 15–4. Alternating the placement of ground covers fills space most efficiently.

Mulches are sometimes used to conserve soil moisture in ground cover plantings. However, the type of material and the time it is done are important. Light, porous materials make the best mulches for ground covers. Materials such as peat moss, corncobs, and peanut hulls are excellent. *Caution:* Hay and straw should be avoided at all times because they contain seeds which can become weeding nightmares.

The initial mulching is done after the ground has frozen for the winter. This insulates the soil against thawing and refreezing. Thereafter, the mulching can be renewed at the same time each year. In areas where the ground does not freeze, the mulch is applied in early spring, prior to weed germination.

VINES

A *vine* is a plant which has a tendency to climb either naturally or when given proper support. Although it has height and width, it lacks the fullness that is normally associated with shrubs. Many ground covers can also be used as vines if they are given vertical support. Figures 15–5 and 15–6 illustrate uses of vines in the landscape.

Aside from their different shape and the different roles they play in the landscape, vines generally are planted and maintained as any other shrub. Some vines require special care, however, to protect them from the damaging effects of exposure to the sun and winter weather.

Using Vines in the Landscape

Vines, the most flexible of all plants, serve many functions in the landscape. In the outdoor room, they create walls, ceilings, or floors, depending upon their supports.

Figure 15–5. The flowering wisteria provides large, grape-like clusters of blossoms.

Figure 15–6. The owner of this Nantucket home is training vines to grow onto the roof for a vine-covered cottage effect.

They are also very effective in relieving the monotony of a large constructed wall, figure 15–7.

There are three ways in which vines climb, figure 15–8. Some vines climb by *twining* themselves around a trellis, fence, or another plant. Others produce fine *tendrils* that wrap around the supporting structure and allow the vine to climb. Still other vines produce *holdfasts* that permit the plant almost to glue itself to the support.

The landscaper should be aware of the climbing methods of vines before selecting

Figure 15–7. Vines growing against this tall building provide an attractive visual pattern.

TWINING

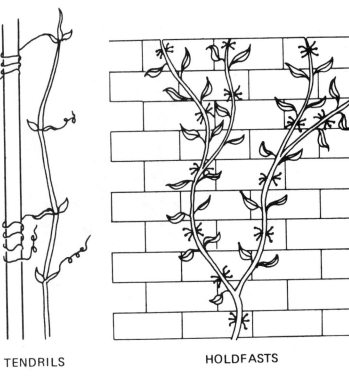

TENDRILS   HOLDFASTS

Figure 15–8. How vines climb

them for use in the landscape. Otherwise, damage to the building could result. For example, vines which produce holdfasts can damage the walls of wooden buildings by pitting the surface and allowing moisture to seep through the wood.

Knowing the method by which vines climb allows the landscaper to

- select the proper species.
- construct the best support.
- avoid moisture damage to structures caused by a vine that is too dense or

that will pit the surface of the supporting structure.
- avoid using a vine that is difficult to remove on a wall that requires frequent painting or maintenance.

The charts on pages 166 and 167 (A Guide to Ground Covers and A Guide to Vines) list some of the more common ground covers and vines available for use in landscape design.

A Guide to Ground Covers

Common Name	Botanical Name	Evergreen	Deciduous	Height	Optimum Spacing	No. Needed to Plant 100 sq. ft.	Light Tolerance	Hardiness Zone Rating	Flower or Fruit Color and Time of Effectiveness
Ajuga or bugle	Ajuga reptans		X	5"	6 inches	400	sun or shade	4	blue or white flowers in summer
Cotoneaster, creeping	Cotoneaster adpressa		X	12"	4 feet	10	sun	4	pink flowers, red fruit in summer and fall
Cotoneaster, rockspray	Cotoneaster horizontalis	semi		18" plus	4 feet	10	sun	4	pink flowers, red fruit in summer and fall
Euonymus, big leaf wintercreeper	Euonymus fortunei radicans	X		18" plus	3 feet	14	sun or shade	5	orange fruit in fall
Euonymus, purple leaf wintercreeper	Euonymus fortunei coloratus	X		18"	3 feet	14	sun or shade	5	not of significance
Honeysuckle, creeping	Lonicera prostrata		X	12"	3 feet	14	sun	5	pale yellow flowers in spring; red fruit in fall
Ivy, Baltic English	Hedera helix baltica	X		8"	18 inches	44	shade	4	none
Mondo	Ophiopogon japonicus	X		12"	10 inches	144	partial shade	8	white or pink flowers in spring
Myrtle or Periwinkle	Vinca minor	X		8"	12 inches	92	shade	4	blue flowers in spring
Oyster plant	Tragopogon porrifolius		X	12"	12 inches	92	sun or shade	9	not of significance
Pachysandra	Pachysandra terminalis	X		12"	12 inches	92	shade	4	white flowers in spring
Sarcococca	Sarcococca ruscifolia	X		tall—requires shearing	3 feet	14	sun or shade	7	white flowers and scarlet berries in fall
Wandering Jew	Tradescantia albiflora	X		6"	12 inches	92	shade	9	red-purple flowers in spring and summer
Weeping lantana	Lantana montevidensis	X		18" plus	24 inches	25	sun	9	lavender flowers all year
Yellowroot	Xanthorhiza simplicissima		X	18" plus	18 inches	44	sun	5	brown-purple flowers in spring

A Guide to Vines

Vines		Broad-Leaved Evergreen	Deciduous	Height	Clinging	Twining or Tendrils	Light Tolerance	Hardiness Zone Rating	Flower or Fruit Color and Time of Effectiveness
Common Name	Botanical Name								
Actinidia, bower	Actinidia arguta		X	30'		X	full sun or semishade	4	white flowers in spring
Actinidia, Chinese	Actinidia chinensis		X	30'		X	full sun or semishade	7	insignificant
Akebia, fiveleaf	Akebia quinata	semi		35'		X	full sun or semishade	4	purple flowers in spring
Ampelopsis, porcelain	Ampelopsis brevipedunculata		X	20'		X	full sun or semishade	4	multicolored fruit in fall
Bignonia (or crossvine)	Bignonia capreolata	X		60'		X	full sun or semishade	6	orange-red flowers in spring
Bittersweet, American	Celastrus scandens		X	20'		X	sun or semishade	2	yellow and red fruit in fall and winter
Boston ivy	Parthenocissus tricuspidata		X	60'	X		sun or shade	4	insignificant
Bougainvillea	Bougainvillea glabra	X		20'	X		full sun	7	multicolored in summer
Clematis	Clematis species		X	3' to 25'*		X	full sun or semishade	4 to 7*	many colors of flowers in late spring
Euonymus, evergreen bittersweet	Euonymus fortunei vegetus	X		25'	X		sun or shade	5	yellow and red fruit in fall and winter
Fig, creeping	Ficus pumila	X		40'	X		sun or shade	9	insignificant
Honeysuckle, trumpet	Lonicera sempervirens		X	50'		X	full sun or semishade	3	orange flowers in summer; red fruit in fall
Hydrangea, climbing	Hydrangea anomala petiolaris		X	75'	X		full sun or semishade	4	white flowers in summer
Ivy, English	Hedera helix	X		70'	X		semishade	5	insignificant
Kudzu vine	Pueraria lobata		X	60'		X	sun or shade	6	insignificant
Monks hood vine	Ampelopsis aconitifolia		X	20'		X	semishade	4	yellow-orange fruit in fall
Rambling roses	Rosa multiflora hybrids and others		X	10' to 20'		support needed	sun	5	flowers of many colors in spring and summer
Trumpet vine	Campsis radicans		X	30'	X		sun	4	orange flowers in summer
Virginia creeper	Parthenocissus quinquefolia		X	50'	X		sun or shade	3	insignificant
Woodbine, Chinese	Lonicera tragophylla		X	50'		X	shade	5	yellow flowers in summer; red fruit in fall

*Dependent upon the actual species selected

167

ACHIEVEMENT REVIEW

A.   Indicate whether the following characteristics describe ground covers (G), vines (V), both ground covers and vines (B), or neither ground covers nor vines (N).

1.   may be deciduous or evergreen
2.   are usually 18 inches or less in height
3.   have great height and width, but lack fullness
4.   often produce colorful flowers and fruit
5.   can serve as ceilings in the outdoor room if properly supported
6.   have the most unreliable hardiness zone ratings
7.   most easily harmed by repeated freezing and thawing of the soil
8.   serve no useful role in the landscape

B.   Describe the proper method of planting and maintaining ground covers. Include the following items.

soil preparation	spacing
adjustment of the soil pH	watering and mulching
fertilization	

C.   Explain the different ways in which vines climb.

SUGGESTED ACTIVITIES

1.   Propagate several ground covers. To accomplish this, take some cuttings (4 to 5 inches in length) from ground cover plantings near the school. Select herbaceous types, since they root faster than woody types. Remove the lower $2\frac{1}{3}$ to 3 inches of leaves and place in flower pots or greenhouse flats of pasteurized sand. Be certain that the container drains well. Keep the sand moist. If a greenhouse and humidity chamber are not available, enclose the pots in a bell jar or within a sealed plastic bag to maintain a high humidity. Check the cuttings for roots in two or three weeks. Transplant into soil after rooting.

2.   Find some areas where ground covers are needed. Visit a nearby park or woodlot. Seek out the spots where grass is not growing well; determine

why it is not. Which areas could be planted to bear ground covers and which could not? Why?

3. Locate vines near the school. Study the ways in which they climb. Look for any signs of injury to the supportive structure. Rate the vines on the basis of foliage density, seasonal color, and how easy removal of the vine would be if necessary. Determine the function of the vine in the landscape.

4. Measure the ability of vines and ground covers to moderate temperature extremes. Place thermometers beneath and atop a ground cover planting and beneath a wall vine under different combinations of sunlight and shade, and during different seasons.

UNIT 16

FLOWERS

OBJECTIVES

After studying this unit, you will be able to

- differentiate among annual, perennial, and biennial flowers.
- list the characteristics of hardy and tender bulbs.
- explain the difference between flower borders and flower beds.
- design a flower planting.
- install and maintain a flower planting.

Flowers are valuable elements of any landscape design, and must be chosen with great care. Flowers have a quality which can easily make them the focal point in a landscape, often in conflict with more important objects. Their value lies in the many colors, fragrances, and seasonal tones that they naturally possess.

Imagine a spring without daffodils and tulips or a summer without geraniums and petunias. Picture an autumn without chrysanthemums or a Christmas season without poinsettias. The flowers of our landscapes are strong reflections of the four seasons. The wise landscape designer uses flowers often but with care.

ANNUALS

An *annual* flower is one which completes its life cycle in one year. That is, it goes from seed to blossom in a single growing season and dies as winter approaches. Generally, annuals are most commonly used in summer landscapes. They bloom throughout the months of June, July, August, and September when the days are long and warm. They offer color, especially in northern regions, when many bulbous perennials are past blooming. There are hundreds of annuals commonly used throughout the country. Some examples of well-known annuals are the petunia, marigold, salvia, and zinnia.

Landscapers obtain annuals by two different methods. In one method, they are directly seeded into the ground after the danger of frost is past. Packages of annual seeds, figure 16–1, are available at most garden centers in the spring. Seeds may also be obtained from mail-order supply houses.

Figure 16–1. Packaged seeds are an easy and inexpensive way to start a flower garden.

Direct seeding of annuals (the placement of seeds in the ground) is the least expensive way to place flowers in the landscape. The major limitations of direct seeding are: (1) the young plants usually require thinning; (2) the plants require more time than the other method to reach blooming age; and (3) it is difficult to create definite patterns in the flower planting.

The other method used to obtain annuals is from *bedding plants*. These are plants which were started in a greenhouse and are already partially grown at the time they are set into the garden, figure 16–2. Very often, the plants are grown in a pressed peat moss container which can be planted directly into the ground. This creates no disturbance for the annual's root system; thus, the flower planting is well established from the very beginning.

Bedding plants are more expensive than seeded annuals. However, there is no need for thinning, and definite patterns can be easily created.

PERENNIALS

A *perennial* flower is one which does not die at the end of its first growing season. While it may become dormant as cold weather approaches, it lives to bloom again the following year. (When a plant is *dormant*, it is experiencing a period of rest in which it continues to live, but has little or no growth.) Most perennials live at least three or four years; many live for much longer.

Nearly all early spring flowers are perennials. Some grow from bulbs; others do not. Many special autumn flowers are also perennials. There are numerous summer perennials which act with annuals to add color to rock gardens and border plantings. Some examples of perennials are the hy-

Figure 16–2. Bedding plants are available from the greenhouse ready to plant in the garden. They give color faster than the direct-seeding method, but cost more.

acinth, iris, daffodil, tulip, poppy, phlox, gladiolus, dahlia, and mum.

Some perennials are available in seed form. However, the majority appear on the market as bedding plants or reproductive structures such as bulbs. Since they do not die at the end of the growing season, most perennials reproduce themselves and may eventually cover a larger area of the garden than was originally intended. This tendency to propagate may be a side benefit or a maintenance nuisance, depending upon the situation.

Bulbous Perennials

The very popular bulb comprises a large number of perennials. Bulbs survive the winter as dormant fleshy storage structures known to botanists as tubers, corms, rhizomes, tuberous roots, and true bulbs. In the landscape trade, they are usually simply called *bulbs*.

Most bulb perennials bloom only once, be it in the spring, summer, or fall. There are a few exceptions, however; these may bloom repeatedly. Bulbs may be classified as hardy or tender.

Hardy bulbs are perennials which are able to survive the winter outside and therefore do not require removal from the soil in the autumn. The only time they must be moved is when they are being thinned. Hardy bulbs usually bloom in the spring. Examples are the hyacinth, iris, daffodil, and tulip.

Tender bulbs are perennials which cannot survive the winter and must be taken up each fall and set out each spring after the

Figure 16–3. Autumn: installing a large bulb planting in front of an outdoor sculpture

Figure 16–4. Spring: the bulb planting in bloom

frost is gone. These bulbs usually bloom during the summer months. Examples are the canna, gladiolus, caladium, and tuberous begonia.

Figure 16–3 illustrates the autumn installation of a sizeable bulb planting around a large piece of outdoor sculpture. Figure 16–4 shows the planting as it appeared the following spring.

BIENNIALS

Flowers known as *biennials* complete their life cycles in two years. They produce only leaves during their first year of growth and flower the second year. After they have bloomed, they die. Biennials include the English daisy, foxglove, Japanese primrose, and pansy.

FLOWER BEDS AND FLOWER BORDERS

A *flower bed* is a freestanding planting made entirely of flowers. It does not share the site with shrubs or other plants. As fig-

ures 16–5 and 16–6 illustrate, flower beds are effective as focal points where sidewalks or streets intersect. They also work well in open lawn areas where they do not conflict with more important focal points and where the lawn is not used for activities that could be damaging to the beds.

Flower beds should never be planted in the public area of a residential landscape. When this is done, the beds attract more attention than the entry to the home, which is the most important part of any public area.

Flower beds must be designed so that they can be viewed from all sides, and must be planted accordingly. Because of this requirement, flower beds contain no woody plants to provide a backdrop for the blossoms. This has given the flower bed the reputation of being the most difficult flower planting to design. Probably for this reason, it is used much less often than the flower border.

The *flower border* is a planting which is placed in front of a larger planting of

Figure 16–5. This freestanding flower bed acts as a traffic divider while adding beauty to the area.

Figure 16–6. Walks on all sides create various points from which this flower bed may be viewed. Despite its size, only two species were used (salvia and dusty miller).

woody shrubs. The foliage of the shrubbery provides a background to set off the colors of the blossoms, figure 16–7. Since the flower border can only be viewed from one side, it is more easily controlled by the designer. Figure 16–8 illustrates the difference between the viewing perspectives of beds and borders.

Modern landscapers are more likely to use flowers in borders than beds for two reasons: they are easier to design, and the strong visual attraction of the flowers is more easily controlled.

DESIGNING FLOWER PLANTINGS

The placement of flowers in a bed or border arrangement is similar to shrub placement in most ways. Flowers are ar-

Figure 16–7. The flower border has a background, as opposed to the flower bed. Here, a vine-covered wall creates a rich contrast for blossoms.

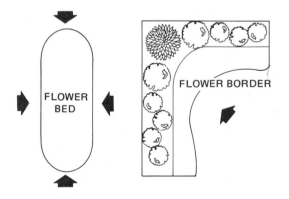

FLOWER BED

FLOWER BORDER

Figure 16–8. Flower beds are viewed from all sides and have no background foliage. Flower borders have a more limited viewing point and have background foliage.

ranged with the tallest to the rear and/or to the center. They are grouped in masses rather than placed as individuals. Flowers, like all other plant materials in the land-

scape, are placed according to the principles of design, figure 16–9.

Additional factors to remember when designing flower plantings are:

- All colors must blend together attractively; orange and red flowers can exist comfortably in the same planting if they do not bloom at the same time.
- Only those flowers blooming at any one time will be noticed.
- Dark, vibrant colors attract the eye strongly and should be used sparingly.
- Pale, pastel colors attract the eye less and can be used in greater quantities.
- Rigid, sharply formed blossoms attract the eye and should be used at the center of the planting.

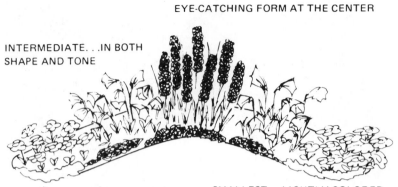

TALLEST. . .DARKLY TONED COLORS. . .
EYE-CATCHING FORM AT THE CENTER

INTERMEDIATE. . .IN BOTH
SHAPE AND TONE

SMALLEST. . .LIGHTLY COLORED. . .
ROUND FORMS AT THE ENDS

Figure 16–9. One example of how to arrange flower shapes, colors, and sizes in the flower border

- Round, loosely formed blossoms attract the eye less and should be used in the foreground and at the ends of the planting.

If an all-seasons flower planting is being designed, species must be selected and arranged so that there will always be a vibrantly colored, rigidly formed flower blooming in the center of the planting. The species will change with each season, but the forms should be similar. Flowers that are shorter, looser, and lighter in color should be selected to complement the central form. They too must be chosen carefully so that one or more species is always in bloom.

INSTALLING AND MAINTAINING FLOWER PLANTINGS

Flowers require a rich, loamy soil that holds moisture yet drains well. Being shallow-rooted, flowers do not do well in soil which allows water to run off rather than soak in, or which has so little organic matter that moisture is not retained. When preparing soil for flower seeding or transplanting, the ground should be cultivated and conditioned to a depth of at least 12 inches. As with trees, shrubs, and other plants, the amount of sand or peat moss to be added is determined by the particular soil conditions at the site.

Directions for installation are given on seed packages for the direct-seeding method. These directions must be followed carefully. Later, the young seedlings may be thinned and transplanted.

With the bedding plant method, the flowers are separated individually and usually spaced between 8 and 12 inches apart. Placement is staggered as with ground covers to maximize coverage. Each young plant is set into the ground so that the soil level is about 1 inch higher than it was around the plants in the greenhouse, figure 16–10. This extra coverage is especially important if the plants are slightly straggly when transplanted. At the time each plant is set into the ground, a cup of water (perhaps containing a weak fertilizer solution) poured into the hole before backfilling helps reduce transplant shock for the young plant.

Bulbs must be set into the ground at

Figure 16–10. Bedding plants are placed in a staggered arrangement for maximum coverage. Peat pots (on left) do not have to be removed before planting.

the proper time of year if they are to bloom on schedule. Hardy bulbs must be planted about October in order to bloom the following spring, since they need the cold winter weather to form their flower buds. Tender bulbs can be set out only after the ground has thawed and there is no danger of frost. In the fall, tender bulbs must be dug up, the soil shaken off, dried, and stored in a cool, dry, dark area until the next summer. It is helpful to dust the bulbs with a fungicide/insecticide mix while they are out of the ground. This helps to protect them from disease and insect problems. All injured or infected bulbs should be discarded rather than stored and replanted.

The chart on page 178 (A Guide to Bulbous Perennials) provides the beginning landscaper with basic information concerning common bulbous perennials.

Following their installation, all flowers should be thoroughly watered and mulched. An organic mulch applied to a depth of about 3 inches helps to conserve soil moisture and reduce weeds.

Maintenance of flower plantings varies with the type. Annuals can be fertilized in midsummer with a low analysis fertilizer to keep them lush and healthy. Bulbs should be fertilized immediately after flowering with a high phosphorus fertilizer such as bone meal. Nonbulbous perennials grow best if fertilized in the early spring. Summer or fall fertilization can actually harm the plants by keeping them too succulent as winter approaches.

All flowers should be watered frequently and deeply during dry periods. Their shallow roots quickly react to drought conditions.

After the bulbs have ceased to flower, their foliage must be allowed to grow until it dies back naturally. It is during this postflowering period that the food needed by the bulbs for the next season's growth is being produced.

A Guide to Bulbous Perennials

Bulb		Flowering Time	Time of Planting	Hardiness	Height	Planting Depth to Top of Bulb	Spacing
Common Name	Botanical Name						
Amaryllis	Amaryllides sp.	summer	spring	tender	15" or more	set top to ground level	12 inches
Anemone	Anemone sp.	summer	spring	semihardy*	7" to 14"	2 inches	12 inches
Bulbous iris	Iris sp.	summer	spring/fall	semihardy*	15" or more	2 inches	12 inches
Caladium	Caladium sp.	summer (foliage color only)	spring	tender	7" to 14"	2 to 3 inches in northern sections; 1 inch in southern sections	8 inches for mass effects
Calla lily	Zantedeschia sp.	summer	spring	tender	7" to 14"	set top at ground level	12 inches
Canna	Canna sp.	summer	spring	tender	36" or more	3 to 4 inches	18 to 24 inches
Crocus	Crocus sp.	spring	fall	hardy	2" to 6"	3 inches	2 to 4 inches
Daffodil	Narcissus sp.	spring	fall	hardy	7" to 12"	4 to 5 inches	6 to 8 inches
Dahlia	Dahlia sp.	summer	spring	tender	20" or more	5 to 6 inches	24 to 36 inches
Gladiolus	Gladiolus sp.	summer	spring	tender	24" or more	3 to 4 inches	6 to 8 inches
Grape hyacinth	Mascari sp.	spring	fall	hardy	1" to 4"	3 inches	2 to 4 inches
Hyacinth	Hyacinthus sp.	spring	fall	hardy	7" to 12"	4 to 6 inches	6 to 8 inches
Lily	Lilium sp.	summer	spring/fall	hardy	15" or more	6 inches	12 inches
Ranunculus	Ranunculus sp.	summer	spring	semihardy*	7" to 14"	2 inches	12 inches
Snowdrop	Galanthus sp.	spring	fall	hardy	1" to 6"	3 inches	2 to 4 inches
Summer hyacinth	Caltonia sp.	summer	spring	tender	1" to 6"	4 inches	6 to 8 inches
Tuberous begonia	Palianthus sp.	summer	spring	tender	7" to 12"	set just below soil surface	6 to 8 inches
Tulip	Tulipa sp.	spring	fall	hardy	7" to 20"	4 to 5 inches	6 to 8 inches

*Semihardy bulbs are regarded as tender in northern sections and hardy in southern sections.

About halfway through the summer, annuals frequently begin to look straggly and set seed, usually reducing their flower show. In these cases, it is common practice to give the flowers a severe pruning. With bushy flowers such as the petunia, a pair of grass clippers is used to cut the plants back. With more stalky annuals, a severe pinching has the same effect. The plants may be unattractive at first, but new shoots and fresh flowers form within two weeks or so. The planting looks fresh and new and carries its bright colors on into the fall season.

As winter approaches, annuals should be cut off at ground level or removed entirely from the planting bed. Perennials can be cut back and mulched. Tender bulbs should be dug up and stored.

ACHIEVEMENT REVIEW

A. Indicate whether the following statements apply to annuals (A) or perennials (P).

1. The plant does not die at the end of the growing season.
2. These plants complete their life cycles in a single year.
3. These plants are most commonly used during the warm summer months.
4. Some forms of these plants are bulbous.
5. Nearly all of our spring flowers are of this type.

B   Indicate whether the following statements apply to hardy bulbs (H), tender bulbs (T), or both (B).

1. The bulbs can survive the winter without being moved inside.
2. The bulbs usually bloom only once each season.
3. These bulbs are planted in the spring and bloom during the summer.
4. These bulbs are planted in the fall and bloom the following spring.
5. The foliage of these bulbs should not be cut back until it has turned brown naturally.

C. Indicate whether the following statements apply to flower beds (BE), flower borders (BO), or both (B).

1. The flowers in this planting are freestanding with no background shrubs.
2. In this planting, the tallest center flowers should have the brightest color.
3. This planting is only viewed from one side, making it easier to design.
4. This planting is mulched to help retain moisture during the season.
5. The flowers in this planting grow best in a rich, loamy soil.

SUGGESTED ACTIVITIES

1. Write to seed companies and request catalogs. The gardening section of your newspaper may have some addresses of suppliers. Posting the pictures around the room will help you become familiar with common flowers in the area.

2. With drafting tools, design a flower bed or border. It should cover an area of at least 40 square feet. Design it so that there are plants in bloom from early spring to late fall.

3. Start annual flowers from seed. The seed can be purchased at a local garden center, supermarket, or hardware store. Plant them in greenhouse flats or flowerpots and place in a greenhouse or near a sunny window. When the weather is warm enough, set them outside around the school building. As an added activity, design a planting for the building first, using the flowers being grown in class.

4. Practice blending flower colors. Cut out patches of colored paper to represent different types and quantities of flowers. Arrange them so that the brightest, most attracting colors are used where the attraction is desired. Pastel colors should be used in greater quantities and placed away from the central color. Follow the suggestions given in the text for arranging flower colors.

5. To understand better the anatomy of bulbs, select several different types for dissection. Carefully peel away each layer. Try to identify those tissues that will become the roots, stem, leaves, and flowers of each bulb. A botany text may be consulted for assistance and exact identification of all parts.

6. Study areas where wildflowers are common. Note how in the natural world, flowers are grouped together in plant masses, not randomly distributed. This can help you attain natural effects when arranging landscape flowers.

THE ARID LANDSCAPE

After studying this unit, you will be able to

- name the regions of the United States where arid landscapes are common.
- explain how landscapes in arid regions differ from others in the country.
- characterize the soils of arid regions.
- describe methods for retaining water in arid soils.
- identify plants that are suitable for arid landscapes.
- explain the methods of transplanting and maintaining cactus plants.

THE ARID LANDSCAPE DEFINED

An *arid* landscape is one whose plants receive little usable water. The water available to the plants may be limited by quantity or quality, by such environmental circumstances as drying winds, or by a combination of factors.

Arid Regions of the United States

Arid landscapes are common to the states of Arizona, Colorado, New Mexico, and Texas, and parts of California, Nevada, Oklahoma, and Utah.

THE SOUTHWEST

In contrast to the soft, lush green, temperate and subtropical regions of the United States, the Southwest stands apart. This region is distinctive not only by its climate, but also by its culture, flora, and fauna. In the past, the Southwest was usually thought of in terms of its native Indians, Mexican and cowboy legacies, Spanish architecture, towering land forms, vast deserts, and strange plant materials. It seemed to be a world apart from the rest of the country and, for most of its history, was home to a very small percent of the population. There were few planned landscapes, and even fewer gardeners who were interested in learning about an area so alien to them.

All of this changed with the onset of the energy crisis, and the resultant shifting of the population. The Sun Belt has the fastest growing population in the country. New homes and businesses are being built throughout the region as individuals and industry seek reduced heating costs and milder winters. The full impact on the Southwest has yet to be seen. Only time will show the effects of the nontraditional and imported architecture, lifestyles, and plant material brought in by people from northern and eastern states.

The Changing Landscape

Changes in the landscape have occurred as the Southwest became home to people transplanted from New England, the Atlantic Northeast, the Midwest, and the Northwest. Some people have attempted to make the strange arid landscape closely resemble the more familiar outdoor rooms of the temperate states. In certain cities, such as Phoenix, large areas of the local flora have been replaced and transformed by out-of-state exotic materials. Bluegrass lawns grow on desert sand, and eastern shrubs bloom from planting beds filled with carefully blended soil mixtures. Those who appreciate the differences unique to each geographical region do not welcome this trend toward uniformity.

The professional landscaper seeking work in the Southwest will find four distinct differences between arid and temperate landscapes:

- *The soil quality is poor* throughout most of the Southwest.
- *Irrigation* is an absolute necessity throughout the year.
- *Altitude variations* result in extremely hot daytime temperatures and very cool nights.
- *High winds* dry out plants quickly and often damage them physically.

SOILS OF THE ARID REGION

Arid soils generally fall into three categories: pure sand or gypsum, adobe, and caliche.

Sand has almost no nutrient content and is without humus, the important organic component of soil. *Adobe* is a heavy claylike soil, used by early residents to make building blocks. Adobe holds moisture better than sand but needs humus to lighten it and improve its aeration. *Caliche* soils are highly alkaline, due to an excessive lime content. They have a calcareous hardpan deposit near the surface that blocks drainage, making plant growth impossible.

Caliche soil is the most problematic soil a landscaper is likely to encounter. Heavy irrigation watering causes the alkaline lime layer to form near the soil surface. The hardpan deposits may lie right at the surface of the soil or at a depth varying from several inches to several feet below ground level. The deposits may occur as a granular accumulation or as a compact, impermeable concretelike layer.

Caliche soils are not a problem in the deep soils of valleys. However, in locations outside of valleys, the land will neither drain naturally nor support healthy plant growth where unaltered caliche is present.

Generally, arid soils

- lack humus.
- require frequent irrigation.
- are nutritionally poor; nutrients are continually leached out by the irrigation water.
- are highly alkaline (pH of 7.5 to 8.5 and higher).
- are low in phosphate.
- lack iron or else contain it in a form unavailable to the plants.

- have a high soluble salt content resulting from alkaline irrigation waters, manures, and fertilizers that do not leach thoroughly.

Organic matter must be added to all southwestern soils to improve their physical structure. The organic matter improves the water retention capability of light sandy soils and breaks up heavy adobe soils. The only way to improve the drainage of caliche soil is to break through it and remove the impermeable layer. The excavated soil can be replaced with a soil mix that will support healthy plant growth.

WATER RETENTION

Water problems are common to landscape gardening throughout the Southwest, whether the landscape is on the valley slopes or the desert floor. An adequate supply of water is never available. What water there is may be so alkaline that it creates as many problems as it cures. Highly alkaline irrigation water can counteract an acidic soil created to support the growth of such plants as azaleas and rhododendrons. It can also contribute to the buildup of soluble salts in the soil. This results in increasingly weakened plant growth.

Nevertheless, irrigation watering is vital to the good health of arid landscapes. However, it is essential that *all* water be retained, whether it is applied naturally or by irrigation.

Methods of Retaining Water

The following methods are used to retain water and moisture in the arid landscape.

- All planting beds in the arid landscape should be recessed several inches below ground level to create a catch basin, figure 17–1. This method traps and holds any applied water, preventing loss through run-off.
- Enough irrigation water should be applied to permeate several inches into the soil, avoiding excessive surface evaporation.
- Organic matter must be incorporated into the soil each year to improve the soil's water retention capacity.
- Organic mulches must be applied to a depth of at least four inches. The mulch slows moisture loss from the soil, and creates a cooler growth environment for the roots.
- Young trees and new transplants can lose enough water through their thin bark to suffer severe damage during a hot summer. For that reason, trunk wraps and whitewash paint should be applied to guard against sun scald. The same remedy is helpful to citrus trees and freshly exposed areas of recently pruned older trees.

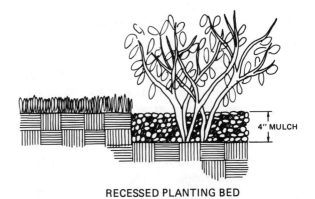

RECESSED PLANTING BED

Figure 17–1. A recessed planting bed creates a catch basin for retaining moisture.

THE SELECTION AND USE OF PLANTS IN THE ARID LANDSCAPE

As landscaping expands in the Southwest, certain questions come to mind. What plants are available and suitable for gardens in arid regions? What types of gardens are appropriate for the area? Can familiar temperate zone plants be expected to survive in arid gardens? Is the landscape profession in the Southwest totally different from that in other regions of the country? The answers to the questions are not clear-cut because the opinions of people vary, just as the many local climates and soils within the Southwest vary. No simple answers will suffice for a region of the country that includes such diverse areas as the Grand Canyon and Palm Springs.

Selecting Plants for the Arid Landscape

Landscapers familiar only with temperate zone plants often are dismayed when they first encounter the flora of arid regions. The succulents and cacti seem stark and strange to the eye. The trees they do recognize are generally regarded as weed trees in the eastern and midwestern states. The lush green cool-season grasses, such as bluegrasses and fescues, are missing. In their place are coarser varieties, tall ornamental grasses, or just sand. Missing also are forested slopes for the landscape to reach toward, and rolling meadow views to see through windows in outdoor walls.

Once the differences are noted, the landscaper must look further to find comforting similarities. Deciduous and evergreen forms of plants can be found. The landscaper will find trees, shrubs, vines, ground covers, and flowers to work with.

The landscaper will still find it necessary to deal with soft irregular plant forms and rigid geometric forms. (In this situation, the geometric, round barrel cactus and the globe arborvitae have something in common. Both are difficult to incorporate into a unified landscape design.) Likewise, the functions of the plants used in southwestern landscapes are similar to those of plants anywhere else in the country. A windbreak is just as important in New Mexico as it is in Kansas. A specimen plant fills the same focal-point role, whether it is a crape myrtle in Georgia or an unusually shaped black locust in Nevada. In short, any species of plant should be judged for its value and function in a particular landscape. One region's weed tree is another region's specimen plant; neither region should claim horticultural superiority.

The "Guide to Selected Southwestern Plants" on pages 188–195 summarizes some of the plants commonly used in landscaping the arid regions of the United States. It is intended not as a complete list, but as a starting point to use when selecting plants. More detailed and complete lists are available from books that deal specifically with southwestern gardening. The Cooperative Extension Service of individual southwestern states can also be of assistance.

Using Plants in the Arid Landscape

The plants in arid regions look quite different from those in other areas. It seems as though the gardens of the arid regions follow a different set of rules in their development. How else could such unusual designs result?

After careful analysis of well-designed southwestern landscapes, it can be seen that the principles of design are as valid in the arid garden as they are in temperate and subtropical gardens. These principles would be weak indeed if they did not apply to all situations. Attention still focuses on the entry to a building and selected points within other use areas. Balance is still important, with the informal, asymmetrical types used most often. Simplicity, which is inherent to the wide-open spaces that characterize the Southwestern landscape, is basic to the man-made landscape.

Proportion is another important consideration. Southwestern architecture, especially residential architecture, is mainly single story. Small trees are more suitable than tall ones to maintain the proper viewer perspective and size relationship between the buildings and the landscape. The principle of rhythm and line, while still valid, leans toward looser, more open space formations than in more populated regions of the country.

Some distinctions do exist. For instance, the space efficiency needed in an urban penthouse garden is seldom a factor in a southwestern garden. Also, arid climates do not have the abundance of moisture and pH neutral soils common to many American gardens which permit the growth of a wide variety of plants. Further, the sheer starkness of the southwestern plants, especially in the desert region, makes the viewer more aware of them individually than in temperate or subtropical gardens. In the latter regions, the massing of foliage is a common practice, and is easily done.

The most successful arid landscapes draw their inspiration and materials from the natural countryside around them. The use of native plant materials, stones, adobe bricks, gravels, and enrichment items that reflect the region's culture creates a garden that suits the locale. Conversely, the use of imported temperate zone plants and turf grasses creates a landscape that is at odds with its natural setting. An example of this is the landscape currently evolving in Phoenix.

Figures 17–2 through 17–6 show a variety of typical landscaping designs suitable for southwestern areas.

Whether the garden is inspired by the surrounding countryside or is an attempt to duplicate a spot in Connecticut, it should be informal in style. The typical southwestern

Figure 17–2. This Arizona home is enframed in a balanced landscape. Attention focuses on the entry, as it should.

Figure 17–3. The public area of this home is nicely designed. The number of species is limited, forms are massed, and the materials used are all native to the area.

Figure 17–4. This landscape would benefit from more massing of plants, with less emphasis on individual plant forms.

Figure 17–5. Massing of plants draws attention away from individual plant forms. These prickly pear cacti lend themselves well to such a use.

Figure 17–6. Southwestern landscaping should reflect the native elements of plants, stones, sand, and space, rather than introducing elements alien to the area.

home is of Spanish or Pueblo architecture. Recent variations in building trends have brought the western ranch and other modern styles into the southwestern cities and suburbs as well. None of these styles lends itself well to formal, symmetrical landscape designs.

As the professional landscaper seeks to meet the needs of the southwestern client, the same concerns arise that are common to landscapers everywhere. How much privacy is desired? How much upkeep will the client accept? How can the climate be modified? Where is the nearest source of supply for materials? How can the indoors and outdoors be tied together most effectively?

Climate Modification

Satisfying the client's needs, while trying to achieve a sense of landscape unity without violating the integrity of the natural site is a complicated challenge. The first factor to consider is climate modification. Most homeowners want relief from the torrid summer sun and the forceful winter winds. Southern and western locations are the best for the planting of small-to-medium-sized trees that will shade the house during the warmest hours of the day. The northern and eastern sides of the house offer the longest periods of shade. Therefore, these are the best sites for the development of family living area patios. This is one significant difference from landscaping in temperate regions, where the southern and western sides of a house are preferred for patio development.

Winter winds blow mostly from the west. They are best controlled by methods that diminish their force and attempt to divert it. Vertical louvered fencing and/or planted windbreaks are best for this purpose. The most effective natural windbreak combines both trees and shrubs. Four or five rows planted 16 feet apart, starting with shrubs on the windward side and building up to trees on the house side, work best, figure 17–7.

The Importance of Natural Features

Whether treated as an on-site or off-site feature, the natural landscape must be respected. Successful southwestern gardens are those that improve upon the natural setting. The use of stones, repetition of earth colors, addition of cooling water features, and native materials all help to tie the man-made and natural landscapes more closely together. Views across the desert or toward a distant mountain range should be enframed to become part of the landscape, figure 17–8. Where appropriate, the off-site natural landscape can be used as a backdrop for an on-site enrichment feature. In such a case, the on-site feature should match the mood of the natural backdrop and be visually dominant, figure 17–9.

Figure 17–8. The foreground trees enframe the distant view.

Figure 17–9. The on-site feature should match the mood of the natural backdrop and be visually dominant.

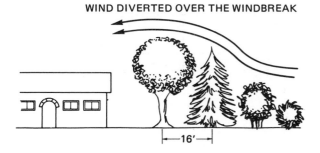

Figure 17–7. How a natural windbreak works

A Guide to Selected Southwestern Plants

Plant		Growth Habit	Mature Height		
Common Name	Botanical Name		1' or less	2'–5'	6'–9'
Ash 　Arizona 　Modesto	Fraxinus velutina Fraxinus velutina var. glabra	T T			
Citrus trees	Citrus sp.	T			
Coral tree	Erythrina sp.	T			
Crabapple, flowering	Malus sp.	T			
Cypress, Arizona	Cupressus arizonica	T			
Elderberry, desert	Sambucus arizonica	T			
Elephant tree	Bursera microphylla	T			
Elm 　Chinese 　Siberian	Ulmus parvifolia Ulmus pumila	T T			
Eucalyptus	Eucalyptus sp.	T			
Hackberry, netleaf	Celtis reticulata	T			
Honeylocust 　Shademaster 　Sunburst 　Thornless	Gleditsia triacanthos var.inermis 'Shademaster' Gleditsia triacanthos var.inermis 'Sunburst' Gleditsia triacanthos var.inermis	T T T			
Ironwood, desert	Olneya tesota	T			X
Jujube, Chinese	Ziziphus jujuba	T			
Locust 　Black 　Idaho 　Pink flowering	Robinia pseudoacacia Robinia pseudoacacia 'Idahoensis' Robinia pseudoacacia 'Decaisneana'	T T T			
Magnolia, southern	Magnolia grandiflora	T			
Mesquite 　Honey 　Screwbean	Prosopis glandulosa var. glandulosa Prosopis pubescens	T T			
Mulberry, white	Morus alba	T			

Mature Height				Season of Bloom					Special Use in the Landscape
10'–15'	15'–30'	30'–50'	Over 50'	Early Spring	Late Spring	Summer	Fall	Winter	
		X		NS					shade tree
		X		NS					shade tree
X				varies with the variety					excellent for containers
	X			X					brilliant flowers
	X				X				specimen plant
		X		NS					screens and windbreaks
	X			NS					screens and windbreaks
	X			NS					
		X		NS					shade tree
		X		NS					windbreak
		X		varies with the variety					many species / prized for flower and/or foliage
		X		NS					shade tree
	X			NS					good in dry, desert conditions
	X			NS					
		X		NS					
	X				X				specimen tree / very salt tolerant
			X		X				frequent pruning makes these attractive flowering trees
		X			X				
		X			X				
			X			X			lawn tree
	X			NS					shade trees and windbreaks
	X			NS					
			X	NS					shade tree

A Guide to Selected Southwestern Plants (continued)

Plant		Growth Habit	Mature Height		
Common Name	Botanical Name		1' or less	2'–5'	6'–9'
Olive, European	Olea europaea	T			
Pagoda tree, Japanese	Sophora japonica	T			
Paloverde					
Blue	Cercidium floridum	T			
Little leaf	Cercidium microphyllum	T			
Mexican	Parkinsonia aculeata	T			
Pine					
Aleppo	Pinus halepensis	T			
Digger	Pinus sabiniana	T			
Italian stone	Pinus pinea	T			
Japanese black	Pinus thunbergii	T			
Pinyon	Pinus cembroides	T			
Pistache, Chinese	Pistacia chinensis	T			
Poplar					
Balm-of-Gilead	Populus balsamifera	T			
Bolleana	Populus alba var. 'Pyramidalis'	T			
Cottonwood	Populus fremontii	T			
Lombardy	Populus nigra 'Italica'	T			
White	Populus alba	T			
Silk tree	Albizia julibrissin	T			
Smoke tree	Dalea spinosa	T			
Sycamore					
American	Platanus occidentalis	T			
Arizona	Platanus racemosa 'Wrightii'	T			
California	Platanus racemosa	T			
Tamarisk					
Athel tree	Tamarix aphylla	T			
Salt cedar	Tamarix parviflora	T			
Umbrella tree, Texas	Melia azedorach 'Umbraculiformis'	T			
Willow					
Babylon	Salix babylonica	T			
Globe Navajo		T			
Wisconsin	Salix x blanda	T			

Mature Height				Season of Bloom					Special Use in the Landscape
10'–15'	15'–30'	30'–50'	Over 50'	Early Spring	Late Spring	Summer	Fall	Winter	
	X			NS					good multi-stemmed tree
	X					X			lawn tree
	X				X				specimen trees
	X				X				
	X				X				
		X		NS					grows well in poor soil
		X		NS					specimen plant
			X	NS					good in desert conditions
	X			NS					good in planters; prune well
X				NS					multi-stemmed effects
			X	NS					good patio tree
									good fall color
		X		NS					narrow columnar form
		X		NS					windbreaks
			X	NS					
		X		NS					
		X		NS					
		X				X			showy shade tree
X					X				
			X	NS					excellent street trees
			X	NS					
			X	NS					
		X				X			wind, drought, and salt resistant
	X					X			
	X				X				shade tree
		X		NS					
			X	NS					
		X		NS					

A Guide to Selected Southwestern Plants (continued)

Plant		Growth Habit	Mature Height		
Common Name	Botanical Name		1' or less	2'–5'	6'–9'
Zelkova, sawleaf	Zelkova serrata	T			
Abelia, glossy	Abelia x grandiflora	S			X
Apache plume	Fallugia paradoxa	S		X	
Arborvitae, Oriental	Platycladus orientalis	S			

Barberry
  Darwin
  Japanese
	
	Berberis darwinii
	Berberis thunbergii
		
		S
		S
				
				X
					
					X

Bird of paradise	Caesalpinia gilliesii	S			X
Brittlebush	Encelia farinosa	S		X	
Butterfly bush	Buddleia davidii	S			X
Cherry laurel, Carolina	Prunus caroliniana	S			
Cotoneaster, silverleaf	Cotoneaster pannosus	S			X
Crape myrtle	Lagerstroemia indica	S			
Creosote bush	Larrea tridentata	S			X
Firethorn, Laland	Pyracantha coccinea 'Lalandei'	S			X

Hibiscus
  Chinese
  Rose of Sharon
	
	Hibiscus rosa-sinensis
	Hibiscus syriacus
		
		S
		S			

Holly
  Burford
  Wilson
  Yaupon
	
	Ilex cornuta 'Burfordii'
	Ilex wilsonii
	Ilex vomitoria
		
		S
		S
		S
					
					X
					X

Hopbush	Dodonaea cuneata	S			
Jojoba	Simmondsia chinensis	S		X	

Juniper
  Armstrong
  Hollywood
  Pfitzer
	
	Juniperus chinensis 'Armstrongii'
	Juniperus californica
	Juniperus chinensis 'Pfitzeriana'
		
		S
		S
		S
				
				X
				
					X

Lysiloma	Lysiloma sp.	S			

Mature Height				Season of Bloom					Use in Landscape
10'–15'	15'–30'	30'–50'	Over 50'	Early Spring	Late Spring	Summer	Fall	Winter	
		X		NS					windbreak
						X			
				X					
X				NS					
				NS	X				barrier plantings
						X			
					X				
						X			vigorous growth
	X			X					screens and hedges
					X				wind screen
	X					X			very colorful
						X			screens and hedges
				X					espaliers well
X		X				X X			
				NS NS NS					Wilson and Yaupon clip and shade well
	X								
X				NS					screens
				NS					hedges
X				NS NS NS					
X					X				good for transition between garden and natural landscape

A Guide to Selected Southwestern Plants (continued)

Plant		Growth Habit	Mature Height		
Common Name	Botanical Name		1' or less	2'–5'	6'–9'
Myrtle	Myrtus communis	S		X	
Ocotillo	Fouquieria splendens	S			
Oleander	Neriam oleander	S			
Photina	Photina glabra	S			
Privet 　California 　Glossy 　Japanese 　Texas	 Ligustrum ovalifolium Ligustrum lucidum Ligustrum japonicum Ligustrum japonicum texanum	 S S S S			 X
Rose, floribunda	Rosa x floribunda	S		X	
Silverberry	Elaeagnus commutatus	S			
Sugar bush	Rhus ovata	S			
Bougainvillea	Bougainvillea glabra	V			X
Ivy 　Algerian 　Boston	 Hedera canariensis Parthenocissus tricuspidata	 G V	 X 		
Jasmine, star	Jasminum multiflorum	V			
Lavender cotton	Santolina chamaecyparissus	G	X		
Periwinkle	Vinca minor	G	X		
Trumpet creeper	Campsis radicans	V			
Virginia creeper	Parthenocissus quinquefolia	V			
Wisteria	Wisteria sinensis	V			

T　Trees
S　Shrubs
V　Vines
G　Ground covers
NS　Flowers are not showy.

Mature Height				Season of Bloom					Special Use in the Landscape
10'–15'	15'–30'	30'–50'	Over 50'	Early Spring	Late Spring	Summer	Fall	Winter	
						X			prunes and shapes well
X					X				specimen plant
X						X	X		does well in heat and poor soil
	X			X					screens
X				X					all species can be pruned to lower heights
X	X			X					
					X				
					X				
					X				massing effects
X				NS					good for containers
X				X					
						X			very colorful
	X			NS					
				NS					
	X					X			very fragrant
						X			effective as edging
					X				
	X					X	X		
	X			NS					
X					X				may be trained as shrubs and weeping trees

Desert Gardens

With desert gardens, there is often a desire to develop the landscape with the native cacti and succulents. Not all desert plants are easily or freely transplanted, though. Some are quite difficult to transplant. Others are protected by law to safeguard them against destruction or theft. Many native plants grow quite slowly, and are endangered species in their natural range. Landscapers should check local laws before collecting from the wild. Many of the desired plants can be purchased from southwestern nurseries where they are grown for sale.

Where desert plants and nondesert plants are combined in the same landscape, it is best to group the species into plantings that have similar cultural requirements. For example, plants that cannot tolerate wind should be grouped against the northeast wall. Plants that require special soil mixtures should not be placed in the same bed as cacti. Plants that need frequent watering should be placed close to the house; plants that need less water may be placed at more distant points.

PLANT INSTALLATION AND MAINTENANCE

The basic methods of plant installation for arid regions are similar to those described in Units 13 through 16. The soil must be conditioned to promote drainage and aeration. Large and frequent applications of humus-making organic material are necessary. Sand must be added to adobe soils. If caliche soil is involved, enough of the soil must be replaced to create a totally new root environment to sustain the plant for its entire lifetime.

Cactus Plants

Cactus plants are sufficiently different from other plants to warrant special mention as to how they can be transplanted successfully.

- Before transplanting, note and mark the north side of the cactus. It is essential that this side of the plant be reoriented to the north in its new location. Otherwise, the intense southern/southwestern sun will harm the plant. The plant will have developed a thicker layer of protective tissue on its south side to withstand the heat.
- By trenching around the cactus, lift as much of the root system as possible.
- Brush as much soil as possible from the roots, then dust them with powdered sulfur.
- Place the cactus in a shaded, open area where air circulates freely. Allow damaged roots to heal for a week before replanting.
- Plant the cactus in dry, well-drained soil. Stake it if necessary.
- Water *after* new growth starts, usually in three or four weeks. Thereafter, water at monthly intervals.

General Guidelines

It is best to plant native desert species before the onset of summer heat. Early spring is a good time, and fall is even better. The soil must drain well, since the roots of most desert plants rot easily if grown in poorly drained soil. Planting during the cool seasons permits strong roots to develop before the summer arrives. This gives the plants a better chance to survive.

Watering depends upon the season and the species of plant. Cacti need water as often as once a week during their period of active growth in the spring. During the fall and winter, they need little or no water and should be allowed to go dormant. Succulents should be watered as soon as the soil surface dries out. It is recommended to water succulents several times weekly during the active season, and once every two weeks during the winter. Lawns must be deeply watered at least twice weekly. All plants should be hosed off periodically to wash away dust. Water must not be applied so late in the day that foliage is still moist in the cool night air.

Desert gardens require far less maintenance than do temperate and subtropical gardens. The dry climate discourages many of the insects and diseases that trouble gardens elsewhere.

Weeds are a maintenance nuisance in desert gardens, as they are everywhere. In small areas, the weeds can be removed by hand. In large areas, weeds can be controlled by chemical herbicides, but there is a possible *hazard* in using chemicals in arid regions. An unexpected rain shower can carry the herbicide from its area of application to nearby desirable trees and plants. For this reason, it is best to use weed killers that kill the weed upon contact and then quickly become inactive in the soil.

Fertilizing the southwestern garden is vital, since the soils are low in natural fertility. A soil test should be made to determine precisely what a local soil needs. For the region in general, phosphates and iron chelates or iron sulphate will need to be added. Organic fertilizers, such as sewage sludge, cottonseed meal, and animal manures are especially good for southwestern soils. Among chemical fertilizers, the 4-12-4 analysis is used most often. As with plants throughout the country, fertilizers should be applied preceding the periods of most rapid growth. They should not be applied later in the growing season when they would encourage soft growth, which would be damaged by winter weather.

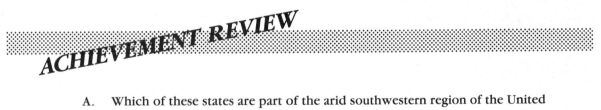

ACHIEVEMENT REVIEW

A. Which of these states are part of the arid southwestern region of the United States?

1. Wyoming	8. Oklahoma
2. Colorado	9. Idaho
3. Texas	10. California
4. Utah	11. Arizona
5. Oregon	12. South Dakota
6. Nevada	13. New Mexico
7. North Dakota	14. Nebraska

B. List four features of southwestern landscapes that make them different from landscapes in other parts of the United States.

C. Name the three distinct soil types of the arid region.

D. Indicate if the following characteristics apply best to adobe soils (A), caliche soils (C), pure sand soils (S), or all soils of the Southwest (AS).

1. lacking in humus
2. very heavy soil; bricklike
3. low in phosphate content
4. impermeable hardpan deposit near surface
5. alkaline pH
6. the poorest nutrient content
7. low in iron content
8. high soluble salt content
9. holds some moisture
10. allows no drainage

E. List five methods of retaining water in southwestern plants and plantings.

F. Select the word or phrase that best completes each of the following statements.

1. The best locations for shade trees in an arid region are off the _____ sides of the house.
   a. north and south   c. east and west
   b. south and west   d. north and east
2. Family living area patios are most desirable on the _____ sides of the house in the Southwest.
   a. north and south   c. east and west
   b. south and west   d. north and east
3. Southwestern winter winds blow mainly from the _____.
   a. north   c. east
   b. south   d. west
4. Windbreaks for a southwestern property are most effective when located off the _____ side of the house.
   a. north   c. east
   b. south   d. west
5. When the natural landscape is used as a backdrop, the enrichment item used against it should match in style and be _____.
   a. dominant   c. inconspicuous
   b. recessive   d. color coordinated
6. Plant groupings in arid landscapes should be based upon a similarity of _____ requirements.
   a. client   c. nutrient
   b. designer   d. cultural
7. Cacti develop a thickened layer of protective tissue on their _____ side, and should be oriented carefully when transplanting.
   a. north   c. east
   b. south   d. west

8. Before replanting, cacti to be transplanted should be _____.
   a. kept moistened for a week
   b. pruned back
   c. balled and burlapped
   d. shaded for a week in an open area so their roots can heal
9. The best season for planting southwestern gardens is _____.
   a. spring   c. fall
   b. summer   d. winter
10. The best herbicides for arid region plantings are those that _____.
    a. kill upon contact and remain active in the soil
    b. kill upon contact and then quickly become inactive in the soil

SUGGESTED ACTIVITIES

1. Collect samples of gypsum, adobe, and caliche soils. Try not to break the calcareous, hardpan layer of the caliche. Compare the soils for water permeability by applying equal measured amounts to each sample and measuring the amount of water collected from the base of each sample after a fixed time period.

2. Using the Guide to Selected Southwestern Plants, identify those plants on the list that are found in your region of the Southwest. Add to the list using a catalog from a nearby nursery.

3. Convert planting designs found in this and other texts that use temperate zone plants into similar arrangements using southwestern plants.

4. In two boxes of soil, each 12 inches deep, place thermometers at depths of 2, 4, 6, and 8 inches. Leave one box unmulched. Cover the other with an organic mulch to a depth of 4 inches. Keep both boxes equally watered and set out in the full sun. Record the temperatures of both boxes at all levels. The cooling influence of the mulch should be apparent. How does the mulch affect water retention? How does it affect soil temperature? How does the soil temperature influence root growth?

SECTION 4

USING
CONSTRUCTION
MATERIALS
IN THE
LANDSCAPE

UNIT 18

ENCLOSURE MATERIALS

After studying this unit, you will be able to

- list five functions of landscape enclosure.
- describe five types of materials used for constructed landscape enclosures.
- explain the need for and means of releasing water pressure from behind solid enclosure materials.

- To provide various degrees of protection and/or privacy
- To serve other engineering needs, such as retaining steep slopes and raising planting beds
- To modify the climate by creating sheltered areas where plants may grow, or by diverting or reducing the wind's force to make the area more comfortable for occupants

FUNCTIONS OF LANDSCAPE ENCLOSURE

The walls of the outdoor room serve to enclose (surround or separate) a section of property which is to act as an outdoor living area. *Enclosure materials* form these walls.

There are several functions of landscape enclosure:

- To define the shape and limits of the landscape
- To control circulation patterns within the landscape

As discussed previously, enclosure is sometimes accomplished with plant materials. Many other types of enclosures are man-made; these may be used alone or in combination with plant materials.

The type of constructed enclosure selected by the landscaper is usually determined by the function it is to perform. If its only purpose is *aesthetic* (to beautify the landscape and make it appealing to the senses), the most important consideration is how well the enclosure material coordinates with the total design. To achieve total unity of design, repeat colors and materials used in the building(s) and in the surfacing and furnishings of the garden in the enclosure materials.

CHOOSING MAN-MADE ENCLOSURES BY FUNCTION

Directing Circulation Patterns

If the purpose is to direct circulation patterns, a fence or wall may be used. Height is usually more important than density when traffic control is the concern. Therefore, open style fencing can be used if the viewer is to be able to see through the enclosure structure, figure 18–1. The higher the enclosure is, the more effective it is in directing movement. A combination of an open style enclosure and plants can create an outdoor wall that is both functional and attractive, figure 18–2.

Protection

If protection is the objective, a solidly constructed fence or wall is a necessity.

Open style fences, such as the chain link, allow the viewer to see through them while discouraging passage. Walls offer the greatest protection since they combine both density and strength. The height of the fence or wall chosen is determined by the type of protection it is to offer. To prevent children or small dogs from wandering into the street may require an enclosure only 3 feet high. To prevent intruders or large animals from entering, a wall 6 feet high or higher is required.

Privacy

For privacy control, the height and density of the enclosure material are again important. Where properties are small and family living areas are closely spaced, as in many older city neighborhoods, enclosure for privacy is a necessity. The enclosure must be solid where total privacy is needed,

Figure 18–1. Post and rail fencing can direct traffic patterns without blocking the view.

Figure 18–2. The combination of constructed and natural enclosure materials is often more attractive and effective than either type would be if used alone.

but a cramped feeling can result when a solid enclosure is used in a small space. Using a combination of plants and constructed enclosures helps to avoid this feeling.

The height of the enclosure necessary for privacy depends upon the location of the persons desiring the privacy and the vantage point of an unwelcome viewer. If a homeowner wishes to be screened from a next-door neighbor when both are in their family living areas at ground level, the enclosure should be about 6 feet high, figure 18–3. If the neighbor looks out a second-floor window onto the patio, the vantage point has been elevated, giving the neighbor an unobstructed view. This requires that the height of the enclosure increase also. Constructed enclosures cannot be much higher than 8 feet without becoming too imposing or threatening in appearance. In addition, there may be local laws limiting fence height. Therefore, trees are fre-

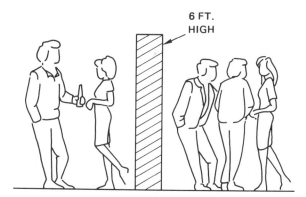

Figure 18–3. Privacy between two properties on the same level requires an enclosure of at least 6 feet in height.

quently used to block views in certain cases, figure 18–4.

When determining the enclosure height needed for privacy, remember:

- When both the viewer and the view are parallel to the ground, privacy can

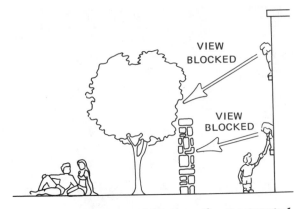

Figure 18–4. The combination of a constructed enclosure and trees gives privacy when the viewer is above ground level.

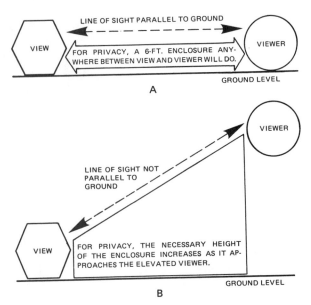

Figure 18–5. The differences in the height of the enclosure necessary for privacy when the line of sight is and is not parallel to the ground.

be obtained by a 6-foot enclosure at any point along the viewing line. It does not matter if the land is flat or sloped as long as the line of sight parallels it, figure 18–5 (A).

• When the viewer and the view do not parallel the ground, the enclosure height necessary for privacy increases as the enclosure approaches the viewer, figure 18–5 (B). The height decreases as it approaches the person desiring the privacy.

Engineering Uses

There are many engineering uses of constructed enclosures. The raised planting bed, for example, is one method of providing grade variation without bulldozing ground. The raised bed also permits plant growth where the existing soil or drainage conditions are unsatisfactory, figure 18–6. An associated benefit of raised planting beds is that they can also help control traffic or function as seatwalls (walls with flat, smooth tops suitable for use as seats).

Constructed enclosures in the form of *retaining walls* can transform slopes that are too steep for human use into smaller,

usable areas. They may also be used to protect steep banks from erosion. For example, the bank can be turned into earthen steps which greatly reduce the downward rush of water, figure 18–7.

When constructed enclosures are used in engineering roles, it is important for the landscaper to choose very strong materials. In some cases, tons of soil may be held back by a retaining wall. The landscaper must also carefully specify the materials to be used, such as stone, poured concrete, or brick.

Releasing Pressure Behind Retaining Walls.

Each construction material has its own special requirements for installation. Some require a footing or internal steel bracing; others need wooden forms during pouring.

One concern with which all landscapers must deal when retaining walls are

Figure 18–6. The raised planting bed adds an interesting effect to this flat rooftop garden. It also offers protection by keeping people away from the edge of the roof.

Figure 18–7. What was once a steep slope has been converted into a series of broad, level planting strips connected by steps. The brick retaining walls provide both strength and beauty.

part of the design is the release of pressure caused by water which can build up behind the walls. Construction of retaining walls often alters the normal drainage pattern of the land. Water which once flowed easily down a bank may have no way of getting past a wall which blocks the direction of flow. If not released, the water may eventually channel under the wall and weaken or burst the wall.

Weep holes, figure 18–8, are the means by which water is allowed to escape from behind retaining walls. Built at the bottom of walls, they provide the necessary drain for water as it seeps down through the soil.

Climate Modification

Where climate modification is the objective of the constructed enclosure, either fences or walls may be used. It may also be desirable to combine a constructed element with plants for even better control or a more attractive appearance. A solid wall or fence built across the path of a prevailing

Figure 18–8. Weep holes

Figure 18–9. A constructed enclosure creates a sheltered area for the growth of marginally hardy plants.

breeze may be able to eliminate the breeze as a factor of the landscape near the wall. If a gentler breeze is desired rather than total stillness, an open style wall or fence is used. This slows down the wind's velocity without totally eliminating air movement.

In areas of borderline hardiness, certain species will survive the winter if they are given protected planting sites. A constructed enclosure provides a sheltered area for marginally hardy plants in figure 18–9. Some of the most commonly used enclosure materials are compared in the chart on pages 208–209.

ACHIEVEMENT REVIEW

A. List five functions of constructed enclosures.

B. Select the best answer from the choices offered to complete each statement.

1. Enclosure can be accomplished with constructed materials or with _____ materials.
   a. design   b. man-made   c. plant   d. solid

2. The _____ an enclosure element is, the more effective it is in traffic control.
   a. wider   b. higher   c. more colorful   d. more solid

3. The type of constructed enclosure selected by a landscaper is usually determined by _____.
   a. the preferences of the client
   b. the function it is to perform
   c. the money available for the job
   d. the past experience of the designer

4. Total privacy for two landscapes which are side by side and at the same level requires an enclosure of _____ in height.
   a. 4 feet   b. 5 feet   c. 6 feet   d. 7 feet

5. When the vantage point for a view is highly elevated, the use of _____ helps to block the view.
   a. awnings   b. trees   c. a chain link fence   d. shrubs

6. Weep holes are necessary for _____.
   a. wall footings
   b. structural strength
   c. water pressure release
   d. appearance

A Comparison of Enclosure Styles and Materials

Style	Material	Security at 6-Foot Height	Privacy at 6-Foot Height	Noise Reduction at 6-Foot Height	Wind Deflection at 6-Foot Height	Grading Structure	Useful for Raised Beds	Comments
BASKETWEAVE FENCE	Wood	Yes	Yes	Moderate	Moderate	No	No	Available in prefabricated sections, attractive on both sides
BRICK WALL	Brick	Yes	Yes	Good	Good	Yes	Yes	An ideal material for free-standing retaining or seat walls; width will vary with height and function
CHAINLINK FENCE	Steel	Yes	No	None	None	No	No	Good for use around pet areas or to safeguard children's play areas
CONCRETE BLOCK WALL	Concrete	Yes	Yes	Good	Good	Yes	Yes	Less expensive than poured concrete, stone, or brick
GRAPE STAKE FENCING	Wood	No	Yes	Moderate	Moderate	No	No	A rustic style that weathers to an attractive gray; also comfortable in urban settings.
LATTICE FENCE	Wood	No	Variable	No	Limited	No	No	Effectiveness as a screen depends upon how closely the lattice is spaced.
LOUVERED FENCE	Wood	Yes	Yes	Moderate	Moderate	No	No	Louvers may be vertical or horizontal and are angled to provide privacy.
PICKET FENCE	Wood or Iron	Depends on the height	No	No	No	No	No	High maintenance costs because of frequent painting needed
POST-AND-RAIL FENCE	Wood	No	No	No	No	No	No	Degree of formality varies with finish of lumber; a style valued for aesthetics more than for security or privacy
POURED CONCRETE WALL	Concrete	Yes	Yes	Good	Good	Yes	Yes	Can be smooth or textured, colored or inset with materials to add interest to the surface; requires reinforcing if it is to provide strength.

From *Ornamental Horticulture*, by Jack E. Ingels, copyright © 1985 by Delmar Publishers Inc.

Style	Material	Security at 6-Foot Height	Privacy at 6-Foot Height	Noise Reduction at 6-Foot Height	Wind Deflection at 6-Foot Height	Grading Structure	Useful for Raised Beds	Comments
RAILROAD TIES	Wood	No	No	No	No	Yes	Yes	Ideal for rustic, natural enclosures; widely used for soil retention; care should be taken to assure that the ties have not been preserved with a phytotoxin.
SLAT FENCE	Wood	Yes	Variable	Moderate	Moderate	No	No	Effectiveness as screen or wind deflector depends upon how closely slats are spaced.
SOLID BOARD FENCE	Wood	Yes	Yes	Moderate	Good	No	No	Expensive but the best for security and privacy combined; maintenance easier than with other styles
SPLIT RAIL FENCE	Wood	No	No	No	No	No	No	A rustic style best used in rural settings; lumber is rough and unfinished
STOCKADE FENCE	Wood	Yes	Yes	Moderate	Good	No	No	A variation of solid board fencing
STONE WALL, ASHLAR	Stone	Yes	Yes	Good	Good	Yes	Yes	The stone is cut, usually at the quarry. Stones vary in their smoothness and finish. They are laid in a horizontal and continuous course with even joints.
STONE WALL, RUBBLE	Stone	Yes	Yes	Good	Good	Yes	Yes	The stone is not cut. No course is maintained. Small stones are avoided. Larger stones are used at the base of the wall.
WOOD RETAINING WALL	Wood	No	No	No	No	Yes	Yes	Wood must be preserved to avoid rapid decay; the preservative should not be phytotoxic; reinforcement necessary to assure strength
WROUGHT IRON GRILLS	Iron	Yes	No	No	No	No	No	Expensive and used mostly for aesthetics; grills may be continuous or used as baffles separately.

SUGGESTED ACTIVITIES

1. Collect photos illustrating fencing styles to become familiar with what is available for use in landscapes. As sources, use mail order catalogs, garden center and lumber company advertisements, and house and garden magazines. Mount each style separately with its name and several examples of how it can be used in the landscape.

2. Make a similar collection of illustrations of houses. Find examples of as many different styles and construction materials as possible. Match the houses with the most appropriate fencing styles. Avoid mixing styles. Example: Split rail fences look fine with ranch style homes, but are inappropriate with Spanish styling; picket fences go well with Cape Cod styles but not ranch styles.

3. Invite a lumber dealer to talk with the class about wood. Which woods last longest? How can less expensive woods that rot quickly be made to last longer? What prefabricated fencing styles are most popular in your town?

4. Demonstrate the different elevations of enclosure needed to provide total privacy in an area. Have two class members sit opposite each other (perhaps one can sit on a staircase or ladder). Two other class members can then separate them by holding a large blanket or other solid material between them. Measure the height needed to block the students' view of each other. Gradually elevate one student's vantage point, each time measuring the height of enclosure needed for blockage of the view. Alter the placement of the enclosure. Place it closer to the viewer first, and then closer to the person being viewed.

5. The ability of certain enclosure materials to deflect or weaken the force of the wind, as well as the patterns of protected and unprotected areas that result, can be demonstrated using a small fan and scaled replicas of enclosure materials. Build some solid and semisolid enclosures from balsa wood or cardboard. Create some shrubs with twigs in clay or styrofoam. To determine the degree of protection offered by each enclosure, moisten a flat surface and observe patterns of drying after the fan (wind) is directed at the enclosure being compared. Note that each enclosure will have to be securely fastened to the surface before testing.

SURFACING MATERIALS

After studying this unit, you will be able to

- select a suitable natural or constructed surface material for a specific area.
- list the advantages and disadvantages of both hard and soft paving.
- determine step dimensions for connecting two different levels of land.

TYPES OF SURFACING MATERIALS

The floor of the outdoor room is formed by the application of surfacing materials. The surfacing is applied only after the soil has been prepared by grading and conditioning. Grading provides for proper water drainage away from buildings and for the movement of water across the soil without harmful erosion. Conditioning of the soil promotes water absorption necessary for the growth of natural surfacings such as grass.

The main reason surfacing is applied is to cover the exposed and disturbed soil surface with a protective material. Without this protection, erosion or compaction of the soil may occur. *Compaction* results when soil particles are pressed tightly together by heavy traffic over the area. Lack of cover can also result in puddling of the soil, which at a severe level can turn a landscape into a mud bath.

There are four basic types of surfacing:

- Paving, for heavy traffic areas
- Turf grass, for areas less subject to use
- Ground covers ⎤ for areas with no
- Flowers ⎦ pedestrians

The chart on the following page compares different types of surfacing. Numbers which are in parentheses in the chart are explained below it.

Paving

Whether or not paving is chosen as a surfacing material depends on how the area in question is to be used. Generally, any area with concentrated foot or vehicular

A Comparison of Types of Surfacing

Surfacing Type	Installation Cost	Maintenance Cost	Walking Comfort	Use Intensity	Seasonal or Constant Appearance
hard paving	highest	low	lowest	highest	constant
soft paving	moderate	moderate (1)	moderate	moderate (1)	constant
turf grass	lowest	high (2)	high	moderate (6)	constant (7)
ground cover	moderate	moderate (3)	N/A (5)	low	constant to seasonal (8)
flowers	moderate	high (4)	N/A (5)	lowest	seasonal

(1) Some replacement is required each year.
(2) Fertilization, weed control, watering, and mowing are necessary.
(3) Initial cost is high due to the hand weeding which is required. Once established, costs are moderate.
(4) Much hand weeding, watering, and fertilizing are required.
(5) Should not be used in areas with pedestrians.
(6) Use intensity is greatest where people do not continuously follow the same path.
(7) Many grasses are dormant in certain seasons and may change color.
(8) Appearance of these materials depends upon whether plants are evergreen or deciduous.

traffic should be paved. Examples are driveways, patios, entries, and areas under outdoor furniture. In these locations, grass quickly wears away, with compaction and mud the result.

There are two subcategories of paving, hard and soft. *Hard paving* includes materials such as brick, stone, poured concrete, tile, paving blocks, and wood planking, figures 19–1, 19–2, and 19–3. The advantages of hard paving are:

Greater Durability. Once installed, hard paving provides the longest service at the least cost.

Lower Maintenance Requirements. Usually, only periodic patching is needed to keep the surfacing attractive.

Strength. Where traffic produces great pressure on the surface, hard paving is superior.

Hard paving also has certain disadvantages:

Heat Absorption. After a length of time in the hot sun, hard paving may become hot to the touch. It also releases the heat slowly at night, making patios warmer than desirable on hot summer evenings.

Hazardous When Wet. Not all pavings are slippery, but smooth concrete, tile, and even wood and stone can be hazardous after a rain. For this reason, they should not be used to surface areas near steps or

Figure 19–1. Patterned brick ends create an interesting and durable surface.

Figure 19–2. Brick and concrete are combined for a durable surface with an attractive pattern.

ramps. Likewise, they should not be used for landscapes that are used by ill or handicapped persons.

Glare.   Smooth-surfaced hard paving reflects sunlight and can be blinding on bright, clear days. Use of a smooth concrete patio next to a glass door can fill the

Figure 19–3. Wood and stone set in mortar give heavy-duty service while complementing the seaside atmosphere.

house with unwanted heat and reflected glare.

Expense.   Hard paving is the most costly way to surface the landscape.

Soft paving includes asphalt and a large group of materials known as *loose aggregates*. Some loose aggregates are crushed stone, marble chips, sand, wood chips, bark chips, and tanbark. These pavings are not ''soft'' in the sense that they would not cause pain if an individual fell on them. While some are actually softer than the hard pavings (such as sand or wood chips), the term *soft paving* indicates that the materials are less durable than hard paving and lack a solid form. They are best used in the landscape where pedestrian or vehicular traffic is not intense, figures 19–4 and 19–5. Soft paving does not perform satisfactorily if it is overused.

The advantages of soft paving are:

Lower Cost of Installation.   Neither the cost of materials nor the cost of soil preparation prior to installation is as great as that for hard paving.

Figure 19–4. Tanbark provides the soft yet durable surface around this playground apparatus.

Figure 19–5. Crushed stone has been used to surface this planting bed. Water can reach plant roots, yet weeds are discouraged.

Faster Installation. Where the surfacing is needed quickly and/or temporarily, soft paving can be applied more rapidly.

Ease of Application in Oddly Shaped Areas. Soft paving can conform more easily to small or unusually shaped places.

Ease of Replacement. If something is spilled on the surfacing and stains it, it can be easily and inexpensively replaced.

Major disadvantages of the soft paving materials vary with the actual materials. Some of the common disadvantages are:

Greater Maintenance Requirements.
Asphalt develops holes. Loose aggregates need to be frequently weeded and raked smooth.

Necessity of Replacing Materials.
Loose aggregates are kicked out of place. A small amount is carried away every time someone walks on it; new material must be added annually.

Tendency to Become Sticky (Asphalt) or Dusty (Aggregates).   When the weather is hot and dry, soft paving may be tracked into the house, damaging carpeting or floors.

SELECTING THE CORRECT SURFACING

The final decision by a landscape designer or contractor concerning the correct surfacing to use requires an analysis of several factors:

- **Cost of materials and the budget of the client.** The ideal surfacing may be too expensive, requiring the substitution of a second choice which makes use of less expensive material. Landscapers must be up-to-date on cost trends in building supplies to make accurate cost decisions.
- **Amount of use the surfacing will receive.** If it is in a primary use area (front entry, patio, driveway), hard paving is needed. If the area receives only secondary use, soft paving or grass may suffice.
- **Aesthetic appearance.** The color and texture of the surfacing should harmonize with the other materials in the landscape.
- **Shape of the area being surfaced.** Some paving materials are fluid and can easily be molded into almost any shape (concrete, asphalt, loose aggregates). Others have definite square, rectangular, hexagonal, or other geo-metric shapes (bricks, patio blocks, paving stones). These are difficult to cut and are therefore most effective if used in designs that require minimal cutting.
- **Effect upon the building's interior.** Surfacing next to a home or other building should not create reflected glare or heat within the building, nor should it produce mud, dust, or oil that might be tracked into the building.
- **Maintenance required.** The amount of maintenance needed to keep the surfacing attractive should be carefully weighed against the amount of maintenance clients are willing to do themselves or pay to have done.

A comparison of some commonly used paving materials can be found on pages 216–223.

STEPS AND RAMPS

If the outdoor room has several levels, each level has a separate surfacing. The surfacing may change or remain the same between levels, depending upon the decision of the designer. Regardless, the levels must be connected with steps, ramps, or ramped steps.

The surfacing of the steps or ramps is usually selected to match that used on the levels being connected. However, there may be variations for either aesthetic or practical reasons. For example, it may be desirable to combine materials used in the surfacing and nearby enclosures in the design of the steps. One practical variation might be the necessity of constructing the steps with a more durable material than that used in the surfacing. Another variation might take into account the fact that some

A Comparison of Surfacing Materials

Material Description	Hard Paving	Soft Paving	Modular	Continuous and Solid
Asphalt: A petroleum product with adhesive and water-repellant qualities. It is applied in either heated or cold states and poured or spread into place.	Semihard; allows weeds to germinate and grow through it			X
Asphalt Pavers: Asphalt combined with loose aggregate and molded into square, rectangular, or hexagonal shapes. They are applied over a base of poured concrete, crushed stone, or a binder.	Semihard if not applied over concrete		X	
Brick: A material manufactured of either hard baked clay, cement, or adobe. While assorted sizes are made, the standard size of common brick is 2 1/4 x 3 3/4 x 8 inches.	X		X	
Brick Chips: A byproduct of brick manufacturing. The chips are graded and sold in standardized sizes as aggregate material.		X	X	
Carpeting, Indoor/Outdoor: Waterproof, synthetic fabrics applied over a concrete base. They are declining in popularity. Their major contribution is to provide visual unity between indoor and outdoor living rooms.				X
Clay Tile Pavers: Similar to clay brick in composition, but thinner and of varying dimensions (most commonly 3 x 3-inch, or 6 x 6-inch squares). They are installed over a poured concrete base and mortared into place.	X		X	

From *Ornamental Horticulture*, by Jack E. Ingels, copyright © 1985 by Delmar Publishers Inc.

Slippery When Wet	Permeable to Water	Suitable for Vehicles	Suitable for Walks	Suitable for Patios
		X	X	Certain formulations are suitable. Others may become sticky in hot weather. *Note:* The application of a soil sterilant before applying the asphalt can eliminate the weed problem in walks, drives, and patios.
	If installed over crushed stone		X	X
	If installed in sand	X	X	X
	X		Edging needed to hold them in place	
	Provision must be made for surface water drainage or the carpeting becomes soggy.			X
X			X	X

A Comparison of Surfacing Materials (continued)

Material Description	Hard Paving	Soft Paving	Modular	Continuous and Solid
Concrete: A versatile surfacing that can be made glassy smooth or rough. It can also be patterned by insetting bricks, wood strips, or loose aggregates into it. Concrete is a mixture of sand or gravel, cement, and water. It pours into place, is held there by wood or steel forms, then hardens.	X			X
Crushed Stone: Various types of stone are included in this umbrella term: limestone, sandstone, granite, and marble. Crushed stone is an aggregate material of assorted sizes, shapes, and durability.		X	X	
Flagstone: An expensive form of stone rather than a kind of stone. Flagstone can be any stone with horizontal layering that permits it to be split into flat slabs. It may be used as irregular shapes or cut into rectangular shapes for a more formal look. It is usually set into sand or mortared into place over a concrete slab.	X		X	
Granite Pavers: Granite is one of the most durable stones available to the landscaper. The pavers are quarried cubes of stone, 3 1/2 to 4 1/2 inches square, that are mortared into place. Various colors are available.	X		X	
Limestone: A quarried stone of gray coloration. Limestone can be cut to any size. It adapts to formal settings.	X		X	

Slippery When Wet	Permeable to Water	Suitable for Vehicles	Suitable for Walks	Suitable for Patios
Only when smoothly finished		X	X	X
	X	X	Edging needed to hold the material in place	Limited use except beneath picnic tables where stains might spoil hard paving
Depends upon the rock used and how smooth the surface is			X	X
		X	X	Too rough
		X	X	X

A Comparison of Surfacing Materials (continued)

Material Description	Hard Paving	Soft Paving	Modular	Continuous and Solid
Marble: An expensive quarried stone of varied and attractive colorations. It has a fine texture and a smooth surface that becomes slippery. Its use as surfacing is limited. It can be inset into more serviceable surfaces such as poured concrete.	X		X	
Marble Chips: A form of crushed stone, marble chips are more commonly used as a mulch than a surfacing. They are expensive compared to other loose aggregates; still they enjoy some use as pavings for secondary walks and areas that are seen more than walked upon.		X	X	
Patio Blocks: Precast concrete materials available in rectangular shapes of varied dimensions and colors. Limitless patterns can be created by combination of the sizes and colors. The blocks are set into sand or mortared over concrete.	X		X	
Sandstone: A quarried stone composed of compacted sand and a natural cement such as silica, iron oxide, or calcium. Colors vary from reddish brown to gray and buff white. The stone may be irregular or cut to rectangular forms.	X		X	
Slate: A finely textured stone having horizontal layering that makes it a popular choice for flagstones. Black is the most common color, but others are available.	X		X	

Slippery When Wet	Permeable to Water	Suitable for Vehicles	Suitable for Walks	Suitable for Patios
X				Best used in dry climate where slipperiness will not be a frequent concern
	X		X	
			X	X
		X	X	X
X			X	X

A Comparison of Surfacing Materials (continued)

Material Description	Hard Paving	Soft Paving	Modular	Continuous and Solid
Stone Dust: A by-product of stone quarrying. Stone dust is finely granulated stone, intermediate in size between coarse sand and pea gravel. It is spread, then packed down with a roller. The color is gray.		X		X
Tanbark: A by-product of leather tanning. The material is processed oak bark. It has a dark brown color and a spongy soft consistency. It is ideal for children's play areas.		X	X	
Wood Chips: A by-product of saw mills, wood chips are available from both softwoods and hardwoods. The latter decompose more slowly than the former. Wood chips have a spongy soft consistency. They are often used as mulches.		X	X	
Wood Decking: Usually cut from softwoods, the surfacing can be constructed at ground level or elevated. The deck is valuable as a means of creating level outdoor living spaces on uneven terrain. Space should be left between the boards to allow water to pass through and the wood to dry quickly. Use of a wood preservative will slow decay.	X		X	
Wood Rounds: Cross-sections of wood cut from the trunks of trees resistant to decay, such as redwood, cypress, and cedar. The rounds are installed in sand. Individual rounds are replaced as they decay.	X		X	

Slippery When Wet	Permeable to Water	Suitable for Vehicles	Suitable for Walks	Suitable for Patios
	X		X	
	X		Edging needed to hold the material in place	
	X		X	
	X		X	X
	X		X	X

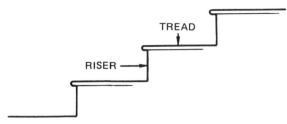

Figure 19–6. The parts of a step

materials suitable for surfacing flat areas are slippery as steps or ramps.

A step is constructed of two parts: an elevating portion, or *riser*, and the part on which the foot is placed, or *tread*, figure 19–6.

Outdoor steps are usually not restricted to the same space limitations as indoor steps, figures 19–7 and 19–8. For this reason, treads can be built wider and risers lower to create a stairway that is more comfortable than indoor steps. The design and construction of outdoor steps should be such that users of the landscape are allowed to maintain the most natural stride pattern possible. This is best accomplished by constructing steps in accordance with a widely accepted formula: the total length of two risers and one tread should equal 26 inches ($T + 2R = 26''$). Furthermore, the tread should be at least wide enough so that an entire foot can be placed upon it (12-inch minimum). Using this formula, if outdoor steps are built with a 12-inch tread, each riser will be 7 inches high ($12'' + (2 \times 7'') = 26''$), figure 19–9. As the tread dimension increases, the riser dimension decreases:

Riser	Tread
7 inches	12 inches
6 inches	14 inches
5 inches	16 inches
4 inches	18 inches

Figure 19–7. Solid risers of wood are combined with treads of loose aggregates for coordination with the surrounding landscape.

Figure 19–8. Because of the log risers and earthen treads, these steps blend in comfortably with the woodland setting.

The number of steps required to connect two levels is calculated by dividing the elevation by the riser dimension desired. For example, if two levels are 48 inches apart and a 6-inch riser is desired, eight steps are required (48″ ÷ 6 = 8 steps), figure 19–10. The amount of horizontal space required for the steps is determined by multiplying the tread dimension by the number of steps. In the example, the eight steps, having seven 14-inch treads, require 98 inches (8.16 feet) of space in the landscape for their construction (14″ × 7 treads = 98″ ÷ 12″ = 8.16′). It should be noted that the number of treads is always one less than the num-

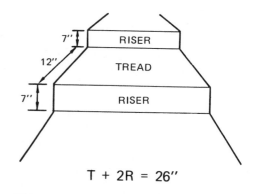

$$T + 2R = 26″$$

Figure 19–9. Calculating the dimensions of outdoor steps

ber of risers, since the top riser connects with the upper level, not another tread.

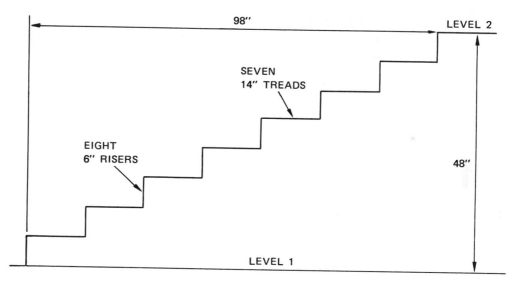

Figure 19–10. Planning space for outdoor steps

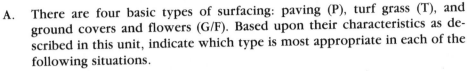

A. There are four basic types of surfacing: paving (P), turf grass (T), and ground covers and flowers (G/F). Based upon their characteristics as described in this unit, indicate which type is most appropriate in each of the following situations.

1. This surface receives moderate foot traffic. There is no reason for fixed patterns to develop across it.
2. This surface receives heavy vehicular traffic.
3. This surface receives no traffic. It functions as a natural element of the outdoor room.
4. This surface must be durable and long lasting. It receives little or no maintenance during the year.
5. This surfacing offers seasonal variation in the landscape.
6. This surface is in a picnic grove where tables are moved to a different spot each week.
7. This surface is in a picnic grove where tables are never moved.
8. This surfacing must tolerate foot traffic while offering a high degree of walking comfort.
9. This surface must be suitable for dancing and shuffleboard.

B. Label the following paving materials as hard or soft.

1. wood rounds
2. crushed stone
3. flagstone
4. wood chips
5. brick
6. poured concrete
7. tanbark
8. asphalt
9. marble chips
10. sand

C. Indicate which paving type, hard or soft, is most suitable in the following situations.

1. The surface is in an eating area and may receive frequent food spills.
2. The surface is next to a heavily used exit from a building.
3. The surface will receive heavy and frequent auto traffic.

4. The surface is located where a dog will play in a service area.
5. The surface must allow rapid drainage of water through it.
6. The surface is to be a patio in a family living area.
7. The surfacing is to be as comfortable to the feet as possible.
8. The surfacing will receive little or no maintenance.
9. The surface must be constructed of the least expensive paving material available.

D. List the six factors which must be considered when selecting surfacing.

E. Using the formula T + 2R = 26″, what size riser is best for a step with a 15-inch tread? Show how you find the answer.

F. How many steps having 5-inch risers are necessary to reach an elevation of 5 feet? Show your work.

G. How much horizontal space would the above steps require? Show your work.

H. How high above level B is level A in the following plan view?

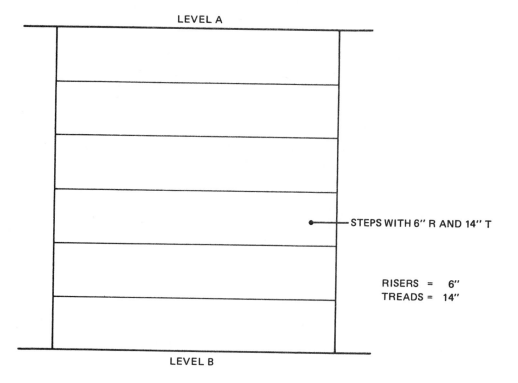

LEVEL A

STEPS WITH 6″ R AND 14″ T

RISERS = 6″
TREADS = 14″

LEVEL B

SUGGESTED ACTIVITIES

1. Select an assortment of surfacings near the classroom (turf grass, asphalt, hard paving, and loose aggregates). Rate them according to foot comfort and appearance. Make comparisons in sun and shade, with and without shoes, and early in the day as opposed to late in the day. Are there any observable differences related to the surfacings' color or texture, softness or firmness, and whether the sun is able to reach them or not?

2. Fill waxed milk containers with oven-dried loose aggregates ranging from coarse to fine textures. Punch several holes in the bottom of each container. Compare the speed with which a measured amount of water drains through each aggregate. Measure the amount of water recovered from each. Which aggregate drains most quickly? Which retains the greatest amount of water?

3. Measure the risers and treads of a set of outdoor steps near the school or in a nearby park. Do the measurements follow the formula $T + 2R = 26''$?

4. Measure the heat retention of selected landscape surfacings. Choose as many types of hard and soft surfacings as possible, plus samplings of turf and ground cover as well. Take surface temperature readings on all surfaces on a hot, sunny afternoon. Rank the surfacings in order of increasing heat retention.

5. Similar comparative studies can be made for slipperiness, staining, or light reflection. Keep testing conditions as standardized as possible while measuring each surface.

6. Take a field trip to a brick works or a stone quarry to see how bricks are made and how stone is cut for paving purposes.

SECTION 5

SELECTING ENRICHMENT ITEMS FOR THE LANDSCAPE

NATURAL ENRICHMENT ITEMS

After studying this unit, you will be able to

- explain what a natural enrichment item is, as opposed to other natural elements in the landscape.
- list examples of natural enrichment items commonly available for use in landscaping.

To understand the concept of enrichment, picture again the indoor room. When the basic structure of an indoor room is completed, it has walls, a ceiling, and a floor, but is still lacking in many ways. To make it a usable and personal room, such things as furniture, lighting, pictures, music, and pets must be added. Although these items do not function as walls, ceilings, or floors, they nevertheless play a valuable role.

The outdoor room has a similar need to be made usable and personal. *Enrichment items* are elements of the outdoor room which are not essential to the formation of its walls, ceiling, or floor. *Natural enrichment items* are those elements which have been formed by nature and are either present at the site or moved to the site by the landscaper.

Natural enrichment items may be either *tangible* (touchable) or *intangible* (not touchable).

TANGIBLE ENRICHMENT ITEMS

Stones

Rocks, boulders, and natural outcroppings are valuable additions to any landscape. Of course, the landscape must be sizeable enough to accept the stones without being overpowered by them. The use of stone as a tangible enrichment item is different from its use in walls or surfacings. As enrichment items, stones are natural outdoor sculptures.

Viewed in a setting where they occur naturally, stone outcroppings can be appreciated for the strong impact they have on

Figure 20–1. This natural stone ledge contributes to the beauty of a lakeside home.

Figure 20–2. Large stones provide an enriching backdrop for the rock garden plants growing among them.

the mood of the landscape, figures 20–1 and 20–2. The outcroppings of bedrock in New York's Central Park are one famous example. Another example is illustrated in figure 20–3, where the large boulders on a college campus create a spot for quiet conversation.

The Japanese were the first to recognize the enriching quality of stones in the landscape. Japanese gardens are often designed to represent nature in miniature. In this type of design, large stones are used to suggest mountains, animals, or other features. The western world has made great use of the rock garden as a way of combining plants and stones in an enriching manner.

Specimen Plants

While the majority of plants function as wall, ceiling, or surfacing elements in the landscape, some play double roles as tangi-

Figure 20–3. Rock formations add natural enrichment to a college campus.

ble enrichment items. Specimen plants may be used as sculpture for their unusual growth habits and for their blossoms or foliage colors, figure 20–4. When pruned into unusual shapes, the plants become highly styled objects of art, figure 20–5. The pruning of plants into unusual shapes is termed *topiary pruning*. This use of a natural enrichment item creates a high maintenance requirement in the garden. Topiary pruning is done sparingly for this reason.

Water

Whether it occurs as still, quiet pools, figure 20–6, or cascading falls, figure 20–7, water possesses natural qualities that are both tangible and intangible. Water can be touched, but it also can be heard. It moves, reflects light, and sparkles. These are important properties, even though they are not tangible.

Should water exist on a site to be developed, the designer should carefully consider its potential. Water is a strong attraction for people. They like to be near it, to listen to it, to watch it ripple or fall. They fish in it, swim in it, and sail on it. It is the most popular of all recreational and aesthetic enrichments.

Figure 20–4. The unusual silhouette of this spruce gives it strong eye appeal. It becomes an enriching focal feature.

Figure 20–5. The topiary pruned shrub as an enrichment item requires high maintenance and is used only in very formal settings.

Figure 20–6. A still pond enriches with its own natural beauty and reflection of the surrounding setting.

Figure 20–7. Cascading water provides an enriching quality through its sparkle, sound, and movement.

Animals

Animals give a sense of life to a landscape that no other enrichment item can duplicate, figure 20–8. The songs of birds and the color of their flitting wings, the scurrying of a chipmunk, and the deep croak of a frog all affirm the presence of nature in the outdoor room. Our parks, campuses, and backyards can easily possess some form of wildlife enrichment if a little care is taken to develop a landscape which also acts as a habitat for them. Many plants produce berries which attract birds and other small animals. A hedgerow can supply suitable nesting sites. The addition of feeding stations assures the presence of wildlife throughout the winter as well.

While city and suburban landscapes may require some planning to encourage the presence of wildlife, rural landscapes usually do not. A landscape designer is free to incorporate views of grazing cattle, sheep, horses, or other domestic animals into the farm landscape. In every case, whether urban or rural in setting, the enrichment provided by animal life is natural and desirable.

INTANGIBLE ENRICHMENT ITEMS

Intangible but invaluable are those enrichments which appeal to the senses other than sight. Many plants are noted for their fragrances or for the tasty fruits they produce. What could be a better reason for using them in the landscape? An aromatic (fragrant) plant beneath a bedroom window or near a patio is a sign of thoughtful landscape development.

Figure 20–8. Water fowl enrich this garden setting.

Also pleasant is the feel of certain enrichment items. White pines, for example, are noted for their soft texture. When wind blows through pine trees, the sound which is produced helps to create a mood that is distinct to the outdoors. Birds and running water, already mentioned as tangible enrichment items, have intangible qualities as well. The landscape designer should attempt to include these intangible natural enrichment features in gardens whenever possible.

ACHIEVEMENT REVIEW

A. Indicate which of the following characteristics apply to enrichment items (E), nonenrichment items (N), or both (B).

1. Their major function is to provide shelter.
2. Their major function is to shape the outdoor room.
3. Their major function is something other than serving as a wall, ceiling, or floor element in the outdoor room.

4. They may be tangible items.
5. They may be tangible or intangible.
6. They could be used as focal points of the design.
7. They could protect people from a rainstorm.
8. They may require periodic maintenance.
9. They are sometimes created by nature.

B. Indicate if the following natural enrichment items are tangible (T) or intangible (I).

1. a boulder
2. a lake
3. the sound of a bird
4. a distorted old pine tree
5. wind whistling through trees
6. a waterfall
7. the sparkle of a waterfall
8. the sound of a waterfall
9. berries on a shrub
10. the taste of berries

C. Give four examples of natural, tangible enrichment items. Do not use any of those listed in question B.

D. Give four examples of natural, intangible enrichment items. Do not use any of those listed in question B.

SUGGESTED ACTIVITIES

1. List all of the natural enrichment items in your home landscape. Indicate if they are tangible, intangible, or have characteristics of both.

2. Do a similar study of a park near the school. Which landscape has more natural enrichment, the park or the home?

MAN-MADE ENRICHMENT ITEMS

After studying this unit, you will be able to

- list three types of man-made enrichment items available for use in landscape development.
- list five ways in which lighting can be used to create an attractive landscape at night.
- determine the contribution made by an enrichment item.

Enrichment items that are created through a manufacturing process are known as *man-made enrichment items.* Subject to the influence of supply and demand, man-made enrichment items are usually available in a wide range of qualities and prices.

TYPES OF MAN-MADE ENRICHMENT ITEMS

Outdoor Furniture

Just as the indoor room needs furniture to be comfortable and usable, so does the outdoor room. At the residential level, outdoor furnishings may include chairs, lounges, and tables. Park benches, trash containers, playground equipment, and other specialized items are considered furniture in a public landscape.

The landscaper should encourage the client to select outdoor furniture appropriate to the quality of the outdoor room in which it will be placed. For the home landscape, outdoor furniture is sold in many places, ranging from grocery stores to department stores. One familiar type of outdoor chair is made of lightweight aluminum tubing with plastic mesh stripping. It is comparatively inexpensive, moderately comfortable, brightly colored, and lasts two or three seasons. Over a period of several

Figure 21-1. Metal chairs and tables make attractive yet durable outdoor furniture. In northern areas, this type of furniture must be stored indoors during winter months.

years, more durable furniture might be a better investment, figure 21-1. It may cost more at first, but this type of furniture usually gives greater comfort and satisfaction for a longer period of time.

In some situations, it is desirable to develop permanent furniture for landscapes. In these cases, it must be durable enough to withstand constant contact with the weather, figure 21-2.

Outdoor Art

Many indoor rooms have pictures on walls and sculpture on coffee tables. These enrichment items help to personalize the room and make it different from all others. The outdoor room also benefits from the enrichment of art. In many large cities, the walls of old buildings are looking fresh and new as local artists turn gritty brick into bright multistory murals. Hotels, corporations, and college campuses are making sculpture an important part of their landscapes. Because of this, the public is gaining a greater appreciation of outdoor art in landscapes, figure 21-3.

One problem concerning the addition of good quality, original outdoor sculpture

Figure 21-2. Permanent seating, a fountain, litter receptacles, and containerized plants complete the enrichment of this public plaza.

Figure 21-3. This large sculpture and reflecting pool enrich the pedestrian mall of the New York State governmental center.

Figure 21-4. This modern sculpture, combined with the falling water, adds original and personal enrichment to the patio.

to the landscape is that it is often very expensive. For this reason, the individual situation should be analyzed carefully before sculpture is selected. When the budget allows, the use of original artwork can be highly rewarding, figure 21-4. Good quality reproductions can also be attractive.

Pools and Fountains

There are many ways that water in man-made forms can be used to enrich landscapes. Swimming pools are enjoying greater popularity each year. From large inground installations to small aboveground forms, the pool has caught the interest of many homeowners. The wise designer considers this use of water where space, weather, and the budget permit.

Also adding to the public's appreciation of man-made water features are the large fountains being used in shopping malls and pedestrian plazas, figure 21-5. While some cities of the world have used richly sculptured fountains in their designs for centuries, many smaller towns are beginning to recognize their value to city living.

The residential landscape can also be designed to incorporate the enriching qualities that water offers. Small recirculating fountains, available at a modest price, can bring new life to a patio area. All such fountains are self-contained, electrically powered units that operate by use of a simple wall switch. Also within the price range of most homeowners are small fish ponds such as the one illustrated in figure 21-6.

Student designers today face an excit-

Figure 21–5. This large splashing fountain, located in a pedestrian plaza, adds a refreshing coolness to the surroundings.

ing challenge: to develop more and better uses of water in home and commercial landscapes. Water and another enrichment item, night lighting, are among the fastest growing areas of development in the landscaping business.

Night Lighting

When night falls, the enjoyment of the landscape can come to an end if no provision has been made for night lighting. With the addition of imaginative lighting, the night landscape can be made both usable and attractive.

Night lighting is used

- to increase the amount of time a garden may be enjoyed each day.
- to provide safety and security for users of the landscape.

Figure 21–6. A backyard fish pond can bring enjoyment to the smallest family living area.

Figure 21–7. Globe lights illuminate while giving the area an aesthetic benefit.

- to create special effects such as colored lighting, silhouette lighting, shadow effects, or patterns against buildings.
- to maintain the same visual relationships between house and garden that exist during the daylight hours.

Until recently, most backyard lighting consisted of floodlights mounted on the roof of the house or garage. The glare of white light was not attractive and often created a prison yard effect. Such floodlights are still excellent security lights, but lighting design has advanced to softer, more attractive forms for the outdoor room, figures 21–7 and 21–8.

There are five common methods of night lighting, figure 21–9.

Walk lights offer both safety and decorative effects. They should be used wherever it is necessary to warn pedestrians that the walk is about to change direction or elevation (such as on steps or ramps).

Figure 21–8. Lighting in the style of an earlier era helps give this small park a restful atmosphere.

Silhouette lighting outlines plants when placed behind them. The viewer sees a dark plant form against a background of light.

SILHOUETTE LIGHTING. . .
THE LAMP IS PLACED
BEHIND THE PLANT.

UP LIGHTING GIVES HIGH-
LIGHT AND SHADOW
PATTERNS TO OBJECTS
ABOVE THE LAMP.

LAMP

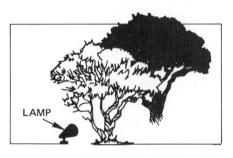

SHADOW LIGHTING. . .THE
LAMP IS IN FRONT AND
THE WALL IS BEHIND THE
PLANT.

LAMP

DOWN LIGHTING DOES
THE SAME FOR OBJECTS
BELOW THE LAMP.

WALK LIGHTS GIVE
SPECIAL EFFECTS, MARK
CHANGES IN DIRECTION,
AND OFFER SAFETY.

Figure 21–9. Five common outdoor lighting techniques

Shadow lighting places the light source in front of the plant and causes a shadow to be cast onto a wall behind the plant.

Down lighting creates patterns of light and leaf shadows on the ground. The light fixture is placed high in a tree and directed downward.

Up lighting is the reverse of the above. The light fixture is placed at the base of the object being illuminated. It is directed upward.

There are two precautions for beginning designers when planning the illumination of landscapes. One is to position the lights so that they do not shine into the eyes of the landscape's users. The other precaution is to be sure that the level of brightness outside the building equals that inside. If the brightness levels are not equal, the separating glass door or window reflects like a mirror. The value of outdoor lighting is then lost to the indoor viewer looking out.

IS THE ENRICHMENT ITEM NECESSARY?

It is possible to design a landscape with too many enrichment items. When this is done, the effect is one of clutter rather than harmonious design. Beginning landscapers may find it difficult to determine the proper number of items to use in a landscape.

A few simple guidelines can be helpful to the new designer. First, be sure the item being considered is truly enriching to the landscape. It must fulfill a role other than the one of walls, ceiling, or surfacing in the outdoor room. Second, most enrichment items attract the viewer's eye strongly and should be used sparingly as focal points in the landscape. Finally, when in doubt concerning the value of an enrichment item, remove it. Then stand back and observe. If nothing appears to be missing in the landscape, it is probably unnecessary. If it leaves a visual hole in the design, the enrichment item probably belongs there.

ACHIEVEMENT REVIEW

A.   Indicate whether the following enrichment items are natural (N) or man-made (MM).

   1.   bird bath
   2.   sun dial
   3.   lake
   4.   statue
   5.   large boulder
   6.   chaise lounge
   7.   picnic table
   8.   chipmunk
   9.   outdoor lights
   10. wind in pine trees

B.   Select the best answer from the choices offered.

1.   Where is the light for silhouette lighting located?
a.   behind the plant   b.   above the plant   c.   in front of the plant

2.   Where is the light for shadow lighting located?
a.   behind the plant   b.   above the plant   c.   in front of the plant

3.   What is a good way to test the value of an enrichment item in a landscape?
a.   Sell it and determine its worth.
b.   Remove it temporarily.
c.   Add another one like it.

4.   Permanent outdoor furniture should be attractive and _____.
a.   lightweight   b.   weather resistant   c.   upholstered

SUGGESTED ACTIVITIES

1.   Demonstrate different lighting techniques in the classroom. Use a small flashlight for the light source. Use a box to represent the building or wall background. Select a small leafed branch from a shrub to represent the plant. Darken the classroom and try up lighting, down lighting, silhouette lighting, and shadow lighting the plant and building.

2.   This activity demonstrates the necessity of designing outdoor lighting so that the level of brightness is close to that of the indoors. Go outside on a bright sunny day and try to see into the school building from the road or sidewalk. The windows, acting as mirrors, will cause the inside of the building to appear dark.

3.   Study the sidewalk system around the school building. Where are walk lights needed for safety?

4.   Invite a sculptor to visit the class to discuss original outdoor art: its costs, common locales, time needed for production, and modern preferences. If possible, arrange a class visit to the artist's studio or to a museum of modern art.

5.   Make a bulletin board display of outdoor furniture, including pictures and information about materials and costs. As sources, use newspapers, department store catalogs, landscape trade journals, and gardening magazines.

The starkness of desert plants makes their use a pleasure and a challenge for the Southwestern landscaper.

Desert plants are used in a traditional grouping. Species are repeated to retain the desired simplicity. A planting such as this functions effectively as a divider of space, a screen for partial privacy, or a traffic director.

Existing trees provide the shaded setting for this attractive home. Foundation plantings are used to complement but not conceal the architecture.

Complementary shades of green contrast richly against the grey of the stone. Effects such as these require time to develop. Their appearance can only be partially predicted by a landscape designer.

oto by Jack E. Ingels

This Family Living Area features a whirlpool. A sense of ceiling is provided, but without blocking the welcomed sunlight.

Design and Photo by Goldberg and Rodler, Landscape Contractors, Huntington, N.Y.

The brick walk, plant materials, and formal planters work together to lead the eye directly to the entrance of this home. Ground cover has been used in place of turf grass to form the floor of the outdoor room.

Photo by Jack E. Ingels

Photo by Jack E. Ingels

This planting of coleus and dusty miller creates a striking outdoor wall between a cafe and pedestrian walkway. Excellent color effects are attained by using plants which have colored foliage in addition to colored flowers.

Photo by Jack E. Ingels

Flowers are best used for bold, dramatic color effects. The selection of colors should be limited and individual colors massed.

This entry is richly designed with textured paving, walk lighting, a bench, and plantings. It reaches forward from the house in welcome.

The building serves as the focal point for this informal vista. Pastel colors in the distance enhance the depth of the setting, making the house appear farther away.

Photo by Jack E. Ingels

Hanging gardens contribute
aesthetically to the
architectural design
of this hotel in
Kona, Hawaii.

Grading of this site permitted the development of a
swimming pool and large patio on a steeply sloping
property.

*Design and Photo by Goldberg and Rodler,
Landscape Contractors, Huntington, N.Y.*

SECTION 6

LAWN
INSTALLATION

SELECTING THE PROPER GRASS

After studying this unit, you will be able to

- list six factors used in the comparison of different turfgrasses.
- list the information required by law on grass seed labels.
- explain the differences between single-species plantings, single-species blends, and mixtures of species.

Turfgrasses are among the oldest plants used for landscaping. They are the most common choice for surfacing the outdoor room. A neatly trimmed lawn of good quality is not only comfortable to walk on, but ideal for many athletic and recreational activities. Because the growing point of the turfgrass is at the crown of the plant, near the soil, it is protected. This permits turfgrasses to be mown and walked upon repeatedly.

COMPARISON OF TURFGRASSES

Most turfgrasses used in landscapes are perennial, surviving from one year to the next. Nearly all species reproduce from seed, although several can be reproduced vegetatively, without pollination and seed production. A typical grass plant produces new leaves throughout the growing season. During the growing season, the turfgrasses will increase beyond the number of seeds sown. One of the objectives of good lawn development is to encourage turf growth as quickly and as evenly as possible.

Growth Habits

Grasses have differing growth habits which result from the three different ways that new shoots are produced, figure 22–1.

- Rhizome-producing (rhizomatous): A *rhizome* is an underground stem. New shoots are sent to the surface some distance out from the parent plant. Each new plant develops its own root

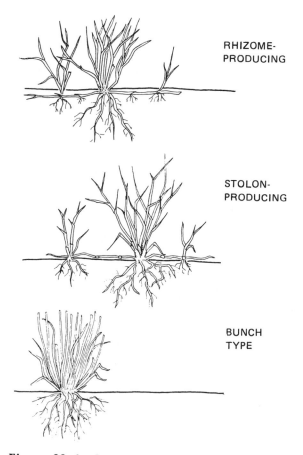

RHIZOME-
PRODUCING

STOLON-
PRODUCING

BUNCH
TYPE

Figure 22–1. Growth habits of grasses. (From Ornamental Horticulture, *by Jack E. Ingels, copyright © 1985 by Delmar Publishers Inc.)*

system and is independent of the parent plant.
- Stolon-producing (stoloniferous): The shoots extending out from the parent plant are above ground. They are called *stolons.* New plants develop independently as described above.
- Bunch-type: New shoots are produced from the sides of the plant, gradually increasing the plant's width.

Rhizome and stolon-producing grasses tend to reproduce more quickly and evenly than bunch-type grasses. Therefore, the bunch-type require more seed and closer spacing in order to cover an area quickly and without clumps.

Texture, Color, and Density

Grass *texture* is mostly a way of describing the width of the grass leaf (blade). The wider the blade is, the coarser will be the texture. Generally, fine-textured grasses are more attractive than coarse-textured grasses. They are also more expensive. The color of a grass and its density will also differ among species. Colors can vary from pastel greens to dark, bluish tones. *Density* refers to the number of leaf shoots that a single plant will produce. It can range from sparse to thick depending upon the type of grass.

Size of Seed

The size of the seed is another reason for variation in the quality and quantity of grass seed mixes. Fine-textured grasses have very small seeds. Coarse-textured grass seeds usually are much larger. Thus, a pound of fine-textured grass seed contains considerably more seeds than a pound of coarse-textured grass seed.

Because of the greater number of seeds per pound, a pound of fine-textured grass seed plants a larger area of land. For example, a pound of fine-textured Kentucky bluegrass contains approximately 2,000,000 seeds. That number of seeds plants about 500 square feet of lawn. A pound of coarse-textured tall fescue contains 227,000 seeds; therefore, only 166 square feet can be planted with a pound of this particular seed.

There are other comparisons that further point out the difference in seed sizes. For example, there are as many seeds in 1 pound of bluegrass as there are in 9 pounds of ryegrass; and as many seeds in a pound of bentgrass as there are in 30 pounds of ryegrass.

Soil and Climatic Tolerance

Most grasses, like almost all other plants, do best in good quality, well-drained soil. Unit 23 describes soil conditioning, pH control, aeration, and fertilization of lawns. However, in every state there are landscape sites that fall short of the ideal conditions preferred for turfgrass success. Some grasses can adapt to a wide range of soil conditions, while others are very limited in their adaptability.

Similarly, some grasses tolerate high humidity and reduced sunlight; others do not. Some thrive in the subtropics and tropics; others are better-suited for temperate and subarctic regions.

Grasses are often grouped into two categories based upon the temperatures at which they grow best:

- Cool-season grasses are favored by daytime temperatures of 60° to 75°F.
- Warm-season grasses are favored by daytime temperatures of 80° to 95°F.

Figure 22–2 shows the peak growth rates of the two types of grasses. Knowl-

edge of the optimum growing temperatures of grasses explains why northern lawns are often brown and dormant in midsummer when the days are very warm. Likewise, warm-season grasses do not really flourish in early spring and late fall when temperatures fall below the optimum temperature.

Common Warm-Season Grasses	Common Cool-Season Grasses
Bermuda grass	Kentucky bluegrass
zoysia grass	red fescue
centipede grass	colonial bentgrass
carpet grass	ryegrass
St. Augustine grass	
Bahia grass	

Figure 22–3 illustrates the climatic regions of the continental United States which are favorable for the growth of the grasses listed and others. Any seed purchased for planting in a certain climatic region should be composed of the appropriate grasses.

Use Tolerance

Under the same conditions of use, some grasses will survive and others will quickly wear away. Some will accept heavy use and recover quickly, while others will recover much more slowly. Some can accept the compaction of heavy foot traffic and still look good; yet others may discolor and slow their rates of growth.

Disease and Insect Resistance

Certain grasses possess a greater resistance than others to insect and disease pests. The resistance may be natural or may have developed through the efforts of plant breeders. Many grasses are continually being improved by horticultural scientists

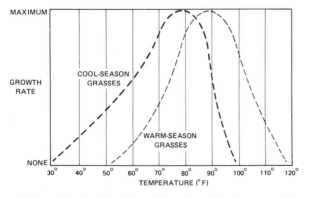

Figure 22–2. Relation of temperature to growth rate in cool-season and warm-season grasses

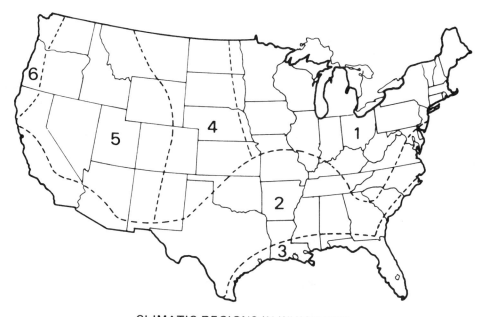

CLIMATIC REGIONS IN WHICH THE
FOLLOWING GRASSES ARE SUITABLE FOR LAWNS:

1. Kentucky bluegrass, red fescue, and colonial bentgrass. Tall fescue, Bermuda, and zoysia grasses in the southern part.
2. Bermuda and zoysia grasses. Centipede, carpet, and St. Augustine grasses in the southern part; tall fescue and Kentucky bluegrass in some northern areas.
3. St. Augustine, Bermuda, zoysia, carpet, and Bahia grasses.
4. Nonirrigated areas: crested wheat, buffalo, and blue grama grasses. Irrigated areas: Kentucky bluegrass and red fescue.
5. Nonirrigated areas: crested wheatgrass. Irrigated areas: Kentucky bluegrass and red fescue.
6. Colonial bentgrass, Kentucky bluegrass, and red fescue.

Figure 22-3. Regions of grass adaptations

searching for features such as better color, resistance to drought, shade tolerance, and pest resistance.

In "A Comparison Chart for Turfgrasses" on pages 250–255, many of the most commonly used turfgrasses are compared.

PURCHASING GRASS SEED

Grass seed is sold in small quantities through retail outlets such as garden centers, supermarkets, hardware stores, and department stores. It is also sold in bulk amounts through wholesale suppliers. Professional landscapers usually purchase seed wholesale. However, most clients have purchased packaged seed from retailers in the past. They may not understand why the seed selected by the landscaper is priced higher than expected. Landscapers must be prepared to explain why all grass seeds are not alike and how the quality of seed is measured.

The key to determining the quality of

A Comparison Chart for Turfgrasses

Grass Species	Cool Season or Warm Season	Growth Habit	Leaf Texture	Mowing Height/Inches	Fertilization Pounds of Nitrogen Per 1000 Square Feet Per Year
Bahiagrass	Warm	Rhizomatous	Coarse	1 1/2 to 2	1 to 4
Bermudagrass	Warm	Stoloniferous and rhizomatous	Fine	1 to 2	4 to 9
Bentgrass, Colonial	Cool	Bunch-type (with short stolons and rhizomes)	Fine	1/2 to 1	2 to 4
Bentgrass, Creeping	Cool	Stoloniferous	Fine	1/2 or less	4 to 8
Bentgrass, Redtop (see Redtop)					
Bentgrass, Velvet	Cool	Stoloniferous	Fine	1/2 or less	2 to 4
Bluegrass, Annual	Cool	Bunch-type or stoloniferous	Fine	1	2 to 6
Bluegrass, Canada	Cool	Rhizomatous	Medium	Does not mow well	1 or less
Bluegrass, Kentucky	Cool	Rhizomatous	Fine	1 to 2 1/2	2 to 6
Bluegrass, Rough	Cool	Stoloniferous	Fine	1 or less	2 to 4
Bromegrass, Smooth	Cool	Rhizomatous	Coarse	Does not mow well	1 or less
Buffalograss	Cool	Stoloniferous	Fine	1/2 to 1 1/2	1/2 to 2
Carpetgrass, Common	Warm	Stoloniferous	Coarse	1 to 2	1 to 2
Carpetgrass, Tropical	Warm	Stoloniferous	Coarse	1 to 2	1 to 2

From *Ornamental Horticulture*, by Jack E. Ingels, copyright © 1985 by Delmar Publishers Inc.

Soil Tolerances	Climate Tolerances	Uses	How Established If Seeded, Pounds Per 1000 Square Feet
Infertile, acidic, and sandy	Subtropical and tropical	Utility turf; good for use along roadways	Seeded at 6 to 8
Does well on a wide range of soils	Warm temperate and subtropical	Sunny lawn areas; good general purpose turf for athletic fields, parks, home lawns	Plugging or seeded at 1 to 1 1/2
Moderately fertile, acidic, and sandy	Temperate and sea-coastal	Areas where intensive cultivation is practical	Seeded at 1/2 to 2
Fertile, acidic, and moist	Subarctic and temperate	Golf greens and other uses where intensive cultivation is practical	Sprigging or seeded at 1/2 to 1 1/2
Moderately fertile, acidic and sandy	Temperate and sea-coastal	Shaded, intensively cultivated areas	Seeded at 1/2 to 1 1/2
Fertile, neutral to slightly acidic	Temperate and cool subtropical	Not planted intentionally; but common in intensively cultivated turfs during spring and fall	Does not apply
Infertile, acidic and droughty	Subarctic and cool temperate	A soil stabilizer	Seeded at 1 to 2
Fertile, neutral to slightly acidic	Subarctic, temperate, and cool subtropical	Sunny lawn areas; good general purpose turf for home lawns, athletic fields, and parks	Seeded at 1 to 2
Fertile and moist	Subarctic and cool, shaded temperate	Some use on shaded, poorly drained sites	Seeded at 1 to 2
Infertile and droughty	Dry and temperate	A soil stabilizer	Seeded at 1 to 2
Does well on a wide range of soils; tolerant of alkaline soils	Dry, temperate and subtropical	Useful in semiarid sites as a general purpose lawn grass	Seeded at 3 to 6
Infertile, acidic, and moist	Subtropical and tropical	Utility turf; good for use along roadways and as a soil stabilizer	Seeded at 1 1/2 to 2 1/2
Infertile, acidic, and moist	Humid subtropical and tropical	Utility turf; good for use along roadways and as a soil stabilizer; can be used as a lawn grass in tropics	Seeded at 1 1/2 to 2 1/2

A Comparison Chart for Turfgrasses (continued)

Grass Species	Cool Season or Warm Season	Growth Habit	Leaf Texture	Mowing Height/Inches	Fertilization Pounds of Nitrogen Per 1000 Square Feet Per Year
Centipedegrass	Warm	Stoloniferous	Medium	1 to 2	1 to 2
Fescue, Chewings	Cool	Bunch-type	Fine	1 1/2 to 2	2
Fescue, Creeping Red	Cool	Rhizomatous	Fine	1 1/2 to 2	2
Fescue, Hard	Cool	Bunch-type	Medium	Does not mow well	1 or less
Fescue, Meadow	Cool	Bunch-type	Coarse	1 1/2 to 3	1 or less
Fescue, Sheep	Cool	Bunch-type	Fine	Does not mow well	1 or less
Fescue, Tall	Cool	Bunch-type	Medium to Coarse	1 1/2 to 3	1 to 3
Gramagrass, Blue	Warm	Rhizomatous	Fine	Does not mow well	1 or less
Redtop (a bentgrass)	Cool	Rhizomatous	Coarse	1 1/2 to 3	1 to 2
Ryegrass, Annual	Cool	Bunch-type	Medium	1 1/2 to 2	2 to 4
Ryegrass, Perennial	Cool	Bunch-type	Fine	1 1/2 to 2	2 to 6
St. Augustinegrass	Warm	Stoloniferous	Coarse	1 to 2 1/2	2 to 6
Timothy, Common	Cool	Bunch-type	Coarse	1 to 2	3 to 6
Wheatgrass, Crested	Cool	Bunch-type	Coarse	1 1/2 to 3	1 to 3

Soil Tolerances	Climate Tolerances	Uses	How Established If Seeded, Pounds Per 1000 Square Feet
Infertile, acidic, and sandy	Subtropical and tropical	Utility turf; also usable as a low-use lawn grass	Seeded at 1/4 to 1/2
Infertile, acidic, and droughty	Subarctic and temperate	Shaded sites with poor soil	Seeded at 4 to 8
Infertile, acidic and droughty	Subarctic and temperate	Shaded sites	Seeded at 3 to 5
Fertile and moist; not tolerant to droughty soil	Moist and temperate	A soil stabilizer	Seeded at 4 to 8
Widely tolerant of all but droughty soils	Moist and temperate	Utility turf; good for use along roadways	Seeded at 4 to 8
Infertile, acidic, well-drained, and droughty	Dry and temperate	A soil stabilizer	Seeded at 3 to 5
Does well on a wide range of soils	Warm temperate and subtropical	Utility turf; good for use along roadways; new cultivars (Brookston, Olympic, and Rebel) good for lawns	Seeded at 4 to 8
Does well on a wide range of soils	Dry and subtropical	Utility turf; good for use along roadways and in arid sites	Seeded at 1 to 2
Does well on a wide range of soils	Subarctic, temperate, and cool subtropical	Utility turf; good for use along roadways and in poorly drained areas	Seeded at 1/2 to 2
Fertile, neutral to slightly acidic and moist	Temperate and subtropical	Useful for quick and temporary lawns in the temperate zone and for winter color in the subtropic zones	Seeded at 4 to 6
Fertile, neutral to slightly acidic and moist	Mild and temperate	Used in mixed species lawns and as an athletic turf	Seeded at 4 to 8
Does well in a wide range of moist soils	Subtropical and tropical seacoastal	A good lawn grass with excellent shade tolerance	Sprigging
Fertile, slightly acidic, and moist	Subarctic and cool temperate	Utility turf; good for athletic fields in cold regions where preferable species won't survive	Seeded at 1 to 2
Does well in a wide range of soils	Subarctic and cool temperate	Useful as a general purpose turf on droughty sites	Seeded at 3 to 5

A Comparison Chart for Turfgrasses (continued)

Grass Species	Cool Season or Warm Season	Growth Habit	Leaf Texture	Mowing Height/Inches	Fertilization Pounds of Nitrogen Per 1000 Square Feet Per Year
Zoysiagrass (Japanese lawngrass)	Warm	Stoloniferous and rhizomatous	Medium	1/2 to 1	2 to 3
Zoysiagrass (Manilagrass)	Warm	Stoloniferous and rhizomatous	Fine	1	2 to 3
Zoysiagrass (Mascarenegrass)	Warm	Stoloniferous and rhizomatous	Fine	Does not mow well	2 to 3

grass seed is the seed analysis label. The *seed analysis label*, which by law must appear on every package of seeds to be sold, gives a breakdown of the contents of the seed package on which it appears. The analysis label may be on the package itself, or, if the seed is being sold in large quantities, on a label tied to the handle of the storage container.

While legal definitions vary somewhat from state to state, most analysis labels contain the following information:

Purity.   The percentage, by weight, of pure grass seed. The label must show the percentage by weight of each seed type in the mixture.

Percent Germination.   The percentage of the pure seed which was capable of germination (sprouting) on the date tested. The date of testing is very important and must be shown. If much time has passed since the germination test, the seed is older and less likely to germinate satisfactorily.

Crop Seed.   The percentage, by weight,

of cash crop seeds in the mixture. These are undesirable species for lawns.

Weeds.   The percentage, by weight, of weed seeds in the mixture. A seed qualifies as a weed seed if it has not been counted as a pure seed or a crop seed.

Noxious Weeds.   Weeds which are extremely undesirable and difficult to eradicate. The number given is usually the number of seeds per pound or per ounce of weed seeds.

Inert Material.   The percentage, by weight, of material in the package which will not grow. In low-priced seed mixes, it includes materials such as sand, chaff, or ground corn cobs. Inert material is sometimes added to make the seed package look bigger. At other times, the inert material is already present in the seed and is not removed because the cost involved would raise the price of the seed.

Three sample analyses follow. Study the contents of each mixture and determine which would probably cost the most and which the least.

Soil Tolerances	Climate Tolerances	Uses	How Established If Seeded, Pounds Per 1000 Square Feet
Does well in a wide range of soils	Temperate, subtropical, and tropical	Useful as a general purpose turf for home lawns, parks, and golf courses, especially in warmer regions	Plugging
Does well in a wide range of soils	Subtropical and tropical	A good lawn grass	Plugging
Does well in a wide range of soils	Warm subtropical and tropical	A soil stabilizer and groundcover	Plugging

Mixture A

Fine-Textured Grasses
    12.76% red fescue   85% germ.
    6.00% Kentucky
        bluegrass   80% germ.
Coarse Grasses
    53.17% annual ryegrass   95% germ.
    25.62% perennial ryegrass   90% germ.
Other Ingredients
    2.06% inert matter
    0.39% weeds—no
        noxious weeds

Mixture B

Fine-Textured Grasses
    38.03% red fescue   80% germ.
    34.82% Kentucky
        bluegrass   80% germ.
Coarse Grasses
    19.09% annual ryegrass   85% germ.
Other Ingredients
    7.72% inert matter
    0.34% weeds—no
        noxious weeds

Mixture C

Fine-Textured Grasses
    44.30% creeping red
        fescue   85% germ.
    36.00% Merion bluegrass   80% germ.
    13.54% Kentucky
        bluegrass   85% germ.
Coarse Grasses
    None claimed
Other Ingredients
    5.87% inert matter
    0.29% weeds—no
        noxious weeds

It is likely that Mixture C would be the most expensive. It contains the highest percentage of fine-textured grasses, no coarse grasses, and the lowest percentage of weeds. Mixture A would probably cost the least, since it contains a high percentage of coarse-textured grasses, the lowest percentage of fine grasses, and the greatest percentage of weeds. None of the mixtures is very poor in quality, since there are no crop or noxious weed seeds claimed by any.

MIXTURES, BLENDS, AND SINGLE SPECIES LAWNS

Grass seed is commonly purchased either as a mixture or a blend. It is also available as a single species (such as all Kentucky bluegrass or all Chewings fescue). A *mixture* combines two or more different species of grass. A *blend* combines two or more cultivated varieties of a single species. Both mixtures and blends have their places depending upon the site and circumstances. Mixtures are most common in temperate zone landscapes; single species plantings are more common in subtropical and tropical landscapes.

Mixtures sometimes have the disadvantage of variegated color and texture. This is a result of the different species they contain. They have the advantage of being able to tolerate mixed environmental conditions and can recover from insect and disease pests that would wipe out a single species.

Single species turf plantings offer a more uniform appearance than mixtures. However, a single species planting is often unable to adjust to severe changes in environmental conditions. It can also be completely destroyed by a single insect or disease invasion.

Blends attempt to retain the advantages of both mixtures and single species plantings. If the cultivated varieties of the blend are carefully selected, a blend offers these advantages: uniform color and texture, resistance to damage from environmental changes, resistance to wear, resistance to pest injury, and the varieties in the blend will have similar maintenance needs.

ACHIEVEMENT REVIEW

A. Not all turfgrasses are alike. They can be compared using different factors. Insert the correct factor into each of the following sentences.

1. Adapting to differences in pH, aeration, fertility levels, humidity, light, and temperatures measures a turf's _____.
2. Rhizomatous, stoloniferous, and bunch-type are different _____ of grasses.
3. Blade width, color variation, and the number of shoots per plant are measures of _____.
4. The ability of turf to withstand the compaction of foot traffic indicates its level of _____.
5. Certain grasses will suffer pest damage more than other grasses because of their _____.
6. One pound of fine-textured grass differs from a pound of coarse-textured grass in many ways. One way is in the number and _____ of the seeds.

B. What could cause a very high quality grass seed purchased in the south to be unsuitable for planting in the north?

C. Of the three seed mixtures A, B, and C shown in this unit, which mixture is most likely to result in a sparse second-year lawn? Why?

D. Why is a grass seed mixture usually preferable to a pure, single-species seed?

E. List and define the important terms found on a grass seed analysis label.

SUGGESTED ACTIVITIES

1. Grow some grasses. Start flats or flower pots of pure grass species in the classroom. Compare fine-leaf and broad-leaf types. If possible, also grow samples of warm-season and cool-season grasses for comparison.

2. Obtain several grass seed mixtures from various sources and in as many price ranges as possible. Rank the mixtures on the basis of package appearance, advertised claims, and brand names. Rank the mixtures again, using the seed analysis labels as the measure. How closely do the package claims match the actual facts about the mixture as shown on the labels? How closely does the price ranking follow the quality ranking?

3. Make a seed count. Weigh ¼-ounce quantities of a fine-textured grass and a coarse-textured grass. Be as accurate as possible. Count the number of seeds in each measure. Do the fine-textured seeds outnumber the coarse-textured seeds? (Note: Do not use redtop for the coarse-textured grass in this exercise. Its seeds are atypically small for a coarse grass.)

UNIT 23

LAWN CONSTRUCTION

OBJECTIVES

After studying this unit, you will be able to

- describe four methods of lawn installation.
- outline the steps required for proper lawn construction.
- explain how to calibrate a spreader.

SELECTING THE METHOD OF LAWN INSTALLATION

There are four methods that may be used to install a turfgrass planting:

- seeding
- sodding
- plugging
- sprigging and stolonizing

The method selected depends upon the species of grass, the type of landscape site, and how quickly the turf must be established. See A Comparison Chart for Turfgrasses in Unit 22.

Seeding

Seeding is the most common and least expensive method of establishing a lawn. The seed can be applied by hand or with a spreader on small sites. On large sites, a cultipacker seeder (pulled by a tractor) or a hydroseeder (a spraying device that applies seed, water, fertilizer, and mulch at the same time) may be used. The hydroseeder is especially helpful for seeding sloped, uneven areas, figure 23–1.

Sodding

When a lawn is needed immediately, *sodding* may be selected as the method of installation. *Sod* is established turf which is moved from one location to another. A sod cutter is used to cut the sod into strips. These are then lifted, rolled up, and placed onto pallets for transport to the site of the new lawn, figure 23–2. At the new site, the sod is unrolled onto the conditioned soil bed. The effect is that of instant lawn, figure 23–3. Sod is produced in special nurseries where it can be grown and harvested efficiently and in large quantities. Sodding is much more costly than seeding. However, the immediacy is important to some

Figure 23–1. Use of the Hydroseeder gives rapid stabilization to this steep embankment. *(Courtesy of United States Department of Agriculture)*

Figure 23–2B. The sod cutter removes the growing turf along with a thin layer of soil.

Figure 23–2A. A sod cutter being used on a sod farm

Figure 23–2C. Pallets of fresh cut sod are carried from the field for transport to landscape sites.

Figure 23–3. The sod is unrolled at the new location and laid in place. The effect is one of instant lawn.

clients, and it is necessary on sites where seed might wash away.

Plugging

Plugging is a common method of installing lawns in the southern sections of the United States. Certain grasses, such as Bermuda, St. Augustine, and zoysia, are not usually reproduced from seed. Instead, they are usually placed into the new lawn as plugs of live, growing grass. Since the growing season in the southern regions is longer than elsewhere, the plugs have time to develop into a full lawn. Plugging is a time-consuming means of installing a lawn, which is its major limitation. However, plugging is necessary for many warm-season grasses that are poor seed producers. On large sites, some mechanization of the planting is possible.

Sprigging and Stolonizing

Like plugging, *sprigging and stolonizing* are more commonly used with warm-season grasses than cool-season grasses. A *sprig* is a piece of grass shoot. It may be a piece of stolon or rhizome or even a lateral shoot. Sprigs do not have soil attached and so are not like plugs or sod. They are planted at intervals into prepared, conditioned soil. Several bushels of sprigs are required to plant 1,000 square feet. If done by hand, the process is slow and tedious. Mechanization can lessen the time required.

Stolonizing is a form of sprigging. The sprigs are *broadcast* (distributed evenly) over the site and covered lightly with soil. Then they are rolled or disked. Since each sprig is not individually inserted into the soil, this method is faster.

PROPER LAWN CONSTRUCTION

If the lawn is to be of the best quality, it must be given every possible chance for success. Proper construction of the lawn is vital. Six steps should be followed by the landscaper to assure a successful beginning for the lawn.

- Plant at the proper time of year.
- Provide the proper drainage and grading.
- Condition the soil properly.
- Apply fresh, good quality seed, sod, plugs, or sprigs.
- Provide adequate moisture to promote rapid establishment of the lawn.
- Mow the new lawn to its correct height.

Time of Planting

Lawns in southern sections of the country require warm-season grasses. Such grasses grow best in day temperatures of 80° to 95°. It is most effective to plant them in the spring, just prior to the summer season. In this way, they have the opportunity to become well established before becoming dormant in the winter.

Cooler northern regions require cool-season grasses to yield the most attractive lawns. Bluegrasses and fescues germinate best when temperatures are in the range of 60° to 75°. These lawns thrive in locations where days are cool and nights are warm. The best planting time for these grasses is early fall or very early spring, prior to the ideal cool season in which they flourish. If cool-season grasses are planted too close to the intensely hot or cold days of summer and winter, they will die or become dormant before becoming well established.

Grading and Draining the New Lawn

Each time the rain falls or a sprinkler is turned on, water moves into the soil and across its surface. *Grading* (leveling land so that it slopes) directs the movement of the surface water. *Drainage* allows the water to move slowly down into the soil to prevent erosion or puddling.

Even lawns that seem flat must slope enough to move water off the surface and away from nearby buildings. If a slight slope does not exist naturally, it may be necessary to construct one. A *fall* (grade) of between 6 inches and 1 foot over a distance of 100 feet is required for flat land to drain properly. Failure to grade lawns away from buildings can result in flooded cellars and basements.

Drainage of water into and through the soil is important. Without a supply of water to their roots, neither grasses nor any other plants can live. Without water drainage past their roots, turf grasses and other plants can be drowned. Depending upon the soil in the particular lawn area involved, good

drainage may require nothing more than mixing sand with the existing soil to allow proper water penetration. In cases where the soil is heavy with clay, a system of drainage tile may be necessary.

If drainage tile is needed, it should be installed after the lawn's grade has been established, but before the surface soil has been conditioned. Regular 4-inch agricultural tile is normally used, placed 18 to 24 inches beneath the surface. Tile lines are spaced approximately 15 feet apart, figure 23–4. Each of the lateral tiles runs into a larger main drainage tile, usually 6 to 8 inches in diameter. This, in turn, empties into a nearby ditch or storm sewer, figure 23–5.

Where the soil is naturally sandy, no special consideration for drainage may be necessary.

Conditioning the Soil

Proper soil preparation requires an understanding of soil texture and soil pH.

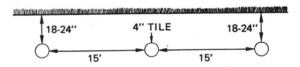

Figure 23–4. Drainage tile installation (Drawing not to scale)

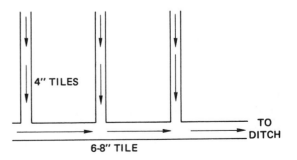

Figure 23–5. The flow of water through tile drainage system (Drawing not to scale)

Soil texture is the result of differing amounts of sand, silt, and clay in the composition of the soil. A soil which has nearly equal amounts of sand, silt, and clay in it is called a *loam* soil. Loam soils are excellent for planting. Soil textures such as *sandy loam, clay loam,* and *silty clay loam* are named for the ingredient or ingredients which make up more than one-third of the composition of the soil. For example, the composition of sandy loam is more than one-third sand. Silt and clay each make up more than one-third of the composition of silty clay loam, and hence, it is less than one-third sand. In conditioning soil for lawn construction, clay, sand, silt, or humus (organic material) may be added to bring the existing soil closer to a medium-loam texture.

Soil pH is a measure of the acidity or alkalinity of soil. A pH measurement of less than 7.0 indicates increasing soil acidity. As the pH increases beyond 7.0, the soil becomes more alkaline or basic. Most turf grasses grow best in soil with a neutral pH (expressed as 7.0) to slightly acidic pH (6.5).

The measurement of soil pH is obtained from a soil test. Soil tests are usually available through county Cooperative Extension Services. Also, pH test kits can be purchased at a reasonable cost, allowing landscapers to make their own determination of pH much more quickly.

If the pH of soil is too acidic, it is usually possible to raise the pH by adding dolomitic limestone. The limestone should be applied in the spring or fall. As the chart in the following column illustrates, the amount applied depends upon the texture of the soil and how far the natural pH is from 6.5 to 7.0.

Where it is necessary to lower the pH

Amount of Dolomitic Limestone Applied Per 1,000 Square Feet of Lawn

Natural Soil	Soil Texture		
	Sandy	Loam	Clay or Silt
pH 4.0	90 lb	172 lb	217 lb
pH 4.5	82 lb	157 lb	202 lb
pH 5.0	67 lb	127 lb	150 lb
pH 5.5	52 lb	97 lb	120 lb
pH 6.0	20 lb	35 lb	60 lb
pH 6.5–7.0	None needed	None needed	None needed

of the soil to attain the desired level of 6.5 to 7.0, landscapers commonly use sulfur, aluminum sulfate, or iron sulfate.

The attainment of a suitable texture and the proper pH are very important in the conditioning of lawn soil. Equally important is the removal of stones from the surface layer of the soil, the loosening of the soil to a depth of 5 or 6 inches, and the incorporation of organic matter into the soil.

Stones may be removed by hand, by rake, or by machine. If the lawn is to be smoothly surfaced, even the smallest surface stones must be discarded.

Decaying organic matter creates *humus,* a valuable ingredient of soil. Humus aids the soil in moisture retention. It also helps air reach the soil. Organic matter can be added to the soil during its conditioning with materials such as peat moss, well-rotted manure, compost, or digested sewage sludge. The landscaper may choose the material which is easily available and relatively low in cost.

All necessary soil additives (pH adjusters, organic matter, sand, and fertilizers) can be worked into the soil at the same time. This is done most effectively with a garden tiller, which also loosens the soil surface and breaks the soil into small particles, figure 23–6. Once the soil has been properly conditioned, it is ready to plant.

Figure 23–6. *A large garden tiller turns the soil while working soil additives into it. For large lawn areas, the tiller is a necessity.*

Planting the Lawn

Seed.   Seed is applied to the prepared soil in a manner that will distribute it evenly. Otherwise, a patchy lawn develops. When applied with a spreader or cultipacker seeder, the seed may be mixed with a carrier material such as sand or topsoil to assure even spreading. The seed or seed/carrier mix is divided into two equal amounts. One part is sown across the lawn in one direction. The other half is then sown across the lawn at a 90° angle to the first half, figure 23–7.

Placing a light mulch of weed-free straw over the seed helps to retain moisture. It also helps to prevent the seed from washing away during watering or rainfall. On a slope that has not been hydroseeded, it is wise to apply erosion netting over the mulched seed to reduce the possibility of the seed washing away, figure 23–8.

Figure 23–7. *Spreader application. Half the material is applied at a 90° angle over the other half.*

Sod.   Sod must be installed as soon after it has been cut as possible. If not, the live grass will be damaged as a result of the excessive temperatures that build up within the rolled or folded strips of sod. Permitting the sod to dry out while awaiting installation can also damage the grass and result in a weak and unsatisfactory lawn.

Figure 23–8. *Erosion netting is used here to prevent the grass seed from washing away until it can become established. Steep slopes such as this one are usually difficult to seed.*

The soil should be moist before beginning installation of the sod. The individual strips are then laid into place much as a jigsaw puzzle is assembled. The sod should not be stretched to fit, as it will only shrink back later, leaving gaps in the lawn surface. Instead, each strip should be fitted carefully and tightly against the other strips. Using a flat tamper or roller, the sod should be tamped gently to assure that all parts are touching the soil.

Plugs.   Plugs are small squares, rectangles, or circles of sod, cut about 2 inches thick. Their installation is similar to that of ground covers. They are set into the conditioned soil at regular intervals (12 to 18 inches) and in staggered rows to maximize coverage. The top of each plug should be level with the surface of the conditioned soil. The soil should be moist but not wet at the time of installation. This prevents some of the plugs from drying out while others are still being installed.

Sprigs.   Sprigs are planted 2 to 3 inches deep in rows 8 to 12 inches apart. In hand installations, rows are not drawn. Instead, the sprigs are distributed as evenly as possible over the prepared soil surface and pushed down into the soil with a stick. As described earlier, stolonizing uses a top-dressing of soil over the sprigs and eliminates the need for individual insertion. The soil should be moist, but not overly wet, when planting begins. If the lawn area is large, planted areas should be mulched and lightly rolled as the installation progresses. Waiting until the entire installation has been completed could result in drying out of the sprigs.

The Importance of Watering

Water is essential to the growth of all plants. As long as grass is dormant in the seed, it needs no water. However, once planted and watered, the seed swells and germinates. At that point, an uninterrupted water supply is very important. The soil surface must not be allowed to dry until the grass is about 2 inches tall. Watering several times a day, every day for a month may be necessary.

Caution should be taken to keep the new seedlings moist without saturating the soil. Too much moisture can encourage disease development. The use of a lawn sprinkler is a much better method than simply turning a garden hose onto the new grass. With a sprinkler, the water can be applied slowly and evenly.

The First Mowing

The first mowing of a new lawn is an important one. The objective is to encourage horizontal branching of the new grass plants as quickly as possible. This creates a thick (dense) lawn. The first mowing should occur when the new grass has reached a height of 2½ to 3 inches. It should be cut back to a height of 1¼ to 1½ inches. Thereafter, different species require differing mowing heights for proper maintenance (See A Comparison Chart for Turfgrasses, in Unit 22). For the first mowing, it is a good practice to collect and remove the grass clippings. After that, clipping removal is usually unnecessary unless the grass has grown so tall between mowings that clumps of grass are visible on the lawn. Grasses used for soil stabilization do not require mowing.

CALIBRATING A SPREADER

Two types of spreaders are used to apply seed, fertilizer, and other granular materials to lawns. These are the *rotary spreader* and the *drop spreader*. The rotary type dispenses the material from a closed hamper onto a rotating plate. It is then propelled outward in a semicircular pattern. The drop spreader dispenses the material through holes in the bottom of the hamper as it is pushed across the lawn, figure 23–7. In both types, the amount of material applied is controlled by the size of the holes through which the material passes, and by the speed of application. Therefore, the spreader must be calibrated to dispense the material at the rate desired. For materials that are applied often and by the same person, the spreader need only be calibrated once, with the proper setting noted on the control for future reference. Different materials usually require different calibrations, even when the rate of application is the same.

The object of calibration is to measure the amount of material applied to an area of 100 square feet. A paved area such as a driveway or parking lot is an excellent calibration site. Afterwards, the seed or other material can be swept up easily for future use. Covering the area with plastic is also helpful in recollecting the material.

The spreader should be filled with exactly 5 pounds of the material being applied. Selection of a spreader setting near the center of the range is a good point at which to begin.

The material is applied by walking at a normal pace in a straight line. The spreader is shut off while it is being turned around. Each strip should slightly overlap the previous one. When an area of 100 square feet has been covered once, the spreader is shut off. The material remaining in the spreader is then emptied out and weighed. By subtracting the new weight from the original weight, the quantity of material applied per 100 square feet is determined. The spreader can then be adjusted to increase or reduce the rate of application.

ACHIEVEMENT REVIEW

Briefly answer each of the following questions.

1. How does the cost of sodding compare to that of seeding?
2. Which method has a more immediate effect, seeding or sodding?
3. Which lawns are commonly started by plugging, sprigging and stolonizing?
4. Which method of lawn installation and establishment requires the most time?
5. At what time of year should warm-season grasses be planted?

6. At what time of year should cool-season grasses be planted?
7. At what time of year should bluegrasses and fescues be planted? Why?
8. Why is it important that soil drain properly?
9. What size of agricultural drainage tile is recommended for lawn use, and how is it spaced?
10. Define soil texture.
11. What type of soil is considered ideal for planting?
12. Explain soil pH.
13. What is a neutral pH level?
14. If soil pH is raised, does the soil become more acidic or more alkaline?
15. If a sandy soil has a pH of 5.0, how many pounds of dolomitic limestone per 1,000 square feet are needed to raise the pH level to that required for a lawn?
16. If the soil mentioned in question 15 covers a lawn area of 3,000 square feet, how much limestone should the landscaper purchase?
17. What are the water requirements of a new lawn?
18. At what height should a lawn mower be set for the first mowing of a new lawn?
19. What is meant by the calibration of a spreader?
20. How is a spreader calibrated?

SUGGESTED ACTIVITIES

1. Invite a Cooperative Extension Service agent to visit the class for a discussion of soil testing. Ask the agent to demonstrate how a soil sample is collected and to explain how landscapers in the state can arrange to have soil tested.

2. Obtain several inexpensive pH testing kits. Bring in soil samples from gardens for testing.

3. Construct a lawn. If materials for proper lawn construction are available at the school, install a new lawn there. If budget restrictions prevent this, volunteer as a class to be a work force for a nearby park, institution, or property owner in return for equipment and materials for the project.

4. Visit a sod farm if one is located in the area.

5. Borrow several spreaders for calibration. (Families of students might be one source.) If there is no budget for seed, substitute sand for demonstration purposes.

SECTION 7

DEVELOPING COST ESTIMATES

UNIT 24

PRICING
THE PROPOSED DESIGN

OBJECTIVES

After studying this unit, students will be able to

- explain the difference between cost and price.
- explain the difference between an estimate and a bid.
- describe landscape specifications.
- prepare a design cost estimate.

One of the questions that every client can be expected to ask is "What is this landscape proposal going to cost me?" The landscape contractor will ask a similar question, "What will it cost my company to build this landscape?" Although both have used the word *cost*, their questions do not seek the same information. The client's question really means, "What will be the total outlay of money necessary to get this landscape done from start to finish? When all is done, how much will I have spent?" The landscape contractor's question really means, "What expenses of constructing this project must I recover to not lose money?" The landscape architect or designer must know the answer to both questions. He or she must design the project to stay within the client's budget for the project. In so doing, the landscape architect or designer must have a realistic understanding of the contractor's costs in order to anticipate the actual cost of building the project.

COST AND PRICE

Although the terms *cost* and *price* are often used interchangeably, they do not always mean the same thing. *Cost* refers to the recovery of expenditures. *Price* refers to an outlay of funds.

The cost of landscape services is the sum of material costs, labor costs, equipment usage costs, and overhead costs.

Cost = Materials + Labor
            + Equipment use + Overhead

These are all expenses assumed by the landscape contractor during the construction of a landscape. If they are not recovered through payment by the client, then the landscaper will lose money.

Price is what the client pays to have the landscape built. It includes the price of the landscape architect or designer's services plus the price of the landscape contractor.

Price = Landscape design services
+ Landscape contracting services

The price of the landscape design services will include the designer or landscape architect's fee for designing the landscape, modifying it as requested by the client, and representing the client whenever necessary. Representation of the client may include obtaining necessary permits, attending zoning meetings, conferring with individuals or groups involved in the project, selecting the landscape contractor, supervising construction of the project, and providing final inspection of the project to certify completion. The landscape architect's services may be calculated as per hour fees or as a percentage of the total value of the project. They will include cost recovery for all the time and any materials expended by the landscape architect. They will also include his or her profit on the project. The profit will be added to the costs to determine the price for landscape design services.

The landscape contractor will use a similar approach to determine the price for landscape contracting services. To the costs of materials, labor, equipment use and overhead will be added two things; contingency and profit. The *contingency* allowance is something like insurance for the landscape contractor. Due to the unpredictable things which can disrupt a construction schedule, it is not possible to calculate precisely the costs of labor and materials. Delays caused by weather, labor problems, miscalculations of material quantities, or builders not finishing on time can wipe out the expected profit. The inclusion of a contingency fee in the price given the client can safeguard the landscape contractor's profit. However, if it is too large it may make the price too high and unacceptable to the client.

Price = Landscape design services + Labor
+ Equipment use + Overhead
+ Contingency + Profit

NOTE: *Overhead costs* include administrative salaries, advertising costs, rent or mortgage payments, office expenses, accountant and attorney fees, subscriptions, memberships, insurance premiums, and equipment maintenance. They are operational costs of the firm. Some are general overhead costs and cannot be assigned just to a specific project. A portion of general overhead costs is charged to each project and included in the price. Other overhead costs can be assigned totally to a particular project. Costs such as portable toilet rental or temporary utility hookups can be fully assigned to the project for which they are needed. These are termed project overhead costs.

ESTIMATES AND BIDS

An *estimate* is an approximation of the price that a customer will be charged for a landscape project. Estimates may be prepared by landscape architects or by landscape contractors. The time of preparation may range from minutes to hours depending upon the size of the project and the level of accuracy needed. To keep a project within the client's budget limits, estimates are done repeatedly during the design stage. Price overruns only result in client disappointment and a waste of the designer's time.

When a price estimate is presented to a client, it is important for the client to understand that the price is not a firm quotation. Rather, it is a close approximation, subject to some change as actual costs are later determined.

A *bid* is a definite offer to provide the services and materials specified in the contract in return for the price agreed upon. Once confirmed by the signature of all parties, the price is binding upon the landscape company to do exactly what it has said it will do. If changes are made by the client or landscaper, the changes must be agreed to by everyone involved. As a result of the changes, the price may be changed, since the changes affect the original bid. Should unforeseen conditions delay the project or otherwise increase costs, the bid price remains fixed. In such cases, the landscaper's profit declines. Therefore, bids must be calculated carefully to assure that all costs are included.

When the landscape project is small, such as a residential property, there may be only one landscape firm working with the client. In such a case, the bidding process is usually informal and negotiable between the landscaper and the client. With larger projects, contracts are certain to require an exact bid, and negotiation may not be possible. On large projects, it is likely that several contractors will be competing for the same job. The firm with the lowest bid has a good chance of being selected, so a bid cannot be greatly overpriced or underpriced. These extremes will lose either jobs or profits for the landscape firm.

SPECIFICATIONS

Large landscape projects usually need more than drawings to explain fully what is required in the design and what quality standard is acceptable. *Specifications* are a listing of the materials, quality standards, and time schedules required to build a particular landscape. They may be prepared by the landscape archihtect or a professional specification writer. Copies of the specifications and the design are provided to each landscape contractor who wants to submit a bid for a project. The specifications must be carefully written to assure that the designer and client get what they are expecting from the landscape contractor. For example, specifications that describe a required species as "eight sugar maples" could result in bids ranging from a few dollars to several thousand dollars. The reason is that there is neither an indication of the size of the plants at the time of installation nor a specific requirement for bare-rooted or balled and burlapped plants. A client expecting a near-mature appearance to the finished landscape would be greatly disappointed by the sparseness of sapling plants. Precisely written specifications prevent client disappointment and discourage deceptive bidding.

Writing specifications can be very tedious work. Every plant in the design must be described by size at planting, root form, soil preparation, and pre- and post-transplant care. Each surfacing installation technique must be explained fully. Mulch depths, lighting fixtures, seed blends, and hundreds of other details must be fully described.

The landscape contractor uses the specifications and the drawings to prepare the bid. Each plant, every brick, every cubic yard of concrete or mulch must be counted. Then the labor and the supervisory time required for their installation are calculated. After that, charges for contingency, overhead and profit are added and the bid is totaled.

PREPARING THE ESTIMATE

Landscape estimates and bids are prepared as spreadsheets. As the data is assembled, it is presented in columns that itemize quantities, descriptions of materials or services, unit costs of materials, unit costs of installation, and total costs for each item. The data is also grouped into categories which organize the estimate for easy reading and referral. A typical design cost esti-

mate includes the following:

- Cost of site clearing and other preparation
- Cost of plant materials
- Cost of construction materials
- Cost of turfgrass
- Allowance for overhead
- Allowance for contingencies
- Fee for landscape designing
- Allowance for profit
- Name of the estimator and date of the estimate

Table 24-1 consists of two partial estimates, including an explanation of each item.

Table 24-1. Estimate for Plant Materials

Quantity (1)	Unit (2)	Description (3)	Material Cost (4)	Installation Cost (5)	Total + 35% (6)	
2	Ea.	*Acer platanoides*, 5', B&B	$35.00	$16.30	$138.51	
1	Ea.	*Betula pendula*, 6', B&B	31.90	23.48	74.76	
4	Ea.	*Cornus florida*, 4', B&B	45.00	13.80	317.52	
15	Ea.	*Euonymus alatus*, 18", BR	8.40	11.60	405.00	
200	Ea.	*Vinca minor*, 2" pots	1.05	.50	418.50	
			Total for plant materials (7)			$ 1,354.29

Estimate for Construction Materials

Quantity (1)	Unit (2)	Description (3)	Material Cost (4)	Installation Cost (5)	Total + 25% (6)	
208	SY	Crushed linestone paving, 4" thick, compacted on a compacted subgrade using a motor grader	$ 7.00	$ 0.32	$1903.20	
90	SF	Timber retaining wall with deadmen, inc. excavation and backfilling	6.00	7.00	1462.50	
1	EA	Fountain, including jet, pump, drain, overflow, water linkage, underwater lighting, electric hookup, and basin	3500.00	700.00	5250.00	
600	SF	Slate pavers, 1¼" thick, irregular fitted in a bed of sand with dry joints.	6.40	4.50	8175.00	
			Total for construction materials (7)			$16,790.70

NOTES: 1. *Quantity* is the number of each separate item used in the design.
2. *Unit* is the form of measurement used to count the item. Examples include square yard (SY), square feet (SF), cubic yard (CY), cubic feet (CF), each (EA),

3. *Description* gives an explanation of what will be done or supplied. For plants it includes the species name, size at installation, and root form (BR for bare root, CT for container, and B&B for balled and burlapped). For construction materials, it includes briefly the materials to be used, means of installation, and other details needed to identify what is to be done.
4. *Material Cost* is the cost of one unit meeting the descriptions given.
5. *Installation Cost* is the charge for labor and any equipment needed to accomplish one unit of the task or service described.
6. *Total + Percent* is the sum of the material and installation cost for one unit multiplied by the quantity of units. To this is added a percentage allowance for overhead and profit. In the examples, 25% is used for O&P of construction and 35% is used for O&P of plant materials. The latter allows for the greater loss of plant items due to their perishability.
7. *Category Subtotals* are underlined and set off to the right for easy totaling later.

Price Estimate for the Design and Development of the Property of Mr. and Mrs. John Doe
1234 Main Street, Cleveland, Ohio

I. PLANT MATERIALS

Quantity	Unit	Description	Material Cost	Installation Cost	Total + 35%
6	Ea.	*Celtis occidentalis*, 1½ " cal. B&B	$ 125.00	$31.00	$1263.60
5	Ea.	*Cornus florida*, 7', B&B	101.00	45.00	985.50
20	Ea.	*Euonymus alatus*, 15", BR	7.00	10.55	473.85
15	Ea.	*Philadelphus coronarius*, 3', BR	5.40	15.63	425.86
50	Ea.	*Vinca minor*, 2" pot	1.05	0.50	104.63
			Total for plant materials		$ 3253.44

II. CONSTRUCTION MATERIALS

Quantity	Unit	Description	Material Cost	Installation Cost	Total + 25%
500	SF	Concrete pavers, 3⅛" thick, interlocking dry joints on 2" sand base, with 4" gravel subbase	$ 2.48	$ 1.53	$2506.25
300	SF	Pressure treated timber wall, 6" × 6" timbers, gravity type, inc. excavation and backfill	6.00	7.00	4875.00
1	EA	Flagpole, aluminum, 25' ht, cone tapered with hardware, halyard and ground sleeve	1060.00	59.02	1398.78
			Total for construction		8780.03

III. TURFGRASS

Quantity	Unit	Description	Material Cost	Installation Cost	Total + 35%
900	SY	Kentucky bluegrass sod, on level prepared ground, rolled and watered	1.00	1.48	3013.20
			Total for turfgrass		3013.20

IV	TOTAL COST OF ALL MATERIALS AND INSTALLATION (See Note 1)	15046.67
V.	CONTINGENCY ALLOWANCE (See Note 2)	1504.67
VI.	FEE FOR LANDSCAPE DESIGN SERVICES (See Note 3)	1805.60
VII.	TOTAL COST FOR COMPLETE LANDSCAPE DEVELOPMENT (See Note 4)	$18356.94

NOTES: 1. The total cost is obtained by adding the subcategory totals.
2. The contingency is taken as a percentage of total costs in IV. In the example, 10% is used.
3. The design fee is taken as a percentage of IV also. In the example, 12% is used.
4. The final figure should be the most distinctive on the spreadsheet. It should be the bottom line figure, with no others below it to create confusion.

The fee for landscape design services is handled in several ways depending upon the size of the project, the credentials of the designer, the policy of the firm, and the laws of the state. In some states, only accredited landscape architects are permitted to charge for their design services. Design-build firms often have salaried designers on the payroll. In such companies, the design costs are usually treated as overhead costs assigned to specific projects. In either case, the fee for designing, drafting, and overseeing the installation of a project to meet full client satisfaction can be estimated at 8 to 15% of the total cost of materials and installation. Usually a large project will use the lower percentage of the range, while a small project will use the higher percentage.

The contingency allowance may be calculated in a similar manner. Using the total cost of materials and installation as a base, a percentage may be added to cover contingencies.

The completed estimate or bid includes a client's name and address, the name of the estimator, and the date of preparation. It may also include an expiration date, after which the figures will no longer be honored because of their unreliability.

A designer will usually present the price estimate at the time the design is shown to the client. A landscape contractor will present the estimate or bid during the negotiation stage of the project. In both cases, the explicit figures shown in the examples are deleted from the proposal given to the client. Only the total figure is presented. The previous page shows a complete price estimate. In this example, no special site preparation was required.

PRACTICE EXERCISE

Prepare a complete price estimate for the property of Mr. and Mrs. Byron Lord, 1238 N. Grand Street, Harwich, Massachusetts. Use the data below and follow the format outlined in this unit. No site preparation is required.

PLANT MATERIALS REQUIRED

   4 Chinese redbud *(Cercis chinensis)*, 5′ ht., B&B, cost $51.00 each and $16.25 to install
20 Golden forsythia *(Forsythia spectabilis)*, 18″ ht., BR, cost $3.00 each and $11.63 to install
   2 Sugar maple *(Acer saccharum)*, 1¼″ cal, B&B, cost $58.00 each and $30.85 to install
12 Carolina rhododendron *(Rhododendron carolinianum)*, 2′ ht., B&B, cost $39.00 each and $12.50 to install
10 Japanese barberry *(Berberis thunbergi)*, 15″ ht., CT, cost $12.50 each and $10.55 to install
20 Vanhoutte spirea *(Spiraea vanhouttei)*, 1 gal. CT, cost $4.35 each and $10.55 to install
300 Japanese pachysandra *(Pachysandra terminalis)*, 2″ pot, cost $0.83 each and $0.50 to install
   1 Babylon Willow *(Salix babylonica)*, 8″ ht., B&B, cost $44.70 and $45.00 to install
12 Floribunda roses *(Rosa floribunda)*, 18″ ht., BR, cost $6.60 each and $11.63 to install
   2 Red oak *(Quercus rubra)*, 6′ ht., BR, cost $21.50 each and $23.48 to install

NOTE: Profit and overhead allowance: 35% of the cost of materials and installation

CONSTRUCTION REQUIRED

90 linear feet (LF) of chain link fencing, 4' high, with galvanized posts and top rail and bonded vinyl 9 gauge fabric @ $4.37 per LF. Installation cost is $1.56 per LF.

1 chain link gate, 4' high, 3' wide, with 2 galvanized gate posts, bonded vinyl 9 gauge fabric @ $218.00 each. Installation cost is $8.49 each.

110 square feet of brick pavers, 2¼" thick, set over a finished subgrade, dry joints, 2" sand base @ $2.31 per SF. Installation cost is $2.71 per SF.

4 walk lights, 10' high, plain steel pole set into a cubic foot of concrete, with distribution system and control switch @ $2,000.00 each. Installation cost is $500.00 each.

NOTE: Profit and overhead allowance: 25% of the cost of materials and installation.

LAWN REQUIRED

1,000 square yards of Kentucky bluegrass sod, rolled and watered @ $1.00 per SY. Installation cost is $0.72 per SY.

NOTE: Profit and overhead allowance: 35% of the cost of materials and installation.

Fee for landscape design services is to be 12% of the total cost of all materials and installation. Contingencies will be included as 10% of the total cost of all materials and installation.

Use your name and the current date as the name of the estimator and the date of the estimate.

ACHIEVEMENT REVIEW

I. Complete the sentences below by inserting the most suitable word.

A. The price of the landscape is of concern to the client. The _____ of building it is of concern to the landscape contractor.

B. All _____ must be determined before a landscape contractor can add on his profit correctly.

C. The _____ of the landscape includes allowances for overhead, contingencies, and profit.

D. The cost of doing business is assigned as a percentage to every client's price estimate. It represents a general _____ cost.

E. The cost of temporary water and electrical hookups at a remote work site while a landscape is being built represent _____ overhead costs.

F. Cost = Materials + _____ + Equipment Use + _____

G. Price = _____ + Materials + Labor + Equipment Use + Overhead + _____ + Profit

II. Define the following terms

A. estimate

B. bid

C. specifications

III. List the components of a typical landscape price estimate.

UNIT 25

PRICING LANDSCAPE MAINTENANCE

OBJECTIVES

After studying this unit, you will be able to

- describe the values of cost analysis to a maintenance firm.
- list the features of a landscape maintenance cost analysis.
- describe unit pricing.
- prepare a maintenance cost estimate.

THE NEED FOR COST ANALYSIS IN LANDSCAPE MAINTENANCE

An accurate analysis of the costs of different tasks done by a landscape maintenance firm has several values:

- It assures that all costs to the firm are recognized.
- It permits a fair price to be charged to the customer.
- It allows a comparison of the profitability of different tasks.

- It can compare the efficiency of different crews performing the same task.

The first two values were discussed in the previous unit. They are equally important in landscape maintenance. The last two values warrant explanation also. A new landscape maintenance firm often believes that all jobs are good jobs. "No job is too big or too small" is the way their advertisements often read. Actually, as a firm grows, not all jobs can be accepted. There may be insufficient time or personnel to respond to every client request. Those tasks that return the greatest profit for the labor invested will need to be emphasized over those that return less profit. A carefully prepared cost analysis can illustrate these different profit potentials.

The performance efficiency of several crews or laborers doing the same task can also be compared with a maintenance cost analysis. Assuming the cost of materials to be the same, the labor time required is the only variable. Carefully kept work records documenting the crew size and hours of labor required to complete a task permit the performance comparison.

FEATURES OF THE MAINTENANCE COST ANALYSIS

A cost analysis of a landscape maintenance job includes

- a listing of all tasks to be performed.
- the total square footage area involved for each service.
- the number of times each service is performed during the year.
- the time required to complete each task once.
- the time required to complete each task annually.
- the cost of all materials required for each task.
- the cost of all labor required for each task.

In order for total job costs to be precisely calculated, each individual cost must be described in a way that can be added easily to all other job costs. *Unit pricing* reduces all area dimensions and material quantities to a common measurement, such as thousand square feet or acre. It is a necessary first step, since materials are often purchased by the truck load, bale, or other bulk measurement. Unit pricing also permits maintenance cost analysis to be adapted for computer use.

CALCULATIONS FOR COST ANALYSIS

To apply the technique properly requires practice. Study the following examples and their explanations.

Example 1

Problem: To calculate the cost of mowing 10,000 square feet of lawn with an 18-inch power mower 30 times each year.

Necessary Information: It takes 5 minutes to mow 1,000 square feet. The laborer receives $5.00 per hour. There are no material costs.

Solution:
Maintenance Operation: Lawn mowing with 18-inch power mower

Square footage area involved	10,000 sq. ft.
Number of times performed annually	30
Minutes per 1,000 square feet	5
Total annual time in minutes (1)	1,500
Material cost per 1,000 square feet	none
Total material cost	none
Wage rate per hour	$5.00
Total labor cost (2)	$125.00
Total cost of maintenance operation per year	$125.00

Note: (1) To obtain the total annual time in minutes:
   a. divide the square footage of area involved by 1,000 [10,000 square feet ÷ 1,000 = 10]
   b. multiply by minutes per 1,000 square feet [10 × 5 = 50 minutes]
   c. multiply by number of times performed annually [50 minutes × 30 = 1,500 minutes]
   d. enter answer under total annual time in minutes.
(2) To obtain the total labor cost:
   a. divide the total annual time in minutes by 60 minutes [1,500 minutes ÷ 60 minutes = 25 hours]
   b. multiply by the wage rate per hour [25 hours × $5.00 = $125.00]
   c. enter answer under total labor cost.

Example 2

Problem: To calculate the cost of mulching 2,000 square feet of planting beds with wood chips, 4 inches deep.

Necessary Information: The task is done once each year. It requires 30 minutes to mulch 1,000 square feet, 4 inches deep. The laborer receives $5.00 per hour. The wood chips cost $165.00 per 1,000 square feet of coverage.

Solution:

Maintenance Operation: Mulching plantings with wood chips, 4 inches deep

Square footage area involved	2,000 sq. ft.
Number of times performed annually	1
Minutes per 1,000 square feet	30
Total annual time in minutes (1)	60
Material cost per 1,000 square feet	$165.00
Total material cost (2)	$330.00
Wage rate per hour	$5.00
Total labor cost (3)	$5.00
Total cost of maintenance operation per year (4)	$335.00

Note: (1) To obtain the total annual time in minutes:
   a.   divide the square footage of area involved by 1,000 [2,000 square feet ÷ 1,000 = 2]
   b.   multiply by minutes per 1,000 square feet [2 × 30 = 60 minutes]
   c.   multiply by number of times performed annually [60 minutes × 1 = 60 minutes]
   d.   enter answer under total annual time in minutes.
   (2) To obtain the total material cost:
   a.   divide the square footage of area involved by 1,000 [2,000 square feet ÷ 1,000 = 2]
   b.   multiply by the material cost per 1,000 square feet [2 × $165.00 = $330.00]
   c.   multiply by the number of times performed annually [$330.00 × 1 = $330.00]
   d.   enter answer under total material cost.
   (3) To obtain the total labor cost:
   a.   divide the total annual time in minutes by 60 minutes [60 minutes ÷ 60 minutes = 1 hour]
   b.   multiply by the wage rate per hour [1 hour × $5.00 = $5.00]
   c.   enter answer under total labor cost.
   (4) To obtain the total cost of maintenance operation per year:
   a.   add total material cost and total labor cost [$330.00 + $5.00 = $335.00]
   b.   enter answer under total cost of maintenance operation per year.

THE COMPLETED COST ESTIMATE

A full cost estimate for maintenance is simply an enlargement of the previous examples. For convenience, all of the maintenance operations that deal with the same area of the landscape are grouped together in the estimate. Study the following example and note the calculation of all figures.

Data
I. A landscape requires the following maintenance tasks and equipment:
   a.   24,500 square feet of lawn cut 30 times each year with a power riding mower
   b.   500 square feet of lawn cut 30 times each year with an 18-inch power hand mower
   c.   all lawn areas fertilized twice each year
   d.   5,000 square feet of shrub plantings fertilized once each year

The Completed Cost Estimate

Maintenance Operation*	Sq. Footage Area Involved*	Number of Times Performed Annually*	Minutes Per 1,000 Sq. Ft.*	Total Annual Time In Minutes**	Material Cost Per 1,000 Sq. Ft.*	Total Material Cost**	Wage Rate Per Hour*	Total Labor Cost**	Total Cost of Maintenance Operation Per Year**
Lawn									
Mowing - rider	24,500 sq. ft.	30	1	735	None		$5.50	$67.38	$ 67.38
Mowing - 18" power	500 sq. ft.	30	5	75	None		$5.50	$ 6.88	$ 6.88
Fertilization	25,000 sq. ft.	2	3	150	$ 5.00	$250.00	$5.50	$13.75	$263.75
Shrubs									
Fertilization	5,000 sq. ft.	1	5	25	$ 6.00	$ 30.00	$5.50	$ 2.31	$ 32.31
Pruning	5,000 sq. ft.	1	60	300	None		$5.50	$27.50	$ 27.50
Flowers									
Soil conditioning	400 sq. ft.	1	200	80	$ 3.00	$ 1.20	$5.50	$ 7.32	$ 8.52
Planting	400 sq. ft.	1	600	240	$125.00	$ 50.00	$5.50	$22.00	$ 72.00
Hand weeding	400 sq. ft.	10	60	240	None		$5.50	$22.00	$ 22.00
Autumn cleanup	400 sq. ft.	1	400	160	None		$5.50	$14.69	$ 14.69
									$515.03

Notes: *All entries in this column came directly from the data given.
**All entries in this column were calculated using methods in the earlier examples. Students should practice the calculations to insure their understanding of the methods.

e. shrubs pruned once each year
f. 400 square feet of flower beds re-
    quiring soil conditioning once
    each spring
g. flowers planted once each year
h. flowers hand weeded 10 times
    each year
i. flower beds cleaned and pre-
    pared for winter once each au-
    tumn

II. Calculated time requirements for the
    maintenance tasks:
    a. a power riding mower cutting
        1,000 square feet of lawn in 1
        minute
    b. an 18-inch power mower cutting
        1,000 square feet of lawn in 5
        minutes
    c. lawn fertilization requiring 3
        minutes per 1,000 square feet for
        spreading
    d. shrub fertilization requiring 5
        minutes per 1,000 square feet
    e. pruning time for shrubs averag-
        ing 60 minutes per 1,000 square
        feet
    f. soil conditioning for flower beds
        requiring approximately 200
        minutes per 1,000 square feet
    g. flower planting requiring 600
        minutes per 1,000 square feet

h. weeding of flowers requiring 60
    minutes per 1,000 square feet
i. cleanup of flower beds in the au-
    tumn requiring 400 minutes per
    1,000 square feet

III. All laborers receive wages of $5.50
     per hour.

IV. Material costs:
    a. lawn fertilizer at $5.00 per 1,000
        square feet
    b. shrub fertilizer at $6.00 per 1,000
        square feet
    c. conditioning materials for flower
        beds at $3.00 per 1,000 square
        feet
    d. flowers for planting averaging
        $125.00 per 1,000 square feet

V. Overhead and Profit. To convert the
   cost analysis to a cost estimate, additional charges for overhead and profit
   must be added. As described in the
   previous unit, these charges may be
   figured as a percentage of the total
   cost of the maintenance operation. In
   this example, overhead costs of 10%
   ($51.50) and profit allowance of 25%
   ($128.76) could be added to the
   $515.03 cost to the firm. The price
   quotation to the client would then be
   $695.29.

PRACTICE EXERCISE

Complete a cost estimate based upon the following data. Add additional overhead costs of 10% and a profit allowance of 25%.
I. A landscape requires the following maintenance tasks and equipment:

    a. 12,000 square feet of lawn cut 25 times a year with a power riding
        mower

    b. 600 square feet of lawn cut 25 times each year with a 25-inch power hand mower

    c. all lawn areas fertilized twice each year

    d. all lawn areas raked once each spring with a 24-inch power rake

    e. 700 square feet of shrub plantings cultivated with hoes twice each year

    f. shrubs pruned once each year

    g. shrubs fertilized once each year

    h. 250 square feet of flower beds requiring soil conditioning once each spring

    i. flowers in 250 square feet planted once each year

    j. flowers in 250 square feet weeded by hand 10 times each year

    k. flower beds in 250 square feet cleaned and prepared for winter once each autumn

II. Time requirements for the maintenance tasks include:

    a. power riding mower cutting 1,000 square feet of lawn in 1 minute

    b. the 25-inch power hand mower cutting 1,000 square feet of lawn in 3 minutes

    c. lawn fertilization requiring 3 minutes per 1,000 square feet for spreading

    d. lawn raking with a 24-inch power rake requiring 10 minutes per 1,000 square feet

    e. hand hoe cultivation of the shrubs requiring 60 minutes per 1,000 square feet

    f. pruning of shrubs averaging 60 minutes per 1,000 square feet

    g. shrub fertilization requiring 5 minutes per 1,000 square feet

    h. soil conditioning for flower beds requiring approximately 200 minutes per 1,000 square feet

    i. flower planting requiring 600 minutes per 1,000 square feet

    j. weeding of flowers requiring 60 minutes per 1,000 square feet

    k. cleanup of flower beds in the fall requiring 400 minutes per 1,000 square feet

III. All laborers receive wages of $5.00 per hour.

IV. Material costs include:

    a. lawn fertilizer at $5.00 per 1,000 square feet

    b. shrub fertilizer at $6.00 per 1,000 square feet

    c. conditioning materials for flower beds at $3.00 per 1,000 square feet

    d. flowers for planting at $125.00 per 1,000 square feet

ACHIEVEMENT REVIEW

A. List four ways in which a cost estimate benefits a landscape maintenance firm.

B. What seven items of data are required before beginning a maintenance cost estimate?

C. Figure the total annual time in minutes for a task which is done 5 times a year, involves 6,000 square feet of area, and requires 7 minutes per 1,000 square feet to accomplish.

D. Figure the total material cost for mulch that is purchased to cover 1,500 square feet of area and costs $125.00 per 1,000 square feet. The mulch is applied once each year.

E. Calculate the total labor cost for a job that requires a total of 420 minutes. The worker assigned to the job is paid $6.00 per hour.

SECTION 8

MAINTAINING
THE
LANDSCAPE

PRUNING TREES AND SHRUBS

OBJECTIVES

After studying this unit, you will be able to

- list the parts of a tree or shrub which are important to consider when pruning.
- explain how to determine when to prune, and why.
- describe which limbs are removed when pruning a tree and how it is done.
- describe which limbs are removed when pruning a shrub and how it is done.

Pruning is the removal of a portion of a plant to attain better shape or more fruitful growth. It is easily done, but not so easily done correctly. Each time that a bud or branch is removed from a plant, it creates both a short-term and long-term effect upon the plant. The *short-term effect* is how the plant looks immediately after pruning, and perhaps through the remainder of the current growing season. The *long-term effect* is how the plant appears

after several seasons of growth without the part that has been pruned.

PARTS OF THE TREE

Before beginning to prune a plant, it is necessary to have a basic understanding of the anatomy of the plant. Figure 26–1 illustrates the parts of a tree.

The *lead branch* of a tree is the most important branch on the plant. It is dominant over the other branches, called the *scaffold branches*. The lead branch usually cannot be removed without losing the distinctive shape of the tree. This is especially true in young trees.

The scaffold branches create the *canopy* of the tree. The amount of shade cast by the canopy of a tree is directly related to the number of scaffold branches and the size of the leaves. When it becomes necessary to remove a branch from a tree, removal usually occurs at a *crotch*, that is, the point at which a branch meets the trunk of the tree or another, larger branch. It is always desirable to leave the strongest

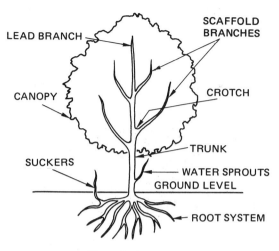

Figure 26–1. The parts of a tree

branches and remove the weakest. Where the crotch union is wide (approaching a right angle), the branch is strong. Where the crotch union is narrow, the branch is weak and may break in a heavy wind, figure 26–2.

Two other types of branches often found on trees are suckers and water sprouts. *Suckers* originate from the underground root system. *Water sprouts* develop along the trunk of the tree. Neither is desirable for a healthy tree and both should be removed.

PARTS OF THE SHRUB

A shrub is a multistemmed plant, figure 26–3. The stems of a shrub (called branches or twigs) differ in age within a single plant. The best flower and fruit production usually occurs on the younger branches. The younger branches are usually distinguished by a lighter color, less bark, and smaller diameter. The older branches have a darker color, are thicker in diameter, and possess a heavier bark.

The point at which the branches and the root system of a shrub meet is the *crown*. New branches originate at the crown, causing the shrub to grow wider. New shoots called *stolons* may spread underground from existing roots to create new shrubs from the parent plant. In cases where the shrub is the result of grafting two plants together to make one, the *graft union* may also be seen at or near the crown. Graft unions are especially common in roses, but may exist on almost any ornamental shrub. Shoots originating below a graft union are from the *stock*, the root portion of the graft. They are cut away, since the quality of their flowers, fruit, and foliage is inferior. Only shoots originating from the *scion*, that portion of

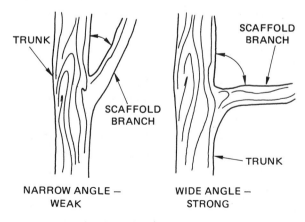

Figure 26–2. Tree crotch structure

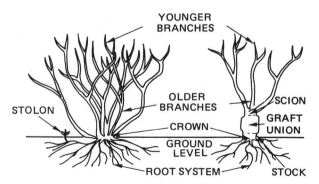

Figure 26–3. The parts of a shrub

the graft occurring aboveground, are allowed to develop.

Even individual twigs have parts that are important to recognize when pruning. As illustrated in figure 26–4, each twig has a *terminal bud* and numerous *lateral buds*. The *bud* represents new growth for the plant. It may contain leaves, flowers, or both. The terminal leaf bud exerts dominance over the other buds. It gives the twig its added length each year. Should the terminal leaf bud be removed, the first lateral bud below it will eventually exert its dominance over the others and become the new terminal shoot.

Not all twigs produce their buds in the same arrangement. As figure 26–5 illustrates, lateral buds may be formed *opposite*

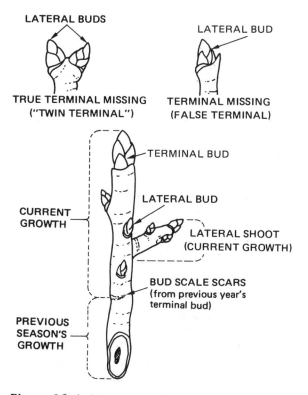

Figure 26–4. The parts of a twig important to pruning

each other, in an *alternate* fashion and, occasionally, in a *whorled* arrangement.

REASONS FOR PRUNING

Unfortunately, many people believe that trees and shrubs should be pruned simply because they have grown since the last pruning. This attitude tends to make the approach to pruning much like a haircut, resulting in a plant that is unnaturally shaped.

By understanding the reasons for pruning, the landscaper is better prepared to determine if a tree or shrub requires pruning. Pruning is done to

- control the size of the plant.
- improve the appearance of the plant by the removal of dead limbs or old wood.
- improve the health of the plant by the removal of diseased, weakened, or injured parts.
- train the plant to grow into a desired shape, such as with topiary pruning (geometric shaping) or espalier pruning (training plants to grow in a vine-like manner).

If a client requests maintenance pruning of plants and none of the above four reasons seem to apply, the landscaper should advise the client that pruning may be unnecessary.

THE PROPER TIME TO PRUNE

Landscapers who perform design and installation as well as maintenance work usually prefer to prune at times of the year when they have little other work. By doing this, their work and income are more evenly distributed throughout the year.

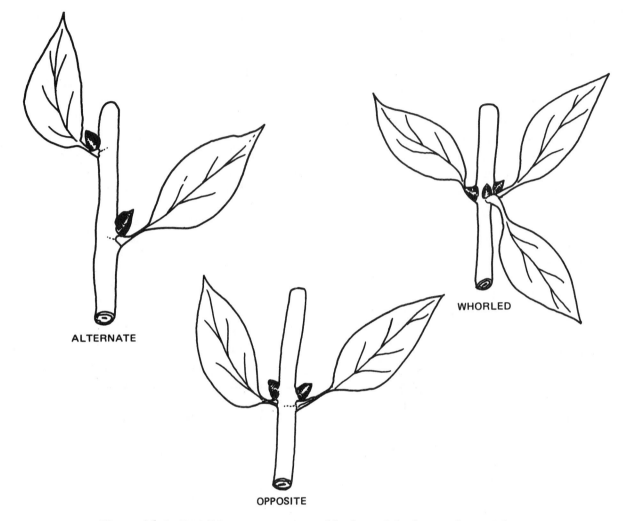

Figure 26–5. Possible arrangements of buds and the leaves they produce

Some plants can accept this off-season attention and remain unaffected by it. Other species accept pruning only during certain periods of the year.

There are advantages and disadvantages to pruning in every season. Since seasons vary greatly from region to region, the following information can be used only as a guide to pruning. Landscapers must determine the influence of local temperatures upon plant growth in their areas.

Winter Pruning

Winter pruning gives the landscaper off-season work. It also allows a view of the plant unblocked by foliage. Broken branches are easily seen, as are older and crossed branches. The major disadvantage of winter pruning is that without foliage, it is difficult to detect dead branches. Because of this, plants can become seriously misshapen if the wrong branches are removed. An additional disadvantage is the damage which can be done to frozen plant parts by cracking. Also, pruning scars have no opportunity to heal during winter, so the plant must carry the open wound throughout the season.

Summer Pruning

Summer pruning also provides off-season work for the landscaper. It allows time for all but very large wounds to heal before the arrival of winter. The major limitation of summer pruning is that problems of plants in full foliage may be concealed. Branches which should be removed are often difficult to see. Especially with trees, it is difficult to shape the branching pattern unless all of the limbs are visible.

Autumn Pruning

Autumn pruning can interfere with the landscaper's second busiest planting season. The income from planting is usually greater and faster than that from maintenance, so pruning in the fall is not welcomed by many landscapers. In terms of the health of the plant, autumn pruning is acceptable as long as it is done early enough to allow healing of the cuts prior to winter.

Autumn pruning should not be attempted on plants that bloom very early in the spring. These early bloomers produce their flower buds the preceding fall. Thus, fall pruning cuts away the flower buds and destroys the spring color show. Autumn pruning should be reserved for those plants that bloom in late spring or summer. They produce their flower buds in the spring of the year in which they bloom. There is no danger of cutting away buds in the fall since there are none present.

Spring Pruning

Spring pruning is usually not welcomed by the landscaper, since spring is the major planting season. However, most plants can be successfully pruned early in the spring as buds begin to swell. This permits a clear view of the live and dead branches. There is not yet any foliage to block the view of the complete plant. If the plant is an early spring bloomer, it is best to prune it immediately after flowering. Spring pruning also provides the plant with time to heal any wounds. Likewise, the unfolding leaves conceal the fresh cuts from the viewer's eye.

There are some exceptions to the guidelines for spring pruning; these are the needled evergreens and any plants which bleed severely when cut in the spring. While needled evergreens or holly can be pruned at any season, people often want to use the cut greens as decoration during the winter holiday season; thus, it is best to prune at this time. When removing branches, care should be taken not to break frozen limbs and twigs.

Also requiring some special attention are plants which have high sap pressure in the early spring. These varieties should not be pruned until the pressure has been reduced naturally by the onset of summer or fall. These are better times to prune such plants as maples, birches, walnuts, or poinsettias, since they will bleed rather than heal quickly after cutting in the spring.

The Parts of the Plant to Prune

The actual limbs and branches that are removed from a tree or shrub are determined by the reason for the pruning. If the objective is to remove diseased portions, the cut should be made through healthy wood between the trunk or crown and the infected part. The cut should never be made through the diseased wood or just behind it. If this is done, the pruning tool

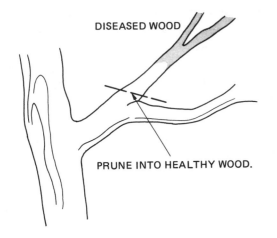

Figure 26-6. The correct way to remove diseased limbs or twigs

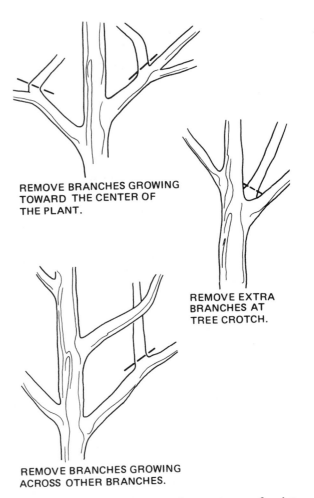

REMOVE BRANCHES GROWING TOWARD THE CENTER OF THE PLANT.

REMOVE EXTRA BRANCHES AT TREE CROTCH.

REMOVE BRANCHES GROWING ACROSS OTHER BRANCHES.

Figure 26-7. Which branches to prune for improved plant appearance

becomes contaminated and may transmit the disease-causing organism to healthy parts that may be pruned later, figure 26-6.

If the pruning is being done for the overall health and appearance of the plant, those branches which are growing into the center of the plant are removed. Limbs and twigs which are growing across other branches can crowd and harm the plant. Such branches should be selected for removal. If more than one limb originates at a tree crotch, the strongest should be left and the others removed. Figure 26-7 illustrates these pruning needs.

If the pruning is being done to reduce the size of the plant without altering its natural shape, careful selection of both the pruned branches and those allowed to remain must be made. Major structural limbs and twigs must be left so that no holes appear in the plant. The fact that many secondary branches stem from one older branch is often overlooked. The result is that removal of the older branch creates a tree or shrub with an entire side missing.

If, as with evergreens, the purpose of the pruning is to create a denser foliage, it is the center shoot which is shortened or removed, figure 26-8. Doing so encourages the lateral buds to grow and create several shoots, where formerly there had been only one. The result is added plant fullness.

HOW TO PRUNE

Pruning Tools

Unit 3 introduced some of the tools used in pruning. A brief review is provided here to aid the student in proper tool selec-

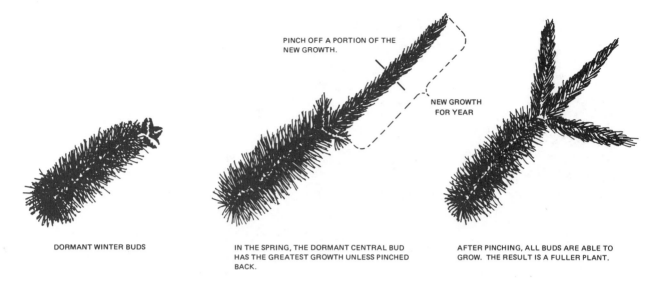

PINCH OFF A PORTION OF THE NEW GROWTH.

NEW GROWTH FOR YEAR

DORMANT WINTER BUDS

IN THE SPRING, THE DORMANT CENTRAL BUD HAS THE GREATEST GROWTH UNLESS PINCHED BACK.

AFTER PINCHING, ALL BUDS ARE ABLE TO GROW. THE RESULT IS A FULLER PLANT.

Figure 26–8. Evergreens are pruned in the spring if a denser foliage is desired.

tion—an essential step in correct pruning methods. Using the proper tool protects the plant against damage which can result from incorrect tool usage.

The *hand pruner*, figure 26–9, is used to cut branches of up to about ½ inch in diameter. It is available in a wide range of prices, with the higher priced tools made of the best steel and having the most durable parts.

Lopping shears, figure 26–10, are used for the removal of branches that would cause a strain on hand pruners. They are effective on wood 1 to 1½ inches in diameter.

The *pruning saw* is needed for tree limbs and shrub wood which exceed 1½ inches in diameter, figure 26–11. It is available with a single blade or a double blade.

Pruning Methods

The method of pruning a tree or shrub depends upon the size and amount of branches being removed.

Figure 26–9. Hand pruners are used to cut woody stems of up to ½ inch in diameter.

Figure 26–10.   Lopping shears are used for removing branches measuring up to 1¹/₂ inches in diameter.

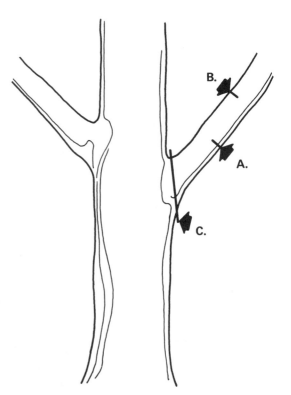

Figure 26–11.   Larger limbs are removed with a pruning saw.

Figure 26–12.   The removal of large limbs using the technique of jump-cutting. The cut at (A) allows the limb to snap off after a cut at (B) without stripping bark from the trunk as it falls. The final cut at (C) removes the stub.

If a limb is being removed from a tree with a pruning saw, the technique is called *jump-cutting*. This method allows the scaffold limb to be removed without stripping off a long slice of bark with it as it falls. The jump-cut requires three cuts for safe removal of a limb, figure 26–12. The final cut should remove the stub of the limb as close to the trunk as possible. The wound is then covered with a wound paint to seal it from insects and disease until the plant has time to heal. Large wounds may require several applications of wound paint until healed.

When shrubs are pruned, one of two techniques is used. *Thinning out* is the re-moval of a shrub branch at or near the crown. It is the major means of removing old wood from a shrub while retaining the desired shape and size. *Heading back* is the shortening, rather than total removal, of a twig. It is a means of reducing the size of the shrub, figure 26–13. In cases where shrubs have become tall and sparse, a combination of thinning out and heading back can rejuvenate old plantings, figure 26–14.

In heading back, the twig is shortened, but not completely removed. The location of the cut is not simply left to chance. Figure 26–15 illustrates three possible placements for twig removal. Twig A has too

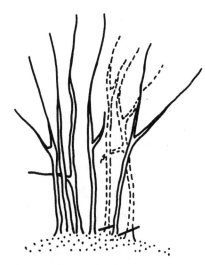

THINNING OUT. As its name implies, this method involves selection of an appropriate number of strong, well-located stems and removal at the ground level of all others. This is the preferred method for keeping shrubs open and in their desired shrub size and form. With most shrubs, it is an annual task; with others, it is required twice a year.

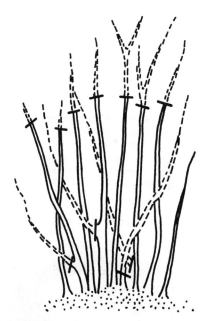

HEADING BACK. This method involves trimming back terminal growth to maintain desired shrub size and form. It encourages more compact foliage development by allowing development of lateral growth. This is the preferred method for controlling the size and shape of shrubs and for maintaining hedges.

Figure 26–13. The techniques of thinning out and heading back

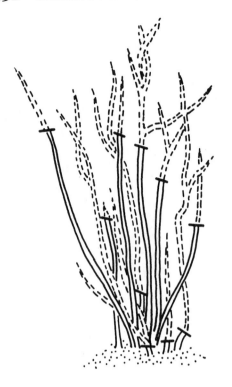

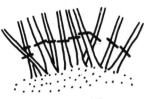

CUT BACK

SELECT SIX OR MORE
WELL-PLACED
VIGOROUS SHOOTS

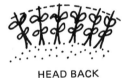

HEAD BACK

GRADUAL RENEWAL. This pruning method involves removal of all mature wood over a 3-to 5-year period. Approximately one-third of the mature wood is removed each season. This is the preferred method for shrubs that have not been recently pruned and are somewhat overgrown.

COMPLETE RENEWAL. This method involves complete removal of all stems at the crown or ground level. Two to three months later the suckers or new growth that emerges is thinned to the desired number of stems. These, in turn, are headed back to encourage lateral branching. Unpruned, seriously overgrown, or severely damaged shrubs are prime prospects for this treatment.

Figure 26–14. Two techniques used to rejuvenate old shrubs

much wood remaining above the bud. It will die from the point of the cut back to the bud, but may not heal over quickly enough to prevent insect and disease entry. The woody stub itself may also decay later. Twig B is cut below the bud, causing the bud to dry out and possibly die. Twig C is pruned correctly. It is cut just above the bud and parallel to the direction in which the bud is pointing. The cut is close enough to the living tissue to heal over quickly.

However, it is not so close to the bud that it promotes drying.

The direction in which the bud grows can be guided by good pruning techniques. Since branches growing into the plant can create congestion, they may be discouraged by the selection of an outward-pointing bud when heading back, figure 26–16. If the twig has buds pointing in opposite directions, the unnecessary one is removed.

Whenever the pruning cut exceeds 1

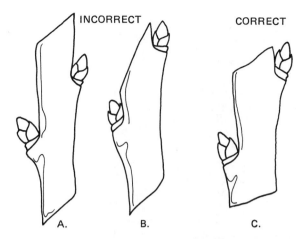

Figure 26–15. Where to prune the twig

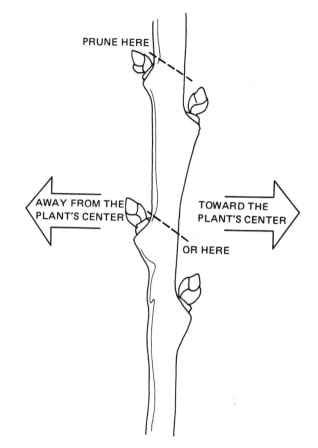

Figure 26–16. Twigs should be pruned to leave an outward pointing bud

inch in diameter, wound paint may be applied to protect the plant from infection during the healing process. Wound paints are available in aerosol cans for small-scale use and in large sizes for professional use. Despite the claims of manufacturers that some offer greater protection than others, there is little evidence to suggest much difference in quality among brands. Some recent research has suggested that wound paints may delay the healing of the plant tissue. Where this is suspected, the landscaper may choose not to use wound paint.

HOW TO PRUNE HEDGES

Creation of a hedge requires close spacing of the shrubs at the time of planting and a special type of pruning. The pruner must shear the plant so that it is as dense as possible. This is usually done with hedge shears, figure 26–17. Hedge shears easily cut through the soft new growth of spring, the time at which most hedges are pruned. For especially large hedges, electric shears are available. However, practice and skill are required for the use of electric shears. Damage occurs quickly if the landscaper does not keep the shears under control.

Proper pruning of a hedge requires that it not only be level on top, but tapered on the sides. It is important that sunlight be able to reach the lower portion of the hedge if it is to stay full. When sunlight cannot reach the lower parts of the hedge, it becomes leggy and top-heavy in appearance. Figure 26–18 illustrates correct and incorrect forms of hedge pruning.

Figure 26–17. Hedge shears

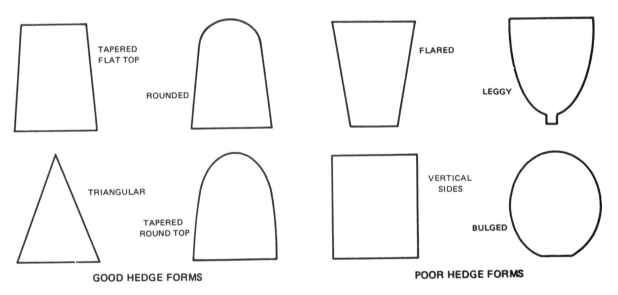

Figure 26–18. Correct and incorrect hedge forms

ACHIEVEMENT REVIEW

A.   Match each term in column 1 with the correct definition from column 2.

Column 1

a.   thinning out
b.   heading back
c.   lateral bud
d.   terminal bud
e.   graft union
f.   tree
g.   shrub
h.   jump-cut
i.   crown

Column 2

1.   the end bud on a branch
2.   a plant having a single, domi-
     nant central trunk
3.   the complete removal of a shrub
     branch at the base of the plant
4.   the point of a shrub at which
     branches and roots meet
5.   a multistemmed plant with no
     central trunk
6.   a technique for removal of large
     tree limbs
7.   the side bud on a branch
8.   the shortening of a shrub
     branch
9.   the junction between a stock
     and a scion

B.   1.   Label the parts of the tree indicated in the following drawing.

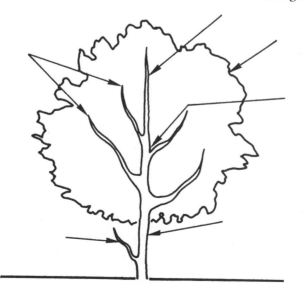

2. The following drawing shows seven numbered branches in the tree. Which three branches should be removed, and why?

3. Indicate the three cuts needed for a correct jump-cut removal of the limb shown in the following drawing. Number the cuts in the order in which they would be made.

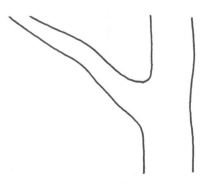

SUGGESTED ACTIVITIES

1. Plan a pruning day. Each student should borrow a pair of hand pruners, lopping shears, or a pruning saw. Try for an assortment of plants needing pruning, such as overgrown, leggy, and sparse. Work in pairs and proceed slowly, discussing major decisions about where to prune.

2. Collect a variety of budded twigs having both opposite and alternate bud arrangements. Practice the correct heading back technique.

3. For a winter activity, select several mature deciduous trees and shrubs for analysis. Study the overall branching patterns. Then discuss which limbs of the trees should be removed; which shrubs need old wood removed; which branches are important to the shape of the plant; and which branches are dispensable.

4. Invite a guest speaker to the class to explain topiary and espalier pruning techniques. Local college instructors, Cooperative Extension specialists, or area garden clubs may be able to furnish names of nearby experts.

CARE OF THE LAWN

After studying this unit, you will be able to

- describe the operations needed to repair a lawn in the spring season.
- explain the meaning of fertilizer analysis statements.
- determine the amount of fertilizer needed to cover a specific area of lawn.
- compare revolving, oscillating, and automatic sprinklers.
- compare reel, rotary, and flail mowers.
- explain the ways lawns can be damaged.

Of all aspects of the landscape which require maintenance during the year, lawns consume the most time. A lawn necessitates both seasonal care and weekly care. Like any other feature of the landscape, it is easier to maintain if it is installed properly. Thus, the landscaper who is hired to install and maintain a lawn may have an easier job than the landscaper hired to maintain a lawn which was poorly installed by someone else.

SPRING LAWN CARE

Cleanup

Spring operations begin the season of maintenance. In areas of the country where winters are long and hard, lawns may be covered with compacted leaves, litter, or semidecomposed thatch. The receding winter may leave behind grass damaged by salt injury, disease, or freezing and thawing.

Small areas can be cleaned of debris with a strong rake. Larger areas of several acres or more require the use of such equipment as power sweepers and thatch removers to accomplish the same type of cleanup.

Rolling of the Lawn

In many central and northern states, the ground freezes and thaws many times during the winter. Such action can cause *heaving* of the turfgrass. Heaving pulls the grass roots away from the soil, leaving them exposed to the drying wind. Heaving also creates a lumpy lawn.

Where heaving occurs, it is advisable to give the lawn a light rolling with a lawn roller in the spring. *Rolling* presses the heaved turf back in contact with the soil. The roller is applied in a single direction across the lawn, followed by a second rolling at an angle perpendicular to the first.

Two precautions should be observed before rolling a lawn. One is that clay soil should never be rolled, since air can be easily driven from a clay soil and the surface quickly compacted. The other precaution is that no soil should be rolled while wet. The roller can be safely used only after the soil has dried and regained its firmness.

The First Cutting

The first cutting of the lawn each spring removes more grass than the cuttings which follow later in the summer. The initial cutting at 1¼ to 1½ inches is done to promote horizontal spreading of the grass. This, in turn, hastens the thickening of the lawn. An additional benefit of the short first cutting is that fertilizer, grass seed, and weed killer which are applied to the lawn reach the soil's surface more easily. Cuttings done later in the year are usually not as short.

Patching the Lawn

If patches of turf have been killed by diseases, insects, dogs, or other causes, it may be necessary to reseed them or add new sod, plugs, or sprigs. Widespread thinness of the grass does not indicate a need for patching. It indicates a lack of fertilization or improper mowing.

Patching is warranted when bare spots are at least 1 foot in diameter. Seed, sod, plugs, or sprigs should be selected to match the grasses of the established lawn. Plugs can be set directly into the soil using a bulb planter or golf green cup cutter to cut the

plug, and then to remove the soil where it is to be planted. With seed, sod, and sprigs, it is best to break the soil surface first with a toothed rake. A mixture of a pound of seed in a bushel of topsoil is handy for patching where seed is to be used, figure 27–1. Mulch and moisture must then be applied as stated earlier.

The timetable for patching is the same as for planting and is related to the type of grass involved.

Aeration

Aeration of a lawn is the addition of air to the soil. The presence of air in the soil is essential to good plant growth. If the lawn is installed properly, the incorporation of sand and organic material into the soil promotes proper aeration. However, where traffic is heavy or the clay content is high, the soil may become compacted. The

Figure 27–1. Patch seeding of thin areas in established lawns is done by breaking the soil surface and applying a small handful of seed.

grounds keeper can relieve the compaction by use of a power aerator, figure 27–2. There are several types of aerators. All cut into the soil to a depth of about 3 inches and remove plugs of soil or slice it into thin strips.

A topdressing of organic material is then applied to the lawn and a rotary power mower run over it. This forces the organic material into the holes or slits left by the aerator. The plugs of soil left on top of the lawn may be removed by raking. If the soil plugs are not too compacted, they can be broken apart and left as topdressing. Equipment is made that can aerate and convert the soil plugs to topdressing in a single operation.

Vertical mowing is a technique that can break up the soil plugs left by an aerator or even remove excessive thatch if nec-

essary. It requires a power rake or a mower whose blades strike the turf vertically. It is done when the lawn is growing most rapidly and conditions for continued growth are favorable. For cool-season grasses, late summer or early autumn is the best time. For warm-season grasses, late spring to early summer is best.

The blades of the vertical mower are adjusted to different heights depending upon the objectives of the operator. A high setting is used to break up soil plugs. A lower setting gives deeper penetration into the thatch layer. This makes it easier to remove and relieves compaction of the soil. Deep vertical mowing is only practiced on deep-rooted turfs. Shallow-rooted turfs often grow mainly in the thatch layer. They can be harmed more than helped by vertical mowing.

LAWN FERTILIZATION

Much like grass seed, lawn fertilizer is sold in an assortment of sizes and formulations and priced accordingly. Stores selling fertilizers range from garden centers to supermarkets. The professional grounds keeper needs to have a basic knowledge of fertilizer products prior to their purchase. Otherwise, it is difficult to choose among the many brands available.

Nutrient Analysis and Ratio

The fertilizer bag identifies its contents. It displays three numbers which indicate its *analysis*, that is, the proportion in which each of three standard ingredients is present. These numbers, such as 10-6-4 or 5-10-10, indicate the percentage of total nitrogen, available phosphoric acid, and water-soluble potash present in the fertilizer, figure 27–3. The numbers are always

Figure 27–2. The aerator is used to remove plugs of soil from compacted lawns, allowing air to enter the soil.

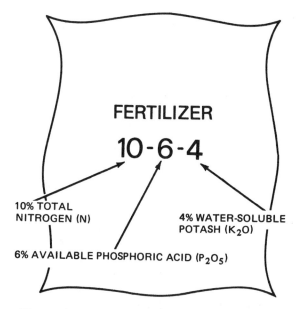

FERTILIZER

10-6-4

10% TOTAL NITROGEN (N)

4% WATER-SOLUBLE POTASH (K$_2$O)

6% AVAILABLE PHOSPHORIC ACID (P$_2$O$_5$)

Figure 27–3. How to interpret fertilizer analysis figures. The nutrients are always shown in the same order.

50 pounds of 5-10-10 fertilizer contain:	50 pounds of 10-20-20 fertilizer contain:
2½ pounds of N (nitrogen)	5 pounds of N
5 pounds of P$_2$O$_5$ (phosphoric acid)	10 pounds of P$_2$O$_5$
5 pounds of K$_2$O (potash)	10 pounds of K$_2$O

given in the same order and always represent the same nutrients.

With simple arithmetic, fertilizers can be compared on the basis of their *nutrient ratios*. For example, a 5-10-10 analysis has a ratio of 1-2-2. (Each of the numbers has been reduced by dividing by a common factor, in this case, 5.) A fertilizer analysis of 10-20-20 also has a ratio of 1-2-2. As the example in the following column illustrates, a 5-10-10 fertilizer supplies the three major nutrients in the same proportion as a 10-20-20 fertilizer, but twice as much of the actual product must be applied to obtain the same amount of nutrients as is contained in the 10-20-20 fertilizer.

The ratio of the fertilizers is the same, but the amount of nutrients available in a bag of each differs. The 5-10-10 mixture should be less expensive than the higher analysis material.

Thus, one measure of the quality of a fertilizer is its analysis. The higher the analysis, the greater is the cost. Whether or not a high analysis fertilizer is needed depends upon the individual plant. Generally, residential lawns do not need a high analysis fertilizer.

Forms of Nitrogen Content

Another factor influencing the quality and cost of fertilizers is the form of nitrogen they contain. Some fertilizers contain nitrogen in an *organic form*. Examples include peat moss, peanut hulls, dried blood, tobacco stems, sewage sludge, and cottonseed meal. The nitrogen content of these materials ranges from 1½ to 12 percent, depending upon the particular material. While sewage sludge is used to some extent on golf course turf, organic fertilizers are not widely used for fertilization of grasses because they are too low in nitrogen. Often, the nitrogen which is present is not in a form which can be used by plants. The best use of organic fertilizers is as soil conditioners which greatly improve the water retention and aeration of the soil.

Chemical forms are the most commonly used fertilizers. They contain a higher percentage of nitrogen. The nitrogen may be quickly available or slowly available; this determines the timing of the nitrogen's release into the soil and uptake by the grass or other plants. It also influences the cost of the fertilizer.

Quickly available fertilizers usually contain water-soluble forms of nitrogen. This means that the nitrogen can be *leached* (washed) through the soil before the plants take it in through their root systems. *Slowly available* fertilizers (also called *slow-release*) make their nitrogen available to the plant more gradually and over a longer period of time. The slow-release effect is possible because the nitrogen used is in a form that is insoluble in water. This gives the plants more time to absorb the nitrogen and prevents fertilizer burn of the plant. Slow-release fertilizers are therefore more expensive than the quickly available forms. Slow-release fertilizers are usually labeled as such. This helps the landscaper to know what is being purchased and what to expect as a response from the plants.

Fillers

A final factor affecting the price and quality of a fertilizer is the amount of filler material it contains. This is directly related to the analysis of the product. In addition to the three major nutrients, fertilizers may contain additional *trace elements* (nutrients which are essential, but needed in smaller amounts) and filler material. *Filler material* is used to dilute and mix the fertilizer. Certain fillers also improve the physical condition of mixtures. However, filler material adds weight and bulk to the fertilizer, thereby requiring more storage space.

The following listing compares high analysis fertilizers (those with a high percentage of major nutrients) and low analysis fertilizers (those with a low percentage of major nutrients) on various points.

High Analysis Fertilizer	Low Analysis Fertilizer
Contains more nutrients and less filler	Contains fewer nutrients and more filler
Cost per pound of actual nutrients is less	Cost per pound of actual nutrients is greater
Weighs less; less labor is required in handling	Is bulky and heavy; more labor is required in handling
Requires less storage space	Requires more storage space
Requires less material to provide a given amount of nutrients per square foot	Requires more material to provide a given amount of nutrients per square foot
Requires less time to apply a given amount of nutrients	Requires more time to apply a given amount of nutrients

In summary, fertilizer cost is determined by three major factors: analysis, form of nitrogen, and amount of bulk filler material. The higher the analysis and the greater the percentage of slow-release nitrogen, the more expensive is the fertilizer.

When to Fertilize Lawns

Lawns should be fertilized before they need the nutrients for their best growth. Cool-season grasses derive little benefit from fertilizer applied at the beginning of the hot summer months; only the weeds benefit from nutrients applied during the late spring. Cool-season grasses should be fertilized in the early spring and early fall. This supplies proper nutrition prior to the seasons of greatest growth. Landscapers should never practice late fall fertilization; it encourages soft, lush growth which is damaged severely during the winter.

Warm-season grasses should receive their heaviest fertilization in late spring.

Their season of greatest growth is the summer.

Amount of Fertilizer

The amount of fertilizer to use is usually stated in terms of the number of pounds of nitrogen to apply per 1,000 square feet. The number of pounds of nitrogen in a fertilizer is determined by multiplying the weight of the fertilizer by the percentage of nitrogen it contains.

Examples

Problem: How many pounds of actual nitrogen are contained in a 100-pound bag of 20-10-5 fertilizer?

Solution: 100 pounds × 20% N = pounds of N

$$100 \times 0.20 = 20 \text{ pounds of N}$$

Problem: How many pounds of 20-10-5 fertilizer should be purchased to apply 4 pounds of actual nitrogen to 1,000 square feet of lawn?

Solution: Divide the percentage of N into the pounds of N desired. The result is the number of pounds of fertilizer required.

4 pounds of N desired ÷ 20% = pounds of fertilizer required
$$4 \div 0.20 = 20 \text{ pounds of 20-10-5 fertilizer required}$$

"A Comparison Chart for Turfgrasses" in Unit 22 lists general fertilizer recommendations for various grasses.

When applying fertilizer to lawns, the recommended poundage should be divided into two or three applications. For example, the 4 pounds of nitrogen per 1,000 square feet for bluegrasses and fescues might be applied at the rate of 2 pounds in

Figure 27–4. Distributing fertilizer by use of a spreader

the early spring and 2 pounds in the early fall. Another possibility is to apply 1 pound in early spring, 1 pound in midsummer, and 2 pounds in early fall. A spreader must be used to assure even distribution of the fertilizer. It is applied in two directions with the rows slightly overlapped, figure 27–4.

WATERING THE LAWN

Turfgrasses are among the first plants to show the effects of lack of water, since they are naturally shallow rooted as compared to trees or shrubs. The grounds keeper should encourage deep root growth by watering so that moisture penetrates to a depth of 8 to 12 inches into the soil. Failure to apply enough water so that it filters deeply into the soil promotes shallow root growth, figure 27–5. Such shallow root systems can be severely injured during hot, dry summer weather.

Infrequent, deep watering is much preferable to daily, shallow watering. The quantity of water applied during an irrigation will depend upon the time of day and the type of soil. Clay soils allow slower water infiltration than coarser textured sandy soils, but clay soils retain water longer. Therefore, less water may need to

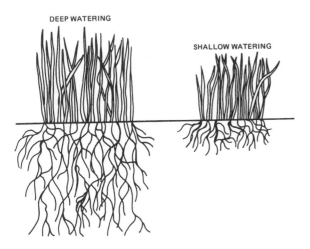

Figure 27–5. Deep watering promotes deep, healthy root growth. Shallow watering promotes shallow rooting and leaves the grass susceptible to injury by drought.

be applied to clay soils or the rate of application may need to be slower or both. The amount of water given off by a portable sprinkler can be calibrated once and a notation made for future reference. To calibrate a portable sprinkler, set several wide-topped, flat-bottomed cans with straight sides (such as coffee cans) in a straight line out from the sprinkler. When most of them contain 1 to 1½ inches of water, shut off the sprinkler. The amount of time required should be noted for future use. Figures 27–6 and 27–7 illustrate two types of portable sprinklers. In addition, permanently installed irrigation systems are available (at considerable cost) for large turf plantings, figure 27–8.

The best time of day to water lawns is between early morning and late afternoon. Watering in the early evening or later should be avoided because of the danger of disease; turf diseases thrive in lawns that remain wet into the evening. Watering prior to evening gives the lawn time to dry before the sun sets.

If watering is done at the proper time and to the proper depth, it is necessary only once or twice each week.

MOWING THE LAWN

There are three types of mowers available for the maintenance of lawns: the reel mower, the rotary mower, and the flail mower. The *flail mower* is used for turfgrasses that are only cut a few times each year. Reel and rotary mowers are used to maintain home, recreational, and commer-

Figure 27–6. One type of lawn sprinkler. An arch of water is cast from side to side. This sprinkler requires periodic relocation.

cial lawns. On a *reel mower*, the blades rotate in the same direction as the wheels and cut the grass by pushing it against a nonrotating bedknife at the rear base of the mower, figures 27–9 and 27–10. The blades of a *rotary mower* move like a ceiling fan, parallel to the surface of the lawn, cutting the grass off as they revolve, figure 27–11. Reel mowers are most often used for grasses that do best with a shorter cut, such as bentgrass. Rotary mowers do not cut as evenly or sharply as reel mowers. However, they are satisfactory for lawn grasses that accept a higher cut, such as ryegrass, bluegrass, and fescue. The riding mower, so popular with homeowners, is a rotary mower. Many campuses, parks, and golf course fairways are mown with a large bank of reel mowers, called a gang mower. It is pulled behind a tractor that has been fitted with tires that will not rut the lawn.

In every situation, the blades must be sharp to give a satisfactory cut. Dull or chipped mower blades can result in torn, ragged grass blades that will die and give the lawn an unhealthy color of gray or

Figure 27–7. This revolving sprinkler covers a limited area and must be manually moved to each new location. Wind gusts can affect the evenness of the coverage. (From Ornamental Horticulture, *by Jack E. Ingels, copyright © 1985 by Delmar Publishers Inc.)*

Figure 27–8. An automatic lawn irrigation system in operation (Courtesy of Weather-Matic Irrigation)

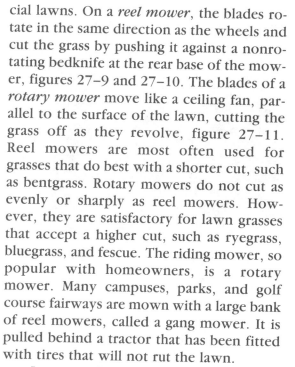

Figure 27–9. A powered reel mower (From Ornamental Horticulture, *by Jack E. Ingels, copyright © 1985 by Delmar Publishers Inc.)*

Figure 27–10. Reel mowers provide the best quality cut. (From Ornamental Horticulture, *by Jack E. Ingels, copyright © 1985 by Delmar Publishers Inc.)*

brown. The sharp blades of any lawn mower should be respected. When powered, they can cut through nearly any shoe. Workers should never mow unless wearing steel-toed work shoes. Hands should never be brought near the blades while the mower is running. No inconvenience caused by shutting off a mower can equal the instant

Figure 27–11. A rotary mower (From Ornamental Horticulture, *by Jack E. Ingels, copyright © 1985 by Delmar Publishers Inc.)*

injury that a power mower can do to a worker's hand or foot.

"A Comparison Chart for Turfgrasses" in Unit 22 illustrates the wide range of tolerable mowing heights that exists between and within species. Within the range, the mowing height selected often depends upon how much care the lawn can be given and what surface quality is expected. Shorter heights require more frequent mowing and watering, and often, greater pest control efforts. In turn, shorter heights give greater density and finer texture to a lawn. A taller lawn surface will have a slightly coarser texture and take longer to thicken. However, it will not require cutting as often. Longer cutting heights will also withstand hot and dry periods better, since the extra blade length will cast cooling shadows over the soil's surface. Often, fewer weeds are an added benefit of a taller lawn surface. Since not all species are mowed to the same height, mixed species lawns should be made up of grasses that have similar cutting requirements.

The frequency of mowing is variable. Because the rate of growth of a lawn can vary with the temperature and with the moisture provided, the frequency of the mowing cannot always be precisely specified. Ideally, a lawn should be mown when it is needed, not because a contract specifies cutting on a certain day.

A long-standing rule of thumb is that mowing should remove about one-third of the length of the grass blade. Thus, if the turf is being kept at 1½ inches, it should be mowed when it reaches a height of 2¼ inches. If the grass gets too long before cutting, the dead clippings can mar the appearance of the lawn. Then the only alternative is to collect the clippings either in a grass-catcher or with a lawn sweeper or rake. If the grass is cut properly, the clippings will not be excessive. They will decompose rapidly and not require collection.

The pattern of mowing should be varied regularly to prevent wheel lines from developing in the lawn. Varying the pattern also encourages horizontal growth of the shoots. An easy variation is to mow at a 90° angle to the last mowing. If done on the same day with a reel mower, an attractive checkerboard pattern develops. The pattern is not so apparent if done with a rotary mower, but the practice is just as healthy for the lawn.

DAMAGES TO LAWNS

Like all plants, turfgrasses are susceptible to assorted injuries. Damage can be visual or physical and frequently is both. Causes of lawn injury include:

- weeds
- pests
- drought
- vandalism

Weeds

There are many definitions of the word *weed*; student landscapers undoubtedly have their own definitions. For discussion purposes, a *weed* may be defined as a plant which (1) is growing where it is not wanted, and (2) has no apparent economic value. Beyond these two qualities, weeds have little else in common. Some weeds have broad leaves (such as dandelion, plantain, and thistle); others are grasses. Some are annuals, others are perennials.

In lawns, weeds are professionally controlled almost entirely by chemical means. A chemical which kills weeds is called an *herbicide*. Some herbicides are *selective*, meaning that they kill only certain weeds and do not harm other plants. Other herbicides are *nonselective*; these kill any plant with which they come into contact. Certain herbicides are classified as *pre-emergence* types. They are applied before the weed seeds *germinate* (sprout) and kill them as they sprout. *Postemergence* herbicides are applied to weeds after they have germinated.

Because the regulations governing the purchase and use of herbicides and other pesticides vary among states, this text contains no recommendations of specific weed controls. Professional grounds keepers in all states can obtain current recommendations for pesticides approved for use in their states by consulting a college of agriculture or the Cooperative Extension Service. The current trend is toward registration of pesticide applicators and restriction of the more poisonous pesticides to use by professionals only. Herbicides are deadly poisons, and the landscaper should handle them cautiously and with a serious attitude.

Good landscaping practices are the best defenses against weeds. However, the need for some herbicides is almost certain to exist in most lawns. They are available in liquid or powdered form. Sometimes herbicides are mixed with fertilizer and sold as combination products which save time and labor.

If an herbicide is applied in liquid form, the sprayer should be cleaned afterward and set aside to be used only for that purpose. Small amounts of herbicide which may remain in the sprayer can kill valuable ornamental plants if the landscaper uses the same sprayer to apply another liquid material directly to plants.

Pests

The following table, "Common Turf Problems," contains a partial list of the pest problems that can injure a typical lawn.

The best defense against most pest injury is the selection of resistant varieties and the creation of a growth environment that favors the grass more than the pest. For example, watering at night promotes the growth of many fungus plants that cause turf diseases. Watering should be done earlier in the day, allowing the grass to dry before nightfall. Another example: allowing a thick thatch layer to develop provides a good habitat for certain insects. Minimizing the thatch layer reduces these insect populations. When soil insects are reduced or eliminated, the turf is not as attractive to rodents, such as moles, that burrow through the soil to feed on them. Thus, solving one problem may indirectly solve another.

As was noted for weeds, the local Cooperative Extension Service can provide information about the appropriate pesticide needed for insect, disease, and rodent control.

Drought

Periods of severe water shortage can harm a lawn. The grass will turn brown and enter a stage of *dormancy* (nongrowth). If the drought continues, the entire lawn can be killed. Irrigation is the major defense against drought. In areas of predictable drought (arid regions), tolerant varieties of grasses should be selected at the time of installation. A greater lawn height is also helpful in withstanding periods of drought.

Common Turf Problems

Turf Insects	Turf Diseases	Other Problems
• Ants	• Anthracnose	• Dogs
• Army worms	• Brown patch	• Gophers
• Bill bugs	• Copper spot	• Ground squirrels
• Chinch bugs	• Dollar spot	• Mice
• Cut worms	• Fairy ring	• Moles
• Grubs	• Fusarium blight	• Human vandalism
• Leaf hoppers	• Leaf spots	• Vehicles and equipment
• Mites	• Net blotch	
• Mole crickets	• Nematodes	
• Periodical cicadas	• Powdery mildew	
• Scale	• Pythium blight	
• Sod webworm	• Red thread	
• Weevils	• Rots	
• Wireworms	• Rusts	
	• Slime molds	
	• Smuts	
	• Snow molds	

From *Ornamental Horticulture*, by Jack E. Ingels, copyright © 1985 by Delmar Publishers Inc.

Vandalism

Vandalism is impossible to control if the vandals are determined. Lawns rutted by vehicles are unattractive and are common abuses of residential and recreational landscapes. Locked gates and the strategic placement of trees can sometimes help by making vehicular access difficult for the would-be vandal. Education to increase public awareness of the value of the landscape and the responsibilities of good citizens is the only real solution to vandalism.

ACHIEVEMENT REVIEW

A. Define the following terms.

1. heaving
2. aeration
3. fertilizer analysis
4. low analysis fertilizer
5. slow-release fertilizer
6. herbicide

B. What does *10-6-4* on a bag of fertilizer mean?

C. Would 10-6-4 fertilizer be considered a high analysis or low analysis product? Why?

D. Of the three fertilizers listed below, which two have the same ratio of nutrients?

10-20-10   5-10-5   5-10-15

E. Why might the prices of two 50-pound bags of fertilizer differ greatly?

F. At what time of the year are warm-season grasses fertilized? Cool-season grasses?

G. How many pounds of actual nitrogen are contained in a 50-pound bag of 12-4-8 fertilizer?

H. How many pounds of 10-10-10 fertilizer should be purchased to fertilize a 2,000 square-foot lawn of bluegrass and fescue if it is applied at the recommended rate?

I. How much water is needed to deeply soak an average lawn?

J.   What is the best time of day to water lawns?

K.   Describe how to repair a lawn by seeding, sodding, sprigging, and plugging. (Review Unit 23 before answering.)

L.   Match the type of sprinkler with its characteristic:

    a.   revolving
    b.   oscillating
    c.   automatic

    1.   casts water in an arched pattern
    2.   permanently installed system for large landscapes
    3.   casts water in a circular pattern

M.   Match the type of mower with its characteristic:

    a.   flail
    b.   reel
    c.   rotary

    1.   blades move like a ceiling fan, parallel to the lawn's surface
    2.   used for grasses that are only cut a few times each year
    3.   the blades rotate in the same direction as the wheels

N.   List four different ways that lawns can be damaged.

SUGGESTED ACTIVITIES

1.   Study "A Comparison Chart for Turfgrasses" in Unit 22 and match grasses growing in your local area that could be blended and grown together successfully. Compare grasses on the basis of texture, frequency of fertilization, mowing height, and preferred soil type.

2.   Calibrate one or more types of portable sprinklers following the directions given in this unit. Determine the length of time each requires to apply 1 inch of water and measure the area of coverage.

3.   Visit a lawn equipment dealership. Ask the owner to show the various models of mowers, spreaders, sprayers, rollers, and rakes that are stocked for lawn maintenance.

4.   Have an equipment field day, perhaps in association with other nearby schools. Invite equipment dealers to bring selected pieces of power equipment to the school for demonstration and/or student use.

WINTERIZATION OF THE LANDSCAPE

OBJECTIVES

After studying this unit, you will be able to

- list those elements of the landscape which require winter protection.
- describe eight possible types of winter injury.
- explain nine ways to protect against winter injury.

Winter injury is any damage done to elements of the landscape during the cold weather season of the year. The injury may be due to natural causes or to human error. It may be predictable or totally unexpected. At times winter injury can be avoided, while at other times it can only be accepted and dealt with.

Winter injury attacks most elements of the outdoor room. Plants, paving, steps, furnishings, and plumbing are all susceptible to damage from one or more causes.

TYPES OF WINTER INJURY

While the types of winter damage are almost unlimited, there are several which commonly occur. The landscaper should be especially aware of these. Injuries are caused by one of two agents: nature or human beings. There are many different examples within these two general categories.

Natural Injuries

The severity of winter weather can cause extensive damage to plant materials in the landscape.

Windburn results when evergreens are exposed to strong prevailing winds throughout the winter months. The wind dries out the leaf tissue, and the dehydrated material dies. Windburn causes a brown to black discoloration of the leaves on the windward side of the plant. Very often, leaves further into the plant or on the side opposite the wind show no damage. Broadleaved evergreens are the most susceptible to windburn because they have the greatest leaf surface area exposed to drying winds. To protect themselves, many broad-leaved evergreens roll their leaves in the winter to reduce the amount of exposed surface area, figure 28–1.

Needled evergreens can also burn. If burn has occurred, brown-tipped branches are apparent in the spring when new growth is beginning. As with broad-leaved forms, windburn on conifers is likely to be confined to the outermost branches on the most exposed side of the plant.

Temperature extremes can also cause injury to plants. Plants which are at the limit of their hardiness (termed *marginally hardy*) may be killed by an extended period of severely cold weather. Others may be stunted when all of the previous season's young growth freezes.

After some cold winters, certain plants may show no sign of injury except that their spring flower displays are absent. This results if the plant produces its flowers and its leaves in separate buds. The weather may not be cold enough to affect the leaf buds, but freezes the more tender flower buds. This is especially common with forsythia and certain spireas in the northern states.

Unusually warm weather during late winter can also cause plant damage. Fruit trees may be encouraged to bloom prematurely, only to have the flowers killed by a late frost. As a result, the harvest of fruit can be greatly reduced or even eliminated. Spring flowering bulbs can also be disfigured if forced into bloom by warm weather that is followed by freezing winds and snow.

Sunscald is a special type of temperature-related injury. It occurs when extended periods of warm winter sunshine thaw the aboveground portion of a plant. The period of warmth is too brief to thaw the root

Figure 28–1. Rolled and discolored leaves show the effects of windburn on this rhododendron.

system, however, so it remains frozen in the ground, unable to take up water. Aboveground, the thawed plant parts require water, which the roots are unable to provide. Consequently, the tissue dries out and a scald condition results.

Sunscald is especially troublesome on evergreens planted on the south side of a building. It also occurs on newly transplanted young trees in a similar location. The young, thin bark scalds easily and the natural moisture content of the tissue is low because of the reduced root system.

Heaving affects turf grass, hardy bulbs, and other perennials when the ground freezes and thaws repeatedly because of winter temperature fluctuations. The heaving exposes the plants' roots to the drying winter wind, which can kill the plants.

Ice and snow damage can occur repeatedly during the winter. The sheer weight of snow and/or ice on plant limbs and twigs can cause breakage and result in permanent destruction of the plant's natural shape, figures 28–2 and 28–3. Evergreens are most easily damaged because they hold heavy snow more readily than deciduous plants. Snow or ice falling off a pitched roof can split foundation plants in seconds.

Plants which freeze before the snow settles on them are even more likely to be injured. Freezing reduces plant flexibility and causes weighted twigs to snap rather than bend under added weight.

Unfortunately, the older and larger a plant is, the greater is the damage resulting from heavy snowfalls and ice storms. There are numerous recorded accounts of the street trees of entire cities being destroyed by a severe winter storm.

Animal damage to plants results from small animals feeding on the tender twigs and bark of plants, especially shrubs. Bulbs are also susceptible. Entire floral displays can be destroyed by the winter feeding of small rodents. Shrubs can be distorted and stunted by removal of all young growth. In cases where the plant becomes *girdled* (with the bark around the main stem completely removed), the plant is unable to take up nutrients and eventually dies.

Figure 28–2. Evergreen trees can be broken and even suffer permanent damage from a heavy snow.

Figure 28–3. The weight of ice on the branches of deciduous plants can break and misshape them.

Human-Induced Injuries

Certain types of injury are created by people during wintertime landscape maintenance. Some types of injury are due to carelessness on the part of grounds keepers. Other types are the predictable result of poor landscape design. A large number are injuries created because the landscape elements are hidden beneath piles of snow.

Salt injury harms trees, shrubs, bulbs, lawns, and paving. Often the damage does not appear until long after the winter season passes. Thus, the cause of the injury may go undiagnosed.

The salt used to rid walks, streets, and steps of slippery ice becomes dissolved in the water it creates. The saline solution flows off walks and into nearby lawns or planting beds. Paving sometimes crumbles under heavy salting. Poured concrete is especially sensitive to this treatment, figure 28–4.

Salt is toxic to nearly all plant life. The resultant injury appears as strips of sterile, barren ground paralleling walks, figure 28–5. Injury can also be seen on the lower branches of evergreens.

Snowplow damage can occur to plant and construction materials for several reasons. A careless plow operator may push snow onto a planting or a bench. This often results when those unfamiliar with the landscape are hired to do the snowplowing. Other injuries from plowing are the result of design errors. Plants, outdoor furniture, and light fixtures should not be placed near walks, parking areas, or streets where they will interfere with winter snow removal.

Figure 28–4. Excess salt had a damaging effect on these concrete steps. This type of damage is unnecessary.

Figure 28–5. Dead grass edging the walk in the summer is a symptom of excessive winter salting.

Damage to lawns can result when the plow misses the walk and actually plows the grass, scraping and gouging the lawn, figure 28–6. The grass may not survive if this occurs repeatedly.

Rutting of lawns is the result of heavy vehicles parking on softened ground. When the surface layer of the soil thaws but the subsoil remains frozen, surface water is unable to soak in. Users of the landscape ac-

customed to finding the ground firm may be unaware of damage caused by vehicles temporarily parked on soft lawns. The soil becomes badly compacted, resulting in unsightly ruts.

REDUCING WINTER INJURY

Some types of winter damage can be eliminated by properly winterizing the landscape in the preceding autumn. Other

Figure 28–6. A scraped lawn is the result of a snowplow which has missed the unmarked sidewalk.

types can be reduced by better initial designing of the grounds. Still other winter injuries can only be minimized, never totally eliminated.

Windburn can be eliminated in the design stage of the landscape if the planner selects deciduous plant materials rather than evergreen materials. This problem can be avoided in the garden by the use of deciduous shrubs on especially windy corners. If evergreens are important to the design or already exist in the garden, windburn can be reduced by erecting burlap shields around shrubs, figure 28–7. The use of an antitranspirant may also reduce water loss from plants and thereby reduce the effects of windburn. The antitranspirant must be applied in the autumn and again in late winter. While antitranspirants are fairly expensive, they are more practical for the protection of large evergreens than burlap shields.

Temperature extremes can be only partially guarded against. Where wind chill (lowering of temperature because of the

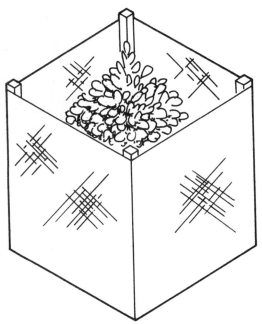

Figure 28–7. A broad-leaved evergreen protected against windburn with a burlap shield.

force of wind) is a factor, plants should be located in a protected area. Wrapping the plant in burlap also helps. This has proven to be an effective technique for protecting tender flower buds on otherwise hardy plants.

Certain plants, such as roses, can be cut back in the fall and their crowns mulched heavily to assure insulation against the effects of winter. Likewise, any plant that can be damaged by freezing and thawing of the soil should be heavily mulched after the ground has frozen to insulate against premature thawing.

If the landscaper is trying to prolong the lives of annual flowers in the autumn, and a frost is forecast, the foliage can be sprinkled with water prior to nightfall. This helps to avoid damage caused by a light frost. The water gives off enough warmth to keep the plant tissue from freezing.

Sunscald of young transplants lessens as the plants grow older and form thicker bark. It can be avoided on trees during the first winter of growth by wrapping the trunks of the trees with paper or burlap stripping. (See Unit 13.) For other types of sunscald, such as that which affects broadleaved evergreens, the same remedies practiced for windburn and temperature extremes are effective. Wrapping the plants in burlap or the use of antitranspirants gives protection.

Some sunscald can be avoided by the designer. Vulnerable species of plants should not be placed on the south side of a building, nor should they be placed against a reflective white wall that will magnify the sun's effect on the aboveground plant parts.

Heaving of the turf is impossible to prevent completely. The best defense against it is the encouragement of deep rooting through proper maintenance and good landscaping practices during the growing season.

Bulbs, ground covers, and other perennials can be protected from heaving through application of a mulch after the ground has frozen. The mulch acts to insulate the soil against surface thawing.

Ice and snow damage to foundation plants can be avoided if the designer is careful not to place plants beneath the overhanging roof line of a building. If the grounds keeper must deal with plants already existing in a danger area, the use of hinged, wooden A-frames over the plants can help to protect them, figure 28–8. As large pieces of frozen snow and ice tumble off the roof, the frame breaks them apart before they can damage the plants.

To aid plants that have been split or bent because of heavy snow accumulation, the grounds keeper must work quickly and cautiously. A broom can be used to shake the snow off the weighted branches. However, the snow removal must be done gently and immediately after the snow stops. If the branches are frozen or the snow has become hard and icy, removal efforts will cause more damage than benefit.

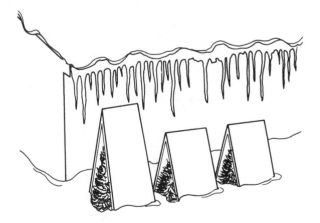

Figure 28–8. Hinged wooden A-frames protect foundation plantings from damage caused by sliding ice and snow.

If breakage of plants occurs during the winter, the grounds keeper should prune the damaged parts as soon as possible. This prevents further damage to the plants during the rest of the winter.

Certain plants, such as upright arborvitae and upright yews, become more susceptible to heavy snow and ice injury as they mature. Often, the damage cannot be repaired. Large and valuable plants in a landscape can be winterized in the autumn by tying them loosely with strips of burlap or twine. (Do not use wire.) When prepared in this manner, the branches cannot be forced apart by the heavy snows of winter, and splitting is avoided.

Animal damage can be prevented by either eliminating the animals or protecting the plants from their feeding. While rats, mice, moles, and voles are generally regarded as offensive, plantings are damaged as much or more by deer, rabbits, chipmunks, and other gentler kinds of animals. Certain *rodenticides* (substances which poison rodents) may be employed against some of the undesirable animals that threaten the landscape. In situations where the animals are welcome but their winter feeding damage is not, a protective enclosure of fine mesh wire fencing around the plants helps to discourage animals from feeding there, figure 28–9.

Figure 28–9. A wire enclosure placed around young plants during the winter helps to protect them from animal damage. Even smaller mesh is needed to discourage rodents.

Salt injury to plants and paving need not be as bad as was illustrated earlier if caution is exercised by the grounds keeper. Salt mixed with coarse sand does a better job than either material used separately. The sand provides traction on icy walks, and a small amount of salt can melt a large amount of ice. Excessive salt has no value; it only kills plants and destroys paving. In very cold temperatures, salt does not melt ice; therefore, in these cases, it serves no purpose. Salt can turn compacted snow, which is comparatively safe for traffic, into inches of slush which is messy and even more slippery. The problem of salt injury can be solved by reducing the amount of salt spread on walks and streets during the winter season. The addition of sand distributes the salt more evenly and provides grit for better traction.

Snowplow damage is to be expected if a designer places plants too close to walks and roadways. Therefore, one obvious solution to the problem begins with the de-

signer. When planning landscapes for areas in which winter is normally accompanied by a great deal of snow, the designer should avoid placing shrubs near intersections or other places where snow is likely to be pushed.

Another type of plow damage is the result of the plow driver's inability to see objects beneath the snow. If possible, all objects such as outdoor furniture and lights should be removed from plow areas prior to the winter season. If it is not possible to move them, low objects should be marked with tall, colored poles that can be seen above the snow.

Whenever possible, snow blowers should be used instead of plows. These machines are much less likely to cause damage.

Rutting of lawns usually results from the practice of permitting individuals to park cars on lawns. The best solution to the problem is to avoid doing so. Otherwise, sawhorses or other barriers offer a temporary solution.

ACHIEVEMENT REVIEW

A. Indicate whether the following types of winter injury are caused by natural conditions (N) or human error (H).

1. crumbled paving resulting from too much salt
2. dry, dead twigs on the windward side of a pine tree
3. dried, blistered bark on the trunk of a recently transplanted tree
4. deep ruts in the lawn in front of a house
5. dead branches in a shrub following an unusually cold winter
6. failure of a shrub to flower in the spring
7. perennials lying on the surface of the soil in the early spring with roots exposed to the drying air

8. dead grass next to a walk heavily salted during the winter
9. an upright evergreen split in the center by snow sliding off a roof
10. a young tree girdled at the base

B. Of the types of winter damage in the following list, which ones could be reduced or prevented by proper winterization of the landscape during the late autumn?

1. crumbled paving
2. sunscald on new transplants
3. breakage of outdoor furniture by snow plows
4. rutting of the lawn by automobiles
5. foundation plants broken by falling snow
6. sunscald on broad-leaved evergreens
7. tree limbs broken off by an ice storm
8. bulbs heaved to the surface of the soil
9. windburn on evergreens
10. flooded basement caused by melting snow

SUGGESTED ACTIVITIES

1. Look for signs of winter injury in nearby landscapes. Find windy corners where evergreens are planted and check for windburned tips. Visit a shopping center, campus, or park where salt is used on walks and parking lots. Look at the paving and nearby plantings for signs of damage. Note the placement of plants in relation to walk intersections and other places where snow may be piled.

2. Conduct ice melting tests. Freeze four pie plates of water. Apply four different mixtures of salt and/or sand to the surfaces and see which melts first. In the first pan, use all salt; in the second, half salt and half sand; in the third, one-quarter salt and three-quarters sand; and in the fourth; all sand. What conclusions can be drawn from the trials? *Note*: Returning the treated pans of ice to the freezer (approximately 20° F) will assure that no natural melting occurs. Check the pans every 15 minutes for observations.

3. Demonstrate the damaging effects of salt upon plant life. Grow some experimental plants in advance. Root each plant in a separate container. Apply only water to some of the plants for a week. To others, apply varying dilutions of a salt and water solution. To a third group, apply water to the soil, but mist the foliage with saltwater several times each day. Record observations of each treatment daily.

4. Demonstrate the reduction of water loss from plant tissue caused by anti-transpirants. Purchase a small bottle of antitranspirant from a garden center, or write to a manufacturer and request a complimentary sample. Dilute with water as specified on the label. Using a small pump sprayer, apply the antitranspirant to one of two comparable samples of cut evergreens in vases of water. Be certain to apply it evenly over all needle surfaces. The untreated sample should dry out sooner than the treated one, indicating greater water loss.

5. Repeat the demonstration in #4 using a sun lamp or a fan to simulate the drying effects of sun and wind and the protection offered by antitranspirants.

LANDSCAPE IRRIGATION

OBJECTIVES

Upon completion of this unit, students will be able to

- describe historic and current uses of landscape irrigation.
- distinguish between sprinkler and trickle irrigation use and understand key irrigation terms.
- select and describe irrigation sprinkler heads.
- explain precipitation rates and the determination of water needs by geographical area.
- describe how irrigation pipe is sized and the available flow and pressure of water are determined.
- explain drip tube and emitter placement.
- explain simple irrigation designs.

BACKGROUND

Irrigation is the supplying of water to land through artificial means. While the delivery systems have varied and changed over the years, the concept is not new. Once humans ceased to be hunters and gatherers and instead became farmers, the realization that water could be directed and relocated to help plants grow soon followed. Canals and channels that connect to nearby rivers have permitted water to flow across fields and plains yielding bounty from an earth otherwise incapable of bearing food. Run-off from the snow capped peaks of distant mountains has been collected and carried to farm fields and communities whose life lines are literally the water pipelines that link their arid locales to the water sources.

As humans became garden builders, not just food producers, irrigation principles were found as applicable to the growth and maintenance of pleasure grounds as they were to agriculture. Princely potentates throughout Europe, Asia, and Africa commonly developed their gardens by redirecting the channels of streams and rivers to bring them into or near their properties. That nearby communities might be either flooded or deprived of their water supply was often not a concern of the aristocratic garden builder.

Today, the irrigation of landscapes is common. Each year more properties receive designed irrigation systems for their lawns and plantings. These systems are gradually replacing the lawn sprinklers, garden hoses, and watering cans of years past. There are several reasons for the increased interest in landscape irrigation. Turf and ornamental plant research continually provides new information regarding the water requirements of specific plant species. Water needs are no longer guessing games. Automated irrigation systems also save water because they only apply the amount that can be absorbed, so there is no run-off, Figure 29–1. That savings is important for economic reasons, since water costs are rising. It is also important for environmental reasons. Controlled water application prevents water laden with fertilizers or pesticides from washing into waterways and sewers. Also, in regions of limited rainfall, landscape irrigation assures that none of the precious liquid is wasted.

TYPES OF LANDSCAPE IRRIGATION SYSTEMS

Landscape irrigation water can be applied in two different ways. *Sprinkler irrigation* applies water under pressure through a delivery system that delivers the water over the tops of plants, Figure 29–2. *Trickle irrigation* supplies water directly to the root zone of the plants, Figure 29–3. The delivery system is low pressure and may be placed atop or within the soil. Table 29–1 compares sprinkler and trickle irrigation systems. The table should be studied before proceeding further.

THE TERMINOLOGY OF LANDSCAPE IRRIGATION

Since landscape irrigation is a somewhat specialized technical field, it has its own specialized vocabulary. An understanding of these terms can provide a basic comprehension of some of the technology of the field.

Figure 29–1. Irrigation **(Photo courtesy of Utah Agricultural Experiment Station)**

Figure 29--2. Sprinkler system (Photo courtesy of Utah Agricultural Experiment Station)

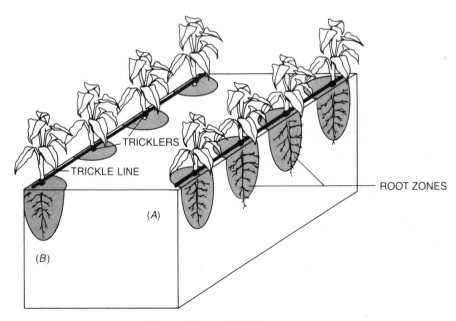

Figure 29–3. Trickle system

Table 29–1. A Comparison of Sprinkler and Trickle Irrigation Systems

Feature	Sprinkler System	Trickle System
Delivery System	Water is sent under pressure through polyethylene or polyvinylchloride pipe and delivered from either *spray heads* or *rotary heads*.	Water is sent under pressure through plastic or poly pipes or tubes and delivered from a small sprinkler head known as an *emitter*.
Delivery Site	Over the tops of the plant and onto the soil beneath	At the roots of the plants
Water Pressure at the Delivery Site	Varies with each system, but always greater than trickle systems. The pressure must propel the water through the air.	Low pressure resulting from either the small openings in the emitters or the long distance traveled through the pipes
Speed of Delivery	Faster than trickle systems. Water delivery is measured in gallons per minute.	Slower than sprinkler systems. Water delivery is measured in gallons per hour.
Delivery of Pesticides and Fertilizers	As long as the materials are water-soluble, they can be delivered in the irrigation water. Some waste and/or chemical burning of foliage may result.	As long as the materials are water-soluble, they can be delivered in the irrigation water. Chemical burn is less likely. Plugging of the emitters is possible. Filtration of the water going into the system will help control the problem.
Water Run-off	Possible if the system is not set to deliver only what the soil can absorb	Little or none due to the slow speed of delivery
Weed Growth	Possible, due to the greater area of coverage	Less of a problem due to the more restricted area of coverage
Evaporated Water Loss	Water is lost to evaporation because it is thrown through the air, left atop foliage, and dispersed into soil outside the root area.	Little water loss because the water is never airborne or left on the tops of leaves to evaporate
Insects and Disease	Excessive moisture on foliage and soil can encourage pests to develop.	By eliminating the amount of wet foliage and soil, pest development is discouraged
Installation Costs	More expensive due to the greater amount of hardware required	Less expensive due to the comparative simplicity of the system
Maintenance	Moderate maintenance. It is quickly apparent when all or parts of the system are malfunctioning.	High maintenance. Because the system cannot be seen working as easily as sprinklers are seen, it requires constant checking.

Sprinkler head: The device through which water leaves the pipe and is propelled onto the lawn or plantings.

Spray pattern: The specific distribution pattern of a specific sprinkler head.

Spray head: One of two types of sprinkler heads. Spray heads are stationary and made of two parts, the sprinkler body and the spray nozzle. The nozzles control the amount of water that leaves the spray head as well as the spray pattern.

Rotary heads: The other type of sprinkler head. Rotary heads move in a circle and propel water in tiny streams under pressure. Rotary heads can dis- tribute water much further than spray heads are able to.

Impact drive heads: One of two types of rotary sprinkler heads. As the pressurized water flows from the head it bumps a spring loaded arm that slowly moves the head around in a circle. The repeating bumping of the arm makes this a somewhat noisy form of irrigation.

Gear drive heads: The other type of rotary sprinkler head. The head contains a number of gears that are turned by the water as it leaves the sprinkler. The movement of these internal gears is what causes the head to turn.

Precipitation rate: The amount of water placed over a landscape area. It is measured in inches of water per hour.

Geographical area: An area of the landscape having a specific water need, based upon the needs of the plants growing there and the rate of water absorption by the soil. A landscape may contain numerous and different geographical areas.

Emitter: The device that functions as a sprinkler head for trickle irrigation.

Discharge rate: The amount of water flowing from the irrigation system over a measured period of time. Sprinkler systems are measured and rated in gallons per minute (gpm). Trickle systems are slower and measured in gallons per hour (gph).

Pressure compensating emitters: Not all emitters can maintain the same discharge rate if the pressure of the water changes. Those that can are termed pressure compensating emitters. They are more expensive than noncompensating types.

Micro spray heads: Similar to the spray head design described earlier, but with a discharge rate more like that of an emitter (in gph). The diameter of water throw is considerably reduced. It is used for small specialized areas of the landscape such as flower beds and groundcover plantings.

Irrigation pipe: Used for sprinkler irrigation systems, there are two types of pipe currently popular due to their superiority over metal pipe. Polyethylene pipe (PE) and polyvinyl chloride pipe (PVC) are widely used both separately and together.

Schedule rated pipe: A PVC pipe used as a covering or sleeve for thinner, weaker pipe when it passes beneath walks, roads, driveways, or walls. The higher the schedule rating is, the stronger the pipe will be.

Pressure rated pipe: A PVC pipe used to carry the water through an irrigation system. It is produced in four forms. Each form guaranteed to withstand a particular water pressure of either 125, 160, 200, or 315 pounds per square inch (psi).

Drip tubing: Used for trickle irrigation systems, the thin black tubing carries the water to the emitters. It is usually black in color and made of plastic.

Flow: The movement of water through the irrigation system.

Friction loss: The loss of pressure during water flow that results from the increasing speed of the water, the increasing length of the pipe, and the roughness of the lining of the pipe.

Velocity: The rate of flow, as expressed in feet of movement per second. For landscape irrigation, the ideal velocity of water is 5 feet per second.

Surge pressure: A shock wave type of pressure that results when water velocity is too high and then is suddenly stopped. Excessive surge pressure over time will weaken the pipe and connections within an irrigation system.

Static pressure: The pressure (in psi) that is present in a closed system, when the water is not flowing.

Dynamic pressure: The pressure (in psi) that is present at any one point in a system as a given quantity of water flows past that point. Dynamic water pressure varies within an irrigation system due to the rise and fall of water as the pipes move up and down across a landscape. Friction losses within the pipes also affect dynamic pressure.

Up to this point both sprinkler and trickle irrigation systems have been discussed simultaneously. Now the discussion will focus on each system separately.

SPRINKLER IRRIGATION

Where large quantities of water must be applied in a controlled manner, sprinkler irrigation systems are the best delivery device. Golf courses and other large lawn areas as well as tree and shrub plantings are suitable for the rapid water delivery of sprinkler systems.

Sprinkler Heads

As noted earlier, there are two types of sprinkler heads, the spray head and the rotary. Spray heads are available as pop-up types that are recessed below mower level when not in use. The same water pressure that allows delivery also forces the spray head nozzle above ground level, giving the pop-up its name. Figure 29–4 illustrates several of the sizes of pop-up spray heads that are available.

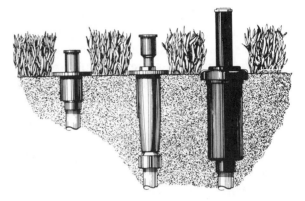

Figure 29–4. Several sizes of the pop-up spray heads that are available

Spray heads that do not recess are also available. They are needed for the irrigation of tall grasses and shrub beds. A plastic riser that may extend several feet above the ground permits a nozzle, specially adapted for shrubs, to deliver water to the plants.

Aside from popping up and down, spray heads have no moving parts. Nozzles are usually purchased separately from the spray head bodies. That permits the system designer to customize the irrigation system for each particular landscape. Nozzles may be selected to distribute water in a full circle, half circle, or quarter circle. They can also deliver water at standard volumes or at low gallonages if site conditions necessitate a slower rate of water application.

Spray heads have their limitations. They can only propel water outward to a distance of 14 to 16 feet from the nozzle before the wind disrupts the spray pattern. A disrupted spray pattern results in non-uniform water application. The overall effect can be inconsistent growth and troublesome wet or dry spots.

Rotary heads have moving parts. They may or may not pop up, depending upon the style, but all rotary heads move in full or partial circles and can propel water further than spray heads. Both the impact drive and gear drive heads are available in sizes that will throw water 110 feet or more from the nozzle. Figures 29–5 and 29–6 illustrate the impact drive and gear drive rotary heads.

In comparison with spray heads, rotary heads do not apply water as quickly. Like spray heads, rotary heads are also affected by the wind.

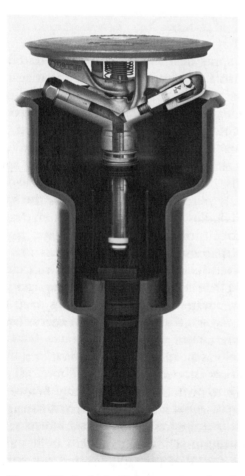

*Figure 29–5. Impact drive rotary head (from Emmons/*Turfgrass Science and Management, *copyright 1984 by Delmar Publishers Inc.)*

Precipitation Rates

Because spray heads apply water faster than rotary heads are able to do, it can be said that they have a higher precipitation rate (in inches of water per hour). Regardless of the type of landscape irrigation system selected, it is necessary to match the discharge rate of the system (in gpm) to the precipitation rate that will permit optimum absorption by the plants and meet their water needs, which are usually stated as so many inches of water per week. To convert from gallons per minute through inches per hour to arrive at inches per week and determine irrigation time is not impossible; but there are some necessary steps along the way.

Step 1   Determine the precipitation rate (PR)
   a. Calculate total gpm by totaling the gpm of all irrigation sprinkler heads in the area of the landscape that is of concern.
   b. Determine the square footage (SF) of the area being covered.
   c. Using a constant figure, 96.3, to aid the conversion, insert the data into the following formula

$$PR = \frac{\text{Total GPM of an area} \times 96.3}{\text{SF of the area}}$$

Step 2   Convert the precipitation rate from inches of water applied per hour to inches per minute using the formula:

$$\frac{PR}{60 \text{ minutes}} = \text{Inches of water per minute}$$

Step 3   Determine how long the sprinklers must run to deliver the plants' weekly water needs.
   a. Learn the water needs of particular plants and plant types. See Table 29–2 for examples.

Figure 29–6. *The Weather-matic Turbo J2 gear drive head (courtesy of Weathermatic Division, Telsco Industries)*

Table 29–2. *A Comparison of Plant Water Needs*

Plant Type	Water Needs
Turf grass	1.5 to 2.0 inches/week
Flowers	1.5 to 2.0 inches/week
Trees and shrubs	1.0 to 1.5 inches/week
Groundcovers	0.5 to 1.0 inches/week

b. Divide the plant's weekly water needs by inches of water per minute.

Example

Given: A 1,000 SF shrub installation needing 1.5 inches of water each week is irrigated by a system that delivers 5.2 gpm.

Question: How much irrigation running time is needed to deliver 1.5 inches of water?

Solution: 1) $PR = \dfrac{5.2 \text{ GPM} \times 96.3}{1000 \text{ SF}}$

= .5 inch per hour

2) $\dfrac{.5 \text{ inches per hour}}{60 \text{ minutes}}$

= .008 inches of water per minute

3) $\dfrac{1.5 \text{ inches}}{.008 \text{ inches/minute}}$

= 188 minutes of operation

4) $\dfrac{188 \text{ minutes}}{60 \text{ minutes}}$

= 3 hours and 8 minutes of operation

Now it is known that in the situation described in the example, the sprinkler irrigation would need to operate 3 hours and 8 minutes or 188 minutes each week in the shrub installation to deliver the amount of water needed by the plants.

Geographical Areas

Table 29–2 illustrates that not all plants require the same amount of water for optimum growth. To landscapers, it is no surprise that not all soils are alike either. They differ greatly in their ability to absorb water. Generally, the more clay that a soil contains the slower is its rate of absorption. The greater the sand content of a soil, the faster will be its rate of absorption. Table 29–3 illustrates some of the characteristics of different types of soil that affect their rate of water absorption.

A landscape that is large enough and of sufficient quality to warrant an irrigation system is likely to have a mixture of plants. It may also have mixture of soil conditions. Therefore one operational schedule that will serve all areas of the landscape is unlikely. Instead the landscape must be divided and grouped into geographical areas. Each geographical area will contain plants that have similar water needs AND similar soil absorption rates. Additionally, allowance must be made for terrain factors such as slopes or depressions that will speed up or slow down water run-off. Other environmental conditions such as temperatures, drying winds, presence or lack of shade, and the number of competing plants can influence the availability of water to the plants' roots.

Once the landscape site has been analyzed and the number of geographical areas has been determined, such follow-up questions as these must be answered.

1. What sprinkler heads are needed for each geographical area?
2. How many are required and of what size?
3. What is the total gpm required by the sprinkler heads in each geographical area and for the total system?
4. How does the total system need compare to the total water flow available from the source of water?
5. What sizes of pipe are needed and what layout is best?
6. What static and dynamic water pressures are available?

Only after these questions and others are answered and the irrigation system is made operational, will there be enough data to determine things such as the amount of running time for the system. Then, if it is found that a single weekly operation of the

Table 29–3. Soil Characteristics and Absorption Rates

Soil Type	Components	Water Intake Rate	Water Retention	Drainage	Rate of Water Absorption
Clay	Clay, with small amounts of silt and/or sand	Low to very low as the amount of clay increases	High to very high due to reduced air space for drainage	Poor to very poor	0.2 inches per hour hour (Low)
Loams	Equal or near-equal mixes of sand, silt and clay	Moderately low to moderately high depending upon the amounts of clay or sand in the loam	Moderately low to moderately high depending upon the amounts of sand or clay in the loam	good	1.0 to 1.7 inches per hour (Moderate)
Sandy	Sand, with lesser amounts of clay and silt	High to very high	Low to very low	good to excessive	Greater than 1.7 inches per hour (High)

system for the calculated amount of time is more than the soil in a geographical area can absorb, it will be necessary to set up a schedule that will apply a lesser amount several times per week. The total amount of water applied will be the same.

SIZING IRRIGATION PIPE

Cost of the pipe is one of the most expensive factors in the price of an irrigation system. The larger in diameter that pipe is, the more costly it will be. Therefore, system designers must specify pipe that is large enough to carry the amount of water required by all sprinklers that lead off it; but it need be no larger. Pipe sizes will vary within an irrigation system, being larger in diameter near the water source and smaller as they are needed further from the source, Figure 29–7. Table 29–4 explains the relationship of irrigation pipe size to the amount of water that can be carried.

Table 29–4. Water Flow and Irrigation Pipe Size

If the pipe must carry	Select a pipe size of
1 to 6 gallons per minute	0.5 inch
7 to 10 gpm	0.75 inch
11 to 16 gpm	1.00 inch
17 to 26 gpm	1.25 inches
27 to 35 gpm	1.50 inches
36 to 55 gpm	2.00 inches

MATCHING WATER FLOW AND PRESSURE WITH PIPE SIZE

To select and specify the most suitable pipe, the irrigation system designer must know the amount of water demanded by the sprinkler heads that are downstream from each section of pipe. *Downstream* is the term to describe the direction of water flow away from the source. Pipe that is upstream will be of wider diameter than pipe which is downstream because it must carry a greater volume of water.

Figure 29–7. Pipe sizes will vary within an irrigation system, being larger in diameter near the water source and smaller as they are needed further from the source. (Photo courtesy of Utah Agricultural Experiment Station)

CALCULATING WORKING WATER PRESSURE

Complicating the match-up of water pressure and quantity with the appropriate pipe size is the problem that pressure varies, depending upon whether the water is static (still) or dynamic (moving). Pressure is also affected by the influence of gravity if water drops or rises from one level to another. Pressure will change as it is released downstream through valves along its route of flow and also in response to the roughness of the inside of the irrigation pipes (friction loss).

Calculating Static Water Pressure

To calculate static water pressure at the system's main valve, the pressure at the mainline source must be adjusted by the pressure created by any elevation change that exists between the mainline and the valve. This is done by multiplying the elevation change in feet by .433 pounds per square inch. This figure (.433 psi) is the constant weight of a 1-foot tall column of water. It is an accepted constant figure used in irrigation calculations. The following example will help clarify the calculation of static pressure.

Problem: The water pressure supplied from the municipal source is 60 psi. From the mainline, a pipe drops 15 feet to the valve that controls the flow of irrigation water. What will be the static pressure at the valve?

Solution: Static pressure at valve = Static pressure at mainline + elevation change × .433 psi

Static pressure at valve =
60 psi + 15(.433 psi) =
60 psi + 6.50 =
66.5 psi

Calculating Dynamic Water Pressure

To calculate moving water pressure it is necessary either to know or to calculate the friction loss as the water rubs against the inside of the pipe. It is also necessary to calculate the pressure lost as the water passes through valves, as it passes through the water meter, and as it rises and falls due to elevation changes.

As this unit can only serve to introduce students to the subject of landscape irrigation, certain concepts must be explained with the understanding that further study and supplemental materials are needed if the student is to develop a true competency. Such is the case in describing the determination of friction loss and appropriate pipe sizes. Manufacturers of irrigation pipe provide irrigation system designers with pipe friction loss charts. There are different charts for different classes and types of pipes. Figure 29–8 illustrates a friction loss chart for a common class of plastic pipe. These charts record the friction loss or pressure loss for a particular size and material of pipe or piece of equipment at different flow rates, and velocities. The charts also aid the system designer in calculating the size of pipe needed, based upon the water flow through the pipe section.

Moving water pressure = Static pressure in mainline; minus the pressure loss in the water meter, the friction loss in the pipe, the pressure loss in valves and fitting; plus or minus elevation pressure gains.

(1120, 1220) SDR 21 C = 150 *PSI Loss Per 100 Feet of Pipe (PSI/100 FT)* *Sizes ¾" thru 6"* *Flow GPM 1 thru 600*

SIZE	¾"	1"	1¼"	1½"	2"	2½"	3"	4"	6"	SIZE
OD	1.050	1.315	1.660	1.900	2.375	2.875	3.500	4.500	6.625	OD
ID	.930	1.189	1.502	1.720	2.149	2.601	3.166	4.072	5.993	ID
WALL THK	0.60	0.063	0.079	0.090	0.113	0.137	0.167	0.214	0.316	WALL THK

Flow G.P.M.	Velocity F.P.S.	P.S.I. Loss	Velocity F.P.S.	P.S.I. Loss	Velocity F.P.S.	P.S.I. Loss	Velocity F.P.S.	P.S.I. Loss	Velocity F.P.S.	P.S.I. Loss	Velocity F.P.S.	P.S.I. Loss	Velocity F.P.S.	P.S.I. Loss	Velocity F.P.S.	P.S.I. Loss	Velocity F.P.S.	P.S.I. Loss	Flow G.P.M.
1	0.47	0.06	0.28	0.02	0.18	0.01	0.13	0.00											1
2	0.94	0.22	0.57	0.07	0.36	0.02	0.27	0.01	0.17	0.00									2
3	1.42	0.46	0.86	0.14	0.54	0.04	0.41	0.02	0.26	0.01	0.18	0.00							3
4	1.89	0.79	1.15	0.24	0.72	0.08	0.55	0.04	0.35	0.01	0.24	0.01							4
5	2.36	1.20	1.44	0.36	0.90	0.12	0.68	0.06	0.44	0.02	0.30	0.01							5
6	2.83	1.68	1.73	0.51	1.08	0.16	0.82	0.08	0.53	0.03	0.36	0.01	0.24	0.00					6
7	3.30	2.23	2.02	0.67	1.26	0.22	0.96	0.11	0.61	0.04	0.42	0.01	0.28	0.01					7
8	3.77	2.85	2.30	0.86	1.44	0.28	1.10	0.14	0.70	0.05	0.48	0.02	0.32	0.01					8
9	4.25	3.55	2.59	1.07	1.62	0.34	1.24	0.18	0.79	0.06	0.54	0.02	0.36	0.01					9
10	4.72	4.31	2.88	1.30	1.80	0.42	1.37	0.22	0.88	0.07	0.60	0.03	0.40	0.01					10
11	5.19	5.15	3.17	1.56	1.98	0.50	1.51	0.26	0.97	0.09	0.66	0.03	0.44	0.01					11
12	5.66	6.05	3.46	1.83	2.17	0.59	1.65	0.30	1.06	0.10	0.72	0.04	0.48	0.02	0.29	0.00			12
14	6.60	8.05	4.04	2.43	2.53	0.78	1.93	0.40	1.23	0.14	0.84	0.05	0.56	0.02	0.34	0.01			14
16	7.55	10.30	4.61	3.11	2.89	1.00	2.20	0.52	1.41	0.17	0.96	0.07	0.65	0.03	0.39	0.01			16
18	8.49	12.81	5.19	3.87	3.25	1.24	2.48	0.64	1.59	0.22	1.08	0.09	0.73	0.03	0.44	0.01			18
20	9.43	15.58	5.77	4.71	3.61	1.51	2.75	0.78	1.76	0.26	1.20	0.10	0.81	0.04	0.49	0.01			20
22	10.38	18.58	6.34	5.62	3.97	1.80	3.03	0.93	1.94	0.32	1.32	0.12	0.89	0.05	0.54	0.01			22
24	11.32	21.83	6.92	6.60	4.34	2.12	3.30	1.09	2.12	0.37	1.44	0.15	0.97	0.06	0.59	0.02			24
26	12.27	25.32	7.50	7.65	4.70	2.46	3.58	1.27	2.29	0.43	1.56	0.17	1.05	0.07	0.63	0.02			26
28	13.21	29.04	8.08	8.78	5.06	2.82	3.86	1.46	2.47	0.49	1.68	0.19	1.13	0.07	0.68	0.02			28
30	14.15	33.00	8.65	9.98	5.42	3.20	4.13	1.66	2.65	0.56	1.80	0.22	1.22	0.09	0.73	0.02	0.34	0.00	30
35	16.51	43.91	10.10	13.27	6.32	4.26	4.82	2.20	3.09	0.75	2.11	0.29	1.42	0.11	0.86	0.03	0.39	0.01	35
40	18.87	56.23	11.54	17.00	7.23	5.45	5.51	2.82	3.53	0.95	2.41	0.38	1.62	0.14	0.98	0.04	0.45	0.01	40
45			12.98	21.14	8.13	6.78	6.20	3.51	3.97	1.19	2.71	0.47	1.83	0.18	1.10	0.05	0.51	0.01	45
50			14.42	25.70	9.04	8.24	6.89	4.26	4.41	1.44	3.01	0.57	2.03	0.22	1.23	0.06	0.56	0.01	50
55			15.87	30.66	9.94	9.83	7.58	5.09	4.85	1.72	3.31	0.68	2.23	0.26	1.35	0.08	0.62	0.01	55
60			17.31	36.02	10.85	11.55	8.27	5.97	5.30	2.02	3.61	0.80	2.44	0.31	1.47	0.09	0.68	0.01	60
65			18.75	41.77	11.75	13.40	8.96	6.93	5.74	2.35	3.92	0.93	2.64	0.36	1.59	0.10	0.73	0.02	65
70					12.65	15.37	9.65	7.95	6.18	2.69	4.22	1.06	2.84	0.41	1.72	0.12	0.79	0.02	70
75					13.56	17.47	10.34	9.03	6.62	3.06	4.52	1.21	3.05	0.46	1.84	0.14	0.85	0.02	75
80					14.46	19.68	11.03	10.18	7.06	3.44	4.82	1.36	3.25	0.52	1.96	0.15	0.90	0.02	80
85					15.37	22.02	11.72	11.39	7.50	3.85	5.12	1.52	3.45	0.59	2.09	0.17	0.96	0.03	85
90					16.27	24.48	12.41	12.66	7.95	4.28	5.42	1.69	3.66	0.65	2.21	0.19	1.02	0.03	90
95					17.18	27.06	13.10	13.99	8.39	4.74	5.72	1.87	3.86	0.72	2.33	0.21	1.07	0.03	95
100					18.08	29.76	13.79	15.39	8.83	5.21	6.03	2.06	4.07	0.79	2.46	0.23	1.13	0.04	100
110					19.89	35.50	15.17	18.36	9.71	6.21	6.63	2.45	4.47	0.94	2.70	0.28	1.24	0.04	110
120							16.54	21.57	10.60	7.30	7.23	2.88	4.88	1.11	2.95	0.33	1.36	0.05	120
130							17.92	25.02	11.48	8.47	7.84	3.34	5.29	1.29	3.19	0.38	1.47	0.06	130
140							19.30	28.70	12.36	9.71	8.44	3.84	5.69	1.47	3.44	0.43	1.59	0.07	140
150									13.25	11.04	9.04	4.36	6.10	1.68	3.69	0.49	1.70	0.08	150
160									14.13	12.44	9.64	4.91	6.51	1.89	3.93	0.55	1.81	0.08	160
170									15.01	13.91	10.25	5.50	6.91	2.11	4.18	0.62	1.93	0.09	170
180									15.90	15.47	10.85	6.11	7.32	2.35	4.42	0.69	2.04	0.11	180
190									16.78	17.10	11.45	6.75	7.73	2.60	4.67	0.76	2.15	0.12	190
200									17.66	18.80	12.06	7.43	8.14	2.85	4.92	0.84	2.27	0.13	200
225									19.87	23.38	13.56	9.24	9.15	3.55	5.53	1.04	2.55	0.16	225
250											15.07	11.23	10.17	4.31	6.15	1.27	2.83	0.19	250
275											16.58	13.39	11.19	5.15	6.76	1.51	3.12	0.23	275
300											18.09	15.74	12.21	6.05	7.38	1.78	3.40	0.27	300
325											19.60	18.25	13.22	7.01	7.99	2.06	3.69	0.31	325
350													14.24	8.05	8.61	2.36	3.97	0.36	350
375													15.26	9.14	9.22	2.69	4.25	0.41	375
400													16.28	10.30	9.84	3.03	4.54	0.46	400
425													17.29	11.53	10.45	3.39	4.82	0.52	425
450													18.31	12.81	11.07	3.77	5.11	0.57	450
475													19.33	14.16	11.68	4.16	5.39	0.63	475
500															12.30	4.58	5.67	0.70	500
550															13.53	5.46	6.24	0.83	550
600															14.76	6.42	6.81	0.98	600

Figure 29–8. A friction loss chart for a common class of plastic pipe

In the sample chart various pipe sizes are listed across the top. Beneath each size, two columns list the velocity in feet per second and the friction loss in pounds per square inch for various rates of water flow. The friction losses are for pipe lengths of 100 feet. For pipe lengths of less than 100 feet, the friction losses would be equivalently reduced.

Example

Given: Water flows through 100 feet of 2″ pipe at the rate of 9 gallons per minute.

Question: What is the velocity of the water and the friction loss?

Answer: Velocity is 0.79 feet per second (fps).
Friction loss is 0.06 pounds per square inch (psi).

Given: Water flows through 50 feet of ¾″ pipe at the rate of 10 gpm.

Question: What is the velocity of the water and the friction loss?

Answer: Velocity is 4.72 feet per second.
Friction loss = 4.31 psi × .50 = 2.16 pounds per square inch.

It is important to know not only the friction loss but also the water velocity in order to minimize surge pressure in the pipes. Also known as the water hammer effect, surge pressure is likely to occur when the velocity goes above 5 fps. Since velocity and pressure loss increase within a pipe as it is required to carry increasing amounts of water, it is necessary to increase the pipe size when friction loss becomes great or when the velocity approaches the 5 fps that will trigger the water hammer effect.

Example

Question: If a 100 feet long pipe has 20 GPM flowing through it, what is the smallest size of pipe that could be used?

Answer: From the chart in Figure 29–8, the first velocity below 5 fps is that for 1¼″ pipe, having a velocity of 3.61 fps.

Question: What would be the friction loss in the above pipe?

Answer: 1.51 psi

Given: Water passes through 100 feet of 1¼″ pipe at the rate of 20 GPM. The static pressure in the mainline equals 66.5 psi, the friction loss in the 1¼″ pipe is 1.51 psi, and the friction loss as water passes through the valve is 6 psi.

Question: What is the working (moving) water pressure?

Answer: Working water pressure = Static pressure – pressure loss in the valve – friction loss in the pipe.
= 66.5 psi – 6 psi – 1.51 psi
= 58.99 psi

Once through the valve, the water flows toward the first sprinkler. Again the pipe must be sized to assume enough pressure to pop the sprinkler out of the ground and deliver the desired amount of irrigation water, while avoiding surge pressure.

If the first sprinkler is 25 feet from the valve, reference to the chart finds the friction loss to be 0.38 psi (1.51 for 100 feet of pipe × .25) in 1¼″ pipe with a flow of 20 gpm. Subtracting the friction loss from the working pressure at the valve reveals a working pressure at the first sprinkler of 58.61 psi.

Sprinkler heads operate within ranges of pressure. Different types of sprinkler heads have different ranges of operation. Continuing with the above example, assume that the sprinkler head being used has a pressure range of 35 to 80 psi. The 58.61 psi of pressure at the first sprinkler head is within the operating range, so the head would pop up and deliver its prescribed amount of irrigation water. As an example, assume that the sprinkler heads of the system deliver 10 gpm. After 10 of the 20 gallons of water per minute are used at the first sprinkler, the remaining 10 gallons per minute flow on toward the second sprinkler, spaced 25 feet further away. Again, the pipe must be sized. From the sample chart in Figure 29–8, the smallest pipe size that will carry the 10 gpm with a velocity of less than 5 fps is ¾″ pipe. In a real situation, with a higher rate of flow and more sprinkler heads, it is sometimes wise to use a size larger than the smallest pipe possible in order to reduce the friction loss that can reduce working pressure. Conversely, when working pressure needs to be reduced to fit within the pressure range of the sprinklers, the use of a smaller pipe will increase the friction pressure and reduce working pressure in the pipe. A pressure regulator can also be placed along the pipe to reduce water pressure.

SELECTING AND LOCATING SPRINKLERS

Upon leaving the sprinklers under pressure, the irrigation water falls across the landscape in a pattern determined by the type of sprinkler head. Either circular or rectangular patterns are possible. The size of the sprinkler head is partly responsible for the amount of area covered. The other factor controlling area of coverage is the trajectory of the spray. Sprinkler head size is matched to the amount of water being delivered. Trajectory is the path of the water as it is propelled through the air. Flat or low trajectories are used in groundcover and beneath shrubs in planting beds. Higher trajectories are used for lawns and for plantings that are watered from overhead.

Sprinkler Pattern

Rectangular patterns fill prescribed areas that are, obviously, rectangular in shape. Circular patterns may be full or partial circles, in radii ranging from several feet to over a hundred feet. Figure 29–9 illustrates common circular patterns. An irrigation system designer must have a thorough knowledge of the hardware available before he or she can design an efficient system.

Locating the Sprinklers

The objective in the positioning of sprinklers is simple: to obtain an even distribution of water. Uneven irrigation causes inconsistent growth and wet and dry areas

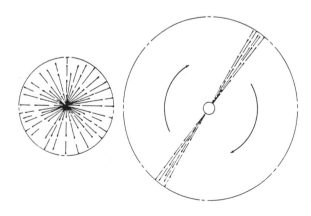

Figure 29–9. Common circular patterns

within the landscape. Sprinkler heads can be set out in either a square pattern or a triangular pattern, Figure 29–10. Triangular patterns are preferred because they give more even water distribution and waste less water. Both patterns rely upon overlapping of the spray arcs because each sprinkler only delivers the full amount of water to ⅔ of its diameter. The outer ⅓ would be drier and the distribution of water uneven were it not for the overlapping.

In a triangular layout, the sprinkler heads are positioned as an equilateral triangle, with equal space between all sprinklers. Where wind is not a predictable factor, the sprinkler arcs should be spaced at a distance that is 60% of the diameter of the arc. If wind is predictable and constant, spacing should be reduced. Manufacturers of sprinkler heads will provide recommendations for spacing of the sprinklers depending upon the various wind speeds. These recommendations should not be stretched.

To do so will only result in uneven water distribution. In free-form or narrow lawn areas, the spacing may be crowded if necessary, but not stretched.

Problem: To lay out the sprinkler heads in a square pattern for a rectangular lawn area that is 75' × 60'. Sprinklers will be used that require 15 feet spacing based upon wind conditions and the manufacturers' recommendations.

Solution: a) Select the bordering edge that most needs to avoid overspray in order to prevent slippery walks or wet people. Divide the length of the border by the recommended spacing of the sprinkler heads. Round up to the next whole number if necessary.

75 feet ÷ 15 feet = 5 spaces

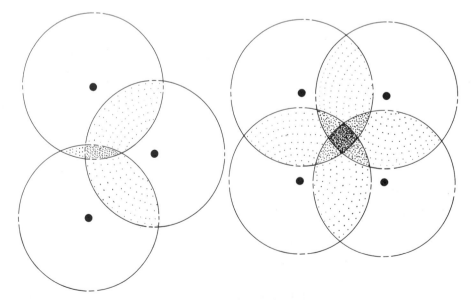

Figure 29–10. Triangular (left) and square (right) spray patterns

b) Divide the other edge length by the recommended spacing of the sprinkler heads. Again round up to the next whole number if necessary.

60 feet ÷ 15 = 4 spaces

c) Draw a grid across the scaled lawn, providing the calculated number of spaces. Locate sprinklers at all grid line intersections.

d) Select the appropriate sprinkler patterns to provide full coverage without overspray.

NOTE: In the example the border lengths divided evenly by the sprinkler spacing. When that is not possible, then an additional calculation is needed to determine the actual spacing of the sprinkler heads.

Example: If the border edge had been 79 feet, rather than 75 feet, the edge length would have been first divided by the ideal spacing:

79 feet ÷ 15 feet = 5.27 = 6 (round up to a whole number)

then divided again by that result to determine the actual spacing of the sprinklers:

79 feet ÷ 6 = 13.17 feet

Problem: To lay out the sprinkler heads for an 80′ × 65′ lawn area using a triangular pattern. Again, the sprinklers used will require 15 feet spacing to compensate for wind conditions.

Solution: a) Select the border edge where overspray must be avoided. Divide the length by the recommended spacing of the sprinkler heads and round up to the next whole number if necessary.

80 feet ÷ 15 = 5.33 = 6 spaces

b) Divide the border edge length by the number of spaces to determine the actual spacing of the sprinkler heads.

80 feet ÷ 6 spaces = 13.33 feet

c) Divide the other edge length by the recommended spacing of the sprinkler heads, rounding up to the next whole number if necessary.

65 feet ÷ 15 = 4.33 = 5 spaces

d) Divide the edge length by the number of spaces to determine the actual spacing of the sprinkler heads.

65 feet ÷ 5 spaces = 13 feet

e) Draw a grid across the scaled lawn, providing the calculated number of spaces. Then locate the sprinkler heads in a pattern that approximates equilateral triangles as closely as possible.

f) Select the appropriate sprinkler patterns to provide full coverage without overspray.

TRICKLE IRRIGATION

For a quick review of the characteristics of trickle irrigation, consult Table 29–1. The system is useful in any situation where slow water application in preferable to sprinkler irrigation due to constraints of space, budget, or limited water supply. Instead of a sprinkler head, water is delivered from an emitter attached to a thin plastic or polyethylene tube. The delivery rate is measured in gallons per hour (gph), and is much slower than the gallons per minute delivery of sprinkler irrigation systems.

Emitters

There are two types of emitters: pressure compensating and non-compensating emitters. The difference is based upon their ability or inability to deliver a constant gph over a wide range of water pressures. In landscapes where there is rolling topography, the rise and fall of the land causes drastic inconsistency in the water pressure in the thin tubes. Pressure compensating emitters are designed to allow for that variation and still deliver the intended amount of water and the desired rate. Non-compensating emitters cannot adjust to varied water pressures. If the pressure changes, their delivery rate changes too. In order to compensate for the effects of topographic variation on water pressure, it is common to use pressure regulators to reduce water pressure at points within the trickle system. Doing this permits the non-compensating emitters to deliver water at their intended rate of flow.

Tube and Emitter Placement

Drip tubing is not visually offensive and can be stretched atop most planting beds or hidden inconspicuously beneath the mulch of the bed. Emitters may be attached directly to the tube or extended away from the tube using micro tubing. For large areas such as shrub plantings, multiple emitters are needed at a plant if sufficient water is to be provided.

In determining the number of emitters needed for a plant, the irrigation designer must consider the soil type and the subsurface wetting pattern that it promotes, the canopy area of the plant, and the percent of the plant's root zone that is to be wetted. It is only necesssary to wet 50% of the root zone of most plants to provide the benefits of irrigation. Placement of the emitters should avoid direct contact with the trunk or stem of the plant. Failure to do so can result in soil pockets that are too wet too long and the health of the plant can be affected.

Subsurface wetting patterns are influenced by the type of soil being irrigated. In sandy soil, with its large particles, the water will move more vertically than horizontally. In fine soils like clay, with small soil particles, the movement of water is more horizontal than vertical.

Where the irrigation water contains high concentrations of sodium or chloride or both, trickle irrigation can encourage a dangerous salt build-up that can kill the plant. Improperly spaced emitters are the usual cause of the problem. Properly spaced, the emitters can both prevent the build-up and encourage the leaching of harmful salts away from the root zone.

Knowing the subsurface wetting patterns is important so that they can be overlapped and enough water applied to leach the salts away. Table 29–5 offers examples of the areas wetted by emitters in different soil types. A designer would need this information to plan for proper emitter placement.

Table 29–5. Soil Types and Emitter Wetting

Soil Type	Area Wetted Per Emitter	Diameter Wetted
Clay soil	65 to 160 square feet	9 to 14 feet
Loam soil	21 to 65 square feet	5 to 9 feet
Sandy soil	5 to 21 square feet	2 ½ to 5 feet

The limitation of an introductory chapter to a complex subject is that it raises more questions in the reader's mind than it is prepared to answer. This chapter is not intended as a full coverage of landscape irrigation. It attempts only to introduce the subject to students and offer a few ideas and examples. Texts devoted solely to this single subject should be consulted before attempting work with irrigation systems.

THE FUTURE

While landscape irrigation is not a technology still in its infancy, neither is it a technology standing still. In most parts of the country, water availability and quality are on-going concerns. While the demand for landscape irrigation of home and commercial landscapes grows, the water resources needed to supply the systems do not grow. Many regions, especially in arid areas, are already using water faster than it can be cleansed and purified or replaced, Figure 29–11. In such regions the mere sight of an irrigation system in operation is, to some people, like waving a red flag in front of a bull. It is seen as a wasteful, aristocratic use of a precious and increasingly expensive resource, Figure 29–12.

For these and other reasons, the future of landscape irrigation will be shaped or altered by many factors. Among them:

- Turfgrasses, groundcovers, and other landscape plants will be bred, select-

Figure 29–11. An arid land (Photo courtesy of Utah Agricultural Experiment Station)

Figure 29–12. Water delivery by concrete canal (Photo courtesy of Utah Agricultural Experiment Station)

ed, and used on the basis of their low water requirements.

- Passive water conservation methods such as the proper placement of trees for shading buildings, lawns, and plantings will become more topical.
- Computer operation of irrigation systems as well as the use of computers to organize preventive maintenance programs for the system is now a reality. Computer aided design of complex irrigation systems is also common today. The future will find even greater reliance upon the computer. It is

not unlikely that the computer will enable the system to detect its own leaks, pinpoint the location and send for repair assistance.

- Alternative sources of water for irrigation systems will be sought. *Effluent* water (treated sewage) and other types of reclaimed water may be possible sources.
- Irrigation systems will become more responsive to the actual need for water rather than merely using a timer that turns on the water whether it is needed or not.

- Systems may have sensors built in that will shut down the system when excessive winds cause inefficiency and waste.
- Systems may be powered by self-contained energy systems such as solar panels.
- The position of water manager will become a valued and professional field of career specialization.

ACHIEVEMENT REVIEW

I. Briefly trace the development of irrigation from its agricultural beginnings to its present use in landscapes. Give examples of landscape irrigation systems in operation within your community.

II. Indicate if the following features are most typical of
(A) sprinkler systems   or   (B) trickle systems

a. less expensive due to the comparative simplicity of the system
b. maintenance is high since the system must be checked constantly to be certain it is working
c. water delivery is over the top of the plants and onto the soil beneath
d. water is delivered through an emitter
e. water is delivered through spray heads or rotary heads
f. water run-off is less due to the slow speed of delivery
g. water pressure at the delivery site is the greatest

III. Insert the proper term to complete the following definitions.

a. _____ heads move in a circle and propel water in a circle.
b. The specific distribution pattern of a sprinkler head is its _____.
c. _____ heads are driven by a spring loaded arm that responds to water pressure and bumps the sprinkler around in a circle.
d. The amount of water placed over a landscape area by a sprinkler is the _____.
e. The _____ is the delivery device for trickle irrigation.
f. The amount of water flowing from an irrigation system over a measured period of time is the _____ rate of the system.

g. The _____ of PVC pipe is a measure of its strength.

h. A PVC pipe used to carry water through an irrigation system is termed _____ pipe.

i. _____ is the loss of pressure during water flow resulting from the increasing speed of water, the increasing pipe length, and the roughness of the lining of the pipe.

j. Velocity is the rate of _____, as expressed in feet per second.

k. When the water velocity is too high and is suddenly stopped, water hammer or _____ pressure can result.

l. The pressure present in a closed system, when the water is not flowing, is termed _____ pressure.

m. As water flows past a point and responds to rises or falls within the system, its pressure becomes _____.

IV. Indicate if the following characteristics of sprinkler heads apply to

    A. spray heads   C. both

    B. rotary heads   D. neither

a. the heads are available in pop up styles

b. they have no moving parts

c. they are able to propel water across the greatest distance

d. water is distributed in full or partial circles

e. water is applied most rapidly

f. their spray pattern is affected by the wind

V. State whether the following statements are (T) true or (F) false

a. Spray heads have a higher precipitation rate than rotary heads have.

b. The discharge rate of the irrigation system must be matched with the rate at which plants can absorb the water.

c. Discharge rate is measured in gallons per minute.

d. Plant water needs are measured in gallons per week.

e. It is not possible to convert from gallons per minute to inches per week.

f. Not all plants require the same amount of water for optimum growth.

g. Sandy soil has a slower rate of absorption than clay soil.

h. Loams drain the best of all soil types.

i. Geographical areas contain a variety of plants and soils having a diversity of water needs and absorption rates.

VI. As concisely as possible, answer the following questions in essay form.

a. Why does the size of irrigation pipe matter?

b. How doe the terms *upstream* and *downstream* relate to water volume in an irrigation pipe?

c. What factors affect working water pressure?

d. What is a friction loss chart?

e. What relationship exists between water hammer, a water velocity of 5 fps and the size of irrigation pipe?

VII. Fill in the blanks to make the following paragraph read correctly.

In a trickle irrigation system, the water is delivered through _____. There are two types of these. They are pressure compensating and _____. Pressure compensating emitters deliver a constant rate of water over a wide range of _____. The use of _____ enables non-compensating emitters to do the same thing. In determining the number of emitters to specify, an irrigation designer must consider the _____ type and the _____ pattern, as well as the canopy of the plant and the percent of the _____ system that is to be wetted. It is only necessary to wet _____ percent of the root system of most plants to provide proper irrigation. Should the irrigation water contain high concentrations of sodium, chloride, or both, dangerous levels of _____ may build up in the soil.

SECTION 9

THE
INTERIOR
PLANTSCAPE

UNIT 30

INTERIOR PLANTSCAPING

OBJECTIVES

Upon completion of this unit students will be able to:

- discuss the current status of the interior plantscape industry.
- list problems unique to the interior use of plants.
- describe the role of light quality, intensity, and duration.
- list the characteristics of a good growing medium.
- explain the steps in proper installation, watering, and drainage.
- describe the interdisciplinary relationship required between architects, landscape architects, interior plantscapers, and maintenance professionals.

CONTAINERIZING PLANTS, PAST AND PRESENT

The human need and pleasure in having plants within our homes and places of business and play are rooted in antiquity. The ancient Greeks, Romans, and Egyptians commonly grew plants in containers to provide herbs for cooking, fragrance, and/or medicinal uses. To some extent most cultures, primitive or civilized, have used plants to add color, texture, softness, and a sense of life to their static, fabricated interior environments.

In America, the residential use of interior plantings has expanded from houseplants and holiday flowers to large trees and exotic desert and jungle species. The soaring popularity of interior plants began in the mid-1970s. America currently leads the world in the development and appreciation of interior plantscapes. Commercially, it is now expected that every new shopping mall, office building, hospital, or hotel will have plants featured prominently in the interior public areas. Most knowledgeable employers are aware of the increased productivity and reduced absenteeism of employees who have living, green plants as part of their working environment. Therefore, interior plantings are not limited just to the public areas; but are now evident within the nation's workplaces as well, Figures 30–1 and 30–2. Architects and interior decorators recognize that plants are as much a part of the indoor room as furniture, carpeting, and wall coverings. Properly selected and displayed, interior plantings duplicate the role and contribution of fine art to the mood and ambiance of a room.

So explosive was the demand for interior plantings in public buildings that the technology necessary to assure the plants' survival was not always able to keep pace. Some of the early efforts, heralded for their aesthetics, became corporate embarrassments a few months later. The lush green lobbies were replaced with dead stalks and leaf littered carpets. Because the architects

and decorators were working with living materials, their failure to consider such foreign requirements as light, water, drainage, and fertilizer is understandable. Now they appreciate the differences between fabrics and philodendrons, and the mistakes of the past are less likely to be repeated.

The past decade has seen the technology needed to sustain plants indoors catch up to the public demand for lavish plantings. The new profession of interior plantscaping is still evolving and is still very labor-intensive. Certainly the next few years will find some advances being made in the way that interior plantings are prepared for installation, irrigated, and drained. New species will be tried. Some will do well and gain public acceptance, while others will

Figure 30–1. Interior plantscaping has expanded throughout the country. It enhances shopping malls and office complexes by providing a natural garden atmosphere. (from Reiley and Shry/Introductory Horticulture, fourth edition, copyright 1991 by Delmar Publishers Inc., Richard Kreh, photographer)

Figure 30–2. Interior plantscaping creates attractive natural barriers to direct the flow of pedestrian traffic. It also provides an area where shoppers or office workers can relax in a peaceful environment. (From Reiley and Shry/Introductory Horticulture, fourth edition, copyright 1991 by Delmar Publishers Inc.)

not adjust to the change from outdoors to indoors. Thus, while the profession is no longer in its infancy, it has not yet reached maturity. It is entering into a new stage of rapid and exciting growth; learning from past mistakes.

THE MATERIALS

As the profession has developed and changed, so has the array of plants used to create the interiorscapes. Yesterday's window sill full of ivy and geraniums has been supplemented with containerized trees, in-ground installations, and lavish, changing displays of seasonal color.

Tropical foliage plants are the most pop-ular and successful indoor plants for long term installations. This is because they do not require the period of cool temperature dormancy that often makes temperate zone plants unsatisfactory. Originally collected from the jungles of South America, Africa, and other exotic locales, these plants are now grown in the greenhouses and nurser-ies of Florida, California, Texas, New York, Ohio, Pennsylvania, and Latin America, Figure 30–3.

Other plants finding their way into the residential and commercial interior plant-scapes of America include subtropical plants such as cacti, traditional and short-lived flowering plants such as poinsettias and mums, and even turf grasses, Figure 30–4.

Figure 30–3. Tropical foliage plants are now grown in greenhouses and nurseries. (from Cooper/Agriscience, copyright 1990 by Delmar Publishers Inc.)

Figure 30–4. Poinsettia varieties grown for the winter holiday season (from Reiley and Shry/ Introductory Horticulture, fourth edition, copyright 1991 by Delmar Publishers Inc.)

UNIQUENESS OF INTERIOR PLANTSCAPES

The transplanting of any plant from its production site to the plantscape site involves some risk, even if it is an exterior plant. When the plant is intended for interior use, the relocation initiates problems that no exterior landscaper faces. Among them:

- A drastic reduction in the quality and intensity of light.
- Reduction and constriction of the plant's root system.
- Replacement of natural rainfall by dependency upon humans for watering.
- A reduction in nutrient requirements and a potential for build-up of soluble salts (fertilizers).
- A lack of air movement and rainfall, allowing dust to accumulate on leaves, often plugging stomata and reducing photosynthesis.
- Potential damage by air conditioners, central heating systems, cleaning chemicals, water additives, and other irritants.

Under these conditions, plants may sustain themselves but they seldom grow. Because of this, it is unnecessary to space plants for expansion; but it is necessary to install them in a manner that permits the replacement of dead or unsightly individuals as needed.

LIGHT AND INTERIOR PLANTINGS

Everyone knows that plants require light to survive and grow. Not everyone knows that there are differences in the *kinds* and *sources* of light. Also, few but horticulturists consider the *amount* of light that plants require. Yet despite how little some people know about the survival needs of interior plantings, expectations for survival of the plantings are always high and frequently disappointed.

How long will plants live indoors? The answer depends upon the plant and the quality of installation and maintenance. However, in interior design as elsewhere, nothing lasts forever. Carpets wear thin; furniture nicks and sags; walls require fresh paint. Plants must be regarded as perishable furnishings as well. If installed correctly into a properly designed setting and maintained properly, the plantscape will serve satisfactorily for a time period that will unquestionably justify its cost. Then it will require at least partial replacement.

Light Intensity

Human activities do not require as much light as that required for the growth of plants. Even modern homes and buildings with extensive windows and skylights are unable to provide a light intensity equaling the outdoors. Glass filters the sun's light such that an unshaded greenhouse still reduces the intensity of sunlight by at least 15 percent.

To understand light intensity requires knowing how light is measured. Light intensity is expressed in the units of *lux* or *foot-candles*. A *lux* is the amount of illumination received on a surface that is 1 meter from a standard light source known as unity. A lux is an international measurement comparable in use to the metric system. In the United States, the footcandle unit is more commonly used and understood. One *footcandle* (fc) is equal to the amount of light produced by a standard candle at a distance of one foot. Direct-reading meters are manufactured that measure light intensity in footcandles up to 10,000. That is the intensity of sunlight on a typical clear, summer day in the temperate zone. In the south, intensity can approach 20,000 fc. A light meter is the only way to measure light intensity accurately and should be the first piece of equipment purchased by a beginning interior plantscaper, Figure 30–5.

The challenge of bringing plants accustomed to outdoor light intensities approaching 20,000 fc into a home or shopping mall is best appreciated through several examples. The average residential living room has a light intensity of 10 to 1,000 fc by day and as few as 5 fc at night. A good reading light provides 20 to 30 fc. A word processor operator may have 40 to 50 fc of illumination on the keyboard's surface. The average shopping mall provides 20 to 30 fc of light in pedestrian circulation areas and up to 100 fc in sales areas.

Figure 30–5. Light meter calibrated in foot candles (from Boodley/The Commercial Greenhouse, copyright 1981 by Delmar Publishers Inc.)

Acclimatization

Long before interior plantings are installed, the plants must be prepared to survive in their new, reduced light setting. The adjustment of an outdoor plant to interior conditions is known as *acclimatization*. Proper acclimatization changes the plant's physiology (biological functioning) and morphology (physical structure). While there is still much to be learned about the adjustment of plants from outdoor to indoor growing sites, it is to the credit of forward-looking industry groups such as the Florida Foliage Association and the Interior Plantscape Division of the Associated Landscape Contractors of America that our present body of knowledge exists.

Acclimatization is directed at the adjustment of four vital factors that determine the survival of all plants: light, nutrients, moisture, and temperature. Under field or greenhouse conditions, the plants' metabolisms have been at or near optimum levels. As the times of harvest, transplanting, and interior installation near, the metabolic activity must be slowed to minimal levels that permit survival and maintain an attractive appearance. Extensive additional growth is seldom an objective.

Light Intensity Acclimatization.

The objective of light intensity acclimatization is to reduce the plant's light needs to a level where *photosynthesis* (the production of food) just slightly exceeds *respiration* (the use of food reserves for growth and maintenance). The point of exact balance is known as the *light compensation point* (LCP). Since a plant's ability to capture the energy of light declines as the plant ages, light levels in the interiorscape must be slightly above the LCP of the plant for long term survival of the plant.

Light intensity acclimatization should begin at the greenhouse or nursery, prior to shipment to the interior site. Plant leaves that are produced in high light intensities are smaller and thicker than those produced under reduced light conditions. The smaller, thicker leaf reduces the potential of radiation damage from the sun. That danger does not exist in the interior setting. During the acclimatization period that may take as long as six months, the new leaves become thinner and larger to permit most efficient capture of the light energy that will sustain them in their interior location. The change in the leaf structure is both morphological and physiological.

Light intensity is reduced gradually over a period of several weeks or months. Each change reduces the light by 50 percent until the desired intensity (usually 100 to 200 fc) is reached. The acclimatization process cannot be rushed without a severe reaction by the plant. That reaction may range from partial leaf drop to death.

Nutrient Acclimatization.

Critical to the survival of the plant in its new interior setting is a healthy root system that is in balance with the leafy greenery of the plant. As the plant's ability to photosynthesize is scaled down by the reduced light intensity, so too is the amount of nutrients that need to be taken up by the roots in support of the plant's growth. Thorough soil *leaching* (flushing with water until it flows freely from the bottom of the container) at the beginning of the acclimatization and occasionally afterwards, will prevent a build-up of soluble salts (fertilizers). Soluble salt accumulations can damage the root system.

Following the leaching process later fertilizations are less frequent than when the plant was growing under high light intensity. The reduction in fertilization must be coordinated with the reduction in light as closely as possible for successful acclimatization.

Moisture Acclimatization.   Both the frequency of watering and the high humidity levels of the production area are gradually reduced as the plant is prepared for relocation. The interior site will be very stressful to the plant since office buildings and malls are kept at low humidity levels for greater human comfort.

Temperature Acclimatization.   Production area temperatures are usually higher than human comfort levels in order to promote more rapid plant growth. During acclimatization, temperatures are gradually reduced to the 65°F to 75°F range that is common to most interior areas.

Light Quality

Once acclimatized to the reduced light intensity of the interior site, the interior plantscape may still prove unsatisfactory if the qaulity of light is incorrect. *Light quality* is the color of light emitted by a particular source. The sun emits all colors of light, some of which the human eye can perceive and others that are unseen by humans but beneficial to plants. The green-yellow light most comfortable for humans is of little use in photosynthesis by plants. They depend on light from the blue and red bands of the visible light spectrum. Visible light is only a narrow region of the radiant light spectrum, Figure 30–6.

As long as both humans and plants can derive their light energy from the sun, the needs of each are satisfied. Indoors, however, where light energy is usually created or supplemented by artificial means, the

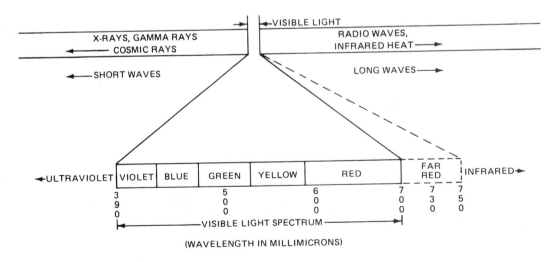

Figure 30–6. Electromagnetic spectrum and spectral distribution of visible light

quality of light can vary considerably. Light selected solely for its benefit to plants may cause the skin tones to human beings to appear ashen and deathly. In similar fashion, an interior decorator may specify a quality of lighting that gives human complexion a healthy glow while making nearby plantings appear brown and dead. Not all lamps provide the same quality of light, nor does any lamp provide a constant quality or intensity as the distance between the lamp and the plants changes. Categories and examples of lamps that have some use in interior plantscaping are shown in Table 30–1. Table 30–2 compares the lamps in all areas important to interior plant survival. You should study these tables thoroughly before proceeding further.

Interior plantings are seldom illuminated from a single source or type of light. For example, consider the plantscape of a typical office. The plants may be permanently set or in movable planters. Their functions may be to serve as room dividers, establish a mood, or relieve a cluttered desk top. The ceiling may be 8 or 10 feet high. Side windows or a skylight may admit some natural light. In such a setting, cool white fluorescent lighting would be ideal for both general lighting and the maintenance of the plants. People, plants, and furnishings look natural beneath cool white light due to its excellent color rendition. If additional task lighting is needed, small desk lights should be used. Special effects such as shadows or textured highlights can be created with incandescent lights installed beneath the plants and directed upward. (These are called uplights.) Some benefit will accrue to the plants from the addition of lighting at the base. However, if supplemental lighting is needed for photosynthesis, it is most efficient when applied from overhead.

A shopping mall presents a different situation. The corridors may have ceilings too high to permit the use of fluorescent lamps, which are not good for illumination when the ceiling is much beyond ten feet. There may be skylights as well as decorative architectural lighting. Overall illumination by mercury or metal halide lamps would be best. As in an office, supplemental or decorative lighting might also be desirable for special effects or the health of the plants. When uplights are used, they should be installed directly into the planters and waterproofed. When supplemental lights are added for overhead illumination, they should be positioned to light the plants fully without shining in the eyes of viewers.

In both examples the total light radiation may be from several sources, some natural and some artificial. Add additional, perhaps uncontrollable, sources of light such as store windows, electrical signs, and reflective surfaces, and the task of determining the total quality and quantity of illumination becomes complex.

Table 30–1. Lamps for Interior Plant Illumination

1. **Tungsten filament incandescent lamps**
   - Standard (the familiar household lightbulb)
   - Reflector (spot or flood lights)
   - Parabolic aluminized reflector (a weather-resistant type of floodlight with a more precise beam)
   - Incandescent plant lamps (not proven to be any better than the standard incandescent)
2. **Fluorescent lamps**
   - Cool white
   - Warm white
   - Plant lamps
   - Wide spectrum plant lamps
3. **High-intensity discharge lamps**
   - Mercury
   - Metal halide
   - High-pressure sodium

Table 30–2. A Comparison of Artificial Lighting Sources for Interior Plantscapes

Lamp Type	How Light Is Produced	Quality of Light Produced	Percent of Visible Light Radiation	Color Rendition	Initial Cost	Operat-ing Cost
Incandescent (all types)	Current flows through a tungsten filament heating it and making it glow.	High in red light; low in blue light	7–11	Good	Low	High
Cool White Fluorescent	Phosphor coating inside the glass tube is acted upon by radiation from a mercury arc.	High in blue and yellow-green light; low in red light	22	Good (blends with natural daylight)	Moderate	Moderate
Warm White Fluorescent	Phosphor coating inside the glass tube is acted upon by radiation from a mercury arc.	Low in blue and green light; more yellow and red light	22	Poor (blends with incandescent light)	Moderate	Moderate
Fluorescent Plant Growth Lamps	Same as other fluorescents. Special phosphors transmit most light energy in blue and red light regions of the spectrum.	High in red and blue light; low in yellow-green light	22	Average (enhances red and blue colors; darkens green colors)	Moderate	Moderate
Wide Spectrum Plant Growth	Same as other fluorescents. Special phosphors transmit most light energy in blue and red light regions of the spectrum.	Less blue and red than standard plant growth lamps; more far-red and yellow-green light	22	Average (favors red and blue colors; darkens green colors)	Moderate	Moderate
Mercury (Deluxe white model, for interior plants)	An electric arc is passed through mercury vapor.	High in yellow-green light; less red and blue light, but still usable for plant growth	13	Poor (favors blue and green colors)	High	Moderate
Metal Halide	Similar to mercury lamps but with metal gas additives to produce a different spectrum	High in yellow-green light; less red and blue light, but usable for growth	20–23	Good (similar to CW fluorescent)	High	Low

Life of the Lamp	Placement Height Above Plants	Plant Responses	Major Advantages	Major Disadvantages
750 to 2000 hours	At least 3 feet to avoid foliage burn	Plants become long and spindly with pale foliage. Flowering is promoted and senescence is accelerated.	• Good for special lighting effects • Compact source of light • Simple installation	• Energy inefficient; too much lost as heat • Light does not distribute evenly over a surface. • Glass blackens with time and light output is reduced. • Frequent replacement is needed.
Up to 20,000 hours	10 feet or less	Plants stay short and compact. Side shoots develop. Flowering extends over a longer period.	• Energy efficient • Heat is radiated over the length of the lamp, allowing closer proximity to plant foliage. • Light distributed more evenly over a flat surface	• Light does not focus well. • They are difficult to start when line voltage drops or humidity is high. • Installation is expensive. • Special fixtures are needed.
Up to 20,000 hours	10 feet or less	Same as CW fluorescent	• Same as CW fluorescent	• Same as CW fluorescent
Up to 20,000 hours	10 feet or less	Rich green foliage color. Large leaf size. Side shoots develop. Plants stay short. Flowering is delayed.	• Same as CW fluorescent • Light emission is from the region of the spectrum most important to photosynthesis.	• Same as CW fluorescent • Greater expense with little increase in benefit to the plants
Up to 20,000 hours	10 feet or less	Stems elongate. Side shoots are suppressed. Flowering is promoted. Plants age rapidly.	• Same as CW fluorescent	• Same as CW fluorescent • Growth may not be desired. • Poor color rendition on nonplant materials
Up to 24,000 hours	10–15 feet or more	Plants respond in a manner similar to CW fluorescent.	• Long life; useful for inaccessible fixtures • Medium energy efficiency	• Not interchangeable with other lamps • Warm-up time required
Up to 20,000 hours	10–15 feet or more	Plants respond in a manner similar to CW fluorescent.	• High energy efficiency, surpassing the mercury lamp • Good for both plant and general lighting	• Warm-up time required • Color and light quality change with operating hours.

Table 30–2. A Comparison of Artificial Lighting Sources for Interior Plantscapes (continued)

Lamp Type	How Light Is Produced	Quality of Light Produced	Percent of Visible Light Radiation	Color Rendition	Initial Cost	Operating Cost
High Pressure Sodium	Sodium is vaporized into an arc.	High in yellow-orange-red light	25–27	Poor (similar to WW fluorescent)	High	Low
Low Pressure Sodium	Sodium is vaporized into an arc	High in yellow-orange-red light	31–35	Poor	High	Low

Determining Total Radiation. Dr. Henry Cathey, director of the U.S. National Arboretum, and Lowell Campbell, an agricultural engineer at the U.S. Department of Agriculture have developed conversion factors that enable light meter measurements of light from different sources to be converted to a common basis of measurement. The unit of measurement is *watts per square meter*, Table 30–3.

By taking independent light meter readings of the footcandles of illumination that

Table 30–3. Conversion Factors for Determining Watts Per Square Meter for Various Light Sources

Light Source	Conversion Factor
Daylight	0.055
High-pressure sodium lamps	0.034
Low-pressure sodium lamps	0.022
Metal halide lamps	0.034
Cool white fluorescent lamps	0.030
Warm white fluorescent lamps	0.030
Fluorescent grow lamps	0.044
Incandescent lamps	0.090
Mercury incandescent lamps	0.070

fall upon the plants from each light source during the brightest periods of the day and during various times of the year, then multiplying by the conversion factor for that particular light source, the amount of radiation is determined. All readings should be taken at plant level. Each reading must be taken when the other light sources are off. Then the interior plantscaper can add the separate measurements together to determine if the proper total illumination is being provided. Cathey and Campbell report that most interior plantings can be maintained in a healthy state if given a minimum of 9 watts per square meter of illumination for 12 hours each day.

Natural Light

Most important of all light sources for interior plantscapes is natural sunlight when it can be planned for and depended upon. Each footcandle of illumination that nature provides is one less that has to be provided and paid for with artificial lighting. In our energy-conscious society, such savings are worth planning for. However,

Life of the Lamp	Placement Height Above Plants	Plant Responses	Major Advantages	Major Disadvantages
Up to 24,000 hours	10–15 feet or more	Typical red-light plant responses; similar to fluorescent plant growth lamps when compared on equal energy	• High energy efficiency. When combined with blue light sources (such as metal halide), they provide good lighting for plants and people. • Long life	• Yellow color makes them unsatisfactory for general indoor lighting by themselves.
Up to 18,000 hours	10 feet or less	Plants respond in a manner similar to HP sodium	• The most energy efficient lamps available	• Yellow color makes them unsuitable where color rendition is important. They must be used at night after closing

knowledge of how to maximize the benefits of natural light is vital; otherwise more heat energy is lost through inefficient windows than is gained in light energy.

Natural light is most helpful when it offers high levels of illumination throughout most of the year. Traditionally sunny areas like the Southwest can make better use of natural light than areas like the Northeast, where clouds block the sun and snow blankets the skylights through much of the winter season.

Sunlight entering from overhead is of greater use in the illumination of interior plantings than light entering from the side, although both are helpful. In neither situation will the natural light be as intense as outside light. It will be significantly reduced by the glass glazing through which it passes and the distance it travels between the point of entry and the leaf surface. Little usable light passes more than 15 feet beyond glass, so skylights in high lobby areas or shopping malls are of no benefit to plantings beneath them. Nevertheless, they can be of great benefit in single-story buildings with lower ceilings. In a similar fashion, a large interior plantscape may derive little benefit from side lighting, since usable light enters at a 45° angle and plants must be placed within that narrow beam if they are to benefit, Figure 30-7. They cannot be too close to the glass or the foliage may burn, however. In a smaller room, as in a residence, natural side light can be of great value.

When skylights are used, they must be designed to permit the most light to enter while insulating against as much winter heat loss as possible. Within the limits allowed by heating and structural engineering, the ceiling well through which the light passes should be as wide and shallow as possible, with the sides painted a reflective white and beveled outward at 45° angles, Figure 30-8. As skylights become more narrow and the ceiling well deeper, there is less area through which the sunlight can enter and a narrower focus of illumination on the surfaces below. The difference between wide, shallow skylights and narrow, deep ones is similar to the difference in illumination between a floodlight

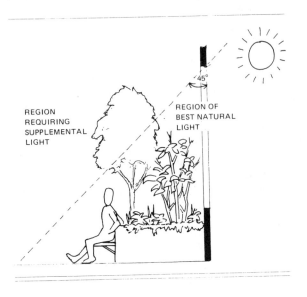

Figure 30–7. Interior plantings receive the best quality of natural light within a 45 degree arc of the side windows

and a spotlight. With natural light and interior plantings, the wide floodlight effect is most desirable.

Selecting the Correct Lighting

In summary, no single recipe for correct lighting can be given. There will be varied settings, needs, and objectives to accommodate. Plants will seldom be the only consideration in the selection of lamps and the quality of illumination. When both plants and people are to be considered, a lamp should be selected that provides the yellow-green visible light needed to render human complexion, clothing, and furnishings attractive, while still providing sufficient blue and red light to allow photosynthesis to exceed respiration in the plants. The cool white fluorescent lamp is ideal for a such a

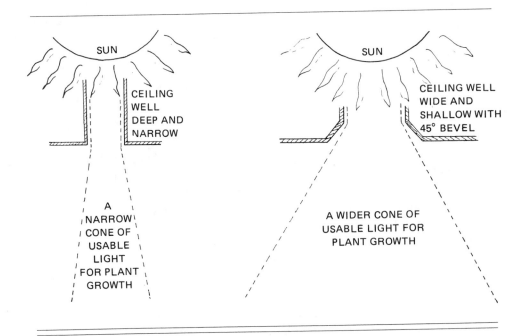

Figure 30–8. Cross-sectional view of skylights, and the influence of their design on the amount of light available to plants.

situation provided that the ceiling is not too high and that growth of the plants is not an objective. If growth is desired, additional incandescent lighting can be focused directly on the plants. The use of more expensive growth lamps is unnecessary since they have not been proven superior to the ordinary cool white fluorescent in maintaining plant health, and they do not render color well. Any natural light that can be used advantageously will reduce the cost of lighting the interior planting.

As for light intensity, not all plants available from growers have been carefully studied to determine the minimum at which they will survive attractively. The ALCA, the FFA, and the colleges of agriculture in the major foliage production states should be queried by anyone responsible for creating an interior plantscape. The many books that purport to give lighting specifications and that stock the shelves of libraries nationwide are satisfactory for home owners but not for professional use. Their information is often dated, usually based upon greenhouse lighting, and my be questionable in its accuracy. Recommendations should be sought that give lighting minimums in footcandles, not in general terms such as high, medium, and low. When plants are installed without documented knowledge of their lighting requirements, the situation is risky at best and the plants must be watched carefully to determine if additional lighting is needed.

To assure that lighting is of the right intensity and duration, a simple timing device may be necessary. The lights must shine on the leaves for enough time each day (twelve hours minimum) to allow adequate photosynthesis to occur. Should the hours of lighting have to be reduced for some reason, the intensity of the lighting must be increased to compensate, Figure 30–9. It does not seem to matter whether foliage plants receive their needed lighting over a short or long period as long as the cumulative photosynthetic activity balances and slightly exceeds respiration. With flowering plants, day length often plays a critical role in determining if and when the blossoms will appear. Since interior plantings are currently valued most for their foliage, day length is of limited importance.

THE GROWING MEDIUM

No less important than light to the successful acclimatization of interior plants is the provision of a proper growing medium. The roots must be placed in an environment that provides structural support, allows the roots to absorb water, and provides essential minerals. Further, the growing medium must allow rapid drainage of water past the root zone and provide the correct pH for growth.

The medium that serves when plants are growing in a nursery field or production container is likely to be inappropriate

Figure 30–9. A timing system can be used to provide supplemental light for an interior plantscape. (from Ingels/Ornamental Horticulture, copyright 1985 by Delmar Publishers Inc.)

for an interior installation. Natural field soil may be:

- too heavy to permit rapid drainage
- too heavy for the floor to support if the container is large
- inconsistent in composition, making standardized maintenance of separate planters difficult
- infested with insects, pathogens, or weeds

Although pasteurized natural soil may be a component of the growing medium for interior plantings, additives will probably be needed. It is even possible that the growing medium selected for the interior plantscape will have no natural soil in it for reasons of improved drainage, hygiene, pH balance, or nutritional consistency. The use of synthetic soils, whose composition is as controlled as a cake recipe, is becoming the rule rather than the exception.

Cornell University and the University of California have been leaders in the formulation of synthetic soils for interior plant production. The Cornell mixes are made from vermiculite or perlite and sphagnum moss. The University of California (U.C.) mixes are made from fine dune sand and sphagnum moss. The ratio of components varies with the species of plants and the maintenance program to be followed.

In addition to the U.C. and Cornell mixes (termed the peat-lite mixes) there are bark mixes, composed of pine bark, sand, and sphagnum moss. These are especially acidic growing media and may require buffering (with dolomitic and hydrated lime) to sustain healthy plants.

All of the synthetic soils are mixed and sold commercially. In large interior installa-

tions, it may be more economical to mix the medium at the site rather than purchase the premixed commercial products. All decisions about the growing medium should be made before the planters are filled and the plants installed. Once planted, errors in the medium's composition are difficult to correct without removing the plant.

Because the artificial media have low nutritional value for the plant, complete fertilizers are required as well as periodic application of the minor elements. Regular soil testing is necessary to assure that the fertilization program is correct.

Installing the Plants

The acclimatization of a plant's root system involves establishment of the correct relationship between roots and foliage. Outdoors, a sizeable root system is needed to supply adequate amounts of water and minerals to the leaves for near-maximal photosynthesis. Indoors, photosynthesis is reduced to survival-maintenance levels, so the root system need not be as large. Thus, one of the first steps at the time of installation is to remove the production medium from around the roots and prune away excess roots, Figure 30–10.

Several methods can be used for setting plants into an interior plantscape, depending upon whether the plants are to be placed in ground beds or raised planters. The anticipated frequency of plant replacement will partially determine the method of installation. For example, large trees are often permanently planted in the floor of an enclosed shopping mall because they are too large and expensive to replace, Figure 30–11. The growing medium around them must permit good drainage and retain nutrients,

Figure 30–10. Excess roots are pruned off the foliage plant before transplanting to establish a more balanced relationship between the foliage and the root mass. (from Ingels/Ornamental Horticulture, copyright 1985 by Delmar Publishers Inc.)

Figure 30–11. The grate around this permanently installed fig tree allows watering and fertilizing while protecting the root system from being trampled or compacted. (from Ingels/Ornamental Horticulture, copyright 1985 by Delmar Publishers Inc.)

while drainage tiles beneath the plant carry away excess water. Plants in such a setting must not be subjected to detergents and waxes used for floor maintenance, so special design provisions, such as raised edging, may be necessary.

Plants that are in raised planters or that require frequent replacement are usually not installed permanently. Instead, they are often planted in a growing medium within a nursery container having good drainage, Figure 30–12. The containerized plant is then placed into a support medium of peat, perlite, sand, or similar well-drained material. The support medium serves to retain the plants as well as permitting excess water to drain away from the root zone and insulating the root system against abrupt temperature or moisture changes. A separating sheet (usually of fiber glass or a rot-resistant fine mesh material) is placed between the support medium and the coarse gravel lining the bottom of the planter. The gravel is needed to facilitate drainage, and without the separator the growing medium and support medium would gradually wash into the gravel and plug it. A plastic tube inserted into the planter permits dip-stick testing to determine if the planter is being overwatered. It also provides a means of pumping out excess water if the planting is endangered by overwatering. Mulch on the surface of the planter serves to discourage moisture loss, provides a decorative appearance, and conceals the rims of the plant containers.

The same techniques used for the planting of containerized plants can be applied to in-ground plantings. If the planter drains directly into the building's drainage system, then the vertical plastic tube is unnecessary. All else remains the same except that there is no outer container.

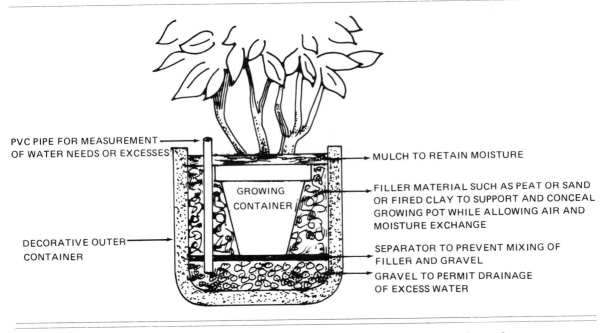

PVC PIPE FOR MEASUREMENT OF WATER NEEDS OR EXCESSES

GROWING CONTAINER

DECORATIVE OUTER CONTAINER

MULCH TO RETAIN MOISTURE

FILLER MATERIAL SUCH AS PEAT OR SAND OR FIRED CLAY TO SUPPORT AND CONCEAL GROWING POT WHILE ALLOWING AIR AND MOISTURE EXCHANGE

SEPARATOR TO PREVENT MIXING OF FILLER AND GRAVEL

GRAVEL TO PERMIT DRAINAGE OF EXCESS WATER

Figure 30–12. Installation of a containerized plant within an indoor planter

WATERING AND DRAINAGE

As noted above, the ability of the growing medium to drain off excess water is critical. More interior plant deaths result from overwatering than for any other reason. All planters must permit the removal of standing water. The layer of coarse gravel already referred to is one method. Other methods include setting containerized plants on top of inverted pots within the larger planter and incorporating drains and spigots into planter bottoms. Where drainage from the planter base is planned, additional planning must assure that carpets, tiles, and other floor surfacings are not damaged by the run-off water. Sitting the plants on gravel beds into which the water can drain and then evaporate is one method.

Hand-in-hand with planning for drainage goes provision for proper watering.

Some interior plantings require continuous moisture; others do better if permitted to dry out between regular waterings. Obviously the two types of plants would not coexist compatibility in the same planter.

An interior plantscape must be watered according to a schedule, and not according to the judgement of a custodian or other unqualified individual. The right watering frequency is most easily determined in controlled environments such as enclosed shopping centers. It is most difficult in locations where environmental variables are not stable, such as by open windows or in drafts near doors.

The need to water a planting can be determined by feeling the soil and observing its color. A gray surface color and failure of soil particles to adhere to the fingers indicate dryness. Moisture meters are also available for a more carefully controlled reading of the growing medium's water content.

Although some automated watering systems exist, there is a suprisingly limited use of them in large installations. Nationwide, there are interior plantscapes utilizing hundreds of plants that are all watered by hand. Most definitely, the technology of watering is still in the developmental stages.

When water is applied, it must be in a quantity adequate to wet the soil deeply, not shallowly. Shallow watering encourages shallow rooting and increases the vulnerability of the plants to damage from drying. Deep watering promotes deep and healthy rooting while providing the soil leaching necessary to prevent soluble salt buildup.

The quality of water used on the interior planting may vary with the location. The most likely source will be municipal water lines. Most public drinking water contains chlorine and often fluoride as germicides and tooth-decay deterrents respectively. Neither additive will harm plants under normal conditions. Although chlorine is potentially harmful, the amounts used in drinking water are dissipated by aeration as the water bubbles from the faucet or hose nozzle. More heavily chlorinated swimming pool or fountain water can damage plants and should never be used as a watering source. *NOTE:* Plants grown around enclosed pools require good air exchange in the room or the chlorine gas from the pool may damage them.

Water is a source of soluble salts. Water that has been softened by means of cation-exchange softeners may be dangerously high in sodium, which can be toxic to plants. In buildings with such water softeners, alternate sources of water should be sought for the plantings. In regions of the country where the need for water conservation causes recycled water to be used on interior plantings, a chemical analysis of the water should be made to determine if any toxic chemicals are present that could damage the planting.

OTHER CONCERNS

As with any planting, certain routine procedures are needed to keep the plants healthy and attractive. The problems that are common to plants grown outdoors are similar to those that trouble plants grown indoors. In addition, indoor plantings often encounter stresses not common in outdoor landscapes.

Fertilization

Fertilization is needed to provide the mineral elements required for photosynthesis. Interior plantings need a complete fertilizer, but not as often as outdoor plantings, because the rate of plant growth is greatly reduced indoors. The ratio of the complete fertilizer should be fairly uniform; for example, 1-1-1 or 2-1-2. Too much nitrogen may lead to spindly, succulent, and unattractive vegetative growth. Trace elements will also need to be applied, especially if the growing medium contains no real soil. Frequent soil testing is necessary, regardless of whether the growing medium is true soil or synthetic. Excessive fertilizing follows only slightly behind overwatering as a major reason why interior plants fail to survive satisfactorily.

Either organic or inorganic fertilizers will work well, but the organics are generally slower in releasing their minerals for use by the plants. This means that soluble salt buildup is less frequently a problem. However, the odor of decomposing organic fertilizers may not be welcomed in such settings as shopping malls or library lobbies.

Therefore, the use of organic fertilizers may not be practical in all situations.

Inorganic fertilizers are applied to large interior plantscapes in liquid form. This is faster and easier than applying dry granulars to each pot. When there are hundreds of pots and planters to maintain, speed is vital.

Humidity

Humidity is seldom a problem for plants growing outdoors, but it can cause problems for interior plantscapes. Because of the drying effects of central heating and air conditioning, interior plantings must adapt to an air environment that may contain half or less of the relative humidity outside. Interior humidities of 40 percent or less are common.

Preparation for the dry air must begin during the acclimatization process. Gradual drying of the plant's aatmosphere will usually allow the plant to survive after transplanting indoors. In some cases, attempts to increase the humidity around plantings by misting the foliage during the day have proven to be of little or no value. Misting may also cause damage to carpeting or furnishings. Proper acclimatization is the best solution at present.

Air Pollution

Air pollution cannot be escaped by bringing the landscape indoors. Pollutants in the exhaust of cars and trucks, the smoke from cigarettes, the chlorine gas escaping from swimming pools, and the chemical soup which passes for air in our major metropolitan areas are all harmful to plants when sufficiently concentrated. Some plant species are more susceptible than others.

Good ventilation is an important element in the health of interior plantings.

Proper ventilation will carry away chlorine vapors, fumes from smokers and chemical cleaning agents, or the ethylene which may be present if a building is heated by some form of hydrocarbon combustion (fossil fuel).

Ethylene can also damage plants as they are shipped to the site. This toxin is present in vehicle exhaust and if permitted to seep into the cabin where plants are stored may result in injury. If packed tightly or in restrictive packaging, the plants also may injure themselves, since their own tissue produces ethylene. Because of the potential harm from ethylene, plants should be unpacked and ventilated immediately upon arrival. At the time the plants are purchased, the grower or shipper should guarantee that the transport vehicles will be ventilated and sealed against exhaust fumes.

Dust

Dust is an air pollutant different from the others in that it is a particulate, not a vapor. When the leaves of a plant are coated with dust, they are not only unattractive, but gas exchange may be reduced due to plugged stomata. Air filtration reduces the amount of dust. Regular cleaning of the plants can also prevent dust buildup. Most plants in a residential interior can be rinsed off under the shower or set outside during a rainfall to wash away the dust. Commercial plantings can be kept clean with regular feather dusting and periodic washing. Cleaning should be a regular task within a total maintenance program for the interior plantscape.

Pruning

Pruning will not be extensive in an interior planting because of the plants' reduced rate of growth. Most pruning will be done to keep the plants shaped for an attractive appearance. Broken or damaged branches will also require removal. If the plants are not intended to grow, in order to avoid crowding, the roots as well as the foliage must be pruned back. Excessive root growth in containers can result in strangulation of the root system.

For pruning the plantings, hand pruners will be suitable for most of the herbaceous material and much of the woody material. Lopping shears will be helpful with larger materials, and pruning saws may be needed for indoor trees. Methods of pruning were described earlier in the text.

Interior plants should be pruned to a shape that suggests the appearance of a full canopy. Due to the restricted lighting in an interior planting, a full canopy seldom forms, however, and the plant's full branching structure may be visible. The pruning must enhance and take advantage of this sparse foliage covering.

Repotting

Repotting of plants is necessary in plantings where growth is allowed. Containers need to be removed from the planter and from the plant, the next larger size selected, and the excess space filled with growing medium. If roots are matted, they should be loosened before repotting. If they have started to grow around themselves, the large and excess roots should be pruned away. The pot should not be filled to the rim with the growing medium. An inch of unfilled space below the pot rim will give water room to flow into the container.

Insects and Diseases

Insects and diseases are not as common to interior plantings as to exterior ones, but they do occur. Insect problems are more common than diseases.

The initial pest presence may be introduced by the plants themselves as they arrive from the grower. Insects or pathogenic inoculum may be present in the foliage, roots, soil, or containers. All should be checked carefully upon arrival, at an area away from the installation site. The same careful check should be made each time replacement plants arrive. Obviously a reputable grower is a first defense against pests.

The most common pest problems of interior foliage plants are:

- aphids
- mealybugs
- spider mites
- white flies
- scale
- thrips
- nematodes
- root mealybugs
- root rots
- leaf spots
- anthracnose
- mildews
- blights

These pests and others are not uncontrollable when modern pesticides and methods of application can be used against them. However, the interior location and the presence of people make the use of sprays, dusts, and fumigants difficult. Whenever there is the possibility of people making contact with the pesticide, it is dangerous to use it. Even furnishings and carpeting can be damaged by many of the corrosive or oil-based chemicals. Where practical, plants can be wrapped in loose plastic bags and sprayed within the bag. This helps reduce the drift and the danger to people and furnishings.

Control measures are restricted to:

- chemical pesticides approved for application indoors
- removal of infected or infested plant parts
- washing away of insects and inoculum from plant foliage
- replacement of plants with healthy new ones

Vandalism and Abuse

Vandalism and abuse to interior plantings may necessitate replacement earlier than expected. Certain locations will bring certain predictable types of abuse. Plantings in cocktail lounges or nightclubs may have alcoholic drinks poured into their soil. Those in college snack bars and dorms may have cigarette holes burned through their leaves. Plantings in shopping malls may be mutilated by home propagators who take cuttings faster than the plants can replace them. Sometimes entire plants are stolen from the planters. The planters themselves are used as litter bins for paper cups, cigarettes, chewing gum, and assorted other debris.

The only real defense against such damage and abuse is public education and cooperation. By keeping the plantings attractive and well maintained, they are less likely to be deliberately damaged. Replacing or repairing damaged plants as soon as they are noticed displays the concern of the owners for an attractive planting that all can enjoy.

Grouping Compatible Species

Grouping compatible species simplifies the maintenance of the interior plantscape. Within any one planter the species selected should have the same requirements for light, moisture, fertilization, and soil mix. While a large plantscape may effectively combine tropical species, desert species, and sometimes even temperate species, they should be in separate planters. When plant replacement is necessary, the new plants should be compatible with the existing ones.

THE INTERDISCIPLINARY TEAM

The popularity of interior plantings has grown faster than the ability of any one profession to stay abreast of it all. A successful interior planting in a commercial building requires the expertise of interior plantscapers, plant growers, interior decorators, landscape architects, architects, maintenance professionals, and building management. Each professional brings his or her point of view to the project. The architect sees the plants as architectural features, not as living organisms. Building management personnel want the plants to attract customers and please employees but they too do not have a horticultural sense of plant needs. Maintenance professionals regard the plants as something to be dusted, watered, and fertilized. They are concerned about the proximity of water, the difficulty of changing lamps, and the ease of reaching the plants. Each has concerns and contributions to the planning process that the others need to know.

The success of the plantscape is measured by its appearance and health. The interior plantscaper should be consulted while the building is still in the planning stage, as errors in lighting quality and intensity can be difficult to correct later. Drainage of planters directly into the building's drainage pipes requires that plantings be sited permanently and near the pipes. Watering of the plantings necessitates a nearby supply of water to which a hose can be attached. A shopping mall or office lobby should have appropriate water outlets every fifty feet along the wall and preferably within each planter. Otherwise hoses will be stretched across walkways, endangering pedestrians and creating puddles. Maintenance of the plantings should be the responsiblity of a contracted professional plant maintenance firm, which should work closely with the architect to assure sufficient water outlets, storage space, accessibility for equipment, and so on. Failure to involve the maintenance firm in the early stages of planning can result in an unattractive plantscape shortly after installation. The managers of the building must be made to understand why specific lamps are needed for plant survival even if less expensive ones are available.

In short, fewer problems will develop for the interior planting if all professionals whose work impacts upon it work together from the beginning. At present, such interdisciplinary cooperation is the exception rather than the rule. The failure to use the team approach is often a case of architects not realizing their own limitations with horticultural materials.

THE FUTURE

No career field in ornamental horticulture holds greater promise than interior plantscaping. The current technology and knowledge of growing plants indoors is comparable to that when Henry Ford and the Wright Brothers began working in their professions. There is a need for fresh approaches to move us beyond *Ficus* trees and hanging baskets. More research is needed to introduce new species and varieties suitable for interior use. Also needed is better data on how to acclimatize plants with less foliage drop and transplant shock. Further study of soil mixes, fertilizer needs, and lighting requirements is needed to replace the guesswork of today. Finally, more professional plant maintenance firms are needed. They need dependable studies of such matters as the time required to dust and clean various leaf sizes and textures. Buildings need to be designed as carefully for their planted occupants as for their human ones. Automated watering and fertilization systems are needed to ease the current labor-intensive methods. There is ample work for young people who wish to train themselves for it.

SUMMARY

The use of plants indoors is not a new idea. Nevertheless, so explosive has been the recent demand for interior plantings in public buildings that the technology necessary to assure their survival has not kept pace.

In general, tropical foliage plants have proven better suited than temperate zone plants for indoor use because they do not require a period of cool temperature dormancy. Nevertheless, when plants are used indoors, a number of problems can occur. The procedures necessary for the successful transplant of tropical foliage plants to an interior locale include acclimatization to reduced light intensity, reduced nutrients, greater moisture stress, and lower temperatures.

Although light acclimatization allows the plant to survive at a reduced light intensity, it is still vital that the proper quality of light be provided. Thus the designer of an interior plantscape must understand the differences in light quality and the lamps that provide them.

The provision of a proper growing medium is equally important to the successful acclimatization of interior plants. The medium must provide structural support, water absorption, essential nutrients, proper pH, and good drainage. It is most often a mixture of natural soil and additives.

Plants may be set into an interior plantscape in ground beds or raised planters. The method of installation will be determined partly by the anticipated frequency of plant replacement. Whether planting in ground or in planters, allowance must be made for the removal of standing water from the planters. More interior plantings die from overwatering than for any other reason.

Watering the plantings, like other procedures, needs to be done as part of a carefully planned program of maintenance. Scheduled maintenance, rather than impromptu attention, is necessary to assure optimum satisfaction with the plantscape.

The most successful interior plantings require the expertise and cooperation of interior plantscapers, plant growers, interior decorators, landscape architects, architects, maintenance professionals, and building management. Each brings a distinct point of view to the project from which all others, and the plantscape, can benefit.

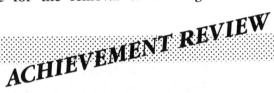

ACHIEVEMENT REVIEW

A. Indicate if the following statements are true or false.

1. Interior use of plants is a new concept.
2. Architects and interior decorators are trained to write correct specifications for interior plantscapes.
3. Tropical plants have proven to be better suited for interior use than temperate plants.
4. Interior plantings require less fertilizer than outdoor plantings.
5. Soluble salts originate from fertilizers and water.
6. Clear glass transmits 100 percent of the sunlight that shines upon it.
7. Light intensity is measured in nanometers.
8. Light wavelength is measured in footcandles.
9. Most plants will survive after being acclimatized to a light intensity of 100 to 200 f.c.

B. Select the answer from the choices offered for each question.

1. The most efficient natural light for interior plantscapes enters from _____.

    a. the sides of buildings
    b. skylights 20 feet overhead
    c. skylights 15 feet or less overhead
    d. incandescent bulbs

2. The most efficient skylight has _____ .
   a. a shallow, wide well with vertical sides
   b. a shallow, wide well with 45° beveled sides
   c. a deep, narrow well with vertical sides
   d. a deep, narrow well with 45° beveled sides

3. In most single-story settings, the best lamp for lighting an indoor planting is _____ .
   a. an incandescent
   b. a cool white fluorescent
   c. a warm white fluorescent
   d. a fluorescent plant growth lamp

4. Interior plantings illuminated with 100 to 200 f.c. of light require _____ hours of lighting each day.
   a. eight
   b. ten
   c. twelve
   d. fourteen

5. The most important reason for using a synthetic soil in an interior planting rather than natural soil is _____ .
   a. drainage
   b. nutrient content
   c. structural support
   d. cost

6. An interior planting that reflects seasonal changes through use of such plants as daffodils, mums, and poinsettias, would be best if designed _____ .
   a. as an in-ground planting
   b. as a containerized planting

7. Deep watering of interior plantings will _____ .
   a. encourage deep rooting
   b. leach away soluble salts
   c. do both of these
   d. do none of these

8. Watering of interior plantscapes is best done _____ .
   a. irregularly
   b. weekly
   c. when convenient
   d. according to an established schedule

9. The two major reasons why interior plants die are overwatering and _____ .
   a. too much light
   b. too much fertilizer
   c. too little fertilizer
   d. incorrect pH

10. Chlorine gas, dust, and ethylene are all possible _____ affecting interior plantings.
   a. pesticides
   b. air pollutants
   c. pathogens
   d. toxins

C. Answer each of the following questions as briefly as possible.
   1. Place X's where appropriate to compare the different lamp types.

Characteristic	Incandescent	Cool White Fluorescent	Fluorescent Plant Lamps	Mercury	Metal Halite	High Pressure Sodium
High in red light						
Low in red light						
High in blue light						
Low in blue light						
Good color rendition						
High initial cost						
Low initial cost						
Moderate initial cost						
Low operating cost						
Moderate operating cost						

   2. Label the parts of this containerized plant.

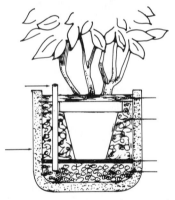

   3. Indicate whether the following are characteristic of interior or exterior plantings.
      a. Rapid growth is encouraged.
      b. Pruning is minimal.
      c. Dusting of foliage is needed.
      d. High-analysis fertilizers are used regularly.
      e. Ventilation of the planting site is needed.
      f. Plants must be acclimatized to low humidity.
      g. Plants are most affected by insects and diseases.
      h. Plants suffer most from vandalism and abuse.

SECTION 10

COMPUTERS

UNIT 31

COMPUTERS IN THE LANDSCAPE INDUSTRY

OBJECTIVES

By completing of this unit, students will be able to:

- describe the ways that landscape firms use computers.
- explain the major types of computer programs currently popular in the landscape industry.
- discuss the benefits and limitations of computers to the industry.
- project the future use of computers in landscaping.

THE TECHNOLOGY AND ITS USES

In the short history of our country most generations of Americans have witnessed some distinctive and unprecedented technological breakthrough thought impossible by earlier generations. The horse and buggy were retired by the automobile. The earth-bound passenger train was swept away by the airplane. The atmosphere dependent plane has been surpassed by the gravity-defying rocket. Less dramatic but equally innovative has been the replacement of the stenographer, typewriter, filing cabinet, T-square, and drawing pencil by the computer. Modern computers are able to process and store vast amounts of data in a variety of forms. They can accelerate calculations, project the effect of changes, allow instant recall of historical data, and never show the slightest sign of fatigue, bad temper, or stress. Given proper instructions, computers permit artists to create exciting graphic displays. Television advertising embraced computer graphics from the outset. Motion pictures, the print media, photographers, and countless others have all jumped aboard the computer bandwagon, using both the data processing and graphic capability of the expanding technology to make their work more efficient, cost effective, and even fun.

The landscape industry was slow to accept the full array of computer services. Like so much of agriculture, landscaping can be very imprecise and subject to unexpected change. The image of the computer as a device demanding precision and consistency was perhaps the reason so many in the industry were skeptical of its applicability. As the industry has refined its cost estimating and pricing techniques and generally upgraded its professional image and business methods, the use of computer technology has found its way to the business mainstream. As an increasing number of computer programs are developed specifically for the landscape industry, the acceptance of the technology grows, Figure 31–1.

At present, landscape architects, landscape contractors, and landscape managers are using computer assistance for:

1. correspondence, records, and other documents previously prepared by the typewriter
2. specification preparation

3. quantifying the materials needed to build a project
4. cost estimating
5. selecting plants
6. designing irrigation systems
7. technical calculations, such as cut and fill
8. landscape design graphics
9. modeling and contouring the terrain of a site

THE POPULAR PROGRAMS

Computer systems require machinery known as *hardware* and instructions to make the machinery operate, termed *software* or *programs*. The hardware sits, unable to do anything until given direction by the software in an electronic language that it can understand. Fortunately the landscape employee using the computer need not understand the electronic language in order to make the program communicate with the hardware.

The hardware requirements logically include a means of entering data into the computer (input devices), a central processor of the data (the computer), a place to store the data once processed (hard or floppy disks), and a means of converting the data from the computer into printed form (output device). Input and output devices vary depending upon whether the data is written or graphic in form, and what quality of output is desired.

The present software programs that find greatest acceptance in the landscape industry are of three types:

Figure 31–1. The tools of the trade have changed, and so has the interaction between drafter and drawing (Courtesy of International Business Machines Corporation)

1. word processing
2. numerical calculations
3. graphic visualization

Word processing is the successor to the typewriter. Letters, labels, reports, memos, and other written documents are prepared and stored on word processors. Paragraphs can be moved or deleted, words can be changed or inserted, envelopes addressed, key phrases visually highlighted, and numerous other techniques applied instantaneously, Figure 31–2. Gone are smudged erasures and impersonal form letters. Even spelling errors and incorrect word choices can be minimized by using the proper software. Many good software programs are available and usable on the IBM personal computers, micro and mini computers, or IBM compatible computers that are now the standard for central processors.

Input for word processing is a keyboard that is similar in many ways to a typewriter. Output is usually from a printer that transfers the image on the computer's monitor to letterhead stationery or other paper being fed into the printer.

Figure 31–2. A word processor in use (Courtesy of Calcomp)

Numerical calculations enlist the capability of some software programs to accomplish mathematical functions. Conventional business needs such as inventory control, accounts receivable and payable, payroll and taxes, billing, time records, and profit and loss statements are all commonly handled by computers. In addition, special calculations distinctive to the landscape industry such as the measurement of material, quantities, or operations, the determination of costs and prices, and the automatic updating of inventory are routinely done by the computer. As a result, less time is spent on calculations that were always time-consuming and tedious and subject to human error. At the same time, the accuracy of the calculations has probably improved since the computers' insistence upon certain data input has compelled companies to keep track of labor hours, material costs, and equipment usage more closely.

While there are a number of good numerical calculating software programs being marketed to the landscape industry, the one enjoying the most widespread use today is the SLICE system developed by Thornton Computer Management Systems of Maineville, Ohio. Unlike earlier programs that were directed to a generic business market, the SLICE system customized its software to the needs of the green industry using either a company's existing hardware or Thornton's own computer product. The developers have made themselves highly visible to the landscape industry and managed to implant their product's name in the minds of industry professionals as the number one computer system for landscape contracting, maintenance, and management needs. It has been a successful marketing campaign, backed up by a good product and customer service. Certainly other producers have and will continue to develop competing software products. Some landscape firms have even developed their own programs, usually as a modification of an existing generic package.

Input devices for numerical calculation programs include the keyboard and the digitizer, Figure 31–3. The *digitizer* permits direct measurements of lengths, areas, volumes, and perimeters from drawings, so it is essential for the conversion of drawn data to numerical equivalents. The output device for numerical calculations is usually the printer.

Figure 31–3. A hand-held stylus is used to select commands and symbols on a digitizer or menu tablet. (Courtesy of GTCO Corporation)

Graphic visualization gained acceptance within the landscape industry more slowly than word processing or numerical calculations. While most graphic artists were suspicious of the electronic art medium at the beginning, many accepted its merits long before landscape architects did.

At present there are two types of graphic visualization systems in use by landscape designers and landscape architects: computer-aided design (CAD) and video imagining.

CAD SYSTEMS

CAD systems are accelerated drafting systems. They do what draftsmen have traditionally done with their T-square and pencils. Computer drafting has increased mainly because of a PC-based CAD software program named *Auto CAD* (a registered trademark of Autodesk, Inc.). Due to the necessity for hardware, software and user training, Auto CAD is an expensive investment for a firm. It is not ready to use upon delivery to the office because it is a general system, marketed to a variety of users. It is the generic nature of Auto CAD that makes it the dominant CAD system. However, to customize it to a specific type of drafting requires a third party, discipline specific software interface. Landscape architects and landscape designers have most frequently selected LANDCADD as their discipline specific software. Developed by a group of practicing professionals and released commercially in 1984, LANDCADD is marketed by LANDCADD, Inc. of Franktown, Colorado. Presently, LANDCADD offers different modular programs which can be selected by firms to fit their needs, not necessarily causing them to purchase programs that they will not use. At the heart of the software system is the Site Planning and Landscape Design Module. It permits the creation of two-dimensional plan views and elevations complete with contour lines, buildings, plant symbols, landscaping, and enrichment items. Surface textures can be added as well as lettering. As the design develops, the plant list is automatically created and tabulated. The module comes with its own menu of symbols to which the user can add his or her own, further customizing the system. Figure 31–4 illustrates a landscape plan developed using a LANDCADD software package. Three dimensional drawings of buildings, terrain and grading plans are also possible using the Planning and Design module.

An Irrigation Design Module is available as well as modules that permit material measurement, cost estimating, and plant selection, Figure 31–5. Another module provides a library of construction detail drawings that can be used directly or modi-

fied by the user before insertion into the landscape plans. Since success breeds competition, a number of competitive discipline specific software systems have entered the market. Each is directed solely or in part to the landscape industry. The competition is good because it assures a free market, innovative research and development, and reduced prices to the consumer.

The input device for computer-aided design is usually a *mouse* or a *digitizing tablet and stylus*. The mouse is held in the designer's hand and rolled around the table surface while the cursor moves about on the screen. The tablet and stylus permit the user to place drawings onto the monitor's screen in a manner remotely similar to that of the traditional draftsman, Figure 31–6.

The output device for CAD system drawings may be the printers used for word processing, but the best quality of printout is obtained from a pen plotter, illustrated in Figure 31–7.

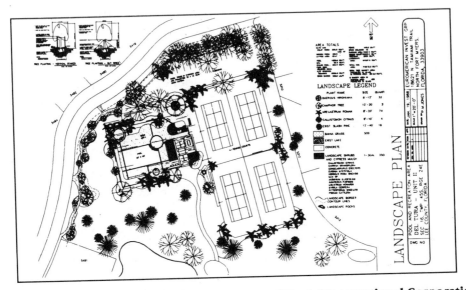

Figure 31–4. A LANDCADD design (Courtesy of Daniel International Corporation)

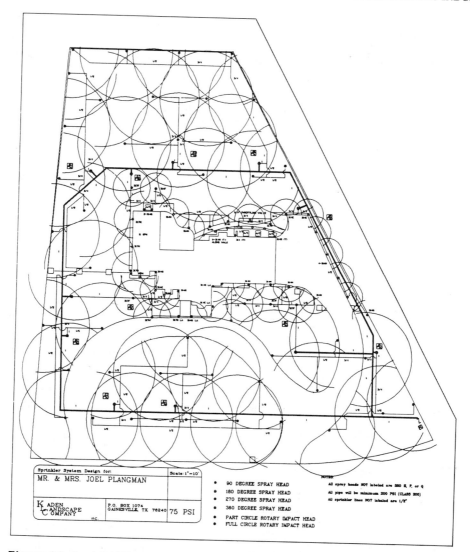

Figure 31–5. A LANDCADD irrigation design (Courtesy of Kaden Landscape)

Video Imaging

Video imaging is a computerized technique that superimposes a landscape concept over a photographic image of the undeveloped landscape. The designer may begin by taking several photographs of the building to be landscaped. Also, the picture may be taken as several minutes of video captured by a camcorder. The photo or video image is then taken to the designer's studio where it is entered into the computer and retained by the system's memory. The designer then directs the computer to apply color photo images of plants, pavings, pools, lawn and

Figure 31–6. The operator can select a command or symbol from a menu tablet (Courtesy of Calcomp)

Figure 31–7. An E-size pen plotter (Courtesy of Hewlett-Packard Company)

other landscape elements over the camcorder or photographic picture. The result is a full color suggestion of how a landscape will look before it is actually installed. It is an excellent sales tool to assist the client's visualization of the designer's ideas.

The leading video imaging system in America is New Image, headquartered in Canoga Park, California. The technology is so new that there is little competition in the marketplace yet. Figure 31–8 illustrates before and after images of landscapes as treated by the video imaging system. In the hands of a skilled operator, the effects possible are realistic and impressive. They permit a variety of design concepts to be presented to a client for reaction before time is spent on plan view designs that may never be constructed. At present, video imaging does not create scaled drawings from which the landscape can be built. However, the New Image system is designed to interact (interface) with CAD systems such as LANDCADD to apply color and realistic surface textures to the line drawings produced by the CAD system.

Input devices for the New Image system are the video camcorder, tablet and stylus, and scanner. The graphic image is composed on the monitor. The graphic image can then be reproduced as a color print or as a videotape for presentation to a client audience of one or a hundred and one.

THE BENEFITS AND LIMITATIONS OF COMPUTERS FOR LANDSCAPERS

Each technological advance carries with it advantages and disadvantages. If the advantages don't greatly outnumber the dis-

Figure 31–8. Before and after examples of video imaging (Courtesy of New Image Industries)

advantages the technology is usually not accepted. While the airplane allows us to travel faster, the view from the windows of the train was better. Computer technology is no longer in its infancy; but neither has it leveled off in its development. Advancements that improve the computer's capabilities and/or offer the manufacturers' a competitive marketing advantage are being announced regularly and internationally. The two edges of the technological sword are thus seen. The great benefits of time saving, reduced errors, greater precision, rapid revisions, and easy replication of tedious tasks are

counterbalanced by technical obsolescence of the equipment, the high costs of replacing or modifying hardware and software and updating employee training, and the danger of putting so much of the revenue producing work of the company into the hands of employee specialists with insufficient back-up replacements.

What was first regarded as a limitation by landscape architects and landscape designers can perhaps be more properly identified as a psychological bias. The designers scoffed at the stiff imagery of the computer generated drawings. Traditionally, the graphic appearance of the landscape plan, including its lettering and symbol styling, has been the hallmark of a designer or a firm. Early CAD designs *were* simplistic and mechanical; however, improved data banks of symbol and lettering styles plus programs that accept the designer's own stylings have removed most of the early objections. Recent software improvements have given CAD design systems the ability to produce perspective drawings and textures for rendering.

While secretaries, estimators and others in landscape firms who deal primarily with words, numbers and calculations have found computer technology easy to adjust to, many landscape architects and designers have not. In the case of the workers whose letters, reports, specifications and spreadsheets are input largely through a keyboard, the computer has not asked them to change much. They still gather or copy data in much the same manner as they have for years. The computer merely accelerates the amount of work they can accomplish and lessens their errors. It also replaces earlier forms of data storage with newer forms of storage, yet the end result is the same.

Designers have not had it as easy. To many landscape architects the fun of designing, as well as the actual development of concepts, forms and relationships have been dependent upon the touch of hand to pencil to paper. Like an electrical current, the flow of creativity is dependent upon contact between all of these elements. The computer does not allow that. It replaces free sketching with menu selections. It offers a data bank of symbols instead of spur-of-the-moment interpretations. It asks questions instead of offering answers, and requires an exact response from the designer if it is to serve. It is that mechanical quality of the input, not just the output, that may prove

to be a limitation of the current technology since many creative individuals are not proficient mechanics.

THE FUTURE

As a mechanical servant the computer's role in the landscape industry will continue to expand and one by one it will overcome all of the current limitations and objections. To be more than mere refinements of existing capabilities, major advances must be made in three areas:

1. the methods by which data can be acquired and input
2. a link between data as it is input and the graphic output from CAD systems
3. a greater variety of output forms

Systems that now use keyboards for data input into word processing and numerical calculation programs can be expected to be voice driven in the future. Such innovative input will permit even faster recording and processing of the data. Instant spelling, checking and grammar checking as well as simultaneous translation into other languages will result from enlarged data bases and more powerful computers. As the computers from one company become linked nationally and internationally to all computers, communications and ordering may bypass not only the postal system and telephone, but send the FAX machine into the gadgeteering history books next to the eight-track musical tape.

Currently CAD systems have no understanding of what the lines and symbols of their graphics represent. Distinction cannot be made between a shape that represents a pool of water and one that symbolizes a brick patio. The designer must tell the estimating software how to interpret the drawing before material calculations and cost estimates can be completed. Once the computer is able to recognize from the symbols what an object is and how it will be constructed, even as it is being drawn, then construction drawings, specifications, and cost estimates can be generated, modified and published simultaneous with the design.

Site analysis data may be entered into the CAD system directly from aerial photos or video images shot from elevated locations such as roof tops, planes or even satellites. Optical and laser scanning systems may be the technology that permits this direct input of data. As some point in the future, voice commands may be used to direct or at least correct computer assisted designing.

Output products can also be expected to change with time. The graphic on the monitor which now prints out as a flat plan, elevation or perspective view may soon appear as a video walk-through of the proposed design. The computer may recognize the differences in size and growth characteristics of the plants selected for the design and project them into the image automatically sized and correctly interpreted. It will easily provide graphic projections of the landscape at maturity or at any earlier age that interests the client or designer.

Still another computer advance will impact on areas of landscape architecture that are beyond the scope of this text. The point to be made is that computers can be expected to move from their present status as an *aid* to the landscaper to the level of an *assistant*. Now they merely record data and do as they're directed. Soon they will be able to analyze data and offer suggestions, while providing graphic illustrations that surpass anything that can be done by conventional drafting or art media. At that point they will have moved the industry to a new level of professionalism.

ACHIEVEMENT REVIEW

I. In the sequence of events below, describe when and how current computer technology could be applied.
   a. initial client contact
   b. site analysis
   c. design development
   d. cost analysis and price determination
   e. billing the client
   f. paying the employees

II. Define the following terms.

   a. word processing
   b. hardware
   c. software
   d. input device
   e. output device

      f. SLICE

      g. CAD

      h. Auto CAD

      i. LANDCADD

      j. New Image

III. Assume the role of a computer systems salesman attempting to convince a hesitant landscape company owner to convert her design-build firm to computers. What would be your complete argument in favor of such action?

IV. Compare the current status of computerization with projections for the future in the following areas:

      a. word processing

      b. cost estimating

      c. land measurements

      d. landscape designing

SUGGESTED ACTIVITIES

1. Using a personal computer and a spreadsheet software program, do the practice exercise at the end of Unit 24 (Pricing the Proposed Design).

2. Contact local dealers for demonstrations of a CAD design program and a video imaging program.

PROFESSIONAL
AND TRADE
ORGANIZATIONS

AGRONOMY, SOIL

AMERICAN SOCIETY OF AGRONOMY
677 S. Segoe Road
Madison, WI 53711

CROP SCIENCE SOCIETY OF AMERICA
677 S. Segoe Road
Madison, WI 53711

PROFESSIONAL GROUNDS
  MANAGEMENT SOCIETY
7 Church Lane
Suite 13
Pikesville, MD 21208

SOIL CONSERVATION SOCIETY OF
  AMERICA
7515 N.E. Ankeny Road
Ankeny, IA 50021

SOIL SCIENCE SOCIETY OF AMERICA
677 S. Segoe Road
Madison, WI 53711

WEED SCIENCE SOCIETY OF AMERICA
309 W. Clark Street
Champaign, IL 61820

BOTANY

AMERICAN ASSN. OF BOTANICAL
  GARDENS AND ARBORETA
P.O. Box 206
Swarthmore, PA 19081

BOTANICAL SOCIETY OF AMERICA
University of Kentucky
Lexington, KY 40506

BULBS

NETHERLANDS FLOWER-BULB
  INSTITUTE
Corporate Plaza II
51 Cragwood
S. Plainfield, NJ 07080

BUSINESS MANAGEMENT

GARDEN INDUSTRY OF AMERICA, INC.
2501 Wayzata Boulevard
Minneapolis, MN 55440

NATIONAL LAWN AND GARDEN
  DISTRIBUTORS ASSN.
1900 Arch Street
Philadelphia, PA 19103

NATIONAL SMALL BUSINESS ASSN.
1604 K Street N.W.
Washington, DC 20006

FERTILIZERS, CHEMICALS

FERTILIZER INSTITUTE
1015 18th Street N.W.
Washington, DC 20036

NATIONAL FERTILIZER SOLUTIONS ASSN.
8823 N. Industrial Road
Peoria, IL 61615

POTASH/PHOSPHATE INSTITUTE
2801 Buford Highway N.E.
Suite 401
Atlanta, GA 30329

FLOWERS, PLANTS

ALL-AMERICAN ROSE SELECTIONS, INC.
P.O. Box 218
Shenandoah, IA 51601

AMERICAN CAMELLIA SOCIETY
P.O. Box 1217
Fort Valley, GA 31030

AMERICAN DAHLIA SOCIETY, INC.
345 Merritt Avenue
Bergenfield, NJ 07621

AMERICAN HIBISCUS SOCIETY
206 N.E. 40th Street
Pompano Beach, FL 33064

AMERICAN IRIS SOCIETY
7414 E. 60th Street
Tulsa, OK 74145

AMERICAN PRIMROSE SOCIETY
2568 Jackson Highway
Chehalis, WA 98532

AMERICAN RHODODENDRON SOCIETY
14635 S.W. Bull Mountain Road
Tigard, OR 97223

AMERICAN ROSE SOCIETY
P.O. Box 30,000
Shreveport, LA 71130

BEDDING PLANTS, INC.
P.O. Box 286
Okemos, MI 48864

BROMELIAD SOCIETY
647 S. Saltair Avenue
Los Angeles, CA 90049

HOLLY SOCIETY OF AMERICA, INC.
407 Fountain Green Road
Bel Air, MD 21014

INTERIOR PLANTSCAPE ASSN.
2000 L Street N.W.
Suite 200
Washington, DC 20036

LIVING PLANT GROWERS ASSN.
1419 21st Street
Sacramento, CA 95814

NORTH AMERICAN LILY SOCIETY, INC.
P.O. Box 476
Waukee, IA 50263

GOVERNMENT AGENCIES

ANIMAL AND PLANT HEALTH
  INSPECTION SERVICE
6505 Belcrest Road
Hyattsville, MD 20782

SOIL CONSERVATION SERVICE
P.O. Box 2890
Washington, DC 20013

GRASS

AMERICAN SOD PRODUCERS ASSN.
4415 W. Harrison
Hillside, IL 60162

BETTER LAWN AND TURF INSTITUTE
  AND THE LAWN INSTITUTE
991 W. Fifth Street
Marysville, OH 43040

PROFESSIONAL LAWN CARE ASSN.
1225 Johnson Ferry Road
Suite B
Marietta, GA 30067

HORTICULTURE

AMERICAN HORTICULTURAL SOCIETY
P.O. Box 0105
Mt. Vernon, VA 22121
and
7931 E. Boulevard Drive
Alexandria, VA 22308

HORTICULTURAL RESEARCH
  INSTITUTE, INC.
2000 L Street N.W.
Suite 200
Washington, DC 20036

LANDSCAPING

INTERNATIONAL FEDERATION OF
  LANDSCAPE ARCHITECTS
Lisbon, Portugal

AMERICAN INSTITUTE OF LANDSCAPE
  ARCHITECTS
602 E San Juan Avenue
Phoenix, AZ 85012

AMERICAN SOCIETY OF LANDSCAPE
  ARCHITECTS
1750 Old Meadow Road
McLean, VA 22101

ASSOCIATED LANDSCAPE CONTRACTORS
  OF AMERICA
405 N. Washington Street
Falls Church, VA 22046

COUNCIL OF TREE AND LANDSCAPE
  APPRAISERS
1250 I Street N.W.
Suite 504
Washington, DC 20005

NATIONAL BARK PRODUCERS ASSN.
301 Maple Avenue W.
Tower Suite 504
Vienna, VA 22180

NATIONAL LANDSCAPE ASSN.
2000 L Street N.W.
Suite 200
Washington, DC 20036

PROFESSIONAL GROUNDS
  MANAGEMENT SOCIETY
7 Church Lane
Suite 13
Pikesville, MD 21208

NURSERIES

AMERICAN ASSOCIATION OF
    NURSERYMEN
230 Southern Building
Washington, DC 20005

MAILORDER ASSN. OF NURSERYMEN,
    INC.
210 Cartwright Boulevard
Massepequa Park, NY 11762

WHOLESALE NURSERY GROWERS OF
    AMERICA, INC.
2000 L Street N.W.
Suite 200
Washington, DC 20036

OUTDOOR LIVING

CALIFORNIA REDWOOD ASSN.
591 Redwood Highway
Suite 3100
Mill Valley, CA 94941

GARDEN INDUSTRY OF AMERICA, INC.
2501 Wayzata Boulevard
Minneapolis, MN 55440

GOLF COURSE SUPERINTENDENTS ASSN.
    OF AMERICA
1617 St. Andrews Drive
Lawrence, KS 66044

KEEP AMERICA BEAUTIFUL, INC.
99 Park Avenue
New York, NY 10016

NATIONAL SWIMMING POOL INSTITUTE
2111 Eisenhower
Alexandria, VA 22314

PEST CONTROL

ENTOMOLOGICAL SOCIETY OF AMERICA
4603 Calvert Road
College Park, MD 20740

INTERNATIONAL PESTICIDE
    APPLICATORS, INC.
a.k.a. Washington Tree Service
20057 Ballinger Road N.E.
Seattle, WA 98155

NATIONAL PEST CONTROL ASSN.
8100 Oak Street
Dunn Loring, VA 22027

WEED SCIENCE SOCIETY OF AMERICA
309 W. Clark Street
Champaign, IL 61820

POWER EQUIPMENT, PARTS

OUTDOOR POWER EQUIPMENT
    INSTITUTE, INC.
1901 L Street N.W.
Washington, DC 20036

SMALL ENGINE SERVICING DEALERS
    ASSN., INC.
P.O. Box 6312
St. Petersburg, FL 33736

SEEDS

AMERICAN SEED TRADE ASSN.
1030 15th Street N.W.
Suite 964
Washington, DC 20005

SOIL CONDITIONERS

CANADIAN SPHAGNUM PEAT MOSS
 INFORMATION BUREAU
928 Broadway
New York, NY 10010

PERLITE INSTITUTION, INC.
6268 Jericho Turnpike
Commack, NY 11725

TREES

AMERICAN FOREST INSTITUTION
1619 Massachusetts Avenue N.W.
Washington, DC 20036

AMERICAN FORESTRY ASSN.
1319 18th Street N.W.
Washington, DC 20036

AMERICAN SOCIETY OF CONSULTING
 ARBORISTS
315 Franklin Road
N. Brunswick, NJ 08902

NATIONAL ARBORISTS ASSN., INC.
1400 Wantagh Avenue
Suite 207
Wantagh, NY 11793

NATIONAL CHRISTMAS TREE ASSN.
611 E. Wells Street
Milwaukee, WI 53202

SOCIETY OF MUNICIPAL ARBORISTS
7447 Old Dayton Road
Dayton, OH 45427

GLOSSARY

Accent plant A plant which is more distinctive than many plants, but does not attract the eye as much as a specimen plant.

Acclimaticization The preparation of plants for a reduced light setting.

Adobe A heavy soil common to the southwestern United States.

Aeration The addition of air into the soil; it is accomplished during soil conditioning with materials such as sand or peat moss. It can be encouraged in established lawns by the use of machines called aerators.

Aesthetic Attractive to the human senses.

Alkaline Characterized by a high pH.

Angle The relationship between two joined straight lines.

Annual A plant which completes its life cycle in one growing season.

Antitranspirant (*also* antidessicant) A liquid sprayed on plants to reduce water loss, transplant shock, windburn, and sun scald.

Arid A term used in the description of landscapes where there is little usable water.

Balled and burlapped A form of plant preparation in which a large part of the root system is retained in a soil ball. The ball is wrapped in burlap to facilitate handling during sale and transplanting.

Bare root A form of plant preparation in which all soil is removed from the root system. The plant is lightweight and easier to handle during sale and transplanting.

Bedding plant An herbaceous plant preseeded and growing in a peat pot or packet container.

Bid A statement of what work, materials, and standards of quality will be provided by a landscape firm in return for the price specified. Once agreed to by a client and the landscape firm, it is legally binding upon both.

B.L.A. Bachelor of Landscape Architecture. The first professional degree for those who study landscape architecture.

Bulb A flowering perennial which survives the winter as a dormant fleshy storage structure.

Calibration The adjustment of a piece of equipment so that it distributes a given material at the rate desired.

Caliche A highly alkaline soil common to the southwestern United States.

Canopy The collective term for the foliage of a tree.

Capital Money used to finance a business.

Closed corporation A business that does not sell its stock publicly. All stock is owned by only a few people, who are often related.

Collateral Item(s) used to guarantee repayment of a loan. The items are of equal or greater value than the money being borrowed.

Compaction A condition of soil in which all air has been driven out of the pore spaces. Water is unable to move into and through the soil.

Compass A graphic design tool used for the construction of circles.

Complete fertilizer A fertilizer containing nitrogen, phosphorus, and potassium, the three nutrients used in the largest quantities by plants.

Conditioning Preparation of soil to make it suitable for planting.

Containerized A form of plant preparation for sale and transplanting. When purchased, the plant is growing with its root system intact within a plastic, metal, or tar paper container.

Contour interval The vertical distance between contour lines.

Contour lines Broken lines found on a topographic map. They represent vertical elevation.

Contract An agreement between two parties that is legally binding.

Cool-season grass A type of grass which grows best in temperate regions and during the cooler spring and fall months.

Corporation A form of business operation that makes the business a legal entity, separate from its owners.

Cost Refers to the recovery of expenditures.

Cost estimate An itemized listing of the expenses in an operation. It can be applied to a single task or a total project.

Crotch The point on a tree at which two branches or a branch and the trunk meet.

Crown The point at which aboveground plant parts and the root system meet.

Cultipacker A large lawn seeder, pulled by a tractor.

Cut A grading practice that removes earth from a slope.

Deciduous A type of plant that loses its leaves each autumn.

Degree The unit of measurement for angles.

Density The number of leaf shoots that a single grass plant will produce.

Design-build firm A landscape business that provides both design and construction services.

Diameter The distance across a circle as measured through the exact center.

Diazo machine A duplicating machine that makes positive copies from vellum tracings onto heavy paper.

Dormancy (adj.: dormant) A period of rest that perennial plants experience during the winter season. They continue to live, but have little or no growth.

Downstream With regard to irrigation, describes the direction of water flow away from the source.

Drainage The act of water passing through the root area of soil. Soil is well drained if water disappears in 10 minutes or less from a shrub or tree planting.

Drainage tile A plastic or clay tube buried beneath the soil that collects excess water from the soil and carries it away.

Drop spreader A device for the application of granular materials such as grass seed and fertilizer. The material is dispensed through holes in the bottom of a hamper as the spreader is pushed across the lawn.

Effluent water Treated sewage.

Enrichment A contribution made to the outdoor room by a landscape item that is not an element of a wall, ceiling, or floor.

Erosion The wearing away of the soil caused by water or wind.

Espalier A form of pruning in which plants are trained against a fence or wall. The effect is vinelike and two dimensional.

Estimate An approximation of the price that a customer will be charged for a landscape project.

Evergreen A type of plant that retains its foliage during the winter. There are needled forms (such as pine, spruce, hemlock, and fir) and broadleaved forms (such as rhododendron, pieris, euonymus, and holly).

Exotic plant A plant that has been introduced to an area by human beings, not nature.

Fauna Animal life.

Fertilization The addition of nutrients to the soil through application of natural or synthesized products called *fertilizers*.

Fertilizer analysis The percentage of various nutrients in a fertilizer product. A minimum of three numbers on the fertilizer package indicates the percentage of total nitrogen (N), available phosphoric acid (P_2O_5), and water-soluble potash (K_2O), in that order.

Fill A grading practice that adds earth to a slope.

Flail mower A mower used for turfgrasses that are only cut a few times each year.

Flora Plant life.

Flower bed A free-standing planting made entirely of flowers with no background of shrub foliage.

Flower border A flower planting used in front of a planting of shrubs. The shrubs provide green background for the blossoms.

Focal point A point of visual attraction. A focal point can be created by color, movement, shape, size, or other characteristics.

Foliage texture The effect created by the combination of leaf size, sunlight, and shadow patterns on a plant.

Footcandle The amount of light produced by a candle at a distance of one foot.

Foundation planting The planting next to a building that helps it blend more comfortably into the surrounding landscape.

Girdling The complete removal of a strip of bark around the main stem of a plant. After girdling, the ability of nutrients to pass from roots to leaves is lost, causing the eventual death of the plant.

Grading Changing the form of the land.

Graft A man-made bond between two different plants, one selected for its aboveground qualities (scion) and the other for its belowground qualities (stock).

Grass seed blend A combination of two or more cultivated varieties of a single species.

Grass seed mixture A combination of two or more different species of grass.

Ground cover A low-growing, spreading plant, usually 18 inches or less in height.

Grounds keeper A professional engaged full-time in landscape maintenance.

Hardiness The ability of a plant to survive through the winter season.

Heading back A pruning technique that shortens a shrub branch without totally removing it.

Heaving An action that causes shallowly rooted plants, such as grasses, ground covers, and bulbs, to be forced to the surface of the soil. The action results from repeated freezing and thawing of the soil surface.

Herbaceous A type of plant that is non-woody. It has no bark.

Herbicide A chemical used to kill weeds.

Holdfasts Special appendages of certain vines that allow them to climb.

Hydroseeder A spraying device that applies seed, water, fertilizer, and mulch at the same time.

Incurve The center of a corner planting bed and a natural focal point.

Inert material Filler material that has no purpose other than to carry and dilute active ingredients in a mixture.

Inorganic Consisting of nonliving materials.

Intangible A quality denoting something that cannot be touched.

Irrigation Supplying water to plants through artificial means.

Jump-cut A pruning technique for the removal of large limbs from trees without stripping bark from the trunk. It involves a series of three cuts.

Landscape architect A licensed professional who practices landscape planning, usually on a scale larger than residential properties.

Landscape contractor A professional who carries out the installation of landscapes.

Landscape designer A professional who devotes all or part of a work day to the design of landscapes.

Landscape installation The actual construction of the landscape.

Landscape maintenance The care and upkeep of the landscape after installation.

Landscape nursery worker A professional who is concerned with the sale and installation of landscape plants and related materials.

Landscaping A profession involving the design, installation, and maintenance of the outdoor human living environment.

Lateral bud Any bud below the terminal bud on a twig.

Leaching The dissolving of materials (such as nutrients) in the water which is present in soil, causing the material to quickly pass the point at which plant roots can benefit from them.

Lettering Machine A device that types an assortment of letter styles and sizes onto a transparent tape. The tape can then be applied to a landscape design.

Light compensation point The point of exact balance between photosynthesis and respiration by plants.

Light quality The color of light emitted by a particular source.

Lime A powdered material used to correct excess acidity in soil.

Loam Soil which contains approximately equal amounts of clay, silt, and sand (a desirable condition).

Lux The amount of illumination received on a surface one meter from a standard light source (an international measurement).

Market The geographic area from which a business attracts most of its customers.

Microcomputer A small computer that adapts well to the business needs of landscape firms.

M.L.A. Master of Landscape Architecture. The second professional degree for those who study landscape architecture.

Morphology Physical structure of plants.

Mulch A material placed on top of soil to aid in water retention, prevent soil temperature fluctuations, or discourage weed growth.

Native plant A plant that evolved naturally within a certain locale.

Naturalized plant A plant that was introduced to an area as an exotic plant, but which has adapted so well that it may appear to be native.

Noxious weeds Persistent weeds defined by law in most states. They are perennial and difficult to control. The presence of these weeds in a grass seed mix indicates that the seed is of low quality.

Nutrient ratio A comparison of the proportion of each nutrient in a fertilizer to the other nutrients in the same fertilizer. Example: A fertilizer with a 5-10-5 analysis has a 1-2-1 ratio of ingredients.

Organic Consisting of modified plant or animal materials.

Outcurve The sides of a corner planting.

Overhead Operational costs of doing business; not individual job costs.

Partnership A form of business operation engaged in by two or more persons.

Perennial A plant which lives more than two growing seasons. It usually is dormant during the winter.

Pesticide A chemical used for the control of insects, plant diseases, or weeds.

pH A measure of the acidity or alkalinity of soil. A pH of 7.0 is considered neutral. Ratings below 7.0 are acidic, above 7.0 alkaline (basic).

Photosynthesis Production of food by the plant.

Physiology Biological functioning of plants.

Plant list An alphabetical listing of the botanical names of plants used in a landscape plan, their common names, and the total number used.

Plug A small square, rectangle, or circle of sod, cut about two inches thick.

Plugging A method of lawn installation that uses cores of live, growing grass.

Price Refers to an outlay of funds.

Private corporation A business that sells its stock publicly and can be owned by many people.

Propagation The reproduction of plants. It may be sexual or asexual (by vegetative cuttings, layering, etc.).

Protractor A graphic design tool for measuring angles.

Pruning The removal of a portion of a plant for better shape or more fruitful growth.

Puddling Compaction of soil to such a degree that water will not soak into it.

Purity The percentage, by weight, of the pure grass seed in a mixture.

Quickly available fertilizer A fast-action fertilizer that has its nitrogen in a water soluble form for immediate release into the soil.

Radius One-half of the diameter of a circle.

Reel mower A mower used for home, recreational, and commercial lawn maintenance. The blades rotate in the same direction as the wheels and cut the grass by pushing it against a nonrotating bedknife at the rear base of the mower.

Respiration The use of food reserves for growth and maintenance by plants.

Rhizome An underground stem. New shoots are sent to the surface some distance out from the parent plant. Each new plant develops its own root system and becomes independent of the parent plant.

Riser The elevating portion of a step.

Rotary mower A mower used for home, recreational, and commercial lawn maintenance. The blades move like a ceiling fan, parallel to the surface of the lawn, cutting the grass off as they revolve.

Rotary spreader A device for the application of granular material such as grass seed and fertilizer. The material drops from a hamper onto a rotating plate and is propelled outward in a semicircular pattern.

Scaffold branch A lateral branch of a tree.

Scale (engineer's) A measuring tool that divides the inch into units ranging from 10 to 60 parts.

Serif A decorative stroke attached to a letter to create an ornate appearance.

Share A unit of ownership for the members of a corporation. A share has monetary value and is the basis for voting and payment of dividends to the owners of corporation stock.

Shrub A multistemmed plant smaller in size than a tree.

Silhouette The outline of an object viewed as dark against a light background.

Site An area of land having potential for development.

Slope A measurement that compares the horizontal length to the vertical rise or fall of land. The measurement can be determined from a topographic map.

Slow-release fertilizer A slow-action fertilizer in which the nitrogen content is in a form not soluble in water. The nitrogen is released more slowly into the soil for more efficient intake by plants.

Sodding A method of lawn installation that uses strips of live, growing grass. It produces an immediate effect on the landscape, but is more costly than seeding.

Software Supportive material that allows a computer to carry out specific functions.

Soil texture The composition of a soil as determined by the proportion of sand, silt, and clay that it contains.

Sole proprietorship A form of business operation in which the owner puts up the capital, reaps all profits, and absorbs all losses. There is no separation between the sole proprietor's personal finances and those of the business.

Species A category of plant classification distinguishing the plant from all others.

Specifications Written requirements for the

installation of a landscape. They are usually prepared by a landscape architect and made available to contractors before the bidding for a contract begins.

Specimen plant A plant that is highly distinctive because of such qualities as flower or fruit color, branching pattern, or distinctive foliage. Its use creates a strong focal point in a landscape.

Spreader A garden tool used for the even distribution of materials such as grass seed and fertilizer.

Sprig A piece of grass shoot. Sprigs are commonly used to establish warm-season grass plantings.

Sprinkler irrigation Water applied under pressure over the tops of plants.

Stolon A stem that grows parallel to the ground. New plants develop from it and become independent of the parent plant.

Sucker A succulent branch that originates from the root system. The vegetation of suckers is abnormal and undesirable.

Sunscald A temperature-induced form of winter injury. The winter sun thaws the above-ground plant tissue, causing it to lose water. The roots remain frozen, and thereby unable to replace the water. The result is drying of the tissue.

Symbols Drawings which represent overhead views of trees, shrubs, or other features of a landscape plan.

Tangible A quality denoting something that is touchable.

Tender A condition of plants which implies their lack of tolerance to cold weather.

Tendrils Special appendages of certain vines that allow them to climb.

Terminal bud The end bud on a twig.

Terrain The rise and fall of the land.

Texture A description of the coarseness or fineness of a plant, compared to other nearby plants.

Thatch Dead, semidecomposed grass clippings on the surface of soil.

Thinning out A pruning technique that removes a shrub branch at or near the crown of the plant.

Topiary A form of pruning in which plants are severely sheared into unnatural shapes such as animals or chess pieces.

Topography A record of an area's terrain.

Trace elements Nutrients essential to the growth of many plants, but needed in far less amounts than the major elements.

Trajectory Path of irrigation water as it is propelled through the air.

Transplant To relocate a plant.

Tread That portion of a step on which the foot is placed.

Triangle A three-sided graphic design tool. It commonly has either a 30°–60°–90° or a 45°–90°–45° combination of angles.

Trickle irrigation Water supplied directly to the root zone of plants.

T-square A long straightedge that takes its name from its shape. It is a graphic design tool.

Twining One method by which certain vines are able to climb.

Unit cost The price of the smallest available form of an item described in a cost estimate.

Unit pricing The reduction of all landscape area dimensions and material quantities to a common measurement, such as thousand square feet or acre.

Vellum A thin, paperlike material on which a landscape plan is traced.

Vertical mowing A technique that requires a power rake or a mower whose blades strike the turf vertically. It is done to break up the soil plugs left by an aerator or to remove excessive thatch.

Warm-season grass A grass that grows best in warmer regions of the country and during the summer months.

Water sprout A succulent branch that grows from the trunk of a tree. The vegetation of water sprouts is abnormal and undesirable.

Weed A plant growing where it is not wanted and having no economic value.

Weep hole A means of preventing water buildup behind a retaining wall.

Windburn Drying out of plant tissue (especially evergreens) by the winter wind.

Winter injury Any damage done to elements of the landscape during the cold weather season of the year.

Working drawing A copy of a landscape design done on heavy paper or plastic film. The working drawing is used repeatedly during actual construction of the landscape and must be very durable.

Wound paint A sealing paint used over plant wounds of 1 inch or more in diameter after pruning.

Zoning The regulations of a community that govern what uses can be made of different areas within the community.

INDEX

393